A SEMANTIC AND STRUCTURAL ANALYSIS OF EPHESIANS

SIL International

SEMANTIC AND STRUCTURAL ANALYSIS SERIES

JOHN BANKER, GENERAL EDITOR

A SEMANTIC AND STRUCTURAL ANALYSIS OF EPHESIANS

Edna Johnson

SIL International

© 2008 by SIL International

Library of Congress Control Number: 2008936831
ISBN: 978-155671-224-1

Printed in the United States of America

The Greek text used in this SSA is from the fourth revised edition
of the United Bible Societies' *Greek New Testament*.

All Rights Reserved

No part of this publication may be reproduced, stored in a retrieval system, or transmitted in any form or by any means without the express permission of SIL International. However, brief excerpts, generally understood to be within the limits of fair use, may be quoted without written permission.

Copies of this and other publications
of SIL International may be obtained from

International Academic Bookstore
SIL International
7500 West Camp Wisdom Road
Dallas, TX 75236-5699, USA

Voice: 972-708-7404
Fax: 972-708-7363
academic_books@sil.org
www.ethnologue.com

CONTENTS

Acknowledgements 7
Abbreviations 8

GENERAL INTRODUCTION 9
The Theory on Which a Semantic and Structural Analysis Is Based 9
Format and Conventions 9
The Use of a Semantic and Structural Analysis 10
The Nature of Propositionalisation 10

INTRODUCTION TO THE SEMANTIC STRUCTURE
OF THE EPISTLE TO THE EPHESIANS 13
Participants in the Communication Situation 13
Occasion and Purpose of the Letter 14
Peak in Ephesians 15
Overview: Thematic Units and Their Theme Statements 18

THE SEMANTIC UNITS OF THE EPISTLE TO THE EPHESIANS 25
Ephesians 1:1–6:24 (Epistle) 25
  Epistle Constituent 1:1–2 (Paragraph: Opening of the Epistle) 26
  Epistle Constituent 1:3–6:20 (Part: Body of the Epistle) 29
    Part Constituent 1:3–3:21 (Subpart: Grounds for 4:1–6:20) 35
      Subpart Constituent 1:3–23 (Expressive Division) 37
        Division Constituent 1:3–14 (Expressive Subdivision) 39
          Subdivision Constituent 1:3a (Expressive Proposition) 41
          Subdivision Constituent 1:3b–14 (Expressive Section) 42
            Section Constituent 1:3b (Expressive Propositional Cluster) 43
            Section Constituent 1:4–6 (Expressive Paragraph) 44
            Section Constituent 1:7–12 (Expressive Paragraph) 48
            Section Constituent 1:13–14 (Expressive Paragraph) 56
        Division Constituent 1:15–23 (Expressive Section) 60
          Section Constituent 1:15–19 (Expressive Paragraph) 62
          Section Constituent 1:20–23 (Expressive Paragraph) 68
      Subpart Constituent 2:1–3:13 (Expository Division) 73
        Division Constituent 2:1–22 (Expository Subdivision) 74
          Subdivision Constituent 2:1–10 (Expository Section) 76
            Section Constituent 2:1–3 (Expository Paragraph) 78
            Section Constituent 2:4–7 (Expository Paragraph) 83
            Section Constituent 2:8–10 (Expository Paragraph) 87
          Subdivision Constituent 2:11–22: (Expository Section) 91
            Section Constituent 2:11–13 (Expository Paragraph) 92
            Section Constituent 2:14–18 (Expository Paragraph) 97
            Section Constituent 2:19–22: (Expository Paragraph) 103
        Division Constituent 3:1–13 (Expository Section) 107
          Section Constituent 3:1 (Propositional Cluster) 109
          Section Constituent 3:2–7 (Expository Paragraph) 111
          Section Constituent 3:8–13 (Expository Paragraph) 118
      Subpart Constituent 3:14–21 (Expressive Section) 126
        Section Constituent 3:14–19 (Expressive Paragraph) 127
        Section Constituent 3:20–21 (Expressive Paragraph) 134
    Part Constituent 4:1–6:20 (Hortatory Subpart: Nucleus of 1:3–6:20) 137
      Subpart Constituent 4:1–6:9 (Hortatory Division) 139
        Division Constituent 4:1–16 (Hortatory Section) 140
          Section Constituent 4:1–6 (Hortatory Paragraph) 142
          Section Constituent 4:7–16 (Expository Paragraph) 148

    Division Constituent 4:17–32 (Hortatory Section) 161
        Section Constituent 4:17–19 (Hortatory Paragraph) 163
        Section Constituent 4:20–24 (Expository Paragraph)...................................... 168
        Section Constituent 4:25–32 (Hortatory Paragraph) 175
    Division Constituent 5:1–6 (Hortatory Paragraph) 183
    Division Constituent 5:7–14 (Hortatory Paragraph) 190
    Division Constituent 5:15–6:9 (Hortatory Section) 198
        Section Constituent 5:15–17 (Hortatory Paragraph) 201
        Section Constituent 5:18–21 (Hortatory Paragraph) 204
        Section Constituent 5:22–33 (Hortatory Paragraph) 209
        Section Constituent 6:1–4 (Hortatory Paragraph) 219
        Section Constituent 6:5–9 (Hortatory Paragraph) 223
    Subpart Constituent 6:10–20 (Hortatory Section)... 227
        Section Constituent 6:10–13 (Hortatory Paragraph) 229
        Section Constituent 6:14–20 (Hortatory Paragraph) 234
  Epistle Constituent 6:21–24 (Complex Section: Closing of the Epistle)............................. 242
    Section Constituent 6:21–22 (Commissive Paragraph).. 243
    Section Constituent 6:23–24 (Expressive Paragraph)... 246

Bibliography 249

Charts
  Chart of Communication Relations 11
  The Constituent Organisation of Ephesians 17

ACKNOWLEDGEMENTS

It is difficult for me to mention by name all those who have contributed to this *Semantic and Structural Analysis of Ephesians*. This is due to the fact that work on it has extended over so many years and has involved so many people. To all who have helped in any way, please accept my thanks.

I am grateful to everybody in the Translation Department of The International Linguistic Centre, Dallas. Whenever I have needed to spend time there working on the SSA they have always accommodated me most cheerfully and have encouraged me by their fellowship as well as by their practical help.

Over the years there have been those who have made significant contributions in different ways to the production of this SSA. My thanks go to Dick Blight for his help with formatting matters, which have always been something of mystery to me; to Betty Eastman, for her advice on editing the manuscript in the early stages; to Ellis Deibler, for his suggestions during the early stages of exegesis and analysis of chapters 1 & 2; to Eugene Minor, for the many hours he spent reading through the manuscript, with a scrupulous attention to detail which enabled me to improve it considerably in the latter stages. James E. Mignard reviewed the SSA from a Greek perspective. My thanks go to him for the time he expended on this, and for his comments and suggestions. I thank all of these most sincerely.

In particular, I should like to thank John Callow and John Banker for their invaluable contribution. Without the input of John Callow I would not have got very far in the analysis of Ephesians, and without the considerable input of John Banker I would certainly never have completed it. John Callow helped me a great deal with the basic exegesis, and in formulating the first draft of the SSA. John Banker built on this foundation, encouraging me to persevere and complete the work. I am indebted to them both for their patient and constructive criticism, and for their illuminating insights into Ephesians.

Last, but certainly not least, my sincere thanks to Sharon Gray for all her hard work in the final editing process. She applied her considerable experience and expertise to this, and her suggestions regarding both content and organisation of the notes were invaluable. I am sure that the application of her skills has contributed greatly to the lucidity and therefore the accessibility of this SSA.

Along with others who spend considerable time studying the Word of God in the course of their work, I am very aware of what a great privilege this is. With that privilege comes responsibility, and I am very conscious of that also. I have tried faithfully to discern the mind of the Lord in what Paul has written in this epistle, but I am very conscious of my own inadequacies in this respect. However, I trust that the Lord will not allow anything I have written to obscure the message which He has for His people. Also, I pray that, despite the shortcomings of this book, through the power of the Holy Spirit, it might be of benefit to each one who reads it.

Edna Johnson

ABBREVIATIONS IN THE DISPLAYS

(exc)	exclusive	[MET]	metaphor
[HEN]	hendiadys	[MTY]	metonymy
[HYP]	hyperbole	(sg)	singular
(inc)	inclusive	[SYN]	synecdoche

ABBREVIATIONS IN THE TEXT

BDAG*	Bauer, Danker, Arndt, Gingrich
BDF	Blass, Debrunner, and Funk
CEV	Contemporary English Version
fn.	footnote
JB	Jerusalem Bible
JBP	J. B. Phillips
KJV	King James Version
LB	Living Bible
LXX	The Septuagint
MS, MSS	manuscript(s)
NAB	New American Bible
NASB	New American Standard Bible
NCV	New Century Version
NEB	New English Bible
NET	New English Translation
NIV	New International Version
NJB	New Jerusalem Bible
NLT	New Living Translation
NRSV	New Revised Standard Version
REB	Revised English Bible
RSV	Revised Standard Version
SSA	Semantic and Structural Analysis
TEV	Today's English Version (Good News Bible)
TNT	Translator's New Testament
UBS	United Bible Societies
UBSGNT	United Bible Societies' Greek New Testament (4th rev. ed.)

*BDAG will be cited by the following formula: page number, period, entry citation (e.g., BDAG, p. 405.12bβ).

GENERAL INTRODUCTION

THE THEORY ON WHICH A SEMANTIC AND STRUCTURAL ANALYSIS IS BASED

This analytical commentary on the Epistle of Ephesians is based on the theory of semantic structure set forth in "The Semantic Structure of Written Communication" by Beekman, J. Callow and Kopesec (1981). *Man and Message* by K. Callow (1998) presents a broader basis for this theory.

This Semantic and Structural Analysis (SSA), like the other studies in the series, has been prepared with the needs of the Bible translator in mind, though it should be useful to all serious students of God's word. It aims to arrive at the meaning the original author intended to communicate to the original recipients, but it differs from most other commentaries in that it is based on a particular theory of the structure of meaning. Consequently, a consistent and comprehensive approach to the analysis of the meaning is applied to the total document, whether that meaning is conveyed by the smallest segments of the written communication (words and their component parts) or by the largest segments (paragraphs and combinations of paragraphs).

In an SSA, the Greek text is analysed in terms of its semantic units, from the highest level to the lowest. Each of these units is presented first as a display. Following the display, features of the unit's intent, structure, boundaries, coherence, prominence and theme are discussed. For a unit on the lowest level (i.e. a single paragraph or propositional cluster), exegetical and other analytical notes are given on each verse.

This SSA does not include a detailed section on the theory and presentation of semantic and structural analyses as some of the earlier SSAs do (Colossians, 2 Thessalonians and their revised editions). Readers may refer to the Colossians or 2 Thessalonians SSA for this information (see bibliography). The Ephesians SSA, however, does include a chart of communication relations, providing easy access to this important tool.

FORMAT AND CONVENTIONS

Each semantic unit of Ephesians is displayed as a chart, with the discourse structure and relational structure shown on the left and the referential contents at the right. Readers should note the following conventions:

1. Italics in the propositions of the display designate implicit material that has been supplied. In some cases, however, it has been difficult to decide what is implicit and what is actually a component of the meaning of the Greek word or words being translated.
2. Parentheses are used to enclose alternative renderings, for example, "my God (*or*, God whom I *worship*)". But if both alternatives are a single word, they are separated simply by a forward slash: "teach/counsel". If they are a short phrase, the phrase is hyphenated: "For-the-rest/Finally". Parentheses are used to enclose specifications for pronouns, as in "we (exc)".
3. Square brackets indicate the clarification of an antecedent, e.g. in proposition 1:6a: "*God did this* [1:4-5] in order that we should praise him". Square brackets also enclose abbreviations for figures of speech that occur in the Greek text, e.g. [MET] for metaphor.
4. In an orienter-content relation where the content consists of more than one proposition, the content label is not used in most cases. Where each proposition in the propositonal cluster immediately following the orienter is oriented by it, a vertical broken line is used between the orienter and the first proposition of the content. See 1:5b-d in the 1:4-6 display for an example. Where the orienter relates principally to the nuclear proposition(s), an unbroken line is used.
5. Boldface type in the propositions of the display indicates words that are emphasised in the Greek text, but which are difficult to emphasise lexically in the display; for example, "**God**" in 2:10a. At the beginning of a note, where the words are already bold, an emphasised word is indicated by underlining.
6. "You" in the display is to be understood as plural. "We" is to be understood as inclusive unless marked exclusive: "we (exc)".
7. Communication relations are tagged not only by labels in the display diagrams, but as much as possible in the display text itself by the use of connectors (conjunctions). For many relations, the connector used for a specific relation is always the same. For example, "because" is used for reason, "since" is used for grounds. They are not interchanged.

Whereas SSAs published during the period 1994–2001 (except for revisions or reprinting of those published earlier) used paragraph pattern labels for relations on the highest level in the paragraph, this SSA uses basic communication relations only. The major reason for this change is to make it easier for readers by reducing the number of distinctions in the labeling.

Like all recent SSAs, this SSA uses the label NUCLEUS instead of HEAD for nuclear units.

THE USE OF A SEMANTIC AND STRUCTURAL ANALYSIS

To a translator who must not only determine the meaning of a passage, but also resolve a myriad of translation problems, it may seem like drudgery to wade through the detailed reasoning backing up the exegetical decisions in an SSA. However, the detailed reasoning is necessary to determine the best analysis. Any interpretation should be backed by solid reasoning and there is no way this can be done without detailed analysis, including reference to the Greek text. To determine whether or not the reasoning is solid, the translator has the option of studying the analysis following each display. The notes, especially, are helpful. They give support for the exegetical decisions made in the displays, deal with problems found in translation into non-Indo-European languages, analyse figures of speech and explain the reason for supplying individual pieces of implicit information.

Instead of reading every part of the SSA, some translators first read the propositions in a display along with other commentaries, versions and other translation aids. Where there is obvious agreement, they may move ahead with confidence. But where there is a difference between the display's renderings and those of other commentaries, the notes on that particular verse or portion of a verse should be consulted to see what led to the decision represented in the display. Translators should then be better able to make their own judgement as to the best interpretation.

The renderings in the display work together with the notes to provide the information translators need. Since the propositions are limited in the information they can provide, the notes contribute to a fuller understanding of them.

To obtain the greatest benefit from an SSA, the discussions of "Intent and Structure" should also be consulted: they orient the reader to the biblical author's development of his argument or thesis on the paragraph level. On the higher levels, the "Intent and Macrostructure" notes help the SSA user to understand the intent of the author in the broader context.

THE NATURE OF PROPOSITIONALISATION

It must be understood that the SSA display text is not, strictly speaking, a translation. Rather, it expresses the analysis of the meaning of the Greek text in English surface-structure form. However it contains various restrictions:

1. Abstract nouns are avoided as much as possible by changing them into verbs and adding obligatory case roles.
2. Finite verb forms are normally used rather than participles.
3. Active constructions are normally used rather than passive ones, except where the focus needs to be maintained on the topic represented by the grammatical subject of the passive rather than on the performer of the action.
4. Words are used only in their primary senses.
5. For live metaphors, the full meaning of the figure intended by the original author is given.

As a result, the sentences in the display do not always sound natural, as they should in a good translation. The inclusion of implicit material often makes them sound overloaded with information and too interpretive. But the primary purpose of the display text is to be a source of information, not a model to be translated word-for-word into a real language.

In some of their patterns, the propositions more closely approximate the patterns of non-Indo-European languages than those of English or Greek. Thus, if the target language naturally uses abstract nouns in more-or-less the same way as English or Greek does, the use of abstract nouns in a translation would be more natural and effective than the form of the display text. But if the target language does not normally use abstract nouns, the display text form may be helpful, since its patterns and obligatory elements are those of verb constructions, not abstract nouns. But even in these languages the display text form ought not to be followed word-for-word. The translator must seek to follow the patterns of the target language.

Likewise, the implicit material provided in the display text is not intended to be translated in its entirety. Only that which is necessary in the target language should be used in translating.

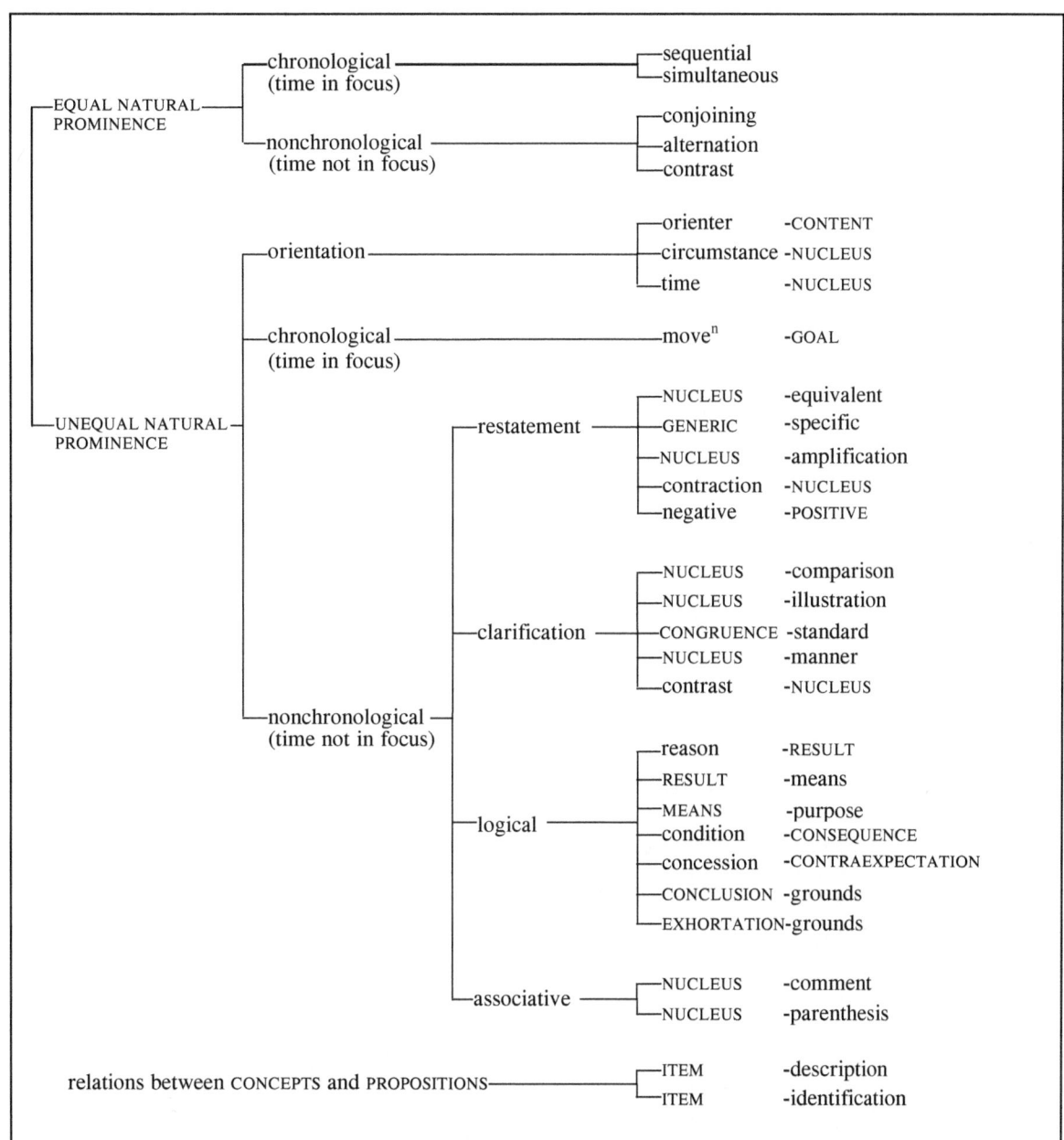

Chart of Communication Relations

Notes:
1. The relations are given in the chart in the usual order in which they are found in New Testament Greek.
2. The naturally prominent member of a paired relation is shown in full capitals. When the author uses marked-prominence devices to increase the prominence of the normally less prominent member, both members will be shown in full capitals in the display.
3. NUCLEUS-amplification and contraction-NUCLEUS are the same communication relation, but with a difference in the position of the nucleus.
4. In the displays, ITEM is shown as a gloss enclosed in single quote marks.

INTRODUCTION TO THE SEMANTIC STRUCTURE OF THE EPISTLE TO THE EPHESIANS

PARTICIPANTS IN THE COMMUNICATION SITUATION

Paul clearly identifies himself as the author of this letter in the first verse: Παῦλος ἀπόστολος Χριστοῦ Ἰησοῦ "Paul, an apostle of Christ Jesus". He refers to himself by name again in 3:1. There appear to be no convincing reasons presented by scholars for rejecting Pauline authorship. It was accepted almost universally by the early church. It was only in the nineteenth century, with the rise of higher criticism, that doubt was cast on Paul's authorship.

Those who dispute that Paul was the author of this letter argue that its style, vocabulary and ideas are not typical of his other epistles. But, as Stott argues,

> ...linguistic and stylistic arguments are notoriously precarious. Why should we expect such an original mind as Paul's to stay within the confines of a limited vocabulary and an inflexible style? Different themes require different words, and changed circumstances create a changed atmosphere (p. 17).

In addition, many of the themes in Ephesians have close parallels in epistles which are indisputably Pauline, e.g. the work of grace in salvation, justification by faith, the place of the Jews and the law.

The relationship to the Epistle to the Colossians is put forward by both sides in the argument over authorship. Those who reject Paul as being the author of Ephesians argue that it would not be possible for one person to write two letters which have such resemblances and yet such significant differences. However, those who hold that Paul is the author argue that the degree of interdependence, blended with individuality, could not have been the product of two minds.

Another argument put forward against Pauline authorship is that the Ephesian letter contains no personal greetings such as are found in his other letters. For example, in the Epistle to the Romans, twenty-six people are mentioned by name in chapter sixteen. Paul spent only a short time in Ephesus on his first visit, at the end of his second missionary journey (Acts 18:19-22). However, his second visit lasted three years (Acts 19:1-20:1, 31). During this second visit, when he spent much time teaching the Ephesian believers and helping to establish the church, he must have built close relationships with those in the church. This is confirmed by the description of his final parting from them in Acts 20:17-38, and, in particular, 20:36-38.

It might be expected, therefore, that there would be specific greetings at the end of the letter, rather than the general ones, τοῖς ἀδελφοῖς "to the brothers" and πάντων τῶν ἀγαπώντων τὸν κύριον ἡμῶν Ἰησοῦν Χριστόν "all who love our Lord Jesus Christ" in 6:23-24. In addition, Paul refers to the fact that he has "heard" of their faith and love (1:15), and that they have "heard" of his stewardship of the gospel (3:2-4), which does not seem to indicate that they knew one another personally.

However, it could be argued that, although the letter may be addressed to the Ephesians, it was also intended to be read by a larger audience with whom Paul had no personal acquaintance, and this would account for the lack of personal greetings.

Despite the arguments *against* Pauline authorship, the majority view is still in support of it, since no satisfactory alternative has been put forward by those who oppose it. As F.F. Bruce states,

> The man who could write Ephesians must have been the apostle's equal, if not his superior, in mental stature and spiritual insight.... Of such a second Paul early Christian history has no knowledge (pp. 11-12).

Also Cadbury (p. 101) says,

> Which is more likely—that an imitator of Paul in the first century composed a writing ninety or ninety five percent in accordance with Paul's style or that Paul himself wrote a letter diverging five or ten percent from his usual style?

When Paul wrote this letter, he was a prisoner (3:1; 4:1; 6:20). Some modern commentators argue that he was imprisoned in Caesarea at this time, most agree that he wrote the letter during his imprisonment in Rome towards the end of his life. During his long imprisonment there, the traditional view is that he also wrote the epistles to the Colossians, the Philippians and Philemon. The reference to Tychicus as the bearer of this letter (6:21), when compared with Colossians 4:7, gives credence to this view. No reasons have been put forward which would cause this theory to be discounted.

Ephesus was an important port on the eastern shore of the Aegean Sea. It was the capital of the Roman province of Asia, the most prosperous province in the empire. Originally a Greek colony, under the Romans it enjoyed to a great extent the right of self-government. It was famous for the temple of Artemis (Diana) and was regarded as sacred to that goddess. The temple served as a bank as well as a temple. Politics, religion and economics were closely intertwined (Acts 19:23–41).

Sorcery was connected with the worship of Artemis and so, from earliest times, the city was the chief centre for magic arts for all Asia (cf. Acts 19:19), with a wide reputation for its exorcists and protection against evil spirits (Acts 19:13–16).

There is some degree of uncertainty as to the intended recipients of this letter. This centres around the phrase ἐν Ἐφέσῳ "at Ephesus" and its omission from some manuscripts. However, the majority of versions include the phrase, sometimes with a footnote noting its omission from some manuscripts (CEV, JBP, KJV, NCV, NIV, NLT, NRSV, REB, TEV). In the commentaries there appears to be a wide acceptance of its inclusion. Against this, some argue that a lack of any personal greetings and other allusions to the time Paul spent in Ephesus make it unlikely that it should be addressed particularly to the Ephesians. In those manuscripts from which ἐν Ἐφέσῳ is omitted, the recipients would be τοῖς οὖσιν καὶ πιστοῖς "the ones being also faithful". This is possible, but is regarded by some scholars as being an awkward grammatical construction in the Greek (Bratcher and Nida, p. 4).

Some commentators suggest that the letter was a circular letter written to more than one church. Possibly a blank was left, to be filled in with the name of the city in which the letter was to be read (see, for example, Mitton, p. 40). That it was intended to be a circular letter seems credible, but the suggestion that a blank was left for such a purpose is unlikely, since there are no other examples recorded of such a practice in ancient history (Lincoln, pp. 2–3).

One possible solution is that suggested by Hodge, i.e. that the letter was written and addressed to the believers at Ephesus, but was intended for the Gentile Christians as a group, rather than for a particular church. So it was written into a form suitable for all such Christians in the neighbouring districts. This would account for a lack of references to the particular circumstances of the believers in Ephesus (p. xiii). Alternatively, O'Brien concludes,

> Ephesians was a general epistle sent to mainly Gentile believers in southwestern Asia Minor, and...it was linked with Ephesus at an early stage, perhaps because of its being a strategic church or because it was one of the several cities to which the letter was sent (pp. 86–87).

In support of both these views, it can be said that, even though believers from both Jewish and Gentile backgrounds may be the intended recipients of this letter (see 1:11–14), Paul explicitly addresses Gentile believers in 2:11 and 3:1, and he describes their former state in 2:11–12 in terms which could apply only to Gentiles. Also, he urges them not to return to their previous Gentile lifestyle (4:17; cf. 2:1–3). In addition, he explicitly states in 3:1 that his imprisonment is "for you Gentiles" and in 3:13 he urges them not to be discouraged because of his sufferings which are "for you" (3:13).

OCCASION AND PURPOSE OF THE LETTER

Although much has been written about the points of similarity between the Epistle to the Ephesians and the Epistle to the Colossians, they differ in one important aspect. The Epistle to the Colossians appears to have been written to a particular group of believers and to address a particular problem, that is, false teaching which was being presented to the believers in Colossae (Col. 2:4, 8, 16–18, 20–23). In contrast, the Epistle to the Ephesians does not appear to address a particular problem or a particular church, although, as stated above, it could be said to address a particular group within the church, that is, those from a Gentile background.

Since an author's purpose determines what he chooses to include in his message, and, in particular, what he stresses as being important, it will be helpful to study those themes which appear consistently throughout the letter in order to discern Paul's purpose.

The BODY of the epistle divides into two parts. The first part (1:3–3:21) is basically expressive and expository. The second part (4:1–6:20) is essentially hortatory.

The theme of the BODY is as follows:

1:3–6:20 God is worthy to be praised, since he has blessed us exceedingly through Christ. He caused Jews and Gentiles who believe in Christ to be at peace with him and with each other, so that now we form one church, with Christ, the supreme ruler over all things, as its head. God's purpose in doing this was to reveal his infinite wisdom to the powerful beings in the heavens. I pray that the Holy Spirit may empower you, that you may experience Christ's infinite love and that God may cause you to be perfect just as he is perfect. May he be glorified through the church and through Christ Jesus forever.

On the basis of all this, behave as God's people should. Imitate him, letting your lives be characterised by love. Under the control of the Holy Spirit and in wholehearted reliance on the Lord Jesus Christ, do all you can to ensure that the church becomes completely united and spiritual mature. To this end, make use of every spiritual resource which God provides for you, in order that you may be able to successfully resist the devil and all his powerful evil spirits. Persevere in prayer for all God's people.

From this theme statement, we may discern that Paul had the following purposes in mind in writing this letter:

1. To praise God because he has so abundantly blessed believers (1:3, 6, 12, 14; 3:20–21) and to cause the Ephesian believers to join Paul in this praise by making them aware of how great is the working of God's grace and power on their behalf (1:3–3:21). Also, to encourage believers to realise that God's power is available to them now (3:20) and will enable them to withstand the attacks of the devil and all his evil powers (6:10–20), since Christ has already defeated them (4:9–10).
2. To reveal to believers that God has a plan to unite the whole of creation under Christ "in the fulness of time" (1:9–10; 3:9–10) and that the church is part of the fulfilment of that larger plan (1:19–23; 3:21).
3. To convince the Ephesians that, by Christ's death, God has caused all believers, whether Jew or Gentile, to be at peace with him and with each other, so that they are now members of one church (2:1–22), with Christ, the supreme ruler over all things, as its head (1:19–23; 4:15; 5:23–24). This is closely connected with point two above.
4. To impress upon both Jewish and Gentile believers the importance of maintaining the unity of the Spirit, which God has given to them (4:3–16). Although the word "unity" is used only in 4:3 and 13, Paul focusses attention on unity in 4:5–6 and also in the metaphors of the body (1:22–23; 4:4, 16), a building (2:19–22) and a bride (5:28–32). In fact, it might be said that the purpose of all the hortatory material in 4:1–6:20 is that unity might be maintained.
5. To encourage believers to behave as God's people should, i.e. imitating God, relying wholeheartedly on Christ, being under the control of the Holy Spirit (4:1–6:9). This is expressed by means of the repeated exhortations on how they are to "walk": "worthy of (their) calling" (4:1); "not as other Gentiles walk" (4:17); "in love" (5:2); "in light" (5:8); "carefully" (5:15). In addition, Paul encourages them to be submissive to one another in the family and master-slave relationship (5:22–6:9). All this is closely connected with points three and four above and the topic of unity.
6. To draw his readers' attention to the qualities of "peace", "love", "knowledge" and "wisdom". The importance of these qualities in the lives of believers and their contribution to unity in the church is made evident by frequent references to the qualities scattered throughout the whole letter.

As can be seen from the purposes listed above, the main focus is on maintaining the unity of the Spirit in the church, as part of God's ultimate purpose of uniting all things in heaven and on earth under the headship of Christ. The intent of all the exhortations to godly living is to this end. Undergirding this is Paul's desire to convince believers that Christ has already defeated the powers of evil, so that they will be encouraged to stand firm against all the attacks of the devil, knowing that the power of God is available to them.

PEAK IN EPHESIANS

Longacre states,

> While discourse has cohesion/coherence and prominence, it just as necessarily involves *progress*, i.e., a well-formed discourse is going somewhere. The progress of a discourse typically issues in some sort of climactic development (or

developments) which I have been accustomed to term *peak(s)* (p. 33).

The peaks in a discourse, to which Longacre refers, are key features in discerning the main purpose of that discourse, since they highlight those aspects of the message on which the author particularly wishes the readers to focus. By using different surface-structure devices, the author ensures that they understand the content and the purpose of the message.

Applying this to Paul's letter to the Ephesians, those units which evidence features of peak are 1:3–14; 1:15–23; 3:14–21 in the first part of the BODY and 4:1–16; 6:10–20 in the second part of the BODY. These occur in initial and final positions in the two parts of the BODY, possibly to indicate their importance in the discourse and draw attention to their content. Although it is acknowledged that peak is not usually analysed as occurring in initial positions in discourse, these initial units in Ephesians have many peak-like features and so, at least in some aspects, have a similar effect as peak in final positions.

These passages which show features of peak highlight the main purposes in the list of purposes above, as follows:

1. To make believers aware of the working of God's power on their behalf in many ways (1:3–23), including the uniting of the church under the headship of Christ (1:22–23), and the ultimate purpose of bringing all things under his headship (1:9–10; 3:9–10).
2. To encourage believers to live godly lives in order to maintain the unity of the Spirit in the church (4:1–16).
3. To convince believers that God's power is available to them now (3:20), so that they will be able to stand firm against the attacks of Satan (6:10–20).

For a more detailed discussion of features of peak in the Epistle to the Ephesians, see the section "Peak in Ephesians" in Intent and Macrostructure for the BODY.

INTRODUCTION TO THE SEMANTIC STRUCTURE OF THE EPISTLE TO THE EPHESIANS 17

THE CONSTITUENT ORGANISATION OF EPHESIANS

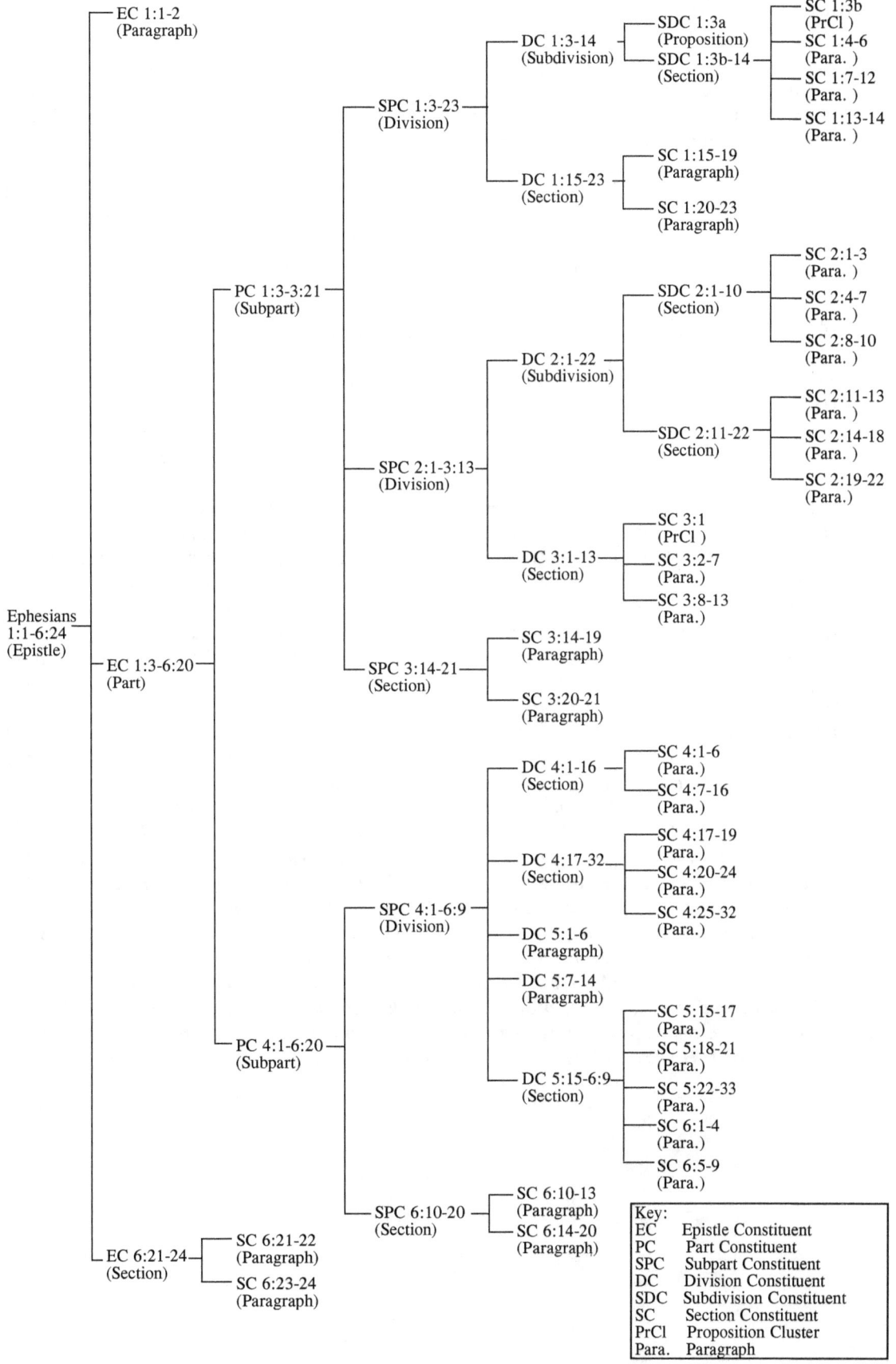

OVERVIEW: THEMATIC UNITS AND THEIR THEME STATEMENTS

EPHESIANS 1:1–6:24 (Epistle)
THEME: I, Paul, write this letter to you who are God's people at Ephesus. God is worthy to be praised, since he has blessed us exceedingly through Christ. By uniting Jews and Gentiles who believe in Christ he established his church, with Christ, the supreme ruler over all things, as its head. God's purpose in this was to reveal his infinite wisdom to the powerful beings in the heavens. May you experience the Holy Spirit's power and Christ's infinite love. And may God be glorified through the church and through Christ Jesus forever. On the basis of all this, behave as God's people should. Let your lives be characterised by love, by the Holy Spirit's control and by wholehearted reliance on Christ, as you do all you can to ensure the unity and spiritual maturity of the church. To this end, make use of every spiritual resource which God provides, so that you may withstand the attacks of the devil. Persevere in prayer for all God's people. I am sending Tychicus to encourage you. I pray that God will continue to bless you all.

> EPISTLE CONSTITUENT 1:1–2 (Paragraph: Opening of the Epistle)
> *THEME: I, Paul, am writing this letter to you who are the people of God in Ephesus. I pray that God will bless you.*
> EPISTLE CONSTITUENT 1:3–6:20 (Part: Body of the Epistle)
> *THEME: God is worthy to be praised, since he has blessed us exceedingly through Christ. He caused Jews and Gentiles who believe in Christ to be at peace with him and with each other, so that now we form one church, with Christ, the supreme ruler over all things, as its head. God's purpose in doing this was to reveal his infinite wisdom to the powerful beings in the heavens. I pray that the Holy Spirit may empower you, that you may experience Christ's infinite love and that God may cause you to be perfect just as he is perfect. May he be glorified through the church and through Christ Jesus forever. On the basis of all this, behave as God's people should. Imitate him, letting your lives be characterised by love. Under the control of the Holy Spirit and in wholehearted reliance on the Lord Jesus Christ, do all you can to ensure that the church becomes completely united and spiritually mature. To this end, make use of every spiritual resource which God provides for you, in order that you may be able to successfully resist the devil and all his powerful evil spirits. Persevere in prayer for all God's people.*
> > PART CONSTITUENT 1:3–3:21 (Subpart: Grounds for 4:1–6:20)
> > *THEME: God is worthy to be praised, since he has blessed us exceedingly through Christ. He chose us, redeemed us and revealed to us his plan to unite all things in heaven and on earth under Christ. He also caused Christ, as supreme ruler over all things, to rule over the church. Because of his grace he saved us, through our faith in Christ. And, through Christ's death, he caused us all, both Jews and Gentiles, to be at peace with him and with each other, so that now we share the same blessings and form one church. He appointed me to make this known to the Gentiles and to make known to everyone that his purpose in forming the church was to reveal his infinite wisdom to the powerful beings in the heavens. I pray that the Holy Spirit may empower you, that you may experience Christ's infinite love and that God may cause you to be perfect just as he is perfect. May God be glorified through the church and through Christ Jesus forever. Amen.*
> > > SUBPART CONSTITUENT 1:3–23 (Expressive Division: Introduction to 2:1–3:13)
> > > *THEME: God is worthy to be praised, since he has blessed us exceedingly through Christ. He chose us, redeemed us and revealed to us his plan to unite all things in heaven and on earth under Christ. He also caused Christ, as supreme ruler over all things, to rule over the church.*

DIVISION CONSTITUENT 1:3-14 (Expressive Subdivision: Nucleus₁ [Eulogy] of 1:3-23)
THEME: God is worthy to be praised, since he has blessed us spiritually and abundantly in every way, because we are united with Christ. Specifically, God has chosen us to be his holy and blameless people. He has redeemed us. He has confirmed this by the Holy Spirit. He has also revealed to us his plan to unite all things in heaven and on earth under Christ at the appointed time. God's purpose in all this is that we should praise him.

    SUBDIVISION CONSTITUENT 1:3a (Expressive Proposition: Conclusion of 1:3b-14)
    THEME: God is worthy to be praised.

    SUBDIVISION CONSTITUENT 1:3b-14 (Expressive Section: Grounds for 1:3a)
    THEME: God has blessed us spiritually and abundantly in every way, because we are united with Christ. Specifically, God has chosen us to be his holy and blameless people. He has redeemed us. He has confirmed this by the Holy Spirit. He has also revealed to us his plan to unite all things in heaven and on earth under Christ at the appointed time. God's purpose in all this is that we should praise him.

        SECTION CONSTITUENT 1:3b (Expressive Propositional Cluster: Generic Nucleus of 1:3b-14)
        THEME: God has blessed us spiritually in every way, with those things which come from heaven, because we are united with Christ.

        SECTION CONSTITUENT 1:4-6 (Expressive Paragraph: Specific₁ of 1:3b)
        THEME: God has chosen us to be his holy and blameless people because we are united with Christ. God did this in order that we should praise him [God].

        SECTION CONSTITUENT 1:7-12 (Expressive Paragraph: Specific₂ of 1:3b)
        THEME: God has redeemed us. He has revealed to us his plan to unite all things in heaven and on earth under Christ at the appointed time. He has also appointed us to receive what he has promised to his people in order that we should praise him.

        SECTION CONSTITUENT 1:13-14 (Expressive Paragraph: Specific₃ of 1:3b)
        THEME: The Holy Spirit within us confirms that we belong to God and guarantees that God will finally redeem us in order that we should praise him.

DIVISION CONSTITUENT 1:15-23 (Expressive Section: Nucleus₂ of 1:3-23 [Thanksgiving and Prayer])
THEME: I thank God for your faith and love. I pray that God may cause you to understand more fully how powerfully he works on behalf of his people, just as he worked powerfully when he caused Christ, who had died, to live again and, as supreme ruler over all things, to rule over the church.

    SECTION CONSTITUENT 1:15-19 (Expressive Paragraph: Nucleus of 1:15-23)
    THEME: I thank God for your faith and love. I pray that God may grant that his Spirit may cause you to be wise and may reveal God to you, that God may grant you to know what you should hope for, what you will finally inherit and how powerfully God works on behalf of us who believe in Christ.

    SECTION CONSTITUENT 1:20-23 (Expressive Paragraph: Amplification of 1:15-19)
    THEME: God worked mightily on behalf of Christ. Specifically, God caused Christ, who had died, to live again, and he placed him in the most highly-honoured position in heaven. God appointed Christ, who rules supreme over all, to rule over the church.

SUBPART CONSTITUENT 2:1-3:13 (Expository Division: Nucleus of 1:3-3:21)
THEME: Because of God's grace he saved us, through our faith in Christ. Through Christ's death, God caused all believers, whether Jew or Gentile, to be at peace with him and with each other, so that now all share the same blessings and form one church. God appointed me to make known to the Gentiles that he is the source of infinite blessings for them, and to make known to everyone that God's purpose in forming the church was to reveal his infinite wisdom to the powerful beings in the heavens.

DIVISION CONSTITUENT 2:1-22 (Expository Subdivision: Nucleus of 2:1-3:13)
THEME: Formerly, we were all spiritually dead and certain to be punished by God, but because of his grace and great love he saved us, through our faith in Christ. Through Christ's death, God has caused all believers, you Gentiles as well as Jewish believers, to be at peace with him and with each other, so that now all share the same blessings and form one church.

    SUBDIVISION CONSTITUENT 2:1-10 (Expository Section: Nucleus$_1$ of 2:1-22)
    THEME: Formerly, we were all spiritually dead and were certain to be punished by God. But because of his grace and great love he saved us, through our faith in Christ. We did nothing at all to save ourselves.

        SECTION CONSTITUENT 2:1-3 (Expository Paragraph: Concession to 2:4-7)
        THEME: Formerly, you were spiritually dead because you were habitually sinning. So also were we all. In this evil state, God would certainly punish us all.

        SECTION CONSTITUENT 2:4-7 (Expository Paragraph: Contraexpectation of 2:1-3)
        THEME: Because God is exceedingly merciful and loved us so much, he caused us to become spiritually alive and to sit victoriously with Christ in heaven. He did this by uniting us with Christ.

        SECTION CONSTITUENT 2:8-10 (Expository Paragraph: Grounds for 2:4-7)
        THEME: It is only because of God's grace that you have been saved, through trusting in Christ. You did not save yourselves. It is God who caused us to become spiritually alive.

    SUBDIVISION CONSTITUENT 2:11-22: (Expository Section: Nucleus$_2$ of 2:1-22)
    THEME: God brought you Gentiles, along with Jewish believers, into his spiritual family by uniting you spiritually with Christ, so that now you all share the same blessings and form one church. Through Christ's death, both Jewish and Gentile believers are at peace with God and one another, which is evidenced by the fact that all believers, whether Jew or Gentile, may approach God freely, by means of the Holy Spirit.

        SECTION CONSTITUENT 2:11-13 (Expository Paragraph: Conclusion$_1$ of 2:11-22)
        THEME: Formerly you were spiritually separated from Christ and not part of God's spiritual family, but now you are spiritually united with Christ and are part of God's family.

        SECTION CONSTITUENT 2:14-18 (Expository Paragraph: Grounds of 2:11-13 and 2:19-22)
        THEME: Christ himself has caused believers, both Jews and Gentiles, to be at peace with God and with one another. He did this by dying on the cross, with the result that the regulations of the Jewish law were made ineffective. The validity of this peace is evidenced by the fact that all believers are able to approach God by means of the Holy Spirit.

        SECTION CONSTITUENT 2:19-22: (Expository Paragraph: Conclusion$_2$ of 2:11-22)
        THEME: So then, you Gentile believers are no longer excluded from God's blessings, but share in them equally with the Jewish believers, and together with them, form one church.

DIVISION CONSTITUENT 3:1-13 (Expository Section: Authoritative grounds for 2:1-22)
THEME: I, Paul, am in prison because I serve Christ on the behalf of you Gentiles. God graciously appointed me to make known to you that Christ is the source of infinite blessings for you, as well as for Jewish believers. He also appointed me to make known to everyone how God accomplished what he had secretly planned, in order that, by means of establishing the church, he might now make known his infinitely wise plan to those beings who exercise power in the heavens.

SECTION CONSTITUENT 3:1 (Propositional Cluster: Conclusion of 3:2–13)
THEME: I want you to know that it is because I serve Christ Jesus on the behalf of you Gentiles that I am in prison.
SECTION CONSTITUENT 3:2–7 (Expository Paragraph: Grounds$_1$ for 3:1)
THEME: God graciously appointed me to be responsible for preaching the gospel to you Gentiles. He revealed to me that he will bless you equally with the Jewish believers, and that you will, with them, belong to one church.
SECTION CONSTITUENT 3:8–13 (Expository Paragraph: Grounds$_2$ for 3:1)
THEME: God graciously appointed me to make known to the Gentiles that Christ is the source of infinite blessings for them, and to cause everyone to understand how God accomplished what he had secretly planned. God's purpose in this was that, by means of establishing the church, he might now make known his infinitely wise plan to those beings who exercise power in the heavens.

SUBPART CONSTITUENT 3:14–21 (Expressive Section: Response to 2:1–3:13)
THEME: I pray that the Holy Spirit may empower you, that you may experience Christ's infinite love and that God may cause you to be perfect, just as he is perfect. May he be glorified through the church and through Christ Jesus forever. Amen.

SECTION CONSTITUENT 3:14–19 (Expressive Paragraph: Nucleus$_1$ of 3:14–21 [Prayer])
THEME: I pray that God may empower you by means of his Holy Spirit, and that you may be able to understand and experience how greatly Christ loves us, and that God may cause you to be perfect, just as he is perfect.
SECTION CONSTITUENT 3:20–21 (Expressive Paragraph: Nucleus$_2$ of 3:14–21 [Responsive Doxology])
THEME: May our infinite God be glorified through the church and through Christ Jesus forever. Amen.

PART CONSTITUENT 4:1–6:20 (Hortatory Subpart: Nucleus of 1:3–6:20)
THEME: Behave as God's people should. Use the spiritual gifts which Christ has given to each of you to ensure that the church becomes completely united and spiritually mature. Do not behave in an evil way or disobey God, but imitate him, letting your lives be characterised by love for one another. By so doing, evil will be exposed and the truth revealed. Behave wisely, be controlled completely by the Holy Spirit and submit yourselves to one another. At all times, rely wholeheartedly on the Lord Jesus Christ to strengthen you. Make use of every spiritual resource which God provides for you, in order to successfully resist the devil and all his powerful evil spirits. Persevere in prayer for all God's people.

SUBPART CONSTITUENT 4:1–6:9 (Hortatory Division: Nucleus$_1$ of 4:1–6:20)
THEME: Behave as God's people should. Use the spiritual gifts which Christ has given to each of you to ensure that the church becomes completely united and spiritually mature. Do not behave in an evil way, but be good to one another. Do not disobey God, but imitate him. Specifically, let your lives be characterised by love for one another. Live righteous lives, since, by doing so, evil is exposed and the truth is revealed. Behave wisely, be controlled completely by the Holy Spirit and submit yourselves to one another.

DIVISION CONSTITUENT 4:1–16 (Hortatory Section: Nucleus$_1$ of 4:1–6:9)
THEME: Behave in a way that shows that you are God's people. Do all you can to ensure that the church remains united. Christ has given different spiritual gifts to each of God's people, in order that they might minister to each other and that, by this means, the church might become completely united and spiritually mature.

SECTION CONSTITUENT 4:1–6 (Hortatory Paragraph: Nucleus of 4:1–16)
THEME: Behave in a way that shows that you are God's people. Do all you can to ensure that you remain united with one another, since there is one church, one Holy Spirit, one Lord Jesus Christ and one God.
SECTION CONSTITUENT 4:7–16 (Expository Paragraph: Grounds for 4:1–6)
THEME: Christ has given different spiritual gifts to each one in his church, in order that the church might remain united and become spiritually mature.

DIVISION CONSTITUENT 4:17–32 (Hortatory Section: Nucleus$_2$ of 4:1–6:9)
THEME: You have learnt that you must behave in a manner which is consistent with your new, godly character. Therefore, stop doing those immoral things which unbelievers do and which are harmful to one another. Rather, act appropriately towards one another.

    SECTION CONSTITUENT 4:17–19 (Hortatory Paragraph: Generic Hortatory Nucleus of 4:17–32)
    THEME: You must no longer behave in the immoral manner in which unbelievers do.
    SECTION CONSTITUENT 4:20–24 (Expository Paragraph [Mitigated Hortatory]: Motivational Grounds for 4:25–32)
    THEME: You have learnt that you must behave in a manner which is consistent with your new, godly character.
    SECTION CONSTITUENT 4:25–32 (Hortatory Paragraph: Appeal of 4:17–32)
    THEME: Stop doing those things which are harmful to one another. Rather, act appropriately towards one another.

DIVISION CONSTITUENT 5:1–6 (Hortatory Paragraph: Nucleus$_3$ of 4:1–6:9)
THEME: Imitate God. Specifically, let everything you do be done because you love one another. Do not let anyone persuade you to disobey God and live immoral lives, since God will punish those people who habitually disobey him.

DIVISION CONSTITUENT 5:7–14 (Hortatory Paragraph: Nucleus$_4$ of 4:1–6:9)
THEME: Live righteous lives, as those who are in the light should. By doing so, expose the evil deeds which evil people do, since, by living righteously, the truth is revealed to ungodly people.

DIVISION CONSTITUENT 5:15–6:9 (Hortatory Section: Nucleus$_5$ of 4:1–6:9)
THEME: Be very careful that you behave wisely, that you be controlled completely by the Holy Spirit, and that you submit yourselves to one another. Wives, submit yourselves to your husbands. Husbands, love your wives. Children, obey your parents. Fathers, bring up your children well. Slaves, obey your earthly masters. Masters, treat your slaves well.

    SECTION CONSTITUENT 5:15–17 (Hortatory Paragraph: Nucleus$_1$ of 5:15–6:9)
    THEME: Be very careful that you behave wisely, that you make good use of your time and that you understand what the Lord wants you to do.
    SECTION CONSTITUENT 5:18–21 (Hortatory Paragraph: Nucleus$_2$ of 5:15–6:9)
    THEME: Let the Holy Spirit control and empower you completely at all times. Praise and thank God for everything. Submit yourselves to one another.
    SECTION CONSTITUENT 5:22–33 (Hortatory Paragraph: Nucleus$_3$ of 5:15–6:9)
    THEME: Wives, submit yourselves to your husbands in the same manner as you should submit yourselves to the Lord. Husbands, love your wives as Christ also loved the church.
    SECTION CONSTITUENT 6:1–4 (Hortatory Paragraph: Nucleus$_4$ of 5:15–6:9)
    THEME: Children, obey your parents since, as believers in the Lord Jesus Christ, it is right that you do so. Fathers, bring up your children well, by training them according to the teaching given by the Lord Jesus Christ.
    SECTION CONSTITUENT 6:5–9 (Hortatory Paragraph: Nucleus$_5$ of 5:15–6:9)
    THEME: Slaves, obey and serve your earthly masters wholeheartedly, since the Lord will reward each person for whatever good thing that person does. Masters, treat your slaves well, since you know that their Lord and yours deals with all people impartially.

SUBPART CONSTITUENT 6:10–20 (Hortatory Section: Nucleus$_2$ of 4:1–6:20 [Climax])
THEME: At all times, rely wholeheartedly on the Lord Jesus Christ to strengthen you. Make use of every spiritual resource which God provides for you, in order to successfully resist the devil and all his powerful evil spirits. At the same time, persevere in prayer to God for all his people.

    SECTION CONSTITUENT 6:10–13 (Hortatory Paragraph: Nucleus of 6:10–20)
    THEME: At all times, rely wholeheartedly on the Lord Jesus Christ to strengthen you. Make use of every spiritual resource which God provides for you, in order to successfully resist the devil and all his powerful evil spirits.

SECTION CONSTITUENT 6:14–20 (Hortatory Paragraph: Amplification of 6:10–13)
THEME: Firmly resist the devil and all his evil spirits. Do this by relying on the truth, on your righteous conduct, on the good news which gives you peace, on your faith in the Lord Jesus Christ, on the fact that God has saved you and on the word which God has given you by means of his Spirit. At the same time, always be alert and persevere in prayer to God for all his people.

EPISTLE CONSTITUENT 6:21–24 (Complex Section: Closing of the Epistle)
THEME: *I am sending Tychicus to tell you what is happening to me and my fellow-workers, and to encourage you. I pray that God will cause you, fellow-believers, to have peace and to love one another. I also pray that he will continue to act graciously towards all who keep on loving our Lord Jesus Christ.*

SECTION CONSTITUENT 6:21–22 (Commissive Paragraph: Nucleus$_1$ of 6:21–24)
THEME: I am sending Tychicus to tell you what is happening to me and my fellow-workers, and to encourage you.

SECTION CONSTITUENT 6:23–24 (Expressive Paragraph: Nucleus$_2$ of 6:21–24 [closing benediction])
THEME: I pray that God will cause you, fellow-believers, to have peace, to love one another and to keep on believing in Christ. I pray that God will continue to act graciously towards all who keep on loving our Lord Jesus Christ.

THE SEMANTIC UNITS OF THE EPISTLE TO THE EPHESIANS
EPHESIANS 1:1–6:24 (Epistle)

THEME: I, Paul, write this letter to you who are God's people at Ephesus. God is worthy to be praised, since he has blessed us exceedingly through Christ. By uniting Jews and Gentiles who believe in Christ he established his church, with Christ, the supreme ruler over all things, as its head. God's purpose in this was to reveal his infinite wisdom to the powerful beings in the heavens. May you experience the Holy Spirit's power and Christ's infinite love. And may God be glorified through the church and through Christ Jesus for ever. On the basis of all this, behave as God's people should. Let your lives be characterised by love, by the Holy Spirit's control and by wholehearted reliance on Christ, as you do all you can to ensure the unity and spiritual maturity of the church. To this end, make use of every spiritual resource which God provides, so that you may withstand the attacks of the devil. Persevere in prayer for all God's people. I am sending Tychicus to encourage you. I pray that God will continue to bless you all.

¶MACROSTRUCTURE	CONTENTS
opening	1:1–2 I, Paul, am writing this letter to you* who are the people of God in Ephesus. I pray that God will bless you.
BODY	1:3–6:20 God is worthy to be praised, since he has blessed us exceedingly through Christ. He caused Jews and Gentiles who believe in Christ to be at peace with him and with each other, so that now we form one church, with Christ, the supreme ruler over all things, as its head. God's purpose in doing this was to reveal his infinite wisdom to the powerful beings in the heavens. I pray that the Holy Spirit may empower you, that you may experience Christ's infinite love and that God may cause you to be perfect just as he is perfect. May he be glorified through the church and through Christ Jesus forever. On the basis of all this, behave as God's people should. Imitate him, letting your lives be characterised by love. Under the control of the Holy Spirit and in wholehearted reliance on the Lord Jesus Christ, do all you can to ensure that the church becomes completely united and spiritually mature. To this end, make use of every spiritual resource which God provides for you, in order that you may be able to successfully resist the devil and all his powerful evil spirits. Persevere in prayer for all God's people.
closing	6:21–24 I am sending Tychicus to tell you what is happening to me and my fellow-workers, and to encourage you. I pray that God will cause you, fellow-believers, to have peace and to love one another. I also pray that he will continue to act graciously towards all who keep on loving our Lord Jesus Christ.

*"You" in the displays is to be understood as plural. "We" is to be understood as inclusive unless marked exclusive: "we (exc)".

COHERENCE

Ephesians follows the established pattern of a Greek letter, of an opening, a BODY and a closing, at this the highest level of the discourse. According to Callow,

> It is this formal structure of the total discourse that constitutes its organizational (or structural) coherence (1983:23; 2002:7).

Other factors which contribute to the coherence (or cohesion) of the discourse will be discussed in the section on Boundaries and Coherence for 1:3–6:20.

PROMINENCE AND THEME

The BODY is the most naturally prominent constituent of the letter since it conveys the main message of the discourse. However, the opening and the closing are also integral to the theme, since they both contain elements which contribute to the rapport which Paul seeks to establish and maintain between himself and the Ephesians. He wants to ensure that they will be receptive to his message and will respond positively to his exhortations.

EPISTLE CONSTITUENT 1:1–2 (Paragraph: Opening of the Epistle)

THEME: I, Paul, am writing this letter to you who are the people of God in Ephesus. I pray that God will bless you.

RELATIONAL STRUCTURE	CONTENTS
NUCLEUS₁ (ADDRESS) — NUCLEUS₁ (AUTHOR)	1:1a *I, Paul, am* an apostle who has been appointed by God to represent Christ Jesus.
NUCLEUS₂ (ADDRESSEES) — 'people of God'	1:1b *I am writing this letter* to you who are the people of God in Ephesus,
— description	1:1c who steadfastly believe *in Christ Jesus and* who are united to Christ Jesus.
NUCLEUS₂ (BLESSING)	1:2 *I pray that* God *our* Father and *our* Lord Jesus Christ will *continue to* act graciously towards you and will *continue to* cause you to have peace.

INTENT AND STRUCTURE

This unit follows the usual formula for the opening of a Greek letter: the name of the author, the name of the addressees and a greeting. The writer is Paul and he addresses the believers at Ephesus. As in all Paul's letters, the greeting takes the form of a prayer, in which he prays that God will bless the Ephesians. It is almost identical with the opening greeting of the letter to the believers at Colossae.

The ADDRESS and BLESSING are distinct constituents and are different in purpose. The ADDRESS has to do with referencing, while the BLESSING is a component of expressive rapport. Since they differ in this way, their relationship would normally be conjoined (co-ordinate) on the macrostructure level. However, the normal features of an opening, such as the non-verb form, tend to mark the entire opening as one paragraph.

Other than the necessary referencing, the purpose of a letter's opening is to state the writer's authority and to establish rapport between the writer and his intended audience. This is what Paul is doing here as he states his own credentials, mentions the faith of the Ephesian believers and asks God to bless them.

NOTES

1:1a *I*, Paul, *am* an apostle who has been appointed by God to represent Christ Jesus. Paul gives his name. He then goes on to describe himself as "an apostle of Christ Jesus by the will of God". This is to ensure that those he is addressing will recognise his authority and listen to what he has to say.

The Greek noun ἀπόστολος "ambassador, delegate, official representative" refers to someone sent as an ambassador to act on behalf of the ruler who sent him. In the New Testament, it is used predominantly to refer to the twelve disciples whom Jesus chose while he was on earth. It is also used often to refer to Paul himself. Here, in the genitive construction ἀπόστολος Χριστοῦ Ἰησοῦ "an apostle of Christ Jesus", the simplest and most obvious meaning is that Paul is an official representative of Christ Jesus. By describing himself as such, he is making the Ephesians aware of the authority which he has to speak and act on behalf of Christ.

The phrase διὰ θελήματος θεοῦ "by the will of God" means that it was God's will that Paul should act as a representative of Christ Jesus. This represents the event "God appointed me/Paul to represent Christ Jesus".

Some manuscripts reverse the order of "Christ Jesus" to "Jesus Christ", but UBSGNT and most versions follow the former. There does not seem to be any semantic distinction signalled by the two different orders. Therefore, it is probably best to follow the order which is most acceptable in the target language.

1:1b *I am writing this letter* to you who are the people of God There is no verb in the Greek, but the participants in the implied event are referred to in the nominative and dative cases, i.e. "Paul...to the saints". The most natural way to complete the sense in English is to supply "*I am writing this letter*," although "*I am sending this letter*" would also be appropriate.

The biblical meaning of the Greek expression οἱ ἅγιοι "the saints" is not the same as the primary sense of "saints" in English. The biblical meaning is "those set apart for, those belonging to God". This is expressed in the display as "to the people of God".

in Ephesus, A number of important Greek manuscripts do not include the words ἐν Ἐφέσῳ "in Ephesus". This is reflected in a number of English versions which include the words but note the issue in a footnote, for example, NIV, NLT, NRSV, TEV. This may mean that the letter was originally meant for a wider audience than just the Ephesians. This idea of a more general readership would explain the variants in this verse and also the lack of greetings to specific individuals in Ephesus.

1:1c who steadfastly believe *in Christ Jesus* and who are united to Christ Jesus. The conjunction καί which joins πιστοῖς ἐν Χριστῷ Ἰησοῦ "believing/faithful in Christ Jesus" to the rest of the verse is understood by the majority of commentators to mean "even/namely". This would indicate that both ἁγίοις and πιστοῖς refer to the one group of people. This analysis is supported by the fact that there is only one article, which occurs before ἁγίοις.

Translations express this in different ways, e.g. "the saints, who are faithful" (TEV), "to the saints, the faithful" (NIV).

The adjective πιστοῖς may mean "faithful" or "believing/believers". Commentators are divided as to which is the more appropriate, because each makes good sense in this context.

Callow (1983:27; 2002:10), when analysing the parallel passage in Colossians 1:2, considers "faithful" to be contextually more suitable than "believing". This analysis is followed here, since those being addressed have already been described as "saints", "the people of God". The sense would seem to be that they are steadfast in what they believe. This is expressed in the display by a relative clause (1:1c) "who steadfastly believe *in Christ Jesus*". This describes those referred to in 1:1b.

The phrase ἐν Χριστῷ Ἰησοῦ "in Christ Jesus" may be connected to both ἁγίοις and πιστοῖς or to only πιστοῖς. Again, commentators are divided, but, because of the occurrence of the single article before ἁγίοις, it seems best to regard it as being connected to both ἁγίοις and πιστοῖς. It is then a further description of the Ephesian believers.

Most commentators agree that, in this context, the phrase "in Christ Jesus" refers to union with Christ. So it is expressed in the display as "who are united to Christ Jesus".

1:2 *I pray that* God our Father and *our* Lord Jesus Christ This verse is regarded as a prayer. It has a stylised form as in Paul's other letters, e.g. 1 Thessalonians (see Callow: 1982:24; 2000:27). There is no verb in the Greek but the implied event is made explicit in the display as "*I pray that*".

In the display proposition, the pronoun "our" occurs in the phrase "our Father and *our* Lord Jesus Christ". It should be noted that whenever the first person plural pronoun appears in the display, it is considered inclusive unless otherwise stated.

will *continue to* act graciously towards you The abstract noun χάρις "grace" represents an event concept and so needs to be re-expressed in a verbal form. This is expressed in the display as "act graciously", in the sense of asking God to bestow undeserved kindness on people. Another option put forward by Callow (1982:24; 2000:27) is to use the verb "to bless", in the sense of asking God to do good to people.

and will *continue to* cause you to have peace. According to Callow,

> [The word εἰρήνη "peace"] reflects the Hebrew greeting of *shalom* 'peace', which expresses much more than lack of strife, or even inner peacefulness. Rather it conveys the idea of "spiritual prosperity," "enjoying God's blessing," general "blessedness." In other words, it is the reciprocal of God's blessing, the recipients' state of blessedness (1982:24; 2000:27).

In this context, the word "peace" is to be understood in this specialised way.

BOUNDARIES AND COHERENCE

The initial boundary of this unit coincides with the beginning of the epistle. The final boundary is marked by the end of the blessing, which is characteristically the last part of the opening.

There are three parts to this unit of Ephesians:

1. The identification of the sender, with a description, using the nominative case.
2. The identification of the addressees, with a description, using the dative case.
3. A wish that God might bless the addressees.

As Paul does in other letters, this is expressed without a verb.

Callow (1983:25; 2002:8) points out with regards to Colossians 1:1–2 that there are relational and lexical aspects of coherence present in the opening unit of an epistle. The reciprocal nature of the sender and the recipients is one relational aspect of coherence. And specifically for Ephesians, the references to the Godhead throughout—"Christ Jesus", "God" (1:1), "God our Father", "the Lord Jesus Christ" (1:2)—provide lexical coherence, along with lexical items belonging to the semantic domain of the Christian faith: "apostle", "saints", "grace" and "peace".

PROMINENCE AND THEME

The ADDRESS and BLESSING have distinctive roles in the opening of the epistle. They are related by conjoining rather than by being in a supportive-type relationship. Therefore, they are equally prominent. So the theme of this unit is based upon both of them.

Again, following Callow's analysis for the theme of Colossians 1:1–2 (1983:25; 2002:9), the content of the second propositional cluster is stated in a generic form, with "God" referring to the Godhead, not just the Father, and "bless" being generic, including both grace and peace.

EPISTLE CONSTITUENT 1:3–6:20 (Part: Body of the Epistle)

THEME: God is worthy to be praised, since he has blessed us exceedingly through Christ. He caused Jews and Gentiles who believe in Christ to be at peace with him and with each other, so that now we form one church, with Christ, the supreme ruler over all things, as its head. God's purpose in doing this was to reveal his infinite wisdom to the powerful beings in the heavens. I pray that the Holy Spirit may empower you, that you may experience Christ's infinite love and that God may cause you to be perfect just as he is perfect. May he be glorified through the church and through Christ Jesus forever. On the basis of all this, behave as God's people should. Imitate him, letting your lives be characterised by love. Under the control of the Holy Spirit and in wholehearted reliance on the Lord Jesus Christ, do all you can to ensure that the church becomes completely united and spiritually mature. To this end, make use of every spiritual resource which God provides for you, in order that you may be able to successfully resist the devil and all his powerful evil spirits. Persevere in prayer for all God's people.

MACROSTRUCTURE	CONTENTS
GROUNDS	1:3–3:21 God is worthy to be praised, since he has blessed us exceedingly through Christ. He chose us, redeemed us and revealed to us his plan to unite all things in heaven and on earth under Christ. He also caused Christ, as supreme ruler over all things, to rule over the church. Because of his grace he saved us, through our faith in Christ. And, through Christ's death, he caused us all, both Jews and Gentiles, to be at peace with him and with each other, so that now we share the same blessings and form one church. He appointed me to make this known to the Gentiles and to make known to everyone that his purpose in forming the church was to reveal his infinite wisdom to the powerful beings in the heavens. I pray that the Holy Spirit may empower you, that you may experience Christ's infinite love and that God may cause you to be perfect just as he is perfect. May God be glorified through the church and through Christ Jesus forever. Amen.
HORTATORY NUCLEUS	4:1–6:20 On the basis of all this, behave as God's people should. Use the spiritual gifts which Christ has given to each of you to ensure that the church becomes completely united and spiritually mature. Do not behave in an evil way or disobey God, but imitate him, letting your lives be characterised by love for one another. By so doing, evil will be exposed and the truth revealed. Behave wisely, be controlled completely by the Holy Spirit and submit yourselves to one another. At all times, rely wholeheartedly on the Lord Jesus Christ to strengthen you. Make use of every spiritual resource which God provides for you, in order to successfully resist the devil and all his powerful evil spirits. Persevere in prayer for all God's people.

INTENT AND MACROSTRUCTURE

The BODY of the epistle consists of two distinct, though related, parts, 1:3–3:21 and 4:1–6:20. These deal with what has been referred to as "doctrine" or "theology" (1:3–3:21) and "duties" or "ethics" (4:1–6:20). Basically, the structure of the BODY is similar to other Pauline letters and consists of prayer and instruction (1:3–3:21), followed by exhortation (4:1–6:20).

The 1:3–3:21 division might be labelled "a reminder". In it, Paul reminds the Ephesians that they are privileged people, since God has blessed them so richly through Christ. He has called them to be his people, made them members of the church and included them in his plan to unite all things under the headship of Christ.

The genre of this unit can be analysed as formally expressive (eulogy, prayer, doxology) and expository, as follows:

A Eulogy (1:3–14)
    B   Prayer (1:15–23)
             C   Expository (2:1–22)
             C'   Expository (3:1–13)
    B'   Prayer (3:14–19)
A' Doxology (3:20–21)

The eulogy and the prayer of 1:3–23 and the prayer and doxology of 3:14–21, as would be expected, are expressive units, as Paul pours out his praise and his petitions to God.

However, 1:3–23 also has expository elements. Paul uses these verses to introduce many of the key ideas which he will further develop in the rest of the letter. These key ideas also provide the grounds for the exhortations of the second half of the BODY.

Among these ideas are God's plan to bring all things together in Christ, God's calling of people to himself and the topics of love, grace, unity, the church, the headship of Christ, power, glory, the heavenlies.

The prayer and doxology unit of 3:14-21 has similar expository elements. Ideas presented in 1:15-23 are restated in these verses, e.g. God's power at work in believers (1:19; 3:16, 20), God's glory (1:17; 3:16, 21), the fulness of God (1:23; 3:19), knowledge (1:17; 3:19).

Conversely, the expository passages of 2:1-3:13 have expressive overtones and a mitigated hortatory element, as Paul seeks to encourage the Ephesians to share in his own great appreciation of all that God has done for his people.

As would be expected in an expository and expressive passage, the mood of the verbs in 1:3-3:21 is, for the most part, indicative. There is only one imperative verb form, μνημονεύετε "remember" (2:11). In contrast, the second half of the BODY, 4:1-6:20, has many imperative and subjunctive verb forms, and is, therefore, clearly hortatory.

This first half of the letter is intended to convince the Ephesians that all believers, whether Jewish or Gentile, are equally blessed by God, and that they are all part of God's purpose for the church. In order to convince them, Paul sets out to strengthen his relationship with them. A strong relationship will make them more likely to accept what he has to say and respond positively to his exhortations in the second part of the letter.

A significant way in which Paul strengthens his relationship with them is by including himself as one who, like them, was "dead in sins" until God saved him. Note also:

1. The use of first person plural verb forms in such passages as 1:3-12, 14, 19; 2:3-7.
2. His thanksgiving to God for the Ephesians in 1:15-16.
3. References to his sufferings on their behalf, e.g. 3:1-13.

In the second half, the hortatory division (subpart) of the BODY (4:1-6:20), Paul's intent is to stimulate the Ephesian believers to respond positively to what he said in 1:3-3:21. He, therefore, urges them to live in such a way that they preserve love and unity and holiness in all aspects of their lives. In this way, they will fulfil God's purpose for them and for his church.

In 1:4, Paul had reminded them of the purpose for which God had called them, i.e. ἐξελέξατο ἡμᾶς ἐν αὐτῷ...εἶναι ἁγίους καὶ ἀμώμους κατενώπιον αὐτοῦ "he chose us in him...to be holy and blameless before him". In 1:18, he prayed that they might know ἡ ἐλπὶς τῆς κλήσεως αὐτοῦ "the hope of his calling", i.e. that they might have a confident expectation that God will fulfil his purpose for those he has called to be his people, as individuals and as part of Christ's body, the church. Now in 4:1, he exhorts them ἀξίως περιπατῆσαι τῆς κλήσεως ἧς ἐκλήθητε "to walk worthy of the calling by which you were called". This implies that God will fulfil what he has promised, but it is their responsibility to live their lives according to God's purpose for them: they are to be "holy and blameless". This applies to them as individuals (1:4) and also as a body, the church (5:27).

The Greek verb περιπατέω "walk" is used to refer to behaviour throughout this letter. It is especially significant in the second half of the BODY, where Paul uses it to introduce a series of exhortations about how they should conduct themselves as God's people. This will be dealt with in more detail in the notes on 4:1-6:20.

The transition from the doctrinal material of 1:3-3:21 to the exhortations and practical instruction of 4:1-6:20 is indicated by the conjunction οὖν "therefore" and by the first person singular form παρακαλῶ "I urge/exhort" in 4:1. Most commentators agree that the series of exhortations introduced in 4:1 has as its basis the whole of 1:3-3:21, not just the immediately preceding paragraph 3:20-21 or even the whole of chapter 3. The two parts of the BODY, therefore, are in a GROUNDS-EXHORTATION relationship.

PEAK IN EPHESIANS

Features of peak that Longacre mentions in *The Grammar of Discourse* which we see as pertinent to Ephesians are:

1. Rhetorical underlining (p. 39). He says, "[The narrator] may employ parallelism, paraphrase, and tautologies of various sorts to be sure that you don't miss" the important point.
2. Heightened vividness (pp. 40-43). Although he doesn't specifically mention metaphor as an example, the extended metaphor of the

Christian soldier's armour in 6:10–17 does produce heightened vividness.
3. Change of pace (pp. 43–45). He says, "The chief devices here are variation in the size of constructions and variation in the amount of connective material".

Expository and hortatory discourse predominate in Ephesians. In Longacre's opinion, of the devices available for marking surface structure peak in expository and hortatory discourse, rhetorical underlining is probably the most frequently used. He considers that both expository and hortatory discourse reflect a struggle. In expository discourse, the struggle is to achieve clarity in the main outlines of its subject. In hortatory discourse, it is to convince the hearers of the soundness of the advice given and to start them on the course of conduct advocated or to discourage them from a course of conduct which is being forbidden. He suggests,

> [A]n artful expository or hortatory discourse will have a meaningful cumulative thrust. This should correlate in at least some discourses with a marked surface structure peak (p. 48).

There are several places in Ephesians where features found in peaks occur. In fact, we could say that the BODY begins with one in 1:3–14, "comparable to the inciting incident of a story" in narrative (Longacre, personal comment, who adds that in this position it might be better to find a different label than "peak"). Among the peak features here are:

1. The repeated occurrence of Εὐλογητός "Blessed (be)" and its cognate forms εὐλογήσας "having blessed" and εὐλογίᾳ "blessing" (all in 1:3).
2. The long sentence (1:3–14), tied together syntactically in a skillful manner with nouns and their corresponding pronouns as the connective links, Christ being the foremost one.
3. The accumulation of lexical forms related to God's will or purpose (1:4–11).
4. The repetition of "to the praise of the glory of" (1:6, 12, 14).

Paul wants to make sure that the Ephesians understand how greatly they have been blessed and that the source of the blessings is God, through Christ. The features listed above underline the importance of what Paul wishes to communicate to the Ephesians and have cumulative thrust in encouraging them to join him in praising God.

The prayer in 1:15–23 also has features of peak, e.g. this is all one Greek sentence and there is repetition of lexical forms dealing with wisdom, knowledge and understanding (1:17, 18). The repetition leads to an accumulation of lexical items from the semantic field of power and greatness (1:19–21). This culminates in τὸ πλήρωμα τοῦ τὰ πάντα ἐν πᾶσιν πληρουμένου "the fulness of the one filling all with all", a phrase containing alliteration and a number of words with superlative sense (1:23).

The main peak of the first half of the letter occurs in its final section (3:14–21). It is marked by:

1. A long sentence (3:14–19).
2. The repetition of lexical items referring to divine qualities such as glory and power (3:16).
3. The emphatic description of the extent of Christ's love (3:18).
4. The oxymoron "to know the love of Christ that is (in fact) unknowable" (3:19).
5. The use of ἵνα πληρωθῆτε εἰς πᾶν τὸ πλήρωμα τοῦ θεοῦ "that you may be filled to/with all the fulness of God" at the end of the prayer (3:19).
6. The doxology in 1:20–21.

In the second half of the BODY, which is largely hortatory, features of peak are found in both the first and final units (4:1–16 and 6:10–20). While peak might be expected at the end of a discourse, here at the beginning of the second half, many features typical of peak are also found. The position of these features of peak, then, is similar to the position of the unit at the beginning of the BODY with its peak-like features (1:3–14).

In 4:2–3, a series of near synonyms (humility, meekness, longsuffering, forbearance) and the closely related terms "love" and "peace" begin the section 4:1–16. These words highlight the theme of "the unity of the Spirit". Thereafter, the following features underline this theme:

1. Repetition of "one" (seven times in 4:4–6) combined with the use of short, non-verbal clauses.
2. Repetition of "all/every" (twelve times in 4:2–16).
3. The explicit references to "the unity of the Spirit" (4:3) and "the unity of the faith"

(4:13) and a number of terms related to "joining together" (4:16).
4. Parallelism in the references to "love" (4:2, 15, 16) and "the body" (4:4, 16) at the beginning and end of the passage.

The use of cognate forms "give/gift" (four times in 1:7–8 and once in 1:11) along with a series of short clauses consisting of "some" as well as a substantive: apostles, prophets, evangelists, pastors and teachers (4:11), draws attention to people God has given to serve the church.

Then, in 4:12–16, there is a list of the different purposes or goals towards which the church should be progressing under the guidance of the above-mentioned people. This is indicated in the surface structure by the repetition of the prepositions πρός "for", εἰς "to, towards, at", μέχρι "until". A further indication is the lexical items from the semantic domain of growing and maturing, e.g. grow up, build up, perfect, complete, fulness, etc.

Also, the metaphor of a mature man (4:13) is in sharp contrast (4:14) with the metaphor of "children". These immature people have not yet attained "the unity of the faith" (4:13). They are open to being deceived by false teachers (described in a list of near synonyms: cunning, craftiness, scheming, deception). These contrasting figures give heightened vividness to the issue of attaining unity and maturity in the church.

Taken together, the multiple features typical of peak have "meaningful cumulative thrust" (Longacre, p. 48) in 4:1–16 in that they focus the reader's attention on the theme of maintaining the unity of the Spirit in the church, which is one of the principal themes of Ephesians.

The final unit of the BODY, 6:10–20, also has features of peak, one being the extended metaphor of the Christian soldier's armour (6:10–17). The use of Τοῦ λοιποῦ "For-the-rest/Finally" in 6:10 indicates a change of topic to Paul's final point in the BODY. The sudden change it introduces, from the domestic matters he has been dealing with in the preceding verses to the military metaphor, highlights the nature of the spiritual struggle facing God's people.

The nature of the struggle is also highlighted by:

1. Repetitive features detailing the strength and wickedness of the enemy (6:11–13).
2. The repetitive surface structure feature of two successive imperative constructions, ἐνδύσασθε τὴν πανοπλίαν τοῦ θεοῦ (6:11) and ἀναλάβετε τὴν πανοπλίαν τοῦ θεοῦ (6:13). These have the same meaning ("put on the full armour of God"). They are followed by a third imperative instruction which is a specific of the first two: "stand, having fastened the belt of truth around your waist" (6:14).

The position of unit 6:10–20 at the end of the BODY is also a factor suggesting a peak/climax, comparable to the denouement of a narrative.

BOUNDARIES AND COHERENCE

The initial boundary of the BODY of the epistle is indicated by the ending of the formalised opening of the epistle, specifically, the ending of the blessing of the addressees (1:2).

The final boundary is indicated by the following features:

1. The δέ in 6:21 introduces a change of subject matter.
2. There is a change of topic, from spiritual warfare to personal matters and Tychicus is introduced.
3. There is a tail-head link between 6:20 and 6:21. In 6:20, as a matter for prayer, Paul refers to himself in relation to proclaiming the gospel and uses this to introduce the communication of his personal situation by Tychicus in 6:21.

There are a number of factors of cohesion and coherence at work in the BODY of the epistle, which unite the two halves. Of these, the theme of "unity" is significant and is expressed in the following ways:

1. Exhortation to unity (τὴν ἑνότητα) occurs in an important exhortation in the first sentence in the Greek text of chapter 4 (4:1–3).
2. The expression τὴν ἑνότητα occurs in a clause expressing a significant purpose of Christ's giving spiritual gifts to his people and appointing them to service (4:13).
3. The phrase ἐν Χριστῷ "in Christ", or its equivalent, occurs more than thirty times in the letter. Although this phrase is used in a variety of ways, and must take its sense from each context, it frequently indicates the means by whom unity is achieved. See 1:3–14; 2:5–6; 3:6; 5:8.

4. The use of Greek terms with the prefix συν- "with, together with". There are fourteen occurrences of this.

   a. In 2:5-6, these compound words refer to the union between Christ and the believers:

   συνεζωοποίησεν "he made us alive with"
   συνήγειρεν "he raised us together with"
   συνεκάθισεν "he seated us with"

   b. Nine occurrences refer to the union of Jewish and Gentile believers:

   συμπολῖται "fellow-citizens" (2:19)
   συναρμολογουμένη "being fitted together" (2:21; 4:16)
   συνοικοδομεῖσθε "are being built together" (2:22)
   συγκληρονόμα "fellow-heirs" (3:6)
   σύσσωμα "fellow-members" (3:6)
   συμμέτοχα "fellow-partakers" (3:6)
   ἐν τῷ συνδέσμῳ τῆς εἰρήνης "in the bond of peace" (4:3)
   συμβιβαζόμενον "being brought together" (4:16)

   c. The other two occurrences are stated negatively, that is, believers are not to become "participants" (συμμέτοχοι) with unbelievers (5:7) nor are they to "participate" (συγκοινωνεῖτε) with them in their evil deeds (5:11).

5. This unity is found in the church, the community of believers. This community is referred to nine times by the term ἐκκλησία (1:22; 3:10, 21; 5:23, 24, 25, 27, 29, 32). It is also described by various metaphors:

   the body of Christ (1:22, 23; 2:16; 4:4, 12, 16; 5:23, 30)
   the holy temple (2:20-22; 4:12, 16)
   the bride (5:21-33)

6. A key verse in relation to "unity" is 1:10. In this verse, Paul refers to God's purpose as ἀνακεφαλαιώσασθαι τὰ πάντα ἐν τῷ Χριστῷ, τὰ ἐπὶ τοῖς οὐρανοῖς καὶ τὰ ἐπὶ τῆς γῆς "to-bring-together/unite all (things) in Christ, the (things) in the heavens and the (things) on the earth" (1:10).

7. The term εἷς "one" is expressive of unity and is used twelve times in the BODY of the epistle: (2:14; 2:15; 2:16; 2:18; 4:4 [three times]; 4:5 [three times]; 4:6; 5:33).

The only direct exhortation to unity is in 4:3. Throughout 4:1-6:9, however, as Paul urges the Ephesians to live in a way which is appropriate for God's people, his intention is to encourage them to live in a way which avoids disunity and maintains unity.

PROMINENCE AND THEME

The theme for the BODY of this epistle is based on both the GROUNDS and the EXHORTATION units of the BODY.

The theme of unity has been referred to in the preceding section on Boundaries and Coherence as a significant coherence factor in the BODY of the epistle, since it is in focus throughout. A basis for this unity is love, which is another prominent theme of the letter.

Hoehner comments,

> The frequent occurrence of the term love in such a short book is phenomenal (p. 104).

He notes that the word occurs, as verb or noun, twenty times in Ephesians. This is twice as many times per thousand words of text than in the other Pauline letters.

The love referred to is both that shown by God and Christ to people and also that between believers. In the second half of Ephesians most of the occurrences are related to the latter, as Paul urges the Ephesians to show love to others in all aspects of their lives. See 4:2; 4:15; 4:16; 5:2; 5:25; 5:28 (three times); 5:33. Clearly Paul attaches great importance to this aspect of the Christian life. Hoehner says,

> This frequent use of love seems to furnish the key to the purpose of the book.... It seems reasonable to conclude that the purpose of Ephesians is to promote a love for one another that has the love of God and Christ as its basis (pp. 105-106).

To this statement it might be added that the further purpose of promoting love among God's people is that it should result in unity.

Notice the occurrence of "through/in Christ" in the theme statement for the BODY of this epistle and also in the themes for lower levels of the discourse. Paul gives prominence to the phrase ἐν Χριστῷ "in Christ", or its equivalent, by constant repetition throughout the letter. He establishes its importance in the eulogy with which the BODY begins (1:3-14) by using it eleven times. This causes us to focus from the start on Christ as the only source, means and agency by whom and in whom God has blessed, and will continue to bless, his people.

The theme of God's working through Christ is inextricably related to the other important themes of love and unity. It is only because God's people are united spiritually with Christ and, through him, have God's power available to them, that they can build up and maintain a church characterised by love and unity which will glorify God. For this purpose, Paul urges the Ephesians to use this power against Satan, whom Christ has already defeated.

PART CONSTITUENT 1:3–3:21 (Subpart: Grounds for 4:1–6:20)

THEME: God is worthy to be praised, since he has blessed us exceedingly through Christ. He chose us, redeemed us and revealed to us his plan to unite all things in heaven and on earth under Christ. He also caused Christ, as supreme ruler over all things, to rule over the church. Because of his grace he saved us, through our faith in Christ. And, through Christ's death, he caused us all, both Jews and Gentiles, to be at peace with him and with each other, so that now we share the same blessings and form one church. He appointed me to make this known to the Gentiles and to make known to everyone that his purpose in forming the church was to reveal his infinite wisdom to the powerful beings in the heavens. I pray that the Holy Spirit may empower you, that you may experience Christ's infinite love and that God may cause you to be perfect, just as he is perfect. May God be glorified through the church and through Christ Jesus forever. Amen.

MACROSTRUCTURE	CONTENTS
INTRODUCTION	1:3–23 God is worthy to be praised, since he has blessed us exceedingly through Christ. He chose us, redeemed us and revealed to us his plan to unite all things in heaven and on earth under Christ. He also caused Christ, as supreme ruler over all things, to rule over the church.
NUCLEUS	2:1–3:13 Because of God's grace he saved us, through our faith in Christ. Through Christ's death, God caused all believers, whether Jew or Gentile, to be at peace with him and with each other, so that now all share the same blessings and form one church. God appointed me to make known to the Gentiles that he is the source of infinite blessings for them, and to make known to everyone that God's purpose in forming the church was to reveal his infinite wisdom to the powerful beings in the heavens.
RESPONSE TO NUCLEUS	3:14–21 I pray that the Holy Spirit may empower you, that you may experience Christ's infinite love and that God may cause you to be perfect, just as he is perfect. May he be glorified through the church and through Christ Jesus forever. Amen.

INTENT AND MACROSTRUCTURE

In considering the structure of the 1:3–3:21 unit as stated in the notes on 1:3–6:20, these verses are analysed as an expository NUCLEUS (2:1–3:13), sandwiched between an INTRODUCTION (1:3–23) and a RESPONSE (3:14–21) to the NUCLEUS. Since the INTRODUCTION consists of eulogy and prayer and the RESPONSE consists of prayer and doxology, they are both expressive units. However, both also have a strong expository component, as stated in the notes on 1:3–6:20.

The INTRODUCTION and the NUCLEUS are connected by καί "and" (2:1), which indicates both a continuity of theme with the preceding unit (1:15–23) and also a new stage in the development of the major theme introduced in it, i.e. how powerfully God acted in and through Christ (1:19–23). Then, in chapters 2 and 3, Paul continues with this theme and describes how that same power of God is effective in the lives of the Ephesian believers.

In this constituent of the epistle Paul's intention is to assure the Ephesians that, because of what Christ has done, they are reconciled to God and, along with all believers, whether Jew or Gentile, they are part of God's church. As such, they are part of God's plan to bring all things in heaven and on earth together under the headship of Christ.

In order to persuade them of these truths, Paul reminds them of several things:

1. The great things that God has done for them through Christ (1:3–14).
2. That the same power which was working in Christ (1:19–20) is available to them.
3. Their former condition when they were alienated from God (2:1–3, 11–12).
4. Their present state of fellowship with him and all who belong to the church (2:13–22).

He wants them to realise fully what they have become "in Christ", so that they will respond to his exhortations in chapters 4–6 and live their lives accordingly.

BOUNDARIES AND COHERENCE

The initial boundary of this unit has been discussed in the section on Boundaries and Coherence for 1:3–6:20.

The final boundary is marked by the doxology of 3:20–21 and the ἀμήν "Amen". It is also marked by those features which indicate the opening of the second half of the BODY in 4:1.

Most notable is the change from expository and expressive genre to hortatory genre. This is clearly signalled by the initial παρακαλῶ οὖν ὑμᾶς...ἀξίως περιπατῆσαι τῆς κλήσεως ἧς ἐκλήθητε "I urge you therefore...to walk worthy of the calling by which you were called". This is the first of a series of exhortations, to encourage the Ephesians to live their lives in accordance with their new position, i.e. as people who have been given new life in Christ and have been incorporated into his church.

There is structural cohesion in the sandwich structure of 1:3–3:21, as stated in the section on Intent and Macrostructure. There is more frequent use of the phrase ἐν Χριστῷ "in Christ", or its equivalent, throughout this part of Ephesians. This is also true of vocabulary belonging to the following semantic fields:

"power/authority" (1:19, 21; 2:2; 3:7, 10, 16, 20)
"the heavenlies" (1:3, 10, 20; 2:6; 3:10)
"glory" (1:6, 12, 14, 17, 18; 3:13, 16, 21)
"fulness" (1:10, 23; 3:19, 20)

PROMINENCE AND THEME

The NUCLEUS (2:1–3:13) is regarded as naturally prominent. The INTRODUCTION (1:3–23) is also considered prominent since all the main topics and themes which are developed in the NUCLEUS are presented in it. Also the καί in 2:1 indicates a co-ordinate relationship with 2:1–3:13.

The RESPONSE is a more appropriate, specific term in this context for result in a basic reason-result relationship. In a reason-result relation, the result tends to be prominent. So 3:14–21 is considered as having equal prominence with 2:1–3:13. Here again we see the mixture of expressive and expository features in 1:3–3:21. The theme statement of 1:3–3:21, therefore, includes prominent elements of the themes of all three units.

SUBPART CONSTITUENT 1:3–23 (Expressive Division: Introduction to 2:1–3:13)

THEME: God is worthy to be praised, since he has blessed us exceedingly through Christ. He chose us, redeemed us and revealed to us his plan to unite all things in heaven and on earth under Christ. He also caused Christ, as supreme ruler over all things, to rule over the church.

MACRSTRUCTURE	CONTENTS
NUCLEUS₁ (Eulogy)	1:3–14 God is worthy to be praised, since he has blessed us spiritually and abundantly in every way, because we are united with Christ. Specifically, God has chosen us to be his holy and blameless people. He has redeemed us. He has confirmed this by the Holy Spirit. He has also revealed to us his plan to unite all things in heaven and on earth under Christ at the appointed time. God's purpose in all this is that we should praise him.
NUCLEUS₂ (Thanksgiving and prayer)	1:15–23 I thank God for your faith and love. I pray that God may cause you to understand more fully how powerfully he works on behalf of his people, just as he worked powerfully when he caused Christ, who had died, to live again and, as supreme ruler over all things, to rule over the church.

INTENT AND MACROSTRUCTURE

The 1:3–23 division consists of a eulogy (1:3–14) and a prayer (1:15–23).

Since 1:3–14 is a eulogy, it is, therefore, an expressive unit. However, it does have expository characteristics, since Paul's intention is to instruct the Ephesians, and by doing so, to enable them to understand how greatly God has blessed them.

Many commentators understand διὰ τοῦτο "because of this" in 1:15 to refer back to the blessings listed in 1:3–14. Others, however, take it to refer most directly to 1:13–14, where specific reference is made to the salvation and faith of the Ephesian believers.

In 1:15–16, Paul refers to the fact that he has heard of their faith in the Lord Jesus and also of their love for all God's people. Because of these things, he never stops thanking God for them. This connection of 1:15–16 with 1:13–14 makes good sense and expresses a natural progression of thought. For more details on this, see the notes on 1:15.

And Paul prays that God will enable the Ephesians to understand more fully how great God's power is and how powerfully he works on behalf of his people through Christ. While this is formally a prayer, and certainly has expressive elements, it is also heavily expository in nature, since Paul wishes to instruct the believers about these matters. The expressive tone is evident as he reveals how he feels about God's great power.

Paul's intention is for the Ephesians to learn from both the eulogy and the prayer, and that what they learn will cause them to join him in praising God. This will, in turn, strengthen his relationship with the Ephesians.

BOUNDARIES AND COHERENCE

The initial boundary of this unit coincides with the initial boundary of the BODY of the epistle. In the case of the final boundary, a break is indicated after 1:23, for the following reasons:

1. There is a change of genre from prayer, albeit a prayer with expository features, to exposition in 2:1.
2. There is a change of topic, from the exaltation of Christ (1:20–23) to a focus on the contrast between the Ephesian believers' past condition of spiritual death, and their present situation as people whom God has made alive spiritually. This is marked by a switch from third person singular to second person plural verb forms, with the independent pronoun ὑμᾶς "you" in the emphatic position in 2:1.
3. After a single long sentence in the Greek (1:15–23), a new sentence begins at 2:1.
4. There is rhetorical bracketing with reference to "the Lord Jesus" and "the saints" in 1:15, and "Christ" and "the church" in 1:22. Christ and the believers are also referred to indirectly in 1:23.

A number of the ideas introduced in the eulogy (1:3–14) are taken up in the thanksgiving and prayer (1:15–23). This gives coherence to 1:3–23. For example, the phrase in 1:17 πνεῦμα σοφίας καὶ ἀποκαλύψεως ἐν ἐπιγνώσει αὐτοῦ "the Spirit of wisdom and revelation in the knowledge of him" recalls ἐν πάσῃ σοφίᾳ καὶ φρονήσει, γνωρίσας ἡμῖν τὸ μυστήριον τοῦ θελήματος αὐτοῦ "making known to us in all wisdom and insight the mystery of his will" (1:8b–9a).

There are also references, both in the eulogy and the prayer, to:

    faith
    glory
    riches
    fulness
    inheritance
    the heavenlies

PROMINENCE AND THEME

The prominent elements of both the eulogy and the prayer are represented in the theme statement.

DIVISION CONSTITUENT 1:3–14
(Expressive Subdivision: Nucleus₁ [Eulogy] of 1:3–23)

THEME: God is worthy to be praised, since he has blessed us spiritually and abundantly in every way, because we are united with Christ. Specifically, God has chosen us to be his holy and blameless people. He has redeemed us. He has confirmed this by the Holy Spirit. He has also revealed to us his plan to unite all things in heaven and on earth under Christ at the appointed time. God's purpose in all this is that we should praise him.

MACROSTRUCTURE	CONTENTS
CONCLUSION ────────────	1:3a God is worthy to be praised,
└─grounds ────────────	1:3b–14 since he has blessed us spiritually and abundantly in every way, because we are united with Christ. Specifically, God has chosen us to be his holy and blameless people. He has redeemed us. He has confirmed this by the Holy Spirit. He has also revealed to us his plan to unite all things in heaven and on earth under Christ at the appointed time. God's purpose in all this is that we should praise him.

INTENT AND MACROSTRUCTURE

The occurrence of εὐλογητός "blessed" as the initial word of this new unit, along with the use of cognate forms εὐλογήσας "having blessed" and εὐλογία "blessing" (1:3), gives prominence to the idea of "blessing" or "praise" and indicates that this is an expressive unit. This is further supported by the references to ἔπαινον "praise" in 1:6, 12, 14. Whereas situation-reaction material is usually analysed as basic cause-effect and would have reason-result labelling, here there seems to be the intention of enhancing the audience's views of God. So this falls more in the category of conclusion-grounds (claim-justification) or even mitigated hortatory.

Paul is expressing what he thinks about God (1:3a). In doing so, he implicitly invites the Ephesians to share in this and to join him in praising God. He goes on to list the many blessings which believers have received from God through Christ (1:3b–14). These verses (1:3b–14) state the grounds for the CONCLUSION of 1:3a.

The three purpose clauses expressing praise to God, which occur in 1:6, 12, 14, are intended to reinforce the statement in 1:3a that God is worthy to be praised.

BOUNDARIES AND COHERENCE

The initial boundary of the 1:3–14 unit coincides with the initial boundary of the BODY of the epistle.

The final boundary of this unit and the initial boundary of the next are marked by the following features:

1. In 1:15, a first person singular authorial reference, κἀγώ "I for my part" or "as for me", is used for the first time in this epistle. Its use marks the beginning of an "I-you" relationship between Paul and the Ephesian believers. It also brings Paul into the foreground as the agent. The significance of κἀγώ as an initial boundary marker is evidenced by its use in 3:1 and 4:1 also. In those places it combines with other evidence to indicate a major boundary.

2. The genre changes from eulogy in 1:3–14 to prayer in 1:15–23. The theme of the eulogy is the many blessings which God has bestowed upon believers. The aim of the prayer is that the Ephesian believers might realise the full extent of those blessings. In 1:16, the orienter μνείαν ποιούμενος "making mention" introduces the unit that is the content of that prayer, the content itself beginning with ἵνα "that" in 1:17.

3. There is a tail-head transition when Paul speaks of the faith of the Ephesians in 1:13 (ἐν ᾧ καὶ πιστεύσαντες "in whom you also having believed") and in 1:15 (τὴν καθ' ὑμᾶς πίστιν ἐν τῷ κυρίῳ Ἰησοῦ "your faith in the Lord Jesus").

God is the agent throughout these verses. There are constant references to the persons of the Trinity, which also provide strong referential cohesion and coherence. God is in focus throughout as the instigator, the one who wills and puts into effect all actions, while it is "in Christ" that they are accomplished.

The coherence of this unit is further strengthened by the use of vocabulary belonging to several sets of semantically related words.

One set concerns God's will or decision-making:

ἐξελέξατο "he chose" (1:4)
προορίσας "having predestined" (1:5)
προορισθέντες "having been predestined" (1:11)
εὐδοκία "good pleasure, purpose" (1:5, 9)
θέλημα "will" (1:5, 9, 11)
προέθετο "he planned, intended" (1:9)
ἐκληρώθημεν "we were chosen" (1:11)
πρόθεσις "plan, purpose" (1:11)
βουλή "purpose, counsel" (1:11)

The second group concerns other attributes of God:

ἀγάπη "love" (1:4)
δόξα "glory" (1:6, 12, 14)
χάρις "grace" (1:6, 7)
ἐχαρίτωσεν "he blessed, favoured" (1:6)

A third set concerns the abundance of blessings which God gives to his people:

πλοῦτος "wealth, abundance" (1:7)
ἐπερίσσευσεν "he caused to abound" (1:8)
πᾶς "all, every kind" (1:8)

PROMINENCE AND THEME

In material such as this, that is intended to change both ideas and behaviour, the CONCLUSION and the grounds must both be represented in the theme statement. The grounds representation is a general statement based on the NUCLEI of all the paragraphs.

SUBDIVISION CONSTITUENT 1:3a
(Expressive Proposition: Conclusion of 1:3b-14)

THEME: *God is worthy to be praised.*

	CONTENTS
	1:3a God, *who is the God* of our Lord Jesus Christ and *who is also* his Father, *is worthy to* be praised.

INTENT AND STRUCTURE

As mentioned in the section on Intent and Macrostructure for 1:3-14, 1:3a is a CONCLUSION based on the grounds of 1:3b-14. It is expressive in nature.

BOUNDARIES AND COHERENCE

The initial boundary has been discussed in the section on Boundaries and Coherence for 1:1-2 and 1:3-14. The basic reason for making a cut between 1:3a and 1:3b is a relational one. All of 1:3b-14 supports the CONCLUSION in 1:3a.

NOTES

1:3a God, *who is the God* of our Lord Jesus Christ and *who is also* his Father, *is worthy of being praised* The occurrence of εὐλογητός "blessed, praised" at the beginning of the verse, along with the use of cognate forms of this word three times in this verse, gives this concept emphasis. See εὐλογήσας "having blessed" and εὐλογία "blessing".

As is common in eulogies, the verb "to be" does not occur. See, for example, 2 Corinthians 1:3; 1 Peter 1:3. Commentators discuss whether the form of the verb to be supplied should be the present indicative "blessed/praised is God", the present imperative "let God be praised" or the present optative "may God be praised". Each of these makes good sense. Most commentators seem to favour the use of the indicative, i.e. that this is a statement about God. See, for example, Eadie (pp. 10-11), Hoehner (p. 162), O'Brien (p. 94).

In the expression ὁ θεὸς καὶ πατὴρ τοῦ κυρίου ἡμῶν Ἰησοῦ Χριστοῦ "the God and Father of our Lord Jesus Christ", the genitive phrase τοῦ κυρίου ἡμῶν Ἰησοῦ Χριστοῦ "of our Lord Jesus Christ" is regarded by the majority of commentators as modifying both θεός "God" and πατήρ "Father". Also the καί has a co-ordinating function. The sense is that God is both the God of our Lord Jesus Christ and also his Father. See also 1:17, where God is again referred to as "the God of our Lord Jesus Christ". Most versions follow this analysis.

Regarding the phrase "our Lord Jesus Christ", it should be noted that, whenever the first person plural pronoun appears in the display, it is inclusive unless otherwise stated.

SUBDIVISION CONSTITUENT 1:3b–14
(Expressive Section: Grounds for 1:3a)

THEME: God has blessed us spiritually and abundantly in every way, because we are united with Christ. Specifically, God has chosen us to be his holy and blameless people. He has redeemed us. He has confirmed this by the Holy Spirit. He has also revealed to us his plan to unite all things in heaven and on earth under Christ at the appointed time. God's purpose in all this is that we should praise him.

MACROSTRUCTURE	CONTENTS
GENERIC	1:3b God has blessed us spiritually in Christ in every way, with those things which come from heaven, because we are united with Christ.
—specific₁	1:4–6 God has chosen us to be his holy and blameless people because we are united with Christ. God did this in order that we should praise him [God].
—specific₂	1:7–12 God has redeemed us. He has revealed to us his plan to unite all things in heaven and on earth under Christ at the appointed time. He has also appointed us to receive what he has promised to his people in order that we should praise him.
—specific₃	1:13–14 The Holy Spirit within us confirms that we belong to God and guarantees that God will finally redeem us in order that we should praise him.

INTENT AND MACROSTRUCTURE

Section 1:3b–14 forms the grounds for Paul's CONCLUSION in 1:3a. These are the abundant spiritual blessings which God has given to us in Christ. This unit might be labelled as either expressive or expository since it has features of both genre.

BOUNDARIES AND COHERENCE

The grounds is presented in GENERIC terms in 1:3b and then in specific terms in the three paragraphs that follow (1:4–6, 1:7–12, 1:13–14). The repetition of the phrase εἰς ἔπαινον (τῆς) δόξης "to the praise of the glory" in 1:6, 12, 14 is a cohesive factor for the section. It also helps to define the respective paragraphs as it closes them.

God is the agent throughout these verses. There are also constant references, both explicit and implicit, to the persons of the Trinity, which also provide strong referential cohesion and coherence. God is in focus throughout as the instigator, the one who wills and puts into effect all actions, while it is "in Christ" that these actions are accomplished.

There is a progression in these paragraphs as the focus changes with each one.

In 1:3b, the focus is generic: "all spiritual blessings".

In 1:4–6, the focus is on past action of God, i.e. he chose believers "before the foundation of the world".

In 1:7–12, the focus moves to the present state of believers, a state brought about through Christ's death on the cross, i.e. they are redeemed and waiting to receive what God has promised to them.

Finally, in 1:13–14, the focus is on the future inheritance of the believers, an inheritance guaranteed by the presence of the Holy Spirit with them.

PROMINENCE AND THEME

For a concise theme, a statement of the GENERIC unit normally would be sufficient, but here the specific units are full of prominence-marking devices, so each specific is represented in summarised form. This includes "God's purpose in all this is that we should praise him", representing the repetitive occurrence of this statement.

SECTION CONSTITUENT 1:3b
(Expressive Propositional Cluster: Generic Nucleus of 1:3b–14)

THEME: God has blessed us spiritually in every way, with those things which come from heaven, because we are united with Christ.

	CONTENTS
	1:3b God has blessed us spiritually in every way, *with those things which come from* heaven, *because we are united* with Christ.

INTENT AND STRUCTURE

The 1:3b propositional cluster forms the GENERIC nucleus of the specifics found in 1:4–14.

NOTES

1:3b God has blessed us spiritually in every way *with those things which come from* **heaven,** In the phrase ὁ εὐλογήσας ἡμᾶς "the one having blessed us", the agent is God and those being blessed are believers.

The Greek word πνευματικῇ "pertaining to the spirit, spiritual", along with πάσῃ "all/every", qualifies εὐλογίᾳ "blessing" in the phrase ἐν πάσῃ εὐλογίᾳ πνευματικῇ "with every spiritual blessing". The term may refer to either the source or the nature of the blessings, or both. The blessings are spiritual in that they come by means of the Holy Spirit and benefit the human spirit. The blessings referred to are election, adoption, redemption, forgiveness, etc. The expression "every spiritual blessing" is a summary statement of the more specific blessings that are listed in the following verses.

The phrase ἐν τοῖς ἐπουρανίοις "in the heavenlies" occurs five times in Ephesians (1:3, 20; 2:6; 3:10; 6:12) and nowhere else in the New Testament. Some ways different versions have translated it are "heavens", "heaven", "heavenly places", "heavenly realms", "heavenly world".

There seems to be consensus that the term denotes location in each of the other occurrences in Ephesians.

In 1:20, it refers to the place where Christ is at the right hand of God.

In 2:6, the place where believers are raised and seated with Christ.

In 3:10, the place where the rulers and authorities are to whom the mystery of the church is made known.

In 6:12, the place where the evil spiritual powers are, against whom believers struggle.

Therefore, here in 1:3, it would also make sense for it to refer to heaven, since the blessings referred to come from God through Christ.

because we are united **with Christ.** The phrase ἐν Χριστῷ "in Christ", or its equivalent, occurs many times in this letter, fourteen of those occurrences being in this section, 1:3–14. Clearly, it is not to be understood in a physical sense. So it must be translated so that its meaning will be understood.

In this context, it can be understood as the reason why or means by which God blessed us. There is not much difference between reason and means here. It is likely that in many languages it will be easier to translate with a reason construction than with means. In the display, therefore, it is expressed as "*because we are united* with Christ".

BOUNDARIES AND COHERENCE

The boundaries of this unit have been discussed in the sections on Boundaries and Coherence for 1:3a and 1:3b–14. The basis for making 1:3b a separate unit is a relational one. It provides the generic statement for the specific explanations of the statement in 1:4–14.

PROMINENCE AND THEME

The theme is based on the single propositional cluster which constitutes this unit.

SECTION CONSTITUENT 1:4–6 (Expressive Paragraph: Specific₁ of 1:3b)

THEME: God has chosen us to be his holy and blameless people because we are united with Christ. God did this in order that we should praise him [God].

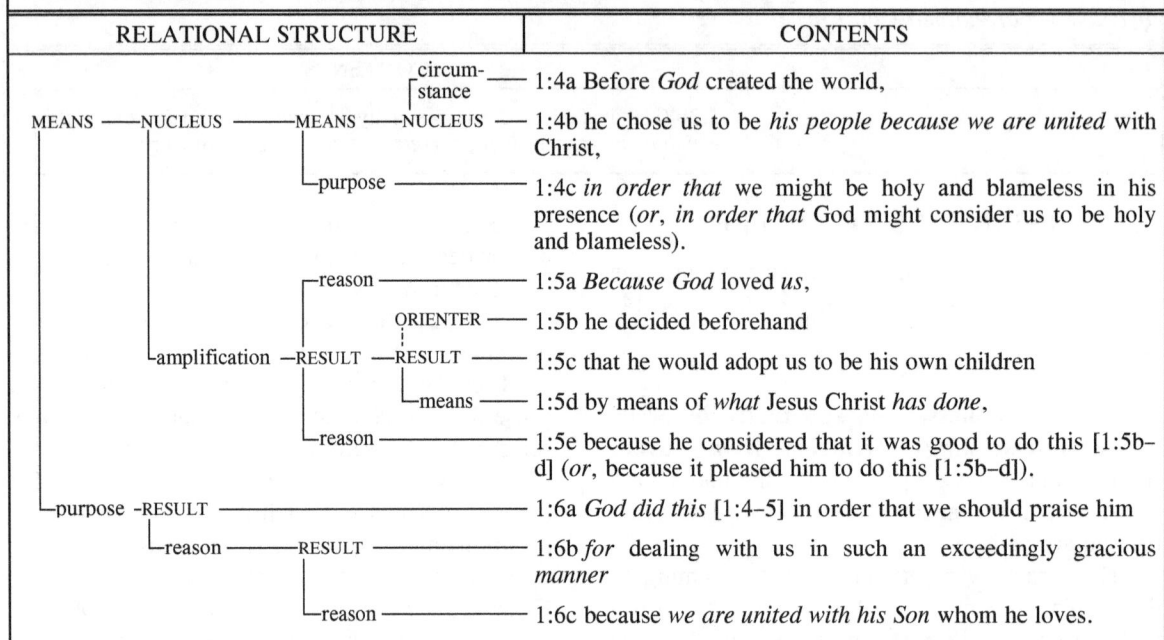

INTENT AND STRUCTURE

This is an expressive paragraph. It is specific₁ of the grounds unit 1:3b–14, which serves as a grounds for the CONCLUSION 1:3a.

NOTES

1:4 The Greek conjunction καθώς "just as, because" may be understood in a comparative sense or a causal sense. Both have good support. However, a third option suggested by some commentators seems most applicable in this context and is followed in this analysis. It is that καθώς introduces the first in a series of specific blessings which were referred to in generic terms in 1:3b. See, for example, Bratcher and Nida (p. 11), Caragounis (p. 61), O'Brien (p. 98).

The specific blessing referred to in 1:4 is that of election.

1:4a Before *God* created the world, See the note on 1:4 for a discussion of καθώς, which begins this verse.

The phrase πρὸ καταβολῆς κόσμου "before the foundation of the world" is temporal. Since καταβολή is an abstract noun representing an event, it is represented in the display by an event proposition, with *God* made explicit as the agent of creation.

In the display, this proposition has been placed before the one containing the main verb "he chose" (1:4b) so that the purpose of that verb should not be separated from the verb itself. Proposition 1:4a states the temporal circumstance in which the event of 1:4b takes place.

1:4b he chose us to be *his people because we are united* with Christ, The verb ἐκλέγομαι means "to choose, select (someone/something for oneself)" (see BDAG, p. 305).

It is important that the target language term used for "choose" does not suggest that the choice is based upon any value or worth in the chosen individual. Rather, it should indicate the purpose of the person doing the choosing. Here, that purpose is indicated by εἶναι ἡμᾶς ἁγίους καὶ ἀμώμους κατενώπιον αὐτοῦ "that we should be holy and blameless before him" (1:4c).

As in 1:4a, the agent is God, referring back to ὁ θεός in 1:3. In 1:4c, the purpose of the choosing is that those chosen might be holy and blameless in God's presence. However, in some languages, it may also be necessary to make explicit the position chosen: *to be his people*.

***because we are united* with Christ** The phrase ἐν αὐτῷ "in him" refers back to ἐν Χριστῷ "in Christ" (1:3). Some commentators suggest that it indicates the *reason* for God's choosing us. See, for example, Meyer (p. 313).

Most versions translate ἐν αὐτῷ "in him" literally. In some languages, however, this may not be possible and a phrase may be needed to describe the "in-Christ" state of believers. This might be expressed as "our being united with Christ".

How this is related to "he chose us *to be his people*" is more difficult to state. Perhaps "God chose us *to be his people* because of our being united with Christ" or "God chose us *to be his people* because we are united with Christ" might express the sense. However, no translation should give the idea that our becoming united with Christ is the primary step in our being chosen. Hodge says,

> God gave a people to his Son in the covenant of redemption. Those included in that covenant, and because they are included in it—in other words, because they are in Christ as their head and representative—receive in time the gift of the Holy Spirit and all other benefits of redemption. Their voluntary union with Christ by faith, is not the ground of their federal union, but, on the contrary, their federal union is the ground of their voluntary union (p. 31).

1:4c *in order that* we might be holy and blameless in his presence (*or, in order that* God might consider us to be holy and blameless). The infinitive εἶναι "to be" indicates the purpose or goal of the preceding verb, ἐξελέξατο "he chose".

Since ἄμωμος "unblemished" was used to describe sacrificial animals, which had to be perfect, some commentators suggest that this should be regarded as a live metaphor. However, since it is frequently used in a moral or religious sense in Scripture (BDAG, p. 56.2a), meaning "blameless", most commentators treat it as a dead metaphor. They, therefore, translate it as "blameless".

Some commentators suggest that "holy and blameless" is a near-synonymous doublet here. Moore (p. 46), however, rejects the analysis that they are synonymous.

There is consensus that the expression κατενώπιον αὐτοῦ "in his presence" means that it is in God's estimation that believers are to be considered holy and blameless. There is some discussion, however, as to *when* this will be the believers' state. Although some commentators think that the focus is on the believers' final state in heaven, the majority consider it to refer to the present time.

1:5a *Because God* loved *us*, Opinions are divided as to whether the phrase ἐν ἀγάπῃ "in love" should be connected to what precedes or to what follows. The views most widely held by commentators are:

1. It should be connected with the following participle προορίσας "having predestined" in 1:5. See, for example, Abbott (p. 8), Best (pp. 122–123), Bratcher and Nida (p. 13), Eadie (pp. 29–30), Ellicott (p. 6), Hendriksen (p. 78, fn. 18). If this analysis is followed, the reference is to God's love for those he has chosen to be his people (NIV, RSV, TEV).
2. It should be connected with the preceding εἶναι ἡμᾶς ἁγίους καὶ ἀμώμους "that we should be holy and blameless" in 1:4. See, for example, Alford (pp. 71–72), Hoehner (pp. 183–184), Lenski (pp. 359–360), Lincoln (p. 17), O'Brien (p. 101). If this analysis is followed, the reference is to the love believers have for others (REB, NJB, NRSV).

In support of the first option, it can be argued that it is more appropriate for the following reasons:

1. The phrase ἐν ἀγάπῃ "in love" is separated from εἶναι ἡμᾶς ἁγίους καὶ ἀμώμους but adjacent to προορίσας.
2. The fact that, in redeeming humanity, God was motivated by love is consistent with other passages in Ephesians. See 2:4; 5:2, 25.

If option one is followed, it provides the reason for God's decision in 1:5b.

Lincoln supports the second option and argues,

> ..."in love" should rather be seen as part of the goal election is intended to achieve in those it embraces—a life before God which is holy and blameless and lived in love. Elsewhere in the letter, with reference to love, its human associations predominate (cf. 1:15; 3:17; 4:2, 15, 16; 5:2, 25, 28, 33; 6:23, 24) (p. 17).

His other reason for his support of the second option is,

> [If ἐν ἀγάπῃ is construed] in this way [it] fits the pattern of the rest of the eulogy where the various sections conclude with a prepositional phrase with ἐν (ibid.).

If the second option is followed, the sense would be that we should be holy and blameless in loving others.

Both options are acceptable and make good sense in the context. In the display, the first option is followed and, since it is understood that God is the agent and "us" the recipients of his love, this is made explicit.

1:5b he decided beforehand In the New Testament, the verb προορίζω "decide upon beforehand, predestine" is used only to describe what God decided from before he created the world.

1:5c that he would adopt us to be his own children The noun υἱοθεσία "adoption" is a legal term borrowed from Roman law. It is only used in a religious sense in the New Testament. The figure is of the adoption of a child/person into a family. Just as a child is adopted into an earthly family, with all the rights and privileges that entails, so those whom God has chosen are adopted into his heavenly family with all the rights and privileges that entails.

The phrase εἰς αὐτόν "unto him" refers to God, not Christ. God is the one who receives believers as his children, through Christ.

There is no consensus among commentators as to the relationship between the aorist participle προορίσας "having predestined" and the aorist finite verb ἐξελέξατο "he chose" in 1:4. The main possibilities are the following:

1. The participle restates the same event as that represented by ἐξελέξατο "he chose" in 1:4, with some additional information. See, for example, Best (p. 123), Candlish (p. 36), Lincoln (p. 25), Hendriksen (pp. 78–79).
2. The participle expresses the reason that God chose people. See, for example, Hodge (p. 35), Hoehner (p. 194).

The aorist participle following the finite verb potentially indicates action prior to that of the finite verb and this would support interpretation 2. However, according to BDF,

> The element of past time is absent from the aorist participle especially if its action is identical with that of an aorist finite verb (§ 339 (1)).

Hendriksen (pp. 78–79) considers the aorist participial clause to be "a further definition of election, showing the form it takes". This makes good sense.

In the display, therefore, 1:5 is regarded as an amplification of 1:4.

1:5d by means of *what* Jesus Christ *has done*, Most versions translate διὰ Ἰησοῦ Χριστοῦ as "through Jesus Christ". The preposition διά "through" indicates the means by which the adoption referred to in 1:5b occurs.

1:5e because he considered that it was good to do this [1:5b–d] (*or,* **because it pleased him to do this [1:5b–d]**). The preposition κατά followed by the accusative case means "in accordance with, because of, on the basis of". Here it introduces a reason for 1:5b–d.

In the genitive construction τὴν εὐδοκίαν τοῦ θελήματος αὐτοῦ "the pleasure of his will", the two Greek nouns are closely related semantically. They might be represented respectively as "it-pleased-him/he-was-pleased to" and "he decided/desired". In the display, their combined sense is expressed as "he considered that it was good to do this [1:5b–d]" or, "it pleased him to do this [1:5b–d]". This proposition parallels the reason given in 1:5a. These two reasons are very similar and bracket the propositional cluster 1:5a–e.

1:6a–b *God did this* [1:4–5] in order that The phrase εἰς ἔπαινον δόξης τῆς χάριτος αὐτοῦ "to the praise of the glory of his grace" brings this paragraph to a close. It is paralleled by εἰς ἔπαινον δόξης αὐτοῦ at the end of 1:7–12 and 1:13–14.

The majority of commentators agree that the preposition εἰς indicates the purpose or goal of election. This is followed in the display, with 1:6a–b providing the purpose of the propositional cluster 1:4a–5e. The ultimate purpose of everything is that "the glory of his grace" should be praised.

we should praise him *for* dealing with us in such an exceedingly gracious *manner* The nouns ἔπαινον "praise", δόξης "glory" and χάριτος "grace" are abstract nouns which represent events or attributes. They are, therefore, expressed as verbs, adjectives or adverbs in the display.

The agent of "praise" is "we". This refers to Paul and all believers, in particular, the Ephesian believers as this letter is specifically for them.

In this SSA, the noun δόξα "glory" is understood to be attributive here. It describes God's gracious actions towards his chosen people. So it can be regarded as an attribute of his grace.

The verb χαριτόω "bestow favour upon, favour highly, bless", which is the verb in the relative clause describing grace, occurs only here and in Luke 1:28. It is used in both passages with God as the agent. The root is the same as that of the noun χάρις "grace". The verb is generally understood to mean "to treat with grace". So the literal meaning of the phrase τῆς χάριτος αὐτοῦ ἧς ἐχαρίτωσεν ἡμᾶς would be "his grace with/of which he has graced us", i.e. God has been gracious towards us. This is the generally accepted sense, and the one expressed in most versions.

The phrase τῆς χάριτος αὐτοῦ ἧς ἐχαρίτωσεν ἡμᾶς "his grace with/of which he has graced us" is an emphatic construction which stresses the superlative nature of God's grace towards his chosen people. So the use of the relative phrase "with/of which he has graced us", in conjunction with δόξα in relation to χάριτος, further emphasises the greatness of God's grace. It might be expressed as "he has dealt with us in such an exceedingly gracious manner" or "he has blessed us so exceedingly abundantly".

Proposition 1:6b expresses the reason for 1:6a, i.e. "we should praise him *for* dealing with us (*or, because* he has dealt with us) in such an exceedingly gracious manner".

1:6c because *we are united with his Son* whom he loves. The phrase ἐν τῷ ἠγαπημένῳ "in the one having been loved" continues the thought that the blessings which believers receive from God are a result of their relationship to Christ (1:3, 4, 5). Because they are "in Christ", i.e. united with him, they are the recipients of God's favour.

Most versions use an "in" prepositional phrase. Exceptions are NLT "because we belong to his dearly loved Son" and CEV "because of the Son he dearly loves". These translations seem appropriate in the context. So, in the display, it is expressed as "because *we are united with his Son* whom he loves".

Proposition 1:6c expresses the reason for 1:6b, i.e. "he has dealt with us in such an exceedingly gracious manner because we are united with his Son whom he loves".

BOUNDARIES AND COHERENCE

The boundaries of this unit have been discussed in the section on Boundaries and Coherence for 1:3b–14.

In the Greek, ἐξελέξατο "he chose" (1:4) is the only non-subordinated finite verb in the paragraph, and the whole paragraph is grammatically related to it.

The paragraph divides into three propositional clusters coinciding with 1:4, 1:5 and 1:6.

The nucleus of 1:6 is 1:6a. This is in a purpose relation with 1:4 and 1:5.

PROMINENCE AND THEME

The relational centre of the paragraph is 1:4b, which has natural prominence. The theme statement for the paragraph should, therefore, be based on this proposition. However, the basic content of 1:6a is repeated at the end of the next two paragraphs. This indicates its significance. Therefore, this is also included in the theme statement.

SECTION CONSTITUENT 1:7–12 (Expressive Paragraph: Specific₂ of 1:3b)

THEME: God has redeemed us. He has revealed to us his plan to unite all things in heaven and on earth under Christ at the appointed time. He has also appointed us to receive what he has promised to his people in order that we should praise him.

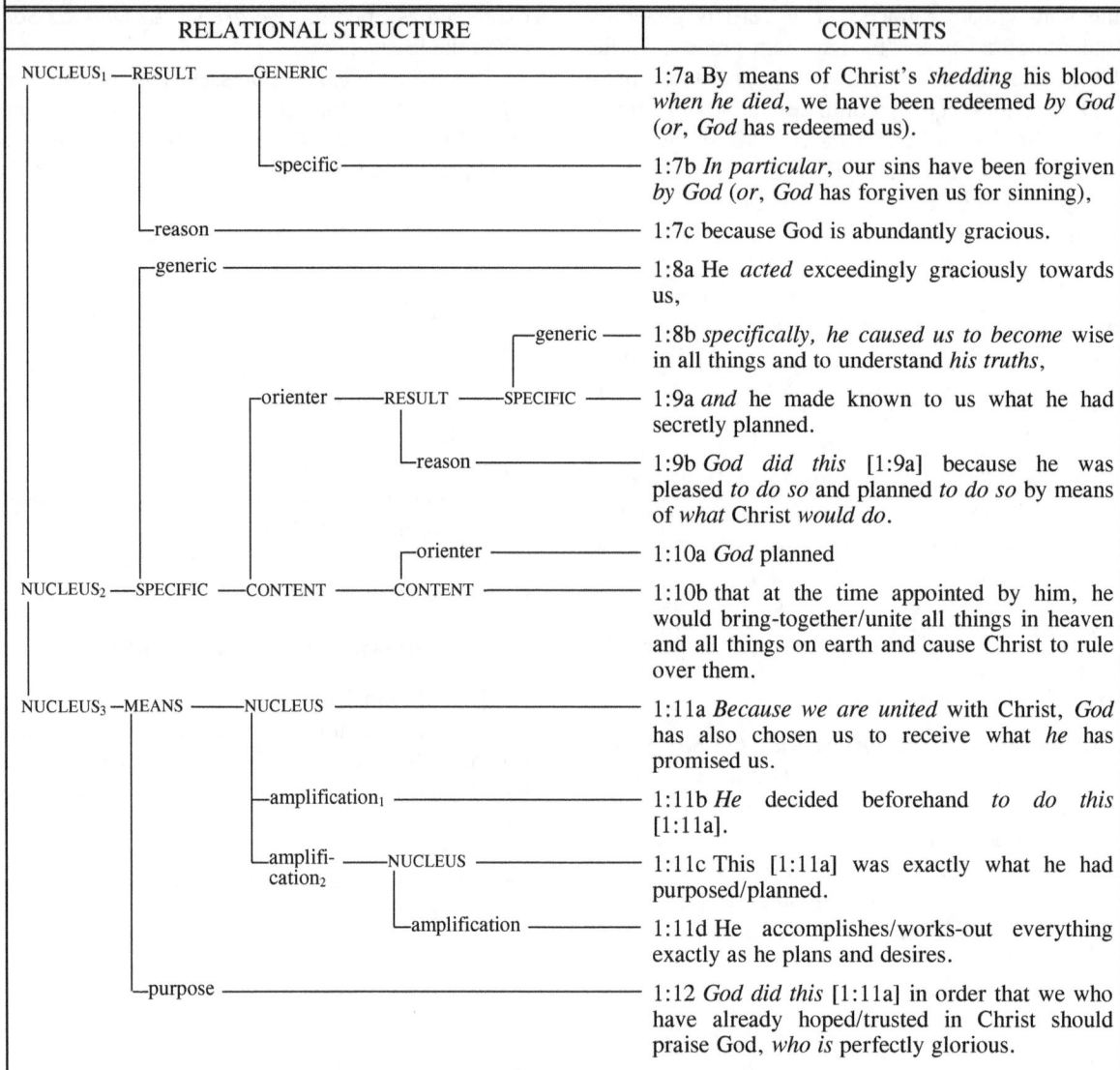

INTENT AND STRUCTURE

This is an expressive paragraph. It states further specific blessings which God has given to his people through Christ. Note also the closing purpose clause (1:12), by which Paul intends to stimulate the Ephesian believers to praise God along with him. The paragraph functions as part of the grounds (1:3b–14) for the CONCLUSION of 1:3a.

Paul has been dealing with past acts of God towards his people in 1:4–6. Now he turns to present blessings in Christ. It is by means of Christ's sacrificial death that we are saved (1:7). He is the one who will be head over all things (1:10). He is the one in whom we hope (1:12).

In 1:9–10, Paul reveals the content of the mystery. This is a significant statement in the introduction of the topic. Different aspects of the mystery are revealed in the rest of Ephesians. See 3:3, 4, 9; 5:32; 6:19. Here, in 1:9–10, the focus is on God's all-inclusive purpose, that, ultimately, all things in heaven and on earth will be united in Christ, i.e. under the headship of Christ. In chapters 2 and 3, Paul deals with a major step in the accomplishment of this goal, when he sets out how Jewish and Gentile believers have been reconciled to God and to each other to form one church. He also explains his part in the accomplishment of this task.

NOTES

1:7a By means of Christ's *shedding* his blood *when he died*, The relative phrase, ἐν ᾧ "in whom", at the beginning of this paragraph provides "the head" of a tail-head link with "in the beloved" at the end of the previous paragraph. Both phrases refer to Christ. The phrase marks a transition to another aspect of his theme of blessings which God has given through Christ: Christ's redeeming work for us.

Callow (1983:70; 2002:42), discussing the parallel passage in Colossians 1:14, suggests that, although the most common meaning of ἐν Χριστῷ in the New Testament is "in union with Christ", it is possible in the context to argue for the sense of agent, i.e. that Christ is the one who in some sense performs the action. This analysis has support elsewhere in Scripture, e.g. in Titus 2:14, it is stated that Christ redeemed us. Also the phrase διὰ αἵματος αὐτοῦ "by means of his blood" makes it clear that Christ is involved in the action here. However, as Callow states for Colossians 1:14, Christ is best seen as the mediate agent, the one through whom we have redemption. This analysis seems equally possible here in Ephesians for similar reasons.

The noun αἷμα literally means "blood". It can also be used to refer to the seat of life or to an atoning sacrifice. In this context, "blood" may be regarded as a metonymy in which it stands for a violent death, or it may be regarded as a non-figurative comparison based on the Jewish sacrificial system. TEV translates it simply as "death", but this seems insufficient since blood is an important theological symbol throughout both the Old and the New Testaments. So the word "blood" should be retained in the translation, but related to the death of Christ, e.g. "Christ's *shedding* his blood *when he died*". This will remove any misunderstanding.

we have been redeemed *by God* (*or, God has redeemed us*). The abstract noun ἀπολύτρωσις "redemption" represents the event "to redeem" or "to ransom". In the clause ἔχομεν ἀπολύτρωσιν "we have redemption", ἔχομεν is active in form, but represents a deep structure passive. It is not we who have redeemed ourselves, but someone else, namely God. In the display, therefore, this is expressed as "we have been redeemed *by God*".

Commentators discuss whether the event "redeem" involves paying of a ransom or simply freeing someone. In some contexts in the New Testament, the more general meaning, freeing someone, is appropriate. See, for example, Luke 21:28; Rom. 8:23. However, in this context, when taken in conjunction with διὰ τοῦ αἵματος "by means of his blood", it seems reasonable to assume that the idea of payment is present. Other Scriptures, such as Matthew 20:28, Mark 10:45, 1 Peter 1:18-19, give support to this.

1:7b *In particular,* our sins have been forgiven *by God* (*or, God* has forgiven us for sinning), The abstract noun ἄφεσιν "forgiveness" represents the event "to forgive". The full clause is ἔχομεν ἄφεσιν τῶν παραπτωμάτων "we have forgiveness of sins". This is regarded as being in apposition with "we have redemption" in 1:7a and it may be in an equivalent or generic-specific relation to it. The latter relationship is probably more appropriate, since "redemption" is usually regarded as including more than the forgiveness of sins. The forgiveness of sins is the one particular aspect on which Paul wishes to focus here. "*In particular*" is used in the display to indicate that this is one specific aspect of redemption.

Again, as in 1:7a, it is good to retain the passive voice if possible, or some other language-specific construction, in order to focus on the blessings which the believers have received.

1:7c because God is abundantly gracious. The Greek word πλοῦτος "wealth, riches" is used figuratively here. Therefore, it means an abundance of something. Paul uses this word frequently in his epistles to modify such qualities as glory, wisdom, grace, assurance. Here in the genitive construction τὸ πλοῦτος τῆς χάριτος αὐτοῦ "the riches of his grace", it describes the nature of this grace—how great or abundant it is.

The pronoun αὐτοῦ "his" refers to God, the one who is abundantly gracious, who acts exceedingly graciously.

Commentators discuss whether κατά "according to" refers to "redemption" or "forgiveness". However, there seems to be greater support for the former. See, for example, Hodge (pp. 41-42), Lincoln (p. 29), O'Brien (p. 107). However, since, in the display, "forgiveness" is represented as being a specific of "redemption", this clause is analysed as qualifying both "redemption" and "forgiveness". It provides a reason for the generic-specific statement of 1:7a–b.

Several versions make a sentence break after 1:7b. See, for example, NJB "Such is the richness of the grace..."; REB "In the richness of his grace..."; TEV "How great is the grace of God...". Bratcher and Nida agree, saying,

> [Although this sentence break may be contested on grammatical grounds,] in terms of essential meaning and of impact on the reader, it may be defended as a faithful translation of the Greek (p 18).

1:8a He *acted* exceedingly graciously towards us, The relative pronoun ἧς "which", with which this verse starts, refers to χάριτος "grace" in 1:7.

It is the direct object of the aorist active indicative of περισσεύω "to lavish, cause to abound, give in large measure" (ἧς is the result of attraction and stands for the accusative ἥν). God is the agent of the verb. So the whole phrase means "he/God caused grace to abound towards us". This might be expressed as "God *acted* exceedingly graciously towards us".

1:8b *specifically, he caused us to become* wise in all things and to understand *his truths*, The connection of the prepositional phrase ἐν πάσῃ σοφίᾳ καὶ φρονήσει "in all wisdom and understanding" is problematic. It needs to be decided whether it is connected to the preceding verb ἐπερίσσευσεν "he caused to abound" or to the following verb γνωρίσας "having made known". In the former case, the "wisdom and understanding" refer to God. In the latter case, the phrase refers to "us".

Most commentators consider that ἐν πάσῃ σοφίᾳ καὶ φρονήσει "in all wisdom and understanding" should be connected with ἧς ἐπερίσσευσεν εἰς ἡμᾶς "he caused to abound in us". The phrase, therefore, refers to the gifts that God has given to his people. See, for example, Ellicott (p. 10), Hendriksen (p. 84), Hodge (p. 43), Hoehner (p. 212), Lincoln (p. 29), O'Brien (p. 107). This analysis is followed in REB, "In the richness of his grace God has lavished on us all wisdom and insight". See also NIV, NJB.

To support this view, commentators refer to two other passages in Ephesians 1. The first is 1:9, where Paul refers to God's making known the mystery of his will to believers. The other is 1:17–19, where he prays that God will give the Ephesian believers "the spirit of wisdom and revelation in the knowledge of him" so that they may know what God has planned for his people. The parallel passage, Colossians 1:9, supports this view.

Few commentators support the alternative analysis, that ἐν πάσῃ σοφίᾳ καὶ φρονήσει "in all wisdom and understanding" should be connected with the following aorist participle γνωρίσας "having made known". This analysis, however, is followed in TEV, "In all his wisdom and insight God did what he had purposed, and made known to us the secret plan...". See also NASB, NRSV. Best, who follows this analysis, says,

> [W]ords dealing with wisdom go fittingly with a word indicating the making known of a mystery (v. 9) (p. 133).

The majority view is followed in the display, but, due to the support in the versions, the alternative is also possible.

Following the majority view, the relationship is, therefore, understood to be that of specific to the generic statement in 1:8a, that God acted exceedingly graciously towards us. However, it is the whole propositional configuration of 1:8b–10b which is in a specific relation with 1:8a rather than the single proposition 1:8b.

Commentators discuss whether there is significant difference between σοφία "wisdom" and φρόνησις "understanding, insight" in this verse. Most consider it to be a generic-specific doublet. So they believe that the difference between the two terms should be preserved. See, for example, Eadie (p. 47), Ellicott (p. 10), Hendriksen (p. 84), Hodge (pp. 43–45). There is no consensus, however, as to what that difference in meaning is. Hendriksen says,

> *Wisdom is knowledge plus*. It is the ability to apply knowledge to the best advantage, enabling a person to use the most effective means for the attainment of the highest goal. *Insight* (cf. Col. 1:9, *understanding*) is the result of *setting one's mind on* God's redemptive revelation in Christ, the mystery of his will, for Paul continues: 9. ...**in that he made known to us the mystery of his will** (p. 84).

Hodge, however, says,

> The wisdom then which the apostle says God has communicated to us, is the divine wisdom in the

Gospel, the mystery of redemption, which had been hid for ages in God, but which he has now revealed...by the Spirit.... The word φρόνησις ...when used in reference to spiritual things...includes all that is meant by spiritual discernment (pp. 44–45).

Bratcher and Nida (p. 19) suggest that it might be translated "he caused us to be wise in all things and to understand".

Following the majority view that these words are not synonyms, it is expressed in the display as "*he caused us to become* wise in all things and to understand *his truths*". In filling out the case frame for the verb "understand", the noun phrase *his truths* is used since there seems to be agreement that the insight gained is into spiritual matters.

1:9a *and* he made known to us that which he had secretly planned. The aorist active participle γνωρίσας "having made known" is related syntactically to the finite verb ἐπερίσσευσεν "he caused to abound" (1:8a). The semantic relationship between 1:9a and 1:8b is that of SPECIFIC (1:9a) to generic 1:8b. This is a part of the propositional configuration 1:8b–10b which is in a SPECIFIC-generic relation with 1:8a. See the notes on 1:8b and 1:10. God has acted in an exceedingly gracious manner towards us. A specific instance of this is that he has made known to us his plan of redemption. This fits the pattern of presentation in the epistle. Paul usually praises the Lord for his gracious acts in general terms and then more specifically. For example, in 1:3, there is praise for "every spiritual blessing", then in each of the following paragraphs—1:4–6, 1:7–12, 1:13–14—various specific blessings are enumerated. Also, within this paragraph (1:7–12) this pattern is seen in 1:7a and 7b.

As is the case throughout the New Testament, the Greek word μυστήριον "mystery" is used to refer to a truth which previously had been known only to God, but which God has now chosen to reveal to believers. It has been translated as "mystery" (NJB, KJV, NIV, NRSV), "secret plan" (TEV), "secret purpose" (REB). Callow (1983:102; 2002:65) represents it as "a secret-message".

The scholarly consensus is that in the genitive phrase τὸ μυστήριον τοῦ θελήματος αὐτοῦ "the mystery of his will", "mystery" describes the contents of what God wills. This phrase is expressed in the display as "that which he had secretly planned".

1:9b *God did this* [1:9a] because he was pleased *to do so* The majority view is that the phrase κατὰ τὴν εὐδοκίαν αὐτοῦ "according to his pleasure" relates to the preceding participle γνωρίσας "having made known". The phrase recalls τὴν εὐδοκίαν τοῦ θελήματος αὐτοῦ "the pleasure of his will" in 1:5. In that verse, and also in 1:7, the preposition κατὰ was understood to indicate a relationship of reason rather than a standard. Although, in this context, there is little semantic difference between the two relationships, it is the relation of reason that is represented in the display.

and planned *to do so* by means of *what Christ would do*. The pronoun ἥν in the relative clause ἥν προέθετο ἐν αὐτῷ "which he planned in him" refers back to τὴν εὐδοκίαν αὐτοῦ "his good pleasure".

There is some debate about whether the phrase ἐν αὐτῷ means "in him" (referring to Christ) or as equivalent to ἐν ἑαυτῷ "in himself" (referring to God). Most versions refer it to Christ. In support of this, Hendriksen says,

> This "in him" must mean "in the Beloved," as the preceding context indicates. The Father "has blessed us with every spiritual blessing...*in Christ*" (1:3), "elected us *in him*" (verse 4), and "graciously bestowed his grace upon us *in the Beloved*" (verse 6). It is natural, therefore, that we should now be referred to the purpose which he cherished for himself "in him" (p. 85).

In the display, the pronoun is taken to refer to Christ and what God planned to accomplish by means of what Christ would do. See Bratcher and Nida (p. 19). TEV also translates it in this way.

1:10 The initial εἰς "for" can be related to the surrounding context in two ways:

1. It is the purpose of the preceding verb προέθετο "he purposed" (1:9). Most commentators favour this option. See, for example, NIV.
2. It connects with τὸ μυστήριον τοῦ θελήματος αὐτοῦ "the mystery of his will" (1:9), making an additional statement about it. See, for example, TEV.

The first option is grammatically correct. However semantically, because there is so much redundancy (i.e. κατὰ τὴν εὐδοκίαν αὐτοῦ ἥν προέθετο ἐν αὐτῷ "according to the good pleasure of him which he purposed in him"), the second option is also possible.

In support of the second option, O'Brien says,

> Although 1:9 is syntactically dependent upon and explains the meaning of God's grace poured upon us (v. 8), with these words about the divine mystery there is a significant development in the eulogy, leading to its climax. God's saving purposes, planned from eternity, had as their final goal the uniting of all things in heaven and earth in Christ, the details of which are spelled out in what follows (pp. 108-109).

Further support for the second option is the importance in this letter of the theme of bringing all things in heaven and earth together "in Christ".

In the context of Ephesians as a whole, therefore, option two seems most appropriate.

So 1:10b is regarded as being the content and 1:8b-9b the orienter. The whole of the propositional configuration 1:8b-10b is in a specific-generic relation with 1:8a. The content of the plan (1:10) would then be given prominence, rather than the orientational material introducing it (1:8-9).

1:10a God planned The abstract noun οἰκονομία "administration, plan" occurs three times in Ephesians (here, in 3:2 and in 3:9). In 3:9, it appears to be used in the sense of "arrangement order, plan" and refers to God's plan of salvation. Here, it seems to refer to putting into action what God has planned. Although, in the Greek, there is no subject stated, in this context the one responsible is God: *God* planned. This acts as an orienter for the rest of the verse, which states the content of what God planned.

1:10b that at the time appointed by him, The genitive phrase τοῦ πληρώματος τῶν καιρῶν "the fulness of the times" has the sense of "the fit, right, appropriate time". The double genitive construction οἰκονομίαν τοῦ πληρώματος τῶν καιρῶν "the plan of the fulness of the times" indicates the time when God is ready to bring his plans or purposes to fruition (cf. Gal. 4:4 and Mark 1:15), i.e. when it is the right/appointed time.

In this context, therefore, "time" does not just refer to the passage of time, of years, months, days. Rather, it refers to what happens, to the events which occur and which contribute to the final, culminating event "to sum up all things in Christ" (1:10).

Commentators do not agree whether this moment has already occurred or is still to come.

The commentators who consider it to have occurred equate it to the first advent of Christ, his death and resurrection, culminating in his second advent and the final judgment. See, for example, Hendriksen (pp. 85-86), Lincoln (pp. 34-35). In support of this view, Lincoln says that, in Colossians (Col 1:26, 27; 2:2; 4:3) and elsewhere in Ephesians (3:3-6, 9-10; 5:32; 6:19), the content of the mystery refers to present reality. This makes it likely that here the "summing up" in Christ has already taken place, that believers are living in "the climactic period when God is administrating the fullness of time" (p. 34).

The commentators who consider the reference to be to a future event equate it to a period of time starting with Christ's second advent and culminating in the uniting of all things in him. See, for example, Hoehner (pp. 218-219), O'Brien (pp. 113-114).

The difference between these two views depends largely upon whether it is the initiating of the process which is in focus or its culmination.

However, since the devil and all the powers of evil are still at work in this world and we have to contend with them (2:2; 5:16; 6:11-13), it would seem better to consider that this "time" has not yet come.

he would bring-together/unite all things in heaven and all things on earth and cause Christ to rule over them. The aorist infinitive ἀνακεφαλαιώσασθαι may have the sense here of "summing up all things" in Christ or "uniting all things under one head" in Christ.

As Lincoln (p. 33) points out, there seems to be little difference between "summing up" and "uniting" in this context.

The display focusses on the "uniting" sense since Paul goes on to amplify the idea of bringing all things together under one head in 1:20-22 and the same doctrine is expressed in some of his other letters. See Philippians 2:9-11; Colossians 1:20.

1:11a Because we are united with Christ, The ἐν ᾧ "in whom" at the beginning of this verse refers to Christ. The phrase "in whom" may be analysed as a reason or means for the following clause, ἐκληρώθημεν "we were chosen". There seems to be more commentary support for means, but, as in 1:3, it is simpler semantically to account for reason here. In the display, therefore, it is expressed as "*Because we are united* with Christ".

God has also chosen us to receive what *he* has promised us. The conjunction καί is translated "also" in KJV, NASB and NIV, "and" in NJB, "furthermore" in NLT and "indeed" in REB. It is left implicit in JBP, RSV. Most commentators consider it to relate only to the event referred to by the verb ἐκληρώθημεν "we were chosen". The sense is not "we also" or "we as well as others", but "we have also been chosen, in addition to all the other benefits we have received from God".

The meaning of the aorist passive indicative ἐκληρώθημεν is not clear in this context. This is the only occurrence of the Greek verb κληρόω in the New Testament, but, in other literature, the active voice originally applied to the casting of lots. It then developed the more general sense of "to allot, assign, choose". The LXX often links it to the idea of inheritance. Following the LXX, many commentators analyse it as relating to inheritance here.

Commentators suggest a number of meanings for ἐκληρώθημεν in this context. There is greatest support for the following two:

1. The believer is God's inheritance. See, for example, Ellicott (pp. 13-14), Hoehner (pp. 225-227), O'Brien (pp. 115-116), Stott (p. 46).
2. The believer receives an inheritance from God. See, for example, Best (pp. 145-146), Eadie (p. 59), Hendriksen (pp. 87-88, fn. 29), Hodge (p. 55).

In support of the first alternative, O'Brien says,

> [T]he rendering 'we were claimed by God as his portion' brings out the passive voice more accurately and is at the same time more in keeping with Old Testament precedent (p.115).

In particular, he refers to Deuteronomy 32:9. Other relevant Old Testament passages are Deuteronomy 4:20; 9:29; 1 Kings 8:51; Psalm 33:12; 106:40.

The reference to "our inheritance" in 1:14 (and similar passages throughout the New Testament, e.g. Acts 20:32; 26:18; Gal. 3:18; Col. 1:12; 3:24; Heb. 9:15; 1 Peter 1:4) supports the second alternative.

Both alternatives are possible in the context. In the display, the second alternative is followed. The sense of "inheritance" is expressed as "what *he* has promised us" and "chosen" is retained to represent God's action in the event.

Another issue with the verb ἐκληρώθημεν "we were chosen" concerns the identity of the "we". This affects the understanding of the pronoun ὑμεῖς "you (pl)" in 1:13.

Commentators suggest two possibilities:

1. Paul is contrasting Jewish believers with Gentile believers, with "we" in 1:11 referring to himself and the former, and "you" in 1:13 referring to the latter. See, for example, Hodge (p. 55), O'Brien (p. 116). In this case, the "we" would be exclusive.
2. Paul is making no contrast and "we" in 1:11 refers to all believers, whether Jew or Gentile. See, for example, Lenski (p. 377), Lincoln (pp. 35, 38). In this case, the "we" would be inclusive and the "you" in 1:13 a matter of focus rather than contrast.

The display follows the second option. See the note on 1:13.

The propositional configuration 1:11a-d, especially nuclear 1:11a, provides the MEANS for 1:12 in the paragraph 1:7-12.

1:11b *He* decided beforehand *to do this* [1:11a]. The verb προορίζω "decide beforehand, predestine" is the same verb used in 1:5. Here it is in the passive, προορισθέντες "having been predestined". God is the agent. This is made explicit in the display.

The clearest way, semantically, of relating προορισθέντες "having been predestined" (1:11b) and ἐκληρώθημεν "we were chosen" (1:11a) is to consider it a relation of circumstance, for example, NIV says "having been predestined". The display follows this interpretation, and 1:11b is presented as an amplification of 1:11a expressing circumstance.

Alternatively, the relationship between προορισθέντες "having been predestined" (1:11b) and ἐκληρώθημεν "we were chosen" (1:11a) could also be analysed as reason. This could be expressed as "because *he* decided beforehand *to do this* [1:11a]".

1:11c This [1:11a] was exactly what he had purposed/planned. The Greek noun πρόθεσις can mean "a setting forth, putting out, presentation" or "plan, purpose, will". The latter is more appropriate in this context, as it also is in its other occurrence in this letter (3:11).

Since πρόθεσις is an abstract noun representing an event, it needs to be expressed by a verb, "to plan" or "to purpose". God is the agent: he does what he planned. What he planned is stated in 1:11a.

The Greek word κατά "according to, because of" can be understood in two ways:

1. It indicates the correspondence of God's predestining with his purpose, i.e. what he predestined was what he had purposed. Most commentators and versions follow this. See, for example, NIV, NRSV.
2. It indicates the reason for God's action of choosing, i.e. God predestined because of his own purpose. See, for example, TEV. This is similar to 1:5, where the same verb, προορίζω, occurs, followed by a clause introduced by κατά which provides the reason for it.

In the display, the first option is followed, with 1:11c providing amplification$_2$ of 1:11a.

1:11d He accomplishes/works-out everything exactly as he plans and desires. The clause τοῦ τὰ πάντα ἐνεργοῦντος κατὰ τὴν βουλὴν τοῦ θελήματος αὐτοῦ "of the one who is working all things according to the counsel of his will" describes God.

When ἐνεργέω is used transitively as here, it means "work, produce, effect". The object of the verb is τὰ πάντα "everything".

There is discussion about the difference in meaning of βουλή "counsel, purpose, plan" and θέλημα "will". Often these two Greek words are used interchangeably. Moore (p. 47) regards them as a near-synonymous doublet (borderline) here.

Others prefer to see a difference in their meanings, for example, θέλημα "will" refers to the activity of the will in general whereas βουλή "counsel, purpose, plan" contains a greater element of deliberate self-determination.

Hendriksen's view (p. 88, fn. 30) is similar when he suggests that God's will (θέλημα) is basic here and that the "plan" or "counsel" (βουλή) springs from it. This indicates that God never acts in an arbitrary manner, but with deliberation. God's πρόθεσις indicates the "purpose" of this plan or the plan itself from the point of view of what it aims to accomplish.

The usual English translation of θέλημα in this verse is "will". The noun βουλή has been translated in different ways, e.g. "counsel" (KJV, NRSV); "purpose" (REB, NIV); "plan" (TEV); and as the verb "decide" (NJB).

Proposition 1:11d is analysed as an amplification of 1:11c. Paul is stating that what God wills and plans is in complete agreement with what he does. In effect, they are one and the same.

It is difficult to express the full sense of the Greek in this verse in clear and idiomatic English. It is also difficult to do justice to the many items belonging to the semantic domain of "will" or "purpose":

προορισθέντες "having decided beforehand"
πρόθεσις "plan"
βουλή "purpose, counsel"
θέλημα "will"

Paul seems to want to emphasise that God's will is absolute, that it is not influenced by other forces, and that everything which happens is determined by God and is according to his will. Paul wants to express these points as emphatically as he can.

1:12 *God did this* [1:11a] *in order that we who have already hoped/trusted in Christ should praise God, who is perfectly glorious.* The phrase εἰς ἔπαινον δόξης αὐτοῦ "to the praise of his glory" is parallel with the phrase that closes 1:4–6 and 1:13–14. See the note on 1:6.

There is some discussion about the relationship indicated by εἰς "so that". There are two possibilities:

1. It may indicate purpose. If so, it would be connected with the main verb of 1:11, ἐκληρώθημεν "we were chosen" or with προορισθέντες "having been decided beforehand", or with both.
2. It may indicate result. If so, it would be connected with ἐκληρώθημεν.

Either of these options would make good sense, but most commentators support the first option and connect it with ἐκληρώθημεν, i.e. God chose us in order that we may be to the praise of his glory. Most versions also translate in this way. So this analysis is followed in the display.

The verb προελπίζω "to hope before, be the first to hope" is found only here in the New Testament and is in perfect active participial form. The complete phrase is τοὺς προηλπικότας ἐν τῷ Χριστῷ "the ones having previously hoped in Christ".

Most commentators understand τοὺς προηλπικότας ἐν τῷ Χριστῷ "the ones having previously hoped in Christ" to refer to Jewish believers. See, for example, Alford (p. 78), Eadie (p. 62), Ellicott (p. 14), Hodge (p. 59).

The interpretation of τοὺς προηλπικότας affects the understanding of the referent of ἡμᾶς "we".

Most commentators take "we" to refer to Jewish believers, contrasting with ὑμεῖς "you" in 1:13, which refers to Gentile believers. However, it seems preferable to understand "we" to be inclusive,

> [since,] in the preceding verses "we" and "us" always refer to Paul and all those addressed (see verses 11, 9, 8, 7, 6, 5, 4, 3). By far the most of those addressed were believers from the Gentiles, not from the Jews. Why, then, the sudden change of meaning in verse 12? (Hendriksen, p. 89, fn. 31).

The ἡμᾶς here then is understood as inclusive and the ὑμεῖς in 1:13 is not contrastive, but refers simply to the Ephesian believers. See the notes on 1:13.

BOUNDARIES AND COHERENCE

The boundaries of this paragraph have been discussed in the section on Boundaries and Coherence for 1:3b–14.

At the beginning of this paragraph, the aorist tense used in the previous paragraph changes to the present tense. There is also a change of subject from "God" to "we". This indicates the change of focus from what God has done in the past to the contemporary state of Paul and the Ephesian believers in Christ.

These verses may be regarded as a single compound paragraph or two shorter paragraphs. In the latter case, the paragraph break would be between 1:10 and 1:11. A number of versions follow the latter analysis, e.g. REB, NIV, RSV, TEV. In support of this, certain parallelisms can be noted:

1. Both paragraphs would begin with ἐν ᾧ "in him" (1:7 and 1:11).
2. Both paragraphs would end with the phrase "in Christ" (1:10 and 1:12).
3. In both paragraphs, the main verb would be first person plural: ἔχομεν "we have" (1:7) and ἐκληρώθημεν "we were chosen" (1:11).

However, in this SSA, regarding 1:7–12 as a single, compound paragraph is preferred. This paragraph would consist of four propositional clusters centred on the four finite verbs:

ἔχομεν "we have" (1:7)
ἐπερίσσευσεν "he caused to abound" (1:8)
προέθετο "he planned" (1:9)
ἐκληρώθημεν "we were chosen" (1:11)

This analysis is supported by the strong parallelism between the three paragraphs, 1:4–6, 1:7–12 and 1:13–14. In particular, there is the recurrent phrase εἰς ἔπαινον δόξης... "to the praise of the glory..." at the close of each unit. See the section on Boundaries and Coherence for 1:3b–14 for more detail.

PROMINENCE AND THEME

In a paragraph such as this with co-ordinate nuclei, each nucleus should be represented in the theme statement. Because the praise expression is recurrent, it is marked as prominent and so thematic.

SECTION CONSTITUENT 1:13–14 (Expressive Paragraph: Specific₃ of 1:3b)

THEME: The Holy Spirit within us confirms that we belong to God and guarantees that God will finally redeem us in order that we should praise him.

RELATIONAL STRUCTURE	CONTENTS
MEANS — NUCLEUS — ┬ circumstance₁ ┬ 'true message'	1:13a *When* you heard the true message,
└ identification	1:13b *that is*, the gospel *which tells how God* saves *you*,
├ circumstance₂	1:13c *and when* you also believed *in Christ*,
├ NUCLEUS	1:13d *God* confirmed *that* you also *belong to him [God] when you were united* with Christ.
├ EQUIVALENT ┬ RESULT	1:13e *God confirmed this*
└ means	1:13f *by means of sending* the Holy Spirit *to be with you, as he had* promised *to do*,
└ comparison	1:13g *just as someone confirms that something belongs to him by* putting *his* seal *on it* [MET].
AMPLIFICATION ─ ┬ comparison	1:14a The Holy Spirit is *like* a deposit/pledge,
├ NUCLEUS	1:14b *that is, the Holy Spirit guarantees that we shall receive from God all that he has promised to give to us*,
└ time	1:14c *at the time* when *God* will finally/completely redeem *his* own people [MET].
purpose	1:14d *God did this* [1:13–14c] in order that *we should* praise him, *who is* perfectly glorious.

INTENT AND STRUCTURE

This is an expressive paragraph which lists further specific blessings received by believers through Christ. It functions as part of the grounds for the CONCLUSION of 1:3a: "God is worthy to be praised".

NOTES

1:13a *When* you heard the true message, The verse begins with ἐν ᾧ καὶ ὑμεῖς "in whom also you". Commentators discuss the reference of "you" and the verb to which it acts as subject.

There are two main viewpoints on the reference of ὑμεῖς "you":

1. It may refer to the Gentile believers in Ephesus, (and, by extension, all other Gentile believers).
2. It may refer to all Ephesian believers, whether Gentile or Jewish.

Most commentators support the first option.

However, in favour of the second option, it should be noted that if Paul had intended to contrast Gentile believers here with Jewish believers in 1:12, he would probably have used δέ, rather than καί at the beginning of this verse. By using καί and the free pronoun ὑμεῖς, he singles out a particular group from among the whole, i.e. "you the readers".

The καί indicates a continuation of the same subject, but with a particular focus. In the display, therefore, the normal use of "you" to refer to the addressees is represented. Paul makes clear that those whom he is addressing are included among the ones who share the inheritance guaranteed to them by the sealing of the Holy Spirit.

Some commentators suggest that the phrase ἐν ᾧ καὶ ὑμεῖς "in whom also you" requires the addition of an implied verb. However, they do not agree what this verb should be. Consider a number of English translations (italics mine):

"And you also *became* God's people" (TEV)
"And you also *were included* in Christ" (NIV)
"So it *is* with you" (NCV)
"In whom also ye *trusted*" (KJV)

An implied verb, however, seems unnecessary. It is better to understand ἐν ᾧ καὶ as connecting with ἐν τῷ Χριστῷ in 1:12 and, therefore, to relate it to the main verb of 1:13, ἐσφραγίσθητε "you were sealed".

The second occurrence of ἐν ᾧ in 1:13 can then be understood as resumptive, i.e. a repetition of the form along with the same grammatical function with ἐσφραγίσθητε "you were sealed". See, for example, Best (p. 148), Hoehner (p. 235).

The main verb in 1:13 is ἐσφραγίσθητε "you were sealed". Its non-figurative meaning is expressed as "confirmed" in the display. It is generally agreed that the two aorist participles ἀκούσαντες "having heard" (1:13a) and πιστεύσαντες "having believed" (1:13c) indicate the temporal circumstances of this main verb. The action of these participles could be regarded as antecedent to the main verb. There is, however, good support for regarding πιστεύσαντες "having believed" as being coincident with it. See, for example, Hoehner (p. 237), Lincoln (p. 39), O'Brien (p. 119).

The clause ἀκούσαντες τὸν λόγον τῆς ἀληθείας "having heard the word of truth" is expressed, therefore, as "*when* you heard the true message". It expresses a temporal circumstance of 1:13d.

1:13b *that is,* **the gospel** *which tells how God saves you,* The genitive phrase τὸ εὐαγγέλιον τῆς σωτηρίας ὑμῶν "the gospel of your salvation" is in apposition to the previous phrase "the word of truth". It further defines or identifies it.

There are two ways to understand the genitive construction τὸ εὐαγγέλιον τῆς σωτηρίας ὑμῶν "the gospel of your salvation":

1. "Salvation" is what "the gospel" effects/accomplishes. See, for example, Hodge (p. 62), Lincoln (p. 39), O'Brien (p. 119).
2. "Salvation" is the content of "the gospel". See, for example, Eadie (p. 64), Ellicott (pp. 15-16), Hoehner (pp. 236-237).

The second option is followed in the display, since the "truth" of the gospel seems to be in focus and, therefore, its content, i.e. it tells about salvation.

1:13c *and when* **you also believed** *in Christ,* The phrase ἐν ᾧ "in whom/which" occurs for the second time here. There is some disagreement about whom or what the pronoun ᾧ refers to, as well as what verb the phrase is connected to.

The pronoun can refer to:

1. Christ
2. the gospel

Most commentators favour the first option, although, grammatically, τὸ εὐαγγέλιον "the gospel" is its closest antecedent.

The second issue to discuss is which verb the phrase ἐν ᾧ "in whom/which" connects with. There are two possibilities:

1. πιστεύσαντες "having believed" (1:13c). The whole expression would then mean "having believed in Christ/the-gospel".
2. ἐσφραγίσθητε "you were sealed" (1:13d). The whole expression would then mean "you were sealed in Christ".

Notice that, in option two, the pronoun ᾧ can only refer to Christ.

Paul does not use the verb πιστεύω "believe" with ἐν "in". It is, therefore, more likely that ἐν ᾧ connects with ἐσφραγίσθητε "you were sealed". The relative pronoun then would refer back to Χριστός rather than τὸ εὐαγγέλιον "the gospel".

This means that there is no explicit object provided for πιστεύσαντες "having believed". In some languages, however, it is necessary to provide an object. This is probably best understood as "Christ".

Since πιστεύσαντες "having believed" is linked to ἀκούσαντες "having heard" by καί, its relationship to ἐσφραγίσθητε "you were sealed" is parallel to that of ἀκούσαντες, i.e. it provides a second temporal circumstance, "*when* you also believed *in Christ*".

1:13d *God* **confirmed** *that* **you also** *belong to him [God] when you were united* **with Christ.** The propositions 1:13d-g form a metaphor. The verb σφραγίζω means "provide with a seal". In the clause ἐσφραγίσθητε τῷ πνεύματι τῆς ἐπαγγελίας τῷ ἁγίῳ "you were sealed with the Holy Spirit of promise", it is used figuratively, in the sense of marking something as a means of identification and ownership.

Just as an owner marks his property with a seal, so God shows that believers belong to him by sending the Holy Spirit to be with them. This can be expressed non-figuratively as "God showed/confirmed that you also belong to him [God]", "you are also united with Christ" or "God identified you as also belonging to him".

1:13e God confirmed this The core of 1:13d is repeated in 1:13e to avoid an excessively long sentence.

1:13f *by means of sending* the Holy Spirit *to be with you, as he had* promised *to do,* The genitive construction τῷ πνεύματι τῆς ἐπαγγελίας τῷ ἁγίῳ "the Holy Spirit of promise" has two possible meanings:

1. "the Holy Spirit whom God promised to send"
2. "the Holy Spirit who brings with him the promise of future blessings".

Most versions (e.g. NIV, NLT, NRSV, TEV) and commentators (e.g. Alford, p. 79; Eadie, p. 65; Ellicott, p. 16; Stott, p. 48) follow the first option. This clause provides the means of 1:13e.

1:13g *just as someone confirms that something belongs to him by* putting *his* seal *on it.* This proposition expresses the illustration (image) part of the metaphor.

1:14a The Holy Spirit is *like* a deposit/pledge, The initial relative pronoun in 1:14a is ὅ ("which") in some manuscripts and ὅς "who" in others. It seems likely that in either case it refers to its nearest antecedent, πνεῦμα "Spirit".

The Greek noun ἀρραβών means "down-payment, deposit, pledge". It refers to the sum of money someone will pay in advance to secure an item he wants to buy.

In the display, it is expressed as a simile, to make explicit that it is used figuratively.

1:14b *that is, the Holy Spirit guarantees that* we shall receive *from God* all that *he* has promised to give to us, The figure of ἀρραβών "down-payment, pledge, deposit" restates or amplifies the figure of putting a seal on something (1:13). Just as a seal establishes and guarantees ownership, so does a deposit. The presence of the Holy Spirit confirms that a person belongs to God and also guarantees that he will receive from God all that God has promised to him. In the display of 1:14b, the meaning is expressed non-figuratively.

The noun κληρονομία "inheritance, possession, property" refers, in Christian usage, to the possession of salvation as the inheritance of God's children (BDAG, p. 548.3).

The comparison is that, as sons inherit their father's property, so God has promised an inheritance to his children. This inheritance consists of all the blessings related to full salvation. In the display, this is expressed as "we shall receive *from God* all that *he* has promised to give to us". An alternative would be "all the blessings that *he* has promised to give to us".

1:14c *at the time* when *God* will finally/ completely redeem *his* own people. Commentators raise a number of questions about the phrase εἰς ἀπολύτρωσιν τῆς περιποιήσεως "until/for the redemption of the possession":

1. What does τῆς περιποιήσεως "the possession" refers to?
2. Is the phrase εἰς ἀπολύτρωσιν τῆς περιποιήσεως "until/for the redemption of the possession" connected to the preceding relative clause or to "sealed" in 1:13.

Relating to the first issue: The meaning of τῆς περιποιήσεως "the possession" needs to be understood within its context, i.e. the genitive phrase εἰς ἀπολύτρωσιν τῆς περιποιήσεως "until/for the redemption of the possession". The noun ἀπολύτρωσις "redemption" originally meant buying back a slave or captive to make them free. The word occurs three times in Ephesians (1:7; 1:14; and 4:30). On each occasion it is used figuratively.

The phrase ἀπολύτρωσιν τῆς περιποιήσεως "the redemption of the possession" can refer to:

1. The inheritance which believers will possess in the future
2. God's inheritance, those people who belong to him.

Most commentators support the second option. God gave the down-payment and, therefore, he will eventually receive what he has purchased, his own/chosen people. Additional support for this can be found in the Old and New Testaments where God's people are often referred to as his [God's] own possession (Deuteronomy 14:2; Malachi 3:17; cf. Acts 20:28); his [God's] own people (Isaiah 43:21; 1 Peter 2:9).

In the display, God is supplied as the agent of redemption, and his "possession" is understood to be "his own people", "those who belong to him".

Relating to the second issue above: The preposition εἰς "until/for" may indicate:

1. Purpose. In this case, it may be the purpose of the immediately preceding phrase or of the main verb "you were sealed" in 1:13.

2. Time. In this case, it connects "the redemption of the possession" to the immediately preceding "who is the down-payment of our inheritance" (1:14b). It may then be translated "when" or "until".

Both options makes good sense. The second option is followed in the display. This can be expressed as, "We shall receive *from God* all that *he* has promised to give to us *at the time* when *God* will completely redeem *his* own people".

1:14d *God did this* **[1:13-14c] in order that** *we* **should praise him,** *who is* **perfectly glorious.** The phrase εἰς ἔπαινον τῆς δόξης αὐτοῦ "to the praise of his glory" occurs in very similar form in 1:6 and 1:12. See the notes on those verses.

Grammatically, the phrase may be connected with either ἐσφραγίσθητε "you were sealed" or ὅ ἐστιν ἀρραβὼν τῆς κληρονομίας ἡμῶν "who is a down-payment of our inheritance". God's purpose in sealing believers with the Holy Spirit is that they should praise him. In the display, it is regarded as the ultimate purpose of all that has gone before in the paragraph 1:13-14.

This final purpose clause parallels, both grammatically and lexically, the clauses in 1:6 and 1:12 which end the two preceding paragraphs. However, not only does it bring paragraph 1:13-14 to a close, it also provides a conclusion to the whole eulogy (1:3-14) which began with the statement (1:3a) that God is worthy to be praised.

BOUNDARIES AND COHERENCE

The boundaries of this paragraph have already been discussed in the sections on Boundaries and Coherence for 1:3-14 and 1:3b-14.

The coherence of this short paragraph derives from its focus on the work of the Holy Spirit in the salvation of God's chosen people. He is referred to in both verses. His presence in the believer is the guarantee of the believer's position as a child of God and of the inheritance which goes with it.

The unity of the passage is strengthened by the use of lexical items belonging to the semantic field of "certainty", "reliability", "trustworthiness":

ἀληθείας "of truth" (1:13)
πιστεύσαντες "having believed/trusted" (1:13)
ἐσφραγίσθητε "you were sealed" (1:13)
ἐπαγγελίας "of promise" (1:13)
ἀρραβών "guarantee, pledge" (1:14)

PROMINENCE AND THEME

A MEANS-purpose relation is not complete without both parts, so both parts are represented in the theme.

The verb ἐσφραγίσθητε "you were sealed" (1:13) is a finite verb. The phrase ἀρραβὼν τῆς κληρονομίας ἡμῶν "down-payment of our inheritance" is an abstract noun construction in a relative clause amplifying the meaning of the finite verb. An abstract noun phrase in a relative clause is not normally prominent. However, the use of the two figures "to seal" and "down-payment" may be intended to give emphasis. So the non-figurative meaning of both are included in the theme statement.

DIVISION CONSTITUENT 1:15-23
(Expressive Section: Nucleus₂ of 1:3-23 [Thanksgiving and Prayer])

THEME: I thank God for your faith and love. I pray that God may cause you to understand more fully how powerfully he works on behalf of his people, just as he worked powerfully when he caused Christ, who had died, to live again and, as supreme ruler over all things, to rule over the church.

MACROSTRUCTURE	CONTENTS
NUCLEUS	1:15-19 I thank God for your faith and love. I pray that God may grant that his Spirit may cause you to be wise and may reveal God to you, that God may grant you to know what you should hope for, what you will finally inherit and how powerfully God works on behalf of us who believe in Christ.
AMPLIFICATION	1:20-23 God worked mightily on behalf of Christ. Specifically, God caused Christ, who had died, to live again, and he placed him in the most highly-honoured position in heaven. God appointed Christ, who rules supreme over all, to rule over the church.

INTENT AND MACROSTRUCTURE

These verses are Paul's response to what he has heard about the faith and love of the Ephesians (1:15) and to what he knows about the many blessings they have received from God through Christ (1:3-14). His intention is to continue to strengthen his relationship with them and to encourage them to understand that God's power is available to them now. This section is expressive in nature, but has many expository elements.

These verses consist of two closely related paragraphs. They constitute a single sentence in the Greek text, if the ἥν "which" (1:20) is treated as a continuing relative construction, rather than the beginning of a new sentence. Relationally, they comprise a NUCLEUS (1:15-19) and an AMPLIFICATION (1:20-23).

Structurally, this unit is made up of a short, introductory thanksgiving (1:15-16a) in which Paul gives thanks for the Ephesian believers. He then goes on to intercede for them (1:16b-19). He ends by praising God for exercising his mighty power in raising Christ from the dead and in exalting him to rule over the church (1:20-23).

BOUNDARIES AND COHERENCE

The initial boundary of this unit has been discussed in the section on Boundaries and Coherence for 1:3-14. In the case of the final boundary, a break is indicated after 1:23, for the following reasons:

1. There is a change of genre from prayer, albeit of an expository nature, to exposition.
2. There is a change of topic, from the exaltation of Christ (1:20-23) to the past and present situation of the Ephesians. This is marked by a switch from third person singular to second person singular verb forms.
3. After a single sentence in the Greek (1:15-23), a new sentence begins at 2:1.
4. There is rhetorical bracketing with reference to "the Lord Jesus" and "the saints" in 1:15, and "Christ" and "the church" in 1:22 and indirectly in 1:23 also.

There is strong evidence for the cohesion and coherence of verses 1:15-23. They form a single sentence in the Greek. There is the repeated use of synonymous terms which refer to the body of believers:

ἅγιοι "the saints" (1:15 and 1:18)
ἐκκλησία "the church" (1:22)
τὸ σῶμα "the body" (1:23)

This vocabulary is not used in either the preceding or following units.

Also Paul uses many terms relating to "knowledge" and "power".

It might be argued that these verses should be analysed as a single paragraph, but it seems better to regard them as two closely related paragraphs for the following reasons:

1. There is a change of topic. The unit 1:15-19 contains thanksgiving and petitionary prayer, while the unit 1:20-23 consists of a statement concerning the power and authority of Christ.
2. There is a tail-head link between 1:19 and the following unit, 1:20-23. In 1:19b, there is

heavy emphasis on God's mighty power aiding believers. This is taken up in the ἥν "which" at the beginning of 1:20. Here there is a switch to the power exerted in Christ when he raised him from the dead and gave him great authority over all things.

PROMINENCE AND THEME

The theme statement of this unit is based on the NUCLEUS, which is naturally prominent, and also on the AMPLIFICATION, which has marked prominence by reason of its subject matter. This subject matter is taken up and developed in chapter 2. The theme consists of a generic representation of the themes of both paragraphs.

SECTION CONSTITUENT 1:15-19 (Expressive Paragraph: Nucleus of 1:15-23)

THEME: I thank God for your faith and love. I pray that God may grant that his Spirit may cause you to be wise and may reveal God to you, that God may grant you to know what you should hope for, what you will finally inherit and how powerfully God works on behalf of us who believe in Christ.

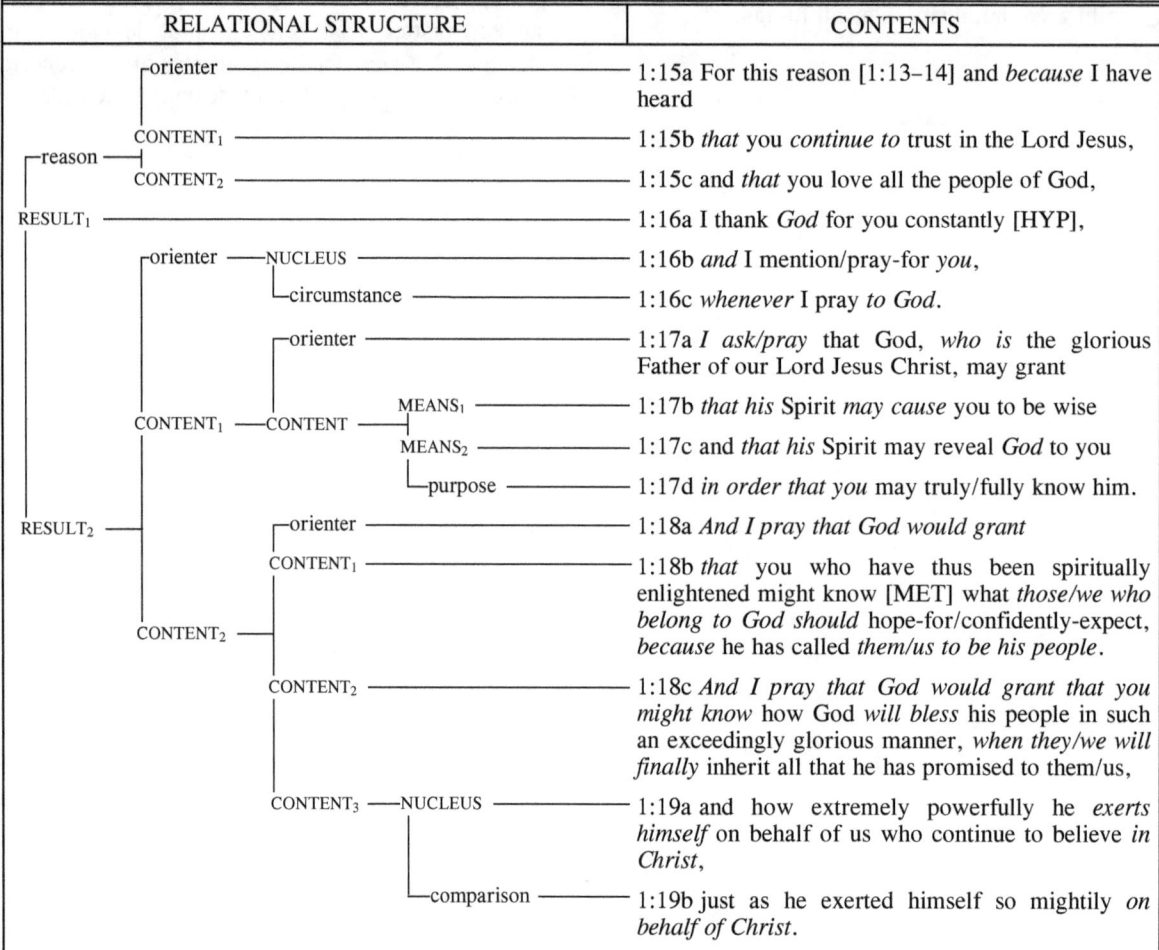

INTENT AND STRUCTURE

This paragraph begins with a short thanksgiving, which is followed by intercessory prayer. See the section on Intent and Macrostructure for 1:15-23.

NOTES

1:15a For this reason [1:13-14] Most commentators consider that διὰ τοῦτο "for this reason, because of this" indicates result. However, they do not agree which verses constitute the reason. There are three possibilities:

1. The phrase διὰ τοῦτο refers back to 1:3-14. See, for example, Abbott (p. 24), Hendriksen (p. 95).

2. The phrase διὰ τοῦτο refers back to 1:13-14. See, for example, Eadie (p. 72), Ellicott (pp. 17-18).

3. The phrase διὰ τοῦτο refers back to 1:3-14, but with special relation to 1:13-14. See, for example, Hodge (p. 68), Hoehner (p. 248), Lincoln (p. 54), O'Brien (p. 124).

An important consideration in deciding between these different analyses is that, in 1:13, specific reference is made to the salvation and faith of those whom Paul is addressing. Now, in 1:15-16, he says that he has heard of their faith in the Lord Jesus and the love they have for all God's people. Because of these things, he never stops thanking God for them. This seems to indicate that 1:15 relates specifically to 1:13-14. as it shows a natural progression of thought.

and *because* **I have heard** The participial clause beginning with ἀκούσας "having heard" may be either a second reason for Paul's thanks or the temporal circumstance in which Paul gives thanks. The former makes more sense in this context.

1:15b *that* **you** *continue to* **trust in the Lord Jesus,** Both πίστις "faith" and ἀγάπη "love" are abstract nouns representing events which are in an addition relation to each other. In both, the agent is "you" referring to the Ephesian believers.

The sense of "faith" in this context is that the Ephesians believe in the Lord. It is not a reference to their initial experience but to their continuing to believe, the constancy of their trust.

This verse is important when discussing whether this letter is addressed specifically to the Ephesians or not. As Paul says that he has *heard* about the Ephesians' faith in Christ, some commentators say that this shows that Paul had not met those to whom he is writing. As Paul had spent much time in Ephesus, then the letter must be addressed to some other church or group of churches. The noun πίστις "faith" would then refer to initial conversion, not on-going trust.

However, it is possible that Paul might simply be mentioning recent news he had received about the church at Ephesus, news not about their initial conversion but news about their continuing faith. This is the analysis used in this SSA.

The noun πίστις "faith" refers to the continuing faith shown by the Ephesian believers since Paul had last been there and which had been reported to him. This might be expressed as "you *continue to* trust".

1:15c and *that* **you love all the people of God,** The adjective ἅγιοι, when used of persons, refers to people who are "consecrated to God". It has been translated as:

"saints" (KJV, NIV, RSV)
"God's people" (REB, TEV)
"members of the church" (NAB)

Here, in the phrase πάντας τοὺς ἁγίους "all the saints", it might be expressed by "all *your* fellow-believers" or "all God's people". In the display, it is expressed as "all the people of God". See the note on 1:1b where the same term is used.

The love referred to here is that of believers for each other.

1:16–19 This propositional cluster is in a result relationship with 1:15 and consists of RESULT₁ (1:16a) and RESULT₂ (1:16b–19b). In the latter configuration, 1:16b-c acts as an orienter for 1:17–19, the CONTENT of the prayer. The conjunction ἵνα "that" usually indicates purpose. However, when following verbs of praying, thanking, etc., it may introduce the content of the prayer. Sometimes it is difficult to decide between purpose and content, since, as O'Brien (p. 129, fn. 156) says, "the content of what is requested may also indicate the purpose of the request". The majority view is that it introduces the content of Paul's prayer.

1:16a I thank *God* **for you constantly,** Most commentators think that οὐ παύομαι "I cease not" connects primarily with the participle εὐχαριστῶν "giving thanks", i.e. "I do not cease giving thanks".

Although the finite verb is παύομαι "cease" and εὐχαριστῶν "giving thanks" is a dependent participle, the event here is "giving thanks" and "cease not" semantically modifies that.

The phrase "I do not cease" generally functions as an emphatic form, with the meaning of the clause here being "I constantly give thanks for you". This can be seen as a hyperbole, having the sense of doing something regularly, many times, but not continuously. It needs to be translated by an appropriate hyperbole in the target language.

1:16b *and* **I mention/pray-for** *you,* Usually the Greek noun μνεία "memory, remembrance" is followed by an objective genitive "of someone/something". Here, in the participial clause μνείαν ποιούμενος "making mention, remembrance", there is no explicit genitive and it needs to be supplied from the context. It may be either "you" or "your faith and love". Most commentators consider that it is "you".

The semantic relationship between the two events represented by εὐχαριστῶν "giving thanks" and μνείαν ποιούμενος "making mention (of you)" is regarded as being co-ordinate. This is how it is presented in the display (1:16a, 1:16b). Paul thanks God for the Ephesian believers and also prays that they should know more of God's blessings.

1:16c *whenever* **I pray** *to God.* The phrase ἐπὶ τῶν προσευχῶν μου "in the prayers of me" represents an event. The preposition ἐπί followed by the genitive τῶν προσευχῶν μου is understood in its temporal sense "in/at-the-time-of" (BDAG, p. 367.18a). The proposition 1:16c, therefore, is regarded as being in a relation of time or circumstance with 1:16b that is, at some point during a time when Paul prays about a variety of matters, he will include the Ephesian believers in those prayers. It is expressed in the display as *"whenever* I pray *to God"*.

1:17a *I ask/pray* **that God,** *who is* **the glorious Father of our Lord Jesus Christ, may grant** There are two nominal phrases here, ὁ θεὸς τοῦ κυρίου ἡμῶν Ἰησοῦ Χριστοῦ "The God of our Lord Jesus Christ" and ὁ πατὴρ τῆς δόξης "the Father of glory". They both describe God.

The phrase τοῦ κυρίου ἡμῶν Ἰησοῦ Χριστοῦ "of our Lord Jesus Christ", taken together with ὁ θεός, is a genitive construction. See the note on 1:3a.

The phrase ὁ πατὴρ τῆς δόξης "the Father of glory" can be understood in two ways:

1. The "Father" [God] is the *source* of "glory".
2. "Glory" functions as an adjectival genitive modifying "Father". The meaning then is "the glorious Father".

Many versions translate the second option. This is the option expressed in the display.

However, it should be noted that, as O'Brien says,

> At the same time [as functioning as an adjectival genitive modifying 'Father'], consistent with similar predicates (e.g., 'the Father of compassion', 2 Cor. 1:3), the genitive is one of origin, meaning that the Father is the *source* of all true glory (p. 131).

1:17b-c *that his* **Spirit** *may cause* **you to be wise and** *that his* **Spirit may reveal** *God* **to you** The noun phrase πνεῦμα σοφίας καὶ ἀποκαλύψεως "spirit of wisdom and revelation" functions in the surface structure as the direct object of the verb δώῃ "he may grant", that is, "he may grant you the Spirit of wisdom and revelation". In the propositionalised English structure, 1:17b-d is the CONTENT of the verb "grant" acting as an orienter.

Commentators discuss whether the word πνεῦμα "Spirit/spirit" refers to the human spirit or the Holy Spirit in this verse.

The majority of commentators consider that it refers to the Holy Spirit. See, for example, Best (pp. 162-163), Eadie (p. 82), Ellicott (p. 20), Hodge (p. 71), Hoehner (pp. 256-257), Lincoln (pp. 56-57), O'Brien (pp. 131-132). This view is reasonable, given that, in 1:13, it was stated that the Ephesians had been "sealed with the Spirit". So Paul is praying here that the Holy Spirit, already present in the believers, might cause them to be increasingly enlightened. See also the note on 3:16.

A second issue is how the two abstract nouns σοφία "wisdom" and ἀποκάλυψις "revelation" relate to πνεῦμα "Spirit/spirit" and what, therefore, are the meanings of the genitive phrases. The καί shows that the two genitive phrases themselves are in a co-ordinate relation.

The genitive construction πνεῦμα σοφίας "the spirit of wisdom" is the easiest to understand. It represents the event "*his* Spirit *may cause* you to be wise".

However, πνεῦμα...ἀποκαλύψεως "the spirit...of revelation" is more complex. It is clear that the Spirit is the one who is doing the revealing, but what is revealed? As ἀποκαλύψεως is modified by ἐν ἐπιγνώσει αὐτοῦ "in the knowledge of him", this is also a factor in understanding the phrase. Commentators offer many suggestions, but there is no consensus. TEV translates it as "reveal God to you" and this is followed in the display, since it includes most of the other suggestions.

1:17d *in order that you* **may truly/fully know him.** The phrase ἐν ἐπιγνώσει αὐτοῦ "in the knowledge of him" is generally regarded as relating to both σοφίας and ἀποκαλύψεως. It indicates the purpose or goal of wisdom and revelation, i.e. "so that you may know him".

There are two ways to treat the abstract noun ἐπίγνωσις:

1. It is synonymous with γνῶσις "knowledge".
2. It is not synonymous with γνῶσις "knowledge" but has its own distinctive difference.

A majority of commentators maintain that they are not synonymous, one of the possible senses of ἐπίγνωσις being "knowing something more completely, truly or fully". Examples of this sense from the versions are:

> "you may know him better" (NIV)
> "to bring you to full knowledge of him" (NJB)
> "to know more of him" (JBP)

1:18a-b *And I pray that God would grant that* **you who have thus been spiritually enlightened might know** The clause πεφωτισμένους τοὺς ὀφθαλμοὺς τῆς καρδίας "the eyes of your heart having been enlightened" is figurative. The "heart" is frequently used in Scripture to represent the human spiritual nature, the centre of spiritual life. It is translated in English as "understanding" (KJV), "mind" (NJB), "heart" (RSV).

The point of comparison may well be as follows: Light enables the physical eye to see, and so to guide what a person does physically. In the same way, God's Spirit enables the "heart" to understand spiritual truth, and so to guide what a person does spiritually. If there is no word or expression in the target language like "enlightened" in English, which has both a figurative and a non-figurative meaning, then possibly "you whom the Holy Spirit has enabled to understand the-truth/what-is-true" might express the meaning.

Syntactically, there are a number of problems with the connection of this clause. These are not discussed in detail in this SSA. Further information can be found in many of the commentaries. See, for example, Eadie (pp. 86–87), Hoehner (pp. 261–262), Lincoln (p. 47).

In this analysis, the view taken is that the participial clause πεφωτισμένους τοὺς ὀφθαλμοὺς τῆς καρδίας "the eyes of your heart having been enlightened" is an accusative absolute that refers back to ὑμῖν "you" in 1:17. The case of this clause has been influenced by the case of the following construction εἰς τὸ εἰδέναι ὑμᾶς "that you should know" (1:18). So this participial clause is in the accusative rather than the more usual dative case. See, for example, Hoehner (p. 262), Lincoln (p. 47), O'Brien (p. 133, fn. 167).

The main grammatical structure is δῴη ὑμῖν...εἰς τὸ εἰδέναι ὑμᾶς "he may grant you...that you should know..." and the participial clause "the eyes of your heart having been enlightened" qualifies "you". Display 1:18a is a clarification of the connection to "he may grant you" in 1:17a. Proposition 1:18a acts as an orienter for 1:18b–19b, which is the CONTENT.

Paul now lists the things which he wants the Ephesians to know. He introduces each one with the indirect interrogative pronoun τίς "what" (1:18b; 1:18c; 1:19a–b).

It seems best to analyse them as a list of three items, i.e. "hope", "inheritance", "power", with the καί "and" at the beginning of 1:19a taken as introducing the final item. This would give three conjoined NUCLEI (CONTENTS) in the display.

The full propositional configuration consists of an orienter (1:18a) and CONTENT$_1$ (1:18b), CONTENT$_2$ (1:18c) and CONTENT$_3$ (1:19a–b).

what *those/we who belong to God should hope-for/confidently-expect, because* he has called *them/us to be his people*. In the genitive construction ἡ ἐλπὶς τῆς κλήσεως αὐτοῦ "the hope of his calling", the two abstract nouns, ἐλπίς "hope" and κλήσεως "calling", represent events.

Most commentators understand the noun κλήσεως "calling" to refer to the call made by God to those whom he has chosen to be his people. This is the usual sense in the epistles.

Paul wants the Ephesian believers to know that, as a result of being called by God, they have a great hope: they can look forward with certainty to the many blessings that God promised to his people. Those "who belong to God" are the ones who "should hope".

God is the agent of the call, "he has called *them to be his people*".

1:18c *And I pray that God would grant that you might know* how God *will bless* his people in such an exceedingly glorious manner, *when they/we will finally* inherit all that he has promised to them/us, This clause τίς ὁ πλοῦτος τῆς δόξης τῆς κληρονομίας αὐτοῦ ἐν τοῖς ἁγίοις "what (is) the riches of the glory of the inheritance of him in the saints" states the second concept which Paul wants the Ephesians to understand.

This clause raises a number of points for consideration.

Firstly, although αὐτοῦ clearly refers to God, it is not clear whether God is the giver or the receiver of the inheritance. However, the focus of this prayer is Paul's request to God to *give* (see δῴη 1:17). Therefore, it is appropriate in this context to understand God to be the source/giver of the inheritance and his people the recipients.

Secondly, it is not clear what is the relationship of the three nouns in the triple genitive construction ὁ πλοῦτος τῆς δόξης τῆς κληρονομίας αὐτοῦ "the riches of the glory of the inheritance of him".

The noun πλοῦτος "wealth, riches" is used several times in a figurative sense in Ephesians (1:7; 2:7; 3:8, 16) to express an abundance of something. In this verse, where Paul wants to express something which is virtually indescribable, it seems that πλοῦτος "wealth, riches" alone is not sufficient. So he uses the combination ὁ πλοῦτος τῆς δόξης τῆς κληρονομίας αὐτοῦ "the riches of the glory of his inheritance". The important thing in any translation, therefore, is to communicate this overwhelming sense of the blessings in store for God's people. Paul uses similar combinations elsewhere. See, for example, τὸ ὑπερβάλλον μέγεθος τῆς δυνάμεως αὐτοῦ "the exceeding greatness of his power" and τοῦ κράτους τῆς ἰσχύος αὐτοῦ "of the strength of his might" (1:19).

Semantically κληρονομίας "inheritance" is an event: X causes Y to inherit Z. It is understood from the context that God is the source of the inheritance and that "his people" are the recipients. What they are to inherit includes many blessings such as salvation, eternal life. This may be expressed by a general, all-inclusive phrase, such as "*they will finally* inherit *all* that God has promised to them". The other two nouns in the genitive construction, πλοῦτος "riches" and δόξης "glory", are probably best regarded as attributive elements and expressed by a phrase such as "exceedingly glorious".

Thirdly, we need to consider what the phrase ἐν τοῖς ἁγίοις "in the saints" connects with. It may be connected to the whole clause τίς ὁ πλοῦτος τῆς δόξης τῆς κληρονομίας "what (is) the riches of the glory of the inheritance" or just to κληρονομία "inheritance". Semantically, there is little difference.

It is generally agreed that τοῖς ἁγίοις "the saints" refers to all believers, past, present and future. In the display, it is expressed as "God's people". Any term which is used to refer to believers in general would be appropriate.

1:19a and how extremely powerfully he *exerts himself* on behalf of us who continue to believe *in Christ*, The verb ὑπερβάλλω "to exceed, to surpass, to outdo" is used three times in Ephesians (here, 2:7 and 3:19). On each occasion it relates to some quality of God: "power", "grace", "love". The present active participle ὑπερβάλλον used here is usually translated as an adjective or adverb such as "exceeding(ly)", "extraordinary(/ily)", "immeasurable(/ly)".

The abstract noun μέγεθος "greatness" can be translated as an adjective such as "great".

In the genitive construction τὸ ὑπερβάλλον μέγεθος τῆς δυνάμεως αὐτοῦ "the exceeding greatness of the power of him", it is clear that the power referred to is God's power, and that it is directed εἰς ἡμᾶς τοὺς πιστεύοντας "towards/with-respect-to us who are believing". That is, God exercises his power for the benefit of believers. This idea of God's power being at work needs to be expressed in this proposition as "how extremely powerfully he works/exerts himself". See also 1:19b.

The object of πιστεύοντας "believing" is not stated explicitly. It could be God, Christ or the gospel, but it is most likely to be Christ. See the expression τὴν καθ' ὑμᾶς πίστιν ἐν τῷ κυρίῳ Ἰησοῦ "your faith in the Lord Jesus" in 1:15. The use of the present participle here indicates that a characteristic attitude is described, that these are people who keep on believing, "who continue to believe *in Christ*".

This proposition provides the nuclear part of CONTENT₃ of the propositional configuration 1:18b–19b.

1:19b just as he exerted himself so mightily *on behalf of Christ*. A majority of commentators understand the preposition κατά "according to" to indicate conformity to a norm or standard rather than reason. See, for example, Bratcher and Nida (p. 34), Ellicott (pp. 22–23), Hoehner (p. 269). The power that God exercises on behalf of his people is equal to the power which he exercised on behalf of Christ when he raised him from the dead and exalted him to be supreme over all things. In fact, Paul is saying that it is this *same* power which is available to the Ephesians and is working on their behalf. As far as SSA relationships are concerned, CONGRUENCE-standard, or the more generic relation NUCLEUS-comparison, would be the choices here. The latter is chosen for the display since the standard is not one that believers are being told to conform to. God is the agent of the action in both propositions.

Both nouns in the genitive expression τοῦ κράτους τῆς ἰσχύος αὐτοῦ "of the strength of the might of him" may be glossed as "strength, power, might". It seems likely that Paul uses more than one term in order to intensify the effect of what he is saying and to impress upon the Ephesians the greatness of God's power.

The abstract noun ἐνέργεια "working, operation, action" represents the event "to work", with God as the agent.

In the display, the standard against which this power is measured is clarified as the power which God used on behalf of Christ. This is explicit in the Greek text of 1:20a: ἣν ἐνήργησεν ἐν τῷ Χριστῷ "which he exerted in Christ".

BOUNDARIES AND COHERENCE

The initial boundary of this unit has been discussed in the section on Boundaries and Coherence for 1:3–14, and the final boundary in the section for 1:15–23.

The fact that 1:20 begins with a relative pronoun is not a conclusive argument against its beginning a new unit on the paragraph level. Note that 1:7 and 1:13 both begin with relative constructions and there is sufficient evidence that they begin a new unit on a level above the sentence (i.e. at least above the English sentence as normally constructed).

There is lexical unity in the use of several words belonging to the domains of "knowledge" and "glory":

δόξης "of glory" (1:17)
σοφίας "of wisdom" (1:17)
ἀποκαλύψεως "of revelation" (1:17)
ἐπιγνώσει "knowledge" (1:17)
πεφωτισμένους "having been enlightened" (1:18)
εἰδέναι "to know" (1:18)
πλοῦτος τῆς δόξης "riches of the glory" (1:18)

PROMINENCE AND THEME

The theme statement of this unit is based on RESULT₁ and RESULT₂, since these have natural prominence. The first RESULT is Paul's thanksgiving and the second is his prayer. In RESULT₂, the nuclear CONTENTS express the prominent features of the prayer.

SECTION CONSTITUENT 1:20–23
(Expressive Paragraph: Amplification of 1:15–19)

THEME: God worked mightily on behalf of Christ. Specifically, God caused Christ, who had died, to live again, and he placed him in the most highly-honoured position in heaven. God appointed Christ, who rules supreme over all, to rule over the church.

RELATIONAL STRUCTURE	CONTENTS
GENERIC	1:20a God worked *mightily* on behalf of Christ.
SPECIFIC₁	1:20b *Specifically*, God caused Christ, *who* had died, to live again,
SPECIFIC₂ — NUCLEUS	1:20c and he placed him *in the most highly-honoured position* at the right hand of God in heaven.
—amplification₁	1:21a Christ is supreme ruler (*or*, rules supreme) over every powerful *spirit* ruler.
—amplification₂	1:21b His title/rank is above the title/rank of every ruler, not only now but also forever.
SPECIFIC₃	1:22a God has caused all things to be subject to Christ [MET].
SPECIFIC₄ — NUCLEUS — NUCLEUS	1:22b God has appointed Christ, who rules over all things, *to rule over* the church.
—amplification	1:23a The church *relates to* Christ *in the same way as* the body *relates to its head* [MET].
—amplification	1:23b In and through the church, Christ exercises that same infinite power which he exercises throughout the whole universe.

INTENT AND STRUCTURE

This is an expressive paragraph which also contains expository features. It provides an amplification of 1:15–19. Paul here enlarges on the mighty power of God which he referred to in 1:19. The focus changes from a general statement about this power (1:19) to more specific aspects of God's mighty power at work on behalf of Christ (1:20–23). Paul wants to convince the Ephesian believers that this same power is effective for them.

1:20a God worked *mightily* on behalf of Christ. The relative pronoun ἥν "which" occurs initially and could refer to any of the three feminine nouns in the preceding clause:

    δυνάμεως "power"
    ἐνέργειαν "working"
    ἰσχύος "might"

Since the focus is on the effectual working of God's power, the pronoun is best taken to refer to ἐνέργειαν. This means that the verb ἐνήργησεν "he worked/operated" (1:20) relates to its correlate noun ἐνέργειαν "working" (1:19), a structure Paul uses elsewhere in this epistle, for example, εὐλογήσας "has blessed" and εὐλογία "blessing" (1:3); χάριτος "grace" and ἐχαρίτωσεν "he has graced" (1:6); ἀγάπην "love" and ἠγάπησεν "he has loved" (2:4). Such a construction is normally used to intensify what is being said. Here, Paul wishes to impress upon the Ephesian believers that the power which was so effective in raising Christ from the dead is also effective on their behalf.

In this verse, the phrase ἐν Χριστῷ "in Christ" indicates that God's power works "on behalf of Christ", "with respect to Christ" or "in the case of Christ".

This clause is a generic statement, followed by several specifics.

1:20b *Specifically*, God caused Christ, *who* had died, to live again, The two aorist participles, ἐγείρας "having raised" and καθίσας "having seated" can be understood in several different ways:

1. They are temporal clauses. See, for example, Meyer (p. 342, fn. 2). Most versions translate this option, for example, "when he raised

him...and seated him...". See KJV, NET, NIV, NRSV, TEV.
2. They describe the way in which God worked to show his power. See, for example, Bratcher and Nida (p. 35), Ellicott (p. 23).
3. They represent events which provide specific instances of "the working of God's mighty power". See, for example, Hoehner (pp. 274–275).

The third option seems most appropriate in the context. Both actions would then be regarded as simultaneous with ἐνήργησεν "he worked". They are expressions of that power at work. In the display, therefore, this proposition is SPECIFIC₁ in relation to 1:20a which is GENERIC.

1:20c and he placed him *in the most highly-honoured position* at the right hand of God in heaven. The conjunction καί "and", which introduces this clause, is a co-ordinating conjunction. The unit it introduces is of equal prominence with 1:20b. It states a further specific of what God, by his power, has accomplished with respect to Christ, i.e. he has exalted him to the position of supreme power.

God is the agent of the action and Christ is the experiencer. When this verb is used with the phrase ἐν δεξιᾷ "at the right", as it is here, it means "to give a special place of honour" to someone. Since, in this context, the position is at God's right hand, it implies the supreme place of honour and authority, equal to that of God.

1:21a Christ is supreme ruler (*or,* rules supreme) over every powerful *spirit* ruler. This verse continues with the theme of the supremacy of Christ. It is an amplification of 1:20c.

There are a number of issues that need to be considered here.

Firstly, what does ὑπεράνω mean in this context? There are two possibilities:

1. It is synonymous with ἄνω and simply means "above, over".
2. The prefix ὑπερ- "over" gives it intensive force so that ὑπεράνω does not simply mean "above" but "high, far above".

The latter seems most likely in view of the list of powers and authorities which follows. The all-inclusive nature of Christ's authority is emphasised by the repetition of καί "and" before each of the nouns relating to authority and power in the verse. The use of πᾶς "all, every" twice in this verse also serves to emphasise Christ's power. Note too the assertion in 1:22 that all things are in subjection to Christ.

Secondly, is there significance in the order of the list of near synonyms here? They are:

ἀρχή "ruler"
ἐξουσία "authority"
δύναμις "power"
κυριότης "lordship"

Some commentators, for example, Alford (p. 85), Meyer (p. 343), think that the order is significant. However most commentators agree that Paul simply intends the list to be all-inclusive. This is supported by the fact that the same words occur in different orders in other passages in the New Testament, e.g. Colossians 1:16. In many languages, therefore, it may be preferable to use a generic statement in translation rather than trying to match every term in the Greek, and so a generic statement is used in the display.

Thirdly, commentators discuss whether this list of authorities refers to human beings, supernatural beings, or to both? Are both good and evil beings included? There does not appear to be conclusive evidence to support any one view. However, more commentators favour the view that angelic authorities are referred to here.

Verse 6:12 lists the evil forces that believers struggle against. There not only ἀρχαί "rulers" and ἐξουσίαι "authorities" are listed, but also "the world-rulers of this darkness, the spiritual forces of evil in the heavenlies". We would expect that Paul would intend to communicate here in 1:21 that Christ is supreme over these powerful beings as well as human authorities.

1:21b His title/rank is above the title/rank of every ruler not only now but also for ever. The final καί introduces a final, general assertion with the participial clause παντὸς ὀνόματος ὀνομαζομένου "every name being named". In the SSA of Philippians, Banker compares καὶ ἐχαρίσατο αὐτῷ τὸ ὄνομα τὸ ὑπὲρ πᾶν ὄνομα "and gave him a name above every name" (Phil. 2:9) with this verse. He states,

> Rank is a basic component of the meaning of ὄνομα 'name' in τὸ ὄνομα τὸ ὑπὲρ πᾶν ὄνομα 'the name which is above every name'. As ὑπέρ 'above' clearly shows, this idea is in focus here.... Thus, ὄνομα signifies more than just 'name'—an appellation to distinguish one person or thing from another (p. 88).

He expresses this propositionally as "God bestowed upon him a title/rank which is above every *other* title/rank".

1:22 The initial καί "and" continues the description of how God's mighty power was demonstrated in Christ. This description began in 1:20 and was developed in 1:20, 21 with reference to Christ's supremacy over the universe. Now Paul goes on to develop the theme further with respect to the benefit of Christ's universal rule to the church.

1:22a God has caused all things to be subject to Christ. The aorist indicative ὑπέταξεν "he put, placed" is co-ordinate with ἐνήργησεν "he worked" (1:20). It is also co-ordinate with the other finite verb in 1:22, ἔδωκεν "he gave". It expresses SPECIFIC₃ of the GENERIC statement 1:20a. An alternative analysis of the relationship of this clause is that it is a restatement in summary form of 1:21.

The statement πάντα ὑπέταξεν ὑπὸ τοὺς πόδας αὐτοῦ "he has put all (things) under his feet" is a metaphor depicting the complete defeat of a person or nation. The victor would place his foot on the neck of the one he had defeated in order to show his power over him. However, by the time David wrote Psalm 8, it seems to have already become a dead metaphor. See Psalm 8:6, "You made him ruler over the works of your hands; you put everything under his feet" (NIV).

Thus, it does not necessarily need to be translated figuratively. In fact, in many languages, it will need to be expressed non-figuratively in order to make the meaning clear, e.g. "God has caused all things to be subject to Christ" or "God has put Christ in complete control of all things".

Note that, in the Greek text, πάντα "all (things)" is placed in the emphatic position before the verb. The agent in the event is God and αὐτοῦ "of him" refers to Christ.

1:22b God has appointed Christ, As stated above, the aorist indicative ἔδωκεν "he gave" is co-ordinate with ὑπέταξεν "he subjected", connected to it by καί "and". As with πάντα in the previous clause, the object, αὐτόν "him", is in an emphatic position in the Greek text. It refers to Christ. God is the agent of the action.

The majority view among commentators is that the meaning of the verb in this context is "give", in the sense of God *giving* Christ to the church as its head. Several versions, however, translate αὐτὸν ἔδωκεν as "appointed him" (NIV) or "made him" (CEV, NCV, NJB, RSV). According to BDAG, p. 242.7, when δίδωμι occurs with a double accusative, as it does here, it may have the sense *"appoint someone someth[ing]"*, to appoint someone to special responsibility.

who rules over all things, *to rule over* **the church.** In the expression κεφαλὴν ὑπὲρ πάντα "head over all (things)", κεφαλήν "head" is figurative. See also 4:15 and 5:23. It is generally agreed that, in this context, "head" denotes authority.

Some commentators maintain that there is a figurative comparison here, the head and the body representing Christ imparting spiritual life to the church. In this case, "head" and "body" would be live metaphors.

However, it is better to take "head" as a dead metaphor. According to Louw and Nida,

> [κεφαλή is used figuratively of] one who is of supreme or pre-eminent status, in view of authority to order or command - 'one who is the head of, one who is superior to, one who is supreme over' (87.51).

As a dead metaphor it would not necessarily need to be translated literally as "head" (but see the note on 1:23a).

In concluding his remarks about this verse, Hoehner states,

> [T]his verse speaks of two manifestations of power: first, God has subjected everything in creation under Christ's feet; and second, God gave Christ to the church as head over everything, which thus implies that he is head over the church (pp. 289–290).

The first of these two manifestations of power is stated in 1:22a and the second in 1:22b.

This proposition is SPECIFIC₄ of 1:20a, co-ordinate with 1:22a.

1:23a The church *relates to* **Christ** *in the same way as* **the body** *relates to its head.* The initial relative pronoun ἥτις "which" relates back to ἐκκλησία "church" in the previous verse. It is the subject of the clause ἥτις ἐστὶν τὸ σῶμα αὐτοῦ "which is the body of him". This qualifies 1:22b, further explaining Christ's relationship to the church by introducing the term σῶμα αὐτοῦ "his body". The αὐτοῦ refers to Christ. In the previous verse the head was referred to as distinct from the body. Here the two are brought together, as in 4:15-16 and 5:23 and in the parallel passage, Colossians 1:18.

Since this is an important figure in this epistle, occurring again in chapters 2, 4 and 5, it is regarded as a live metaphor. So the point of comparison needs to be made explicit in the display proposition.

1:23b In and through the church, Christ exercises that same infinite power which he exercises throughout the whole universe. The clause τὸ πλήρωμα τοῦ τὰ πάντα ἐν πᾶσιν πληρουμένου "the fulness of the (one) filling all (things) in-every-(way)/with-all-(things)" or "the fulness of the (one) being filled all in all" This clause further explains the relationship between Christ and the church. It is quite complicated, however.

The main issues in meaning are:

1. Who is the agent in the "filling" process?
2. Who or what is being filled?

In discussing these questions, the meaning of the noun phrase τὸ πλήρωμα "the fulness, the filling", and the meaning of the related verb πληρουμένου "filling/being-filled" are the most important items for discussion.

Firstly, the meaning of the noun phrase τὸ πλήρωμα "the fulness, the filling". Commentators suggest two possibilities:

1. It has a passive sense. It refers to the church being filled by Christ or God. See, for example, Best (p. 188), Candlish (p. 50), Ellicott (p. 26), Hoehner (p. 299), Lincoln (p. 75), O'Brien (p. 150), Stott (p. 65).
2. It has an active sense. It refers to the church fulfilling Christ, in the sense of completing him. He is the head, the church is his body. See, for example, Hendriksen (pp. 103-104), Lenski (pp. 404-405).

In all other New Testament uses of πλήρωμα "fulness, filling", the sense is active "that which fills or makes something full" or "completes". However, in other Greek literature, there are contexts where the sense is passive "that which is full of something". In this context, the passive sense would mean "the church is full of Christ", i.e. "Christ fills the church" (BDAG, p. 829.1b and 2)

Secondly, the present participle πληρουμένου "filling/being-filled" is middle or passive in form. The middle voice would give an active meaning. So the same question arises as for the noun phrase τὸ πλήρωμα "the fulness, the filling". Commentators, therefore, say that:

1. It is active (middle). It would, therefore, refer to Christ's filling or completing all things. See Candlish (p. 51), Hodge (p. 91), Lincoln (p. 77), O'Brien (pp. 150-151).
2. It is passive. It would, therefore, refer to Christ being filled by God and that Christ, in turn, fills the church. See Best (p. 188), Hoehner (p. 299).

As this is the only use of the verb πληρόω "to fill" in a potential middle, some commentators use this argument to support the second option. They also cite passages such as Colossians 1:19 and 2:9-10.

However, a middle voice with an active meaning is normal in Greek as a whole. Also, elsewhere in Ephesians, Christ and the Holy Spirit are spoken of as being the active powers of filling (4:10; 5:18). So it seems preferable to understand it in this way here, i.e. it is Christ who is the agent.

To summarise, then: with a number of variables at work, it is difficult to decide the meaning of the entire phrase. Due to good commentary support and consistency with Scripture in general, the display follows the following options:

The phrase τὸ πλήρωμα "the fulness" refers to Christ's filling the church.
The participle πληρουμένου should be understood in its active sense, "he is filling".

The phrase τὰ πάντα ἐν πᾶσιν "all (things) in-every-way/with-all-(things)" is understood to refer to the whole universe, all creation, since there is nothing in the context to restrict the sense of τὰ πάντα. The phrase ἐν πᾶσιν then means "completely" or "in every way".

The clause τὸ πλήρωμα τοῦ τὰ πάντα ἐν πᾶσιν πληρουμένου, therefore, is understood to be saying two things:

1. Christ fills the church.
2. Christ fills all-things/the-universe completely.

It needs then to be decided in what sense Christ fills the church and the universe.

Christ can be said to fill the universe in the sense that he exercises his sovereign power throughout the universe and over all things (1:21; 4:10), including the church (1:22). But his relationship to the rest of the universe is not the same as that between himself and the church. The church, as Christ's body and as a participant in the working out of God's purposes, is the recipient of Christ's special grace and gifts. These include the Holy Spirit (4:7-16; 5:18). God's power is available to believers (1:19). Christ, as their head, is the one who directs and guides them (1:22).

In 3:19, Paul prays for the Ephesian believers that they "might be filled to all the fulness of God". This indicates that this has not yet been completely fulfilled. Nevertheless, God's resources are available to them already through Christ.

It can be said, therefore, that Christ, as the one who exercises infinite power throughout the universe, fills the church with himself, i.e. with his own perfections and with that same power which he exercises over the universe. The propositional representation in the display is based on this analysis, although it is only one of a number of possibilities which might be suggested as expressing the meaning of this complicated clause.

BOUNDARIES AND COHERENCE

Both the initial boundary and the final boundary of this unit have been discussed in the section on Boundaries and Coherence for 1:15-23.

Lexical cohesion evidencing coherence can be seen in the abundance of vocabulary dealing with the authority of Christ. Almost every word in 1:20-23 deals with this.

PROMINENCE AND THEME

The theme statement for this paragraph is extracted from the GENERIC statement and the four SPECIFICS since all are prominent, as shown by the climactic repetition and accumulation of lexical items from the semantic domain of power and lordship.

SUBPART CONSTITUENT 2:1–3:13 (Expository Division: Nucleus of 1:3–3:21)

THEME: Because of God's grace he saved us, through our faith in Christ. Through Christ's death, God caused all believers, whether Jew or Gentile, to be at peace with him and with each other, so that now all share the same blessings and form one church. God appointed me to make known to the Gentiles that he is the source of infinite blessings for them, and to make known to everyone that God's purpose in forming the church was to reveal his infinite wisdom to the powerful beings in the heavens.

MACROSTRUCTURE	CONTENTS
NUCLEUS	2:1–22 Formerly, we were all spiritually dead and certain to be punished by God, but because of his grace and great love he saved us, through our faith in Christ. Through Christ's death, God has caused all believers, you Gentiles as well as Jewish believers, to be at peace with him and with each other, so that now all share the same blessings and form one church.
AUTHORITATIVE GROUNDS	3:1–13 I, Paul, am in prison because I serve Christ on the behalf of you Gentiles. God graciously appointed me to make known to you that Christ is the source of infinite blessings for you, as well as for Jewish believers. He also appointed me to make known to everyone how God accomplished what he had secretly planned, in order that, by means of establishing the church, he might now make known his infinitely wise plan to those beings who exercise power in the heavens.

INTENT AND MACROSTRUCTURE

Paul's intention in this unit is to encourage the Ephesian believers to understand what their position is in relation to Christ and the church. He wants them to realise that, because of their salvation, they are now reconciled to God. They are, therefore, fellow-members of God's church along with Jewish believers. And the church is under the headship of Christ. Paul states this in the discourse of 2:1–22.

Then, in chapter 3, in order to give authority to what he says, he digresses from the prayer he begins in 3:1 and tells the Ephesians that he has been specially chosen by God to reveal these truths to them (3:2–13).

This division 2:1–3:13 is an expository unit. Structurally, it consists of two paragraph clusters, 2:1–22 and 3:1–13. The second of these provides an authoritative or validating grounds for the first, which is best understood as the NUCLEUS.

BOUNDARIES AND COHERENCE

The initial boundary of this unit has been discussed in the section on Boundaries and Coherence for 1:15–23. The initial boundary of the next unit, 3:14–21, is marked by the repetition of the expression τούτου χάριν "for this reason" in 2:14 followed by the orienter to the prayer, κάμπτω τὰ γόνατά μου πρὸς τὸν πατέρα... "I bend my knees to the Father...".

PROMINENCE AND THEME

The NUCLEUS is naturally prominent. So its theme statement (or the most prominent parts thereof) should be included in the theme. The authority of a document is crucial and so prominent enough to be included in the theme here also.

DIVISION CONSTITUENT 2:1–22 (Expository Subdivision: Nucleus of 2:1–3:13)

THEME: Formerly, we were all spiritually dead and certain to be punished by God, but because of his grace and great love he saved us, through our faith in Christ. Through Christ's death, God has caused all believers, you Gentiles as well as Jewish believers, to be at peace with him and with each other, so that now all share the same blessings and form one church.

MACROSTRUCTURE	CONTENTS
NUCLEUS$_1$	2:1–10 Formerly, we were all spiritually dead and were certain to be punished by God. But because of his grace and great love he saved us, through our faith in Christ. We did nothing at all to save ourselves.
NUCLEUS$_2$	2:11–22 God brought you Gentiles, along with Jewish believers, into his spiritual family by uniting you spiritually with Christ, so that now you all share the same blessings and form one church. Through Christ's death, both Jewish and Gentile believers are at peace with God and one another, which is evidenced by the fact that all believers, whether Jew or Gentile, may approach God freely, by means of the Holy Spirit.

INTENT AND MACROSTRUCTURE

Subdivision 2:1–22 has strong ties with 1:15–23, where Paul prayed that the Ephesians might have a greater appreciation of God's power exercised on their behalf. In chapter 2, he now wants to increase their awareness of this power. The two units, 2:1–10 and 2:11–22, which make up this section are related by the parallel nature of their structure and content and are considered co-ordinate NUCLEI.

Both units follow a "once-now" pattern, contrasting the past and present situations of the Ephesian believers. In 2:1–10, the focus is on the contrast between their past condition of spiritual death, characterised by disobedience to God, and their present situation as people whom God has made alive spiritually, in order to live lives of obedience to him.

In 2:11–22, the focus is on their pre-Christian past in relation to the special position of the Jews within God's saving purpose. At that time, as Gentiles, they were alienated from God and, therefore, ineligible for the privileges that belong to those who were God's people. Now, by contrast, they are reconciled with God, as are Jewish believers. They enjoy the same privileges as the Jewish believers do and are united with them to form one church.

This is an expository unit, as can be seen from the predominant use of indicative verbs and cause-effect connectors such as γάρ "for", διό "therefore", ὅτι "that", οὖν "therefore". Paul is reminding the Ephesians about what God has done on their behalf through Christ. His purpose in doing this is to cause them to have a greater awareness of God's great power and also of his love.

Paul wants the Ephesians to appreciate fully the extent to which God has changed them and their situation, so that their response to his exhortations in 4:1–6:20 will be positive and wholehearted.

The conjunction διό "therefore" plus the imperative μνημονεύετε "remember" in 2:11a are not used to exhort some specific behaviour based on the preceding context but to draw the attention of the Ephesians to what he is about to say in 2:11–22. Since verses 2:11–13 repeat some of the same ideas as 2:1–10 and especially of 2:1–3, διό may be functioning as signalling resumption. The resumption in this case would be restating truths for the purpose of emphasis and as a platform for developing further aspects of the theme in 2:14–22.

BOUNDARIES AND COHERENCE

The initial boundary of this unit has been discussed in the section on Boundaries and Coherence for 1:15–23.

The final boundary is marked by the end of the "building" metaphor in 2:22, where Paul was addressing the Ephesians directly, using second person plural pronouns and verb forms. The beginning of the next unit is then marked in 3:1 when Paul refers to himself as ἐγὼ Παῦλος ὁ δέσμιος τοῦ Χριστοῦ Ἰησοῦ ὑπὲρ ὑμῶν τῶν ἐθνῶν "I, Paul, the prisoner of Christ Jesus on behalf of you Gentiles".

It is generally agreed that Paul was intending to pray for the Ephesians at this point. However, he digresses and does not resume the prayer until 3:14.

The subject matter of the two units which make up this expository section relates them closely to each other, as stated in the section on Intent and Macrostructure.

PROMINENCE AND THEME

The theme statement is based on the prominent elements of the two NUCLEI.

SUBDIVISION CONSTITUENT 2:1-10 (Expository Section: Nucleus₁ of 2:1-22)

THEME: Formerly, we were all spiritually dead and were certain to be punished by God. But because of his grace and great love he saved us, through our faith in Christ. We did nothing at all to save ourselves.

MACROSTRUCTURE	CONTENTS
┌─concession ───────────	2:1-3 Formerly, you were spiritually dead because you were habitually sinning. So also were we all. In this evil state, God would certainly punish us all.
CONTRAEXPECTATION ──CONCLUSION ───	2:4-7 Because God is exceedingly merciful and loved us so much, he caused us to become spiritually alive and to sit victoriously with Christ in heaven. He did this by uniting us with Christ.
└─GROUNDS ───────────	2:8-10 It is only because of God's grace that you have been saved, through trusting in Christ. You did not save yourselves. It is God who caused us to become spiritually alive.

INTENT AND MACROSTRUCTURE

This is an expository unit with expressive overtones. Paul intends to influence the Ephesians' ideas and emotions by causing them to recall their former state and compare it with their present one. These verses are parallel with 2:11-22 and provide NUCLEUS₁ of 2:1-22.

Structurally, this unit may be regarded as one paragraph or three closely related paragraphs, 2:1-3, 2:4-7 and 2:8-10.

The subject matter of the whole unit is God's gracious work in bringing sinners to salvation. Each of the above three paragraphs deals with a different aspect of this subject, as follows:

1. In 2:1-3, Paul describes the Ephesians' former sinful state from which God delivered them through Christ. The focus is on ὑμᾶς "you" (for accusative form, see the note on 2:1) and ἡμεῖς "we" as agents. The pronouns are forefronted in 2:1 and 2:3. The vocabulary in these verses is drawn from the semantic domain of evil and wrong-doing:

παραπτώμασιν "trespasses" (2:1)
ἁμαρτίαις "sins" (2:1)
ἀπειθείας "disobedience" (2:2)
ἐπιθυμίαις "lusts" (2:3)
ὀργῆς "wrath" (2:3)

2. In 2:4, Paul changes the focus with the phrase ὁ δὲ θεός "But God". The focus shifts from "we/you" as agents to God as agent. The vocabulary in 2:4-7 contrasts with that in 2:1-3 in that it is drawn from the semantic domain of qualities and actions associated with God, and so refers only to that which is good:

ἐλέει "mercy" (2:4)
ἀγάπην "love" (2:4)
ἠγάπησεν "he loved" (2:4)
χάριτι "by grace" (2:5)
χάριτος "of grace" (2:7)
χρηστότητι "kindness" (2:7)

The cohesion of 2:4-7 is further strengthened by the sandwich structure created by πλούσιος ὢν ἐν ἐλέει "being rich in mercy" in 2:4 and τὸ ὑπερβάλλον πλοῦτος τῆς χάριτος αὐτοῦ "the exceeding riches of his grace" in 2:7.

3. In 2:8, the forefronting of χάριτι "by grace" gives it prominence, so that it is the focus of the 2:8-10 unit. This focus is maintained by references such as δῶρον "gift" (2:8) and οὐκ ἐξ ἔργων "not of works" (2:9). The subordinating conjunction γάρ "for" (occurring here at 2:8a) often is found at a switch in an argument from a claim or inference to the support for it. The switch here is significant enough to analyse 2:8-10 as a paragraph on its own.

BOUNDARIES AND COHERENCE

Evidence for the initial boundary of this unit has been given in the section on Boundaries and Coherence for 1:15-23. As for the final boundary, there is a διό "therefore" at the beginning of the new Greek sentence in 2:11 as well as the imperative μνημονεύετε "remember". This indicates a break of some kind. Paul's presentation in 2:1-3 is similar to that in 2:11-13 (especially 2:11–12), dealing with the Ephesian believers' past life. However, this does not prove that they both belong to the same paragraph-level unit. The intervening verses 2:4–10 deal with the present phase of their lives, which has resulted from the grace of God. Also, 2:11–13 begins the presentation on the Gentile believers' being brought together as one body with the Jewish believers, a presentation that is developed more fully in 2:14–22.

These verses are marked as a unit by the "sandwich structure" created by the use of the verb περιπατέω "walk" in 2:2 and 2:10, which refers to the Ephesians' way of life.

The contrastive expressions, νεκροὺς τοῖς παραπτώμασιν καὶ ταῖς ἁμαρτίαις ὑμῶν "dead in your trespasses and sins" (2:1, stating the Ephesians' condition before their conversion), and κτισθέντες ἐν Χριστῷ Ἰησοῦ "created in Christ Jesus" (2:10, stating their condition after their conversion) might also be viewed as a "sandwich structure".

PROMINENCE AND THEME

Paragraph 2:4–7 is the nuclear unit of the 2:1–10 section. It acts as CONTRAEXPECTATION to the concession unit, 2:1–3, and is supported by the grounds unit, 2:8–10. The concession, 2:1–3, is integral to the theme. The grounds is marked prominent because of the repetition of two contrasting topics: grace as the sole means for salvation and the inability of our own works to save us. This gives emphasis to the grounds. Thus each paragraph is represented in this section theme.

SECTION CONSTITUENT 2:1–3 (Expository Paragraph: Concession to 2:4–7)

THEME: Formerly, you were spiritually dead because you were habitually sinning. So also were we all. In this evil state, God would certainly punish us all.

RELATIONAL STRUCTURE	CONTENTS
NUCLEUS₁ — NUCLEUS — NUCLEUS₁	2:1a Formerly, you were *spiritually* dead [MET],
NUCLEUS₂	2:1b you were habitually sinning.
amplification — NUCLEUS	2:2a You were behaving in the same *evil* manner as those who oppose Christ behave,
amplification — 'Satan'	2:2b *that is*, you behaved in the *evil* manner in which *Satan wants you to behave*.
description — NUCLEUS₁	2:2c He rules over evil spirits in the heavens,
NUCLEUS₂	2:2d and he is the spirit who is now working-powerfully-in/controlling the people who disobey *God*.
NUCLEUS₁ — NUCLEUS	2:3a Formerly, we all used to disobey *God*.
amplification — GENERIC	2:3b We did what our evil human nature wanted *us to do* (*or*, we behaved as our evil human nature caused *us to behave*).
specific	2:3c We were habitually doing *those evil deeds which* our bodies and our minds wanted *to do*.
NUCLEUS₂ — NUCLEUS	2:3d In our natural *evil* state, *God* would certainly punish us,
comparison	2:3e just as *he will certainly* punish all other *evil people*.

INTENT AND STRUCTURE

In this expository paragraph, Paul wants the Ephesians to remember their former desperate condition before they trusted in Christ.

NOTES

2:1 The initial καί "and" resumes the thought of 1:19–23 about how God's power works on behalf of the Ephesian believers. In 1:20, God's power is exemplified in the resurrection and exaltation of Christ. Here, in 2:1–10, Paul presents a further example of that same power: the spiritual life created in those who were "dead in sin".

The pronoun ὑμᾶς "you (pl)" is forefronted in 2:1. Since it is in the accusative case, it seems that Paul intended it to be the object of a verb, probably συνεζωοποίησεν "he made alive" (2:4).

However, he digresses to explain his statement about the Ephesians' being formerly "dead in sins" and that this had also been the position of the Jews (2:2–3).

He then resumes his original thought in 2:4. This resumption is indicated in the Greek text by the word δέ.

In 2:5, the resumption includes a repetition of ὄντας νεκροὺς τοῖς παραπτώμασιν "dead in trespasses", but this time, because of the reference to ἡμεῖς "we" in 2:3, Paul uses the accusative plural pronoun ἡμᾶς "us" rather than ὑμᾶς "you" as object of συνεζωοποίησεν "he made alive".

As for 2:1, in modern English, there is no difference between the second person plural pronoun in the nominative and accusative cases. But there is in other languages. In these languages a nominative (subject) form should be used here.

2:1a Formerly, you were *spiritually* dead, In English, it is more natural for the time orientation of a paragraph to occur at the beginning of the paragraph. Greek, however, tends to focus on the person orientation of the paragraph. In the Greek text here, the word ποτε "formerly" occurs in 2:2a. To make the display less ambiguous, "formerly" has been moved to the beginning of 2:1a.

The pronoun ὑμᾶς "you" in 2:1a refers to the Ephesian believers. In this context, the Ephesians represent all Gentile believers.

The word νεκρός "dead" is used figuratively. This is made clear in the next two verses where Paul describes the sort of lives the Ephesians were living before they believed. This figurative sense is expressed in the display by using the expression "spiritually dead". However, many languages do not have an equivalent to "spiritually". In some of these languages, it may be possible to use a simile instead of a metaphor, e.g. "it was as if you were dead".

2:1b you were habitually sinning. In the Greek text, there are two abstract nouns παραπτώμασιν "transgressions, trespasses" and ἁμαρτίαις "sins". Commentators differ on how they understand them:

1. Some think that there is no difference in meaning.
2. Others think that παράπτωμα "transgression, trespass" refers to outward transgressions, while ἁμαρτία "sin" refers to the inherent principle of sin.
3. Still others think that παράπτωμα is a specific term and ἁμαρτία is more general and abstract.

The important point in this context is that these two terms are comprehensive and cover all possible sins.

Being "dead in sins" (2:1a) makes it clear that sin governed every aspect of the Ephesians' lives. So it is natural to understand that their sinning was habitual. The use of περιεπατήσατε "you walked" (2:2)—a verb often used of habitual conduct—supports this. So, in the display, the verb "sinning" is qualified by "habitually".

There are two ways to understand the dative case in the phrase τοῖς παραπτώμασιν καὶ ταῖς ἁμαρτίαις ὑμῶν "in your trespasses and sins":

1. It indicates the reason the Ephesians were spiritually dead, that is, because of their trespasses and sins.
2. It indicates the state and condition of the death.

Many commentators and versions follow the first option and understand the dative phrase as causal. However, a number of commentators consider that both meanings are present. Eadie, for example, compares it with the corresponding passage in Colossians 2:13 and states,

> "The trespasses and sins" do not merely indicate the cause of death,...but they are descriptive also of the state of death. They represent not simply the instrument, but at the same time the condition of death (p. 119).

See also Best (p. 201), Hoehner (pp. 307–308), Lincoln (p. 93), O'Brien (pp. 156–157).

It would seem, therefore, that the phrase τοῖς παραπτώμασιν καὶ ταῖς ἁμαρτίαις ὑμῶν "in your trespasses and sins" indicates the condition of unbelievers as much as it does the cause of that condition.

One way to express the dative phrase, indicating the condition of unbelievers, would be "you were *spiritually* dead, you were habitually sinning". This would indicate an ongoing state or condition. This is used in the display, because it appears to be more basic—Paul is not necessarily focussing on reason-result factors at this point.

2:2 This cluster of propositions is an amplifycation of 2:1a.

2:2a You were behaving in the same *evil* manner as those who oppose Christ behave, The initial relative pronoun αἷς "which" is plural, referring to both τοῖς παραπτώμασιν "trespasses" and ταῖς ἁμαρτίαις "sins". It is not necessary to literally express ἐν αἷς "in which" in the display, because of the transformation from abstract nouns to verb in 2:1.

The verb περιπατέω literally means "to walk, go". It is, however, frequently used, as here, to mean "to behave, conduct oneself". It often refers to habitual behaviour. See the note on 2:1b.

The preposition κατά "according to", with the accusative case, occurs twice in this verse. Each time the phrase in which it occurs qualifies the verb περιεπατήσατε "you conducted yourselves, behaved". It indicates the standard by which the Ephesians had been living before God made them alive.

Its first occurrence is in the phrase κατὰ τὸν αἰῶνα τοῦ κόσμου τούτου "according to the age of this world". The Greek term αἰών "age" occurs elsewhere in Ephesians (1:21; 2:7; 3:9, 11, 21). In each of these verses, it is understood in a temporal sense.

Here, however, αἰῶνα is qualified by τοῦ κόσμου τούτου "of this world". Although the term κόσμος may be used to refer to the created, material world (see 1:4), in this context, it refers to a world system that is opposed to God. The complete phrase τὸν αἰῶνα τοῦ κόσμου τούτου "the age of this world", therefore, refers to behaviour which is characterised by the prevailing life-style of the time, a world system which is evil and opposed to God. "To live according to the age of this world", therefore, means to live in a sinful manner.

When they were unbelievers, the Ephesians lived like everyone around them, conforming to the standards of a society that did not know Christ. This might be expressed as "you were behaving in the same evil manner as those who oppose Christ behave".

2:2b *that is*, you behaved in the *evil* manner in which *Satan* wants you to behave. This second phrase introduced by κατά "according to" specifies who directs the evil way of life referred to in 2:2a. It is agreed that τὸν ἄρχοντα τῆς ἐξουσίας τοῦ ἀέρος "the ruler of the authority of the air" is Satan.

So the Ephesians had formerly behaved according to the will of Satan, that is, in the evil manner in which he wanted them to behave.

2:2c He rules over evil spirits in the heavens, Both 2:2c and 2:2d describe Satan.

Commentators agree that τὸν ἄρχοντα "the ruler" refers to Satan. However, there is discussion about the sense of the genitive phrase τῆς ἐξουσίας τοῦ ἀέρος "of the power of the air". Commentators suggest the following:

1. The abstract noun ἐξουσία refers to the "domain" or "realm" over which Satan rules (BDAG, p. 353.6). The genitive τοῦ ἀέρος "of the air" then defines that realm.
2. The abstract noun ἐξουσία refers to the evil spirits over whom Satan rules. The genitive τοῦ ἀέρος then describes the place where they live/rule.
3. The genitive τοῦ ἀέρος "of the air" is used metaphorically. So τῆς ἐξουσίας τοῦ ἀέρος "the power of the air" refers to the nature of the powers spoken of, not to the place where they live. They are spiritual or heavenly in their nature.

The first and second options seem most likely. According to the world view of Paul's time, "the air" referred to that intermediate area between earth and heaven, above the earth but beneath heaven where God is. In this context, therefore, it is the region where Satan rules and where spirits, especially evil spirits, are at work. This would fit with the references to the hostile powers which inhabit "the heavenlies" and against which believers are called to fight (6:12). See, for example, the discussions in Candlish (p. 52), Hendriksen (pp. 113–114), Lincoln (p. 96), O'Brien (p. 160).

The difference in meaning between the first and second options is slight. So, in the display, this is expressed as "He rules over evil spirits in the heavens". In translating "in the heavens" care should be taken to choose a term for "heavens" which does not refer to heaven where God lives.

2:2d and he is the spirit who is now working-powerfully-in/controlling the people who disobey *God*. There are two things that need to be decided with regard to the phrase τοῦ πνεύματος τοῦ νῦν ἐνεργοῦντος ἐν τοῖς υἱοῖς τῆς ἀπειθείας "the spirit now working in the sons of disobedience".

Firstly, what does πνεῦμα "spirit" mean in this context? There are two possibilities:

1. It refers to a supernatural being.
2. It refers to an essential principle or characteristic.

Secondly, what is the relationship of πνεῦμα "spirit" to the previous clause? Again there are two main possibilities:

1. It is in apposition to ἐξουσίας "power, authority".
2. It is in apposition to ἄρχοντα "ruler".

These two issues cannot be discussed separately as they are interrelated. The combination of the issues provides four interpretations:

1. πνεῦμα refers to a supernatural being and the phrase is in apposition with ἐξουσίας. The sense then is "that power/authority which is the spirit now working...".
2. πνεῦμα refers to a supernatural being and the phrase is in apposition to ἄρχοντα "ruler". The sense then is "the ruler over the power of the air".
3. πνεῦμα refers to an essential principle or characteristic and the phrase is in apposition to ἄρχοντα. The sense then is "that principle that is now working...".
4. πνεῦμα refers to an essential principle or characteristic and the phrase is in apposition to ἐξουσίας. The sense then is "that

power/authority which is the essential principle now working...".

It is difficult to decide which option is correct and there is much disagreement among commentators. Many commentators agree that πνεῦμα "spirit" likely refers to Satan. It is the connection that causes the most discussion.

In favour of apposition to ἐξουσίας "power, authority", it can be said that it is the most grammatically natural option as it agrees in case with πνεύματος (both genitive).

However, the lack of case agreement with ἄρχοντα "ruler" is not a decisive point. More important is that fact that ἄρχοντα "ruler" is the head noun in the genitive construction, and therefore the natural antecedent. This is how it is understood in the display with πνεῦμα referring to Satan.

The phrase τοῖς υἱοῖς τῆς ἀπειθείας "in/among the sons of disobedience" is a Hebrew idiom which means "those characterised by disobedience". Such idioms were often used for emphasis. The disobedience referred to is usually towards God. Either God himself is disobeyed directly or his laws are disobeyed. In the display, this is expressed as "those people who disobey *God*". "God" is supplied to complete the case frame.

2:3a Formerly, we all used to disobey *God*. Most commentators understand the relative prepositional phrase ἐν οἷς "in/among whom/which" to refer to the immediately preceding phrase ἐν τοῖς υἱοῖς τῆς ἀπειθείας "in/among the sons of disobedience".

The clause ἐν οἷς καὶ ἡμεῖς πάντες ἀνεστράφημεν "among whom also we all behaved" is, therefore, understood to mean that the Ephesians belonged among "the children of disobedience", i.e. they behaved like them, living according to the same standards. They disobeyed God just as "the children of disobedience" did.

It is not clear to whom ἡμεῖς πάντες "we all" refers. There are two options:

1. It refers to only Paul and his fellow-Jews. The "you" of 2:1 and 2:2 then refers to the believing Ephesian Gentiles or believing Gentiles in general. See, for example, Abbott (p. 43), O'Brien (p. 161).

2. Other commentators regard ἡμεῖς as including Paul, his companions and all the Ephesian believers, possibly even all believers in general. See, for example, Best (pp. 207–208), Eadie (pp. 130–131), Ellicott (p. 30), Hoehner (p. 317), Lincoln (p. 97).

There seems to be no reason to follow the first option, since the distinction between Jew and Gentile is not significant in this particular context. Also the use of πάντες "all" suggests universality. So, in these notes, it is assumed that Paul is referring to himself, his companions, as well as all the Ephesians, whether Jew or Gentile.

The forefronting of ἡμεῖς πάντες "we all" is for emphasis. It draws attention to the state of all believers before God called them. In other words, "we, who are believers, at one time thought and behaved in the same way as the 'sons of disobedience' now behave (2:2), that is, we did not obey God".

2:3b We did what our evil human nature wanted *us to do* (*or,* we behaved as our evil human nature caused *us to behave*). The clause ἐν ταῖς ἐπιθυμίαις τῆς σαρκὸς ἡμῶν "in the lusts of our flesh" amplifies 2:3a, explaining the Ephesians' former behaviour.

The word ἐπιθυμία "desire, longing", which may be used in either a good or a bad sense, is used in a bad sense here (also in 4:22). It signifies a desire to have or do something evil, or an excessive desire of any kind.

The word σάρξ "flesh", in this context, refers to the fallen and corrupt human nature as a whole. It should be understood in this general sense in this clause. It is not until the following clause that it is more specifically defined.

The preposition ἐν "in" introduces the definition of "our" behaviour: "we behaved according to our evil human nature".

2:3c We were habitually doing *those evil deeds which* our bodies and our minds wanted *to do*. The present active participle ποιοῦντες "doing" and its direct object τὰ θελήματα τῆς σαρκὸς καὶ τῶν διανοιῶν "the desires of the flesh and of the mind" describe the action of the finite verb ἀνεστράφημεν "we behaved" (2:3b).

This proposition is in a specific relation to 2:3b. In 2:3b, it is stated that the Ephesians behaved according to their evil human nature. Now Paul restates this in the clause ποιοῦντες τὰ θελήματα τῆς σαρκὸς καὶ τῶν διανοιῶν "doing the desires of the flesh and of the mind".

This is the second occurrence of the noun σάρξ "flesh" in this verse. It is likely that this second use is more specific than the generic use in 2:3b.

In combination with τῶν διανοιῶν "of the mind", it gives further details about the things which a person's evil nature causes him to want to do.

In 2:3c, τῆς σαρκός "the flesh" refers to the sensual side of our nature, and would include sexual sins and other sins which indulge our bodies. In contrast, διάνοια "understanding, mind" probably refers to those sins connected with our thoughts. According to BDAG, 234.5, διάνοια may have the meaning of "*sense, impulse*, in a bad sense...pl. Eph. 2:3".

The words σάρξ and διάνοια refer to evil desires of all sorts, both physical and in thoughts, ideas, emotions. In the display, this is expressed as "*those evil deeds which* our bodies and our minds wanted *to do*".

2:3d In our natural *evil* state *God* would certainly punish us, The initial καί "and" in the clause καὶ ἤμεθα τέκνα φύσει ὀργῆς "and were by nature children of wrath" indicates a co-ordinate relation with 2:3a-c.

The expression τέκνα...ὀργῆς "children of wrath" is an idiom (see also 2:2). It means "potential recipients of wrath". Here it describes the Ephesians' former state as being those who were the objects of God's wrath.

The word ὀργή "wrath, anger" is probably a metonymy referring to the outcome of the anger, that is, punishment, rather than the emotion itself. The sense, therefore, is that God would punish them.

The word φύσις "nature, natural condition" indicates a condition that is common to all people by birth. Here it refers to people and the natural evil condition they were in before God saved them.

The sense of the whole clause is "in our natural *evil* state it was certain that God would punish us".

2:3e just as *he will certainly* punish all other *evil people.* The phrase ὡς καὶ οἱ λοιποί "as also the rest" expands the "we" of the previous passage to include all humanity. God will punish anyone who remains in a state of disobedience towards him. The ὡς "as" introduces a comparison between the former state of those who are now believers and the present state of οἱ λοιποί "the rest".

BOUNDARIES AND COHERENCE

The initial boundary of this unit has been discussed under Boundaries and Coherence for 1:15-23. There is a contrastive break at the beginning of 2:4 with the conjunction δέ marking the switch from the "you" and "we" orientation of 2:1-3 to the orientation with God as subject in 2:4-7. There is no explicit reference to God or Christ in 2:1-3.

PROMINENCE AND THEME

The most prominent nuclei, 2:1, 2:3a and 2:3d, are the basis for the theme statement.

SECTION CONSTITUENT 2:4–7
(Expository Paragraph: Contraexpectation of 2:1–3)

THEME: Because God is exceedingly merciful and loved us so much, he caused us to become spiritually alive and to sit victoriously with Christ in heaven. He did this by uniting us with Christ.

RELATIONAL STRUCTURE	CONTENTS
REASON — NUCLEUS₁	2:4a But God is so exceedingly merciful
NUCLEUS₂	2:4b and he loved us so much,
NUCLEUS₁ — NUCLEUS — concession — NUCLEUS₁	2:5a as a result, even when we were *spiritually* dead [MET]
NUCLEUS₂	2:5b *and* were habitually sinning,
CONTRAEXPECTATION	2:5c he caused us to become *spiritually* alive [MET] *by means of uniting us* with Christ
emphatic comment	2:5d —*it is only* because *God* is so gracious that he has saved you.
NUCLEUS₂ — RESULT	2:6a And God has raised *us* up *spiritually* with *Christ Jesus* and caused *us* to sit *victoriously* with him in heaven [MET],
means	2:6b *by means of uniting us* with Christ Jesus.
purpose — RESULT	2:7a *He did this* [2:5c-6] in order that he might demonstrate *to everyone* in-future-times/forever that he has acted in an incomparably gracious and kind way to us
reason	2:7b because of *what* Christ Jesus *did for us*.

INTENT AND STRUCTURE

Throughout this chapter, Paul wants to make the Ephesians aware of how great God's grace and mercy is towards them, and that this affects their lives. This is also true in this paragraph. Here he states three gracious acts that God has done for the Ephesian believers:

1. He has caused them to become spiritually alive with Christ.
2. He has raised them up spiritually with Christ.
3. He has caused them to sit victoriously with Christ in heaven.

This important information is contained in the three main clauses in 2:5 and 2:6 and indicated by the three non-subordinated finite verbs:

συνεζωοποίησεν "he made (us) alive with"
συνήγειρεν "he raised (us) up with"
συνεκάθισεν "he seated (us) with"

These verbs recall 1:20–21. What God did for Christ by his power, he has now done for the Ephesians.

The adjective πλούσιος "rich, wealthy" is forefronted for emphasis. It is used figuratively to intensify the phrase ἐν ἐλέει "in mercy, compassion, pity". It describes the greatness of God's mercy towards sinners.

The participial phrase πλούσιος ὢν ἐν ἐλέει "being rich in mercy" indicates a reason why God raised us to life.

NOTES

2:4a But God is so exceedingly merciful The conjunction δέ is translated "but" in most versions. It indicates a contrast with paragraph 2:1–3.

The combination of ὁ θεός "God" with δέ at the beginning of the verse expresses a switch from the Ephesians, living in an immoral state, to *God* and what he has done for them through Christ.

2:4b and he loved us so much, The clause διὰ τὴν πολλὴν ἀγάπην αὐτοῦ ἣν ἠγάπησεν ἡμᾶς "because of his great love (with) which he loved us" provides the reason for:

1. what follows (2:5-6)
2. or what precedes (2:4a).

In most translations the first option is preferred. This is followed in the display. This then provides a second reason, along with 2:4a, for 2:5-6. The reason-result relation is marked at the beginning of display 2:5a with "as a result".

The pronoun ἡμᾶς "us" includes along with Paul both Jewish and Gentile believers. It refers to the same people as that of ἡμεῖς πάντες "we all" in the preceding verse (2:3).

By using both the noun ἀγάπην "love" and the verb ἣν ἠγάπησεν "with which he loved", Paul is emphasising what he is saying. He wants to convey the strength and intensity of God's love. He further strengthens what he is saying by qualifying ἀγάπην "love" with the adjective πολύς "much, many". When this adjective occurs with a singular noun, as it does here, it denotes degree: "much, great, strong, deep". So the combination of adjective, noun and verb means "he loved us so-much/greatly".

The display indicates the emphasis in these two reason clauses by "so exceedingly" (2:4a) and "so much" (2:4b). In a translation, whatever prominence devices are used in a specific language should be used to communicate the strength of the feeling Paul wishes to convey.

2:5a as a result, even when we were *spiritually* dead Paul returns here to what he began to say in 2:1. However, he now expands the subject to "we" (instead of "you"), in order to include himself and all believers.

A majority of commentators and versions translate καί, as "even" and many commentators say that it has an intensive sense here (Eadie, p. 141; Ellicott, p. 32; Hodge, p. 112; Lincoln, p. 101; O'Brien, p. 166, fn. 50).

In this context the participial phrase καὶ ὄντας ἡμᾶς νεκροὺς τοῖς παραπτώμασιν "even we being dead in trespasses" may express two different relations at the same time, circumstance and concession. *Even when* we were in this state of spiritual death God made us spiritually alive. An alternative would be to translate as "even though".

2:5b *and* were habitually sinning The phrase τοῖς παραπτώμασιν "in the sins" refers to the sins already mentioned in 2:1. As in 2:1b, this constituent further specifies the condition of the Ephesians before they were saved.

2:5c he caused us to become *spiritually* alive *by means of uniting us* with Christ Paul now completes what he began to say in 2:1. The clause συνεζωοποίησεν τῷ Χριστῷ "he made (us) alive with Christ" is a metaphor. It refers to the spiritual life that believers have by means of being united with Christ. See Eadie (p. 143), Hodge (pp. 112-113). God is the agent in the main event "he made *us* alive". He is the one who causes us to become spiritually alive. Those who trust in Christ receive the same life that Christ himself received. This is the first of the three conjoined nuclei which occur in 2:5-6 (the next two occur in display 2:6a).

2:5d —*it is only* because *God* is so gracious that he has saved you. Paul uses this clause to emphasise God's grace, his unmerited favour. Many commentators consider that it is syntactically a parenthetical comment. However, thematically, it is not parenthetical at all but puts increased focus on the theme of God's grace in 2:1-10.

God's grace is one of the most prominent and recurring themes in the epistle. Here in 2:5d, the Greek word χάριτι "by grace" is forefronted for emphasis. This emphasis should be maintained in translation. In the display, this emphasis is indicated by the phrase "it is only" and the intensifier "so".

In this section, Paul switches back and forth between first and second person plural pronouns:

2:1-2:	second person plural
2:3a-5c:	first person plural
2:5d:	second person plural
2:6-7:	first person plural
2:8-9:	second person plural
2:10:	first person plural

Commentators discuss, particularly, the switches to the second person plurals in 2:5 and 2:8. These switches may be to ensure that the Ephesians do not forget that it is God who is the agent in changing their state and not they themselves.

2:6a And God has raised *us* up *spiritually* with *Christ Jesus* There are two ways to analyse the καί "and" at the beginning of this verse:

1. It introduces a further NUCLEUS, conjoined with 2:5c.
2. It introduces an amplification of NUCLEUS 2:5c. The two verbs συνήγειρεν "he raised (us) up with" and συνεκάθισεν "he seated (us) with" are two different aspects of συνεζωοποίησεν "he made (us) alive with" (2:5c).

The first option is the more straightforward and shows the parallels with 1:20 clearly. So this is represented in the display.

Commentators discuss whether there is any significant meaning difference between συνεγείρω "to raise up with" and συνζωοποιέω "to make alive with". Some regard them as being synonymous, while others think that there is a distinction in meaning. However, there is no agreement as to what that distinction is. Most versions make a difference and translate συνεγείρω as "raise up" and συνζωοποιέω as "make alive" or "bring to life".

Most commentators consider that "raised up with Christ" refers to the present state of believers rather than their future physical resurrection. This view is supported by Paul's use of the aorist tense of συνήγειρεν "he raised (us) up with" which refers to a completed action. It, therefore, has a metaphorical, rather than physical sense. So, it, along with the verb "made alive with" refer to the spiritual state of believers.

The combination of verbs "made alive with", "raised up with" and "seated with in heavenly places" obviously parallels what physically happened to Christ (1:20). This implies that "he raised up with" is a live metaphor here. It is handled as such in the propositionalisation and should also be in translation. So, καὶ συνήγειρεν...ἐν Χριστῷ Ἰησοῦ could be expressed as "God has raised *us* up *spiritually* with Christ Jesus" or "and *it is just like* God has raised *us* up with Christ Jesus".

and caused *us* to sit *victoriously* with him in heaven, As discussed in the previous note, συνήγειρεν "he raised (us) up with (Christ)" probably refers to the spiritual state of believers. So συνεκάθισεν "he seated (us) with (Christ)" should be regarded in the same way, i.e. as a metaphor that describes the spiritual exaltation of believers, resulting from Christ's exaltation. In other words, believers share in the authority and honour which Christ receives as a result of his enthronement in heaven.

Most versions translate this part of the verse fairly literally. TEV is most noticeably different as it expresses the meaning of the metaphor: "to rule with him in the heavenly world".

In the display, another aspect of the metaphor is made explicit, namely the significance of the believer's position. In 2:1-2; 3:10; 6:10-20, Paul refers to the hostile spiritual powers who are opposed to God and his people. Christ's exaltation has given him victory and authority over all these powers (see 1:21). As believers share in his exaltation, they also share in his victory (see Lincoln, pp. 108-109). To include this aspect, συνεκάθισεν ἐν τοῖς ἐπουρανίοις ἐν Χριστῷ Ἰησοῦ "he seated (us) with Christ Jesus in heaven" is expressed, in the display, as "has caused us to sit *victoriously* with him in heaven", with "victoriously" representing the significance of the believer's position.

2:6b *by means of uniting us* with Christ Jesus. The phrase ἐν Χριστῷ Ἰησοῦ "in Christ Jesus" is connected to both συνήγειρεν "he raised (us) up with" and συνεκάθισεν "he seated (us) with". These privileges are because of our union with Christ Jesus.

2:7a *He did this* [2:5c-6] in order that he might demonstrate *to everyone* in-future-times/forever that he has acted in an incomparably gracious and kind way to us The initial ἵνα "so that, in order that" introduces the purpose of the preceding two NUCLEI: 2:5c and 2:6.

The agent of ἐνδείξηται "he might show/demonstrate" is God. What he is demonstrating is τὸ ὑπερβάλλον πλοῦτος τῆς χάριτος αὐτοῦ "the exceeding riches of his grace". This is similar to the phrase τὸ πλοῦτος τῆς χάριτος αὐτοῦ in 1:7. Here, the Greek word ὑπερβάλλον "going beyond, surpassing" has been added to the phrase and intensifies the description of God's gracious character and action on behalf of his people. The combination of πλοῦτος and ὑπερβάλλον in qualifying τῆς χάριτος αὐτοῦ "his grace" can be expressed in English by the adverb "incomparably".

It may be necessary in translation to state to whom God is demonstrating his grace. If so, the expression used should be as general as possible, e.g. "to everyone".

Commentators interpret the phrase ἐν τοῖς αἰῶσιν τοῖς ἐπερχομένοις "in the coming ages" in various ways, for example:

1. It refers to the period between Christ's ascension and his second coming.
2. It refers to the unending period following Christ's second coming.
3. It refers to the unending period following the writing of this letter.

It is best in translation to use a general expression, one which refers to the future in general, e.g. "for all time to come", "now and forever".

In the propositionalisation, the rendering of the phrase ἐν χρηστότητι "in kindness, generosity" functions in a co-ordinate relationship with the rendering of τῆς χάριτος "grace": "he has acted in an incomparably gracious and kind way". The phrase ἐφ' ἡμᾶς "towards us" provides the object of his kind action: God acted graciously and kindly towards "us".

2:7b because of *what* Christ Jesus *did for us*. In this context, the phrase ἐν Χριστῷ Ἰησοῦ "in Christ Jesus" can relate to God's grace and kindness as:

1. the means of God's grace and kindness
2. the reason for God's grace and kindness

Among the commentators, there is no consensus on this issue. In the display, a "reason" relationship is expressed.

BOUNDARIES AND COHERENCE

For a discussion on the boundaries and coherence of 2:4–7, see the section on Intent and Macrostructure for 2:1–10.

PROMINENCE AND THEME

The theme statement is based on the naturally prominent NUCLEI and the marked prominent REASON supporting them.

SECTION CONSTITUENT 2:8–10 (Expository Paragraph: Grounds for 2:4–7)

THEME: It is only because of God's grace that you have been saved, through trusting in Christ. You did not save yourselves. It is God who caused us to become spiritually alive.

RELATIONAL STRUCTURE	CONTENTS
CONCLUSION — NUCLEUS — REASON	2:8a *It is only* because of *God's* grace
RESULT	2:8b *that* you have been saved,
means	2:8c through *your* trusting *in Christ*.
amplification — NUCLEUS₁ — negative	2:8d You did not save yourselves.
POSITIVE	2:8e God *saved you because he* freely chose to do so.
NUCLEUS₂ — REASON	2:9a None *of you were saved* by means of anything *you yourselves* did,
result	2:9b with the result that no one *may have any reason for* boasting *about* (*or, being proud of*) *what they have done*.
grounds — NUCLEUS	2:10a It is **God** who made us *new people*.
amplification — MEANS	2:10b By means of uniting us with Christ Jesus, he has caused us to become *spiritually* alive,
purpose	2:10c in order that we should live our lives habitually doing the good deeds which God had planned for us to do.

INTENT AND STRUCTURE

Again, this is an expository paragraph with expressive overtones. Paul makes a strong claim in 2:8a-c which he amplifies in 2:8d-9b. He then gives the grounds for this claim in 2:10a-c. He wants to convince the Ephesians that they have done nothing at all to achieve their own salvation. Rather it was God who freely chose to save them.

NOTES

2:8–10 The γάρ "for", which occurs at the beginning of 2:8, introduces a unit which can be analysed in three ways:

1. A restatement and amplification of the brief interjection in 2:5.
2. A summary of 2:1–7.
3. A confirmation of the statement made in 2:7, explaining the grounds for making it.

The argument in these verses is intense. This probably indicates that the third option is the most appropriate one.

2:8a-b ***It is only*** **because of *God's* grace *that* you have been saved,** The abstract noun phrase τῇ...χάριτι "by grace" is forefronted in the Greek text for emphasis. In the display, this emphasis is reflected by forefronting and the use of the phrase "*It is only*".

As for the relationship of 2:8a with 2:8b indicated by the dative construction τῇ χάριτι, dative constructions in a context like this may indicate either instrument/means or cause (reason). Since "grace" describes God's character, reason appears to be the appropriate relationship.

In some languages there is no direct equivalent for "grace" and so often a word or phrase as close in meaning as possible is used. Bratcher and Nida suggest,

> The statement it is by God's grace that you have been saved [TEV] may be expressed as "because God is so kind, you have been saved" or "because God is so kind, he has saved you" (p. 47).

The periphrastic perfect construction, ἐστε σεσῳσμένοι "you-are having-been-saved", indicates completed action resulting in a present state. Their being saved is a completed action with its state and effects continuing on indefinitely. Again, God is the agent.

2:8c through *your* trusting *in Christ*. The Greek word διά "through/because-of" in the phrase διὰ πίστεως "through/because-of faith" can denote a relationship of means/instrument or reason. In

English, "through", indicating means, seems to be the appropriate word for this context, since it may introduce an action that qualifies the action of the main verb but which may be subsidiary in some sense. Here, God's grace in saving mankind is more primary than people's faith.

As in other New Testament letters (e.g. Gal. 2:16; Rom. 3:22, 26), the object of the "faith" mentioned here is Christ, rather than God, the Father.

2:8d You did not save yourselves. The conjunction καί "and" at the beginning of this clause introduces an amplification of 2:8a–c. The conjunction is not made explicit in the display, since it would not be natural at this point in an English discourse.

It is not clear to whom/what the demonstrative pronoun τοῦτο "this" refers. There are two main options discussed in commentaries:

1. It refers to πίστεως "faith". This is the nearest preceding noun. So, Paul is saying that faith is not of ourselves but the gift of God. See, for example, Hodge (pp. 119–120).
2. It refers to the entire expression, χάριτί ἐστε σεσῳσμένοι διὰ πίστεως "by grace you have been saved through faith" (2:8a–c). So, Paul is saying that our salvation by grace through faith is not of ourselves but a gift of God. See, for example, Abbott (p. 51), Best (p. 226), Lincoln (pp. 111–112), O'Brien (p. 175, fn. 90).

Grammatically, the first option is the less likely. The noun πίστις is feminine whereas the demonstrative pronoun τοῦτο is neuter. As the two words are so physically close in the Greek text, the demonstrative would be more likely to be feminine if it referred to πίστις.

Although the first option expresses the antithesis between "faith" and "works" well, it destroys the parallelism on which 2:8–9 depends for its force.

The second option, however, retains this important parallelism between οὐκ ἐξ ὑμῶν "not of yourselves" and οὐκ ἐξ ἔργων "not of works" in 2:9a. This option is followed in the display.

The contrasts and parallels in 2:8–9 are important. Paul states positively "you have been saved by grace through faith" then goes on to state negatively "this is not of you". Next he emphasises what he has just said by two further parallel statements, one presented positively, θεοῦ τὸ δῶρον "(it is) the gift of God" and the other negatively, οὐκ ἐξ ἔργων "(it is) not of works". These contrasts and parallels should be retained in translation, if possible.

2:8e God *saved you because he* freely chose to do so. The genitive θεοῦ "of God" in the phrase θεοῦ τὸ δῶρον "the gift of God" is in an emphatic position. This shifts the focus from the immediately preceding pronoun ὑμῶν "of you" in 2:8d.

The genitive construction θεοῦ τὸ δῶρον "the gift of God" parallels the idea of χάριτί ἐστε σεσῳσμένοι διὰ πίστεως "by grace you have been saved through faith" (2:8a–c). It emphasises that it is God alone who is the agent of salvation. He is the one who gives "the gift", which is "salvation by grace, through faith". The pronoun "you" in italics represents the recipients of "the gift".

Normally, a gift is something material which someone *gives* to another person. In this context, however, the "gift" which God *gives* believers is something abstract—salvation. It emphasises the fact that people can do nothing to earn or buy salvation; it is something that God does and it is free. God gives this gift because he freely chooses to do so.

This proposition is parallel with 2:8a–c. Both make a positive statement.

2:9a None *of you were saved* by means of anything *you yourselves* did, This negative statement οὐκ ἐξ ἔργων "not of works", concerning the source or cause of salvation, is parallel with, and reiterates, the thought of οὐκ ἐξ ὑμῶν "not of you" in 2:8d.

Most commentators consider that the noun "works" (ἔργων) referred to here should not be limited to the Mosaic law, although it includes that law. The noun ἔργα "works" is a general term which refers to human effort. Paul is making it clear here that no one can be saved by their own efforts.

2:9b with the result that no one *may have any reason for* boasting *about* (*or,* being proud *of*) *what they have done*. Except in the Pauline epistles, the verb καυχάομαι occurs rarely in the New Testament. BDAG defines it as,

> [to] take pride in someth[ing], *boast, glory, pride oneself, brag...in* or *about a person* or *thing* (p. 536.1).

The verb is understood most often to refer to an outward expression of pride in speech and is expressed thus in most versions by a word like "boast", for example, "so that no one can boast" (NIV). In this context, however, it is possible that Paul is referring to an attitude of mind, rather than simply speech that results from that attitude. People may pride themselves about what they have done without showing it openly. This might be expressed as "being proud of what they have done". Of course, here with either "boast" or "be proud of" the attitude is unacceptable.

This clause is introduced by ἵνα "in order that, so that". The relationship it indicates may be:

1. purpose
2. result

God's primary purpose in saving people without their needing to earn or pay for their salvation was for a greater purpose than simply preventing boasting. Therefore, the second option "result" is more appropriate in this context. A number of translations follow this alternative, for example, CEV: "It isn't something you have earned, so there is nothing you can brag about". See also NCV, NLT.

This Greek clause may relate to the preceding text in two ways:

1. It relates to the immediately preceding οὐκ ἐξ ἔργων "not of works" (2:9a).
2. It relates to 2:8d-e as well as 2:9a.

In the display diagram, the first option is followed, because the clause has close semantic ties to "not of works" (2:9a) and is physically close to it in the Greek text.

2:10a It is <u>God</u> who made us *new people*. The introductory γάρ "for" may signal that 2:10 is the grounds for the statement in 2:8-9, that salvation is God's free gift, not a result of human endeavour. Hodge, in support of this, says,

> That salvation is thus entirely the work of God, and that good works cannot be the ground of our acceptance with him, is proved in this verse—
> 1ˢᵗ. By showing that we are God's workmanship.... And 2d. By the consideration that we are created unto good works.

He continues,

> [Our] being created unto good works shows that good works are not the ground on which [we] are made the subjects of this new creation (p. 120).

See also Alford (p. 94), Eadie (p. 157), Ellicott (p. 35).

In the display, 2:10a-c is taken as grounds for 2:8-9.

The pronoun αὐτοῦ "his" is in an emphatic position at the beginning of the clause. It refers to God as the agent in the clause αὐτοῦ...ἐσμεν ποίημα "his handiwork/workmanship we are". The emphasis is maintained in the display.

Apart from Romans 1:20, this is the only place in the New Testament where the noun ποίημα "that which is made, work, creation" occurs. In both passages it refers to a specific creative act of God. Because 2:10a is closely connected with the following clause, κτισθέντες ἐν Χριστῷ Ἰησοῦ "created in Christ Jesus", most commentators agree that here ποίημα refers to the new, spiritual life of believers. Bratcher and Nida (pp. 47-48) suggest that "God made us what we now are" expresses the sense. A more specific rendering would be "God made us new people". The event of "making" expressed in ποίημα "handiwork/workmanship" is rendered as the verb "made" in the display.

In this verse, Paul changes from the direct "you" to the pronoun "we": Paul includes himself with the Ephesian believers as being God's handiwork.

2:10b-c This cluster of propositions amplifies 2:10a. In particular, it explains the preceding noun, ποίημα "handiwork".

2:10b By means of uniting us with Christ Jesus, he has caused us to become *spiritually alive*, The aorist passive participle κτισθέντες "created" is qualified by the phrase ἐν Χριστῷ Ἰησοῦ "in Christ Jesus". This recalls the clause in 2:5, συνεζωοποίησεν τῷ Χριστῷ "he made (us) alive with Christ", which refers to the same event. In both verses, Paul is referring to spiritual life. This is accomplished by means of "our union with Christ Jesus".

This is the nucleus of the 2:10b-c cluster. It functions as a MEANS for 2:10c.

2:10c in order that we should live our lives habitually doing the good deeds The Greek preposition ἐπί followed by a dative may indicate purpose and point to the goal of an event or state (BDAG, p. 366.16). In this context, the purpose is ἔργοις ἀγαθοῖς "for good works", that is, in order that believers should do good deeds. This is in antithesis to οὐκ ἐξ ἔργων "not of works" (2:9a). Good works are not the cause but the consequence of salvation.

which God had planned for us to do. It is generally agreed that the relative pronoun οἷς "which" refers to ἔργοις ἀγαθοῖς "good works". However, commentators do not agree how it relates to the aorist indicative προητοίμασεν "he prepared beforehand". There are two possibilities:

1. It is the direct object. The meaning then is, "God prepared/planned beforehand those good deeds".
2. It is the indirect object. The meaning then is, "God prepared us beforehand for those good deeds".

Both possibilities have difficulties attached to them.

The difficulty with the first option is that οἷς "which" is dative. A direct object would normally be accusative.

The difficulty with the second option is that there is no ἡμᾶς "us" in the text. Also it would be more usual to express the indirect object sense here by the accusative followed by εἰς. See similar structures in Romans 9:23; 2 Timothy 2:21; Revelation 9:7.

Most commentators support the first option and consider that οἷς "which" is the direct object of προητοίμασεν "he prepared beforehand". They explain the dative case by attraction, i.e. the dative ending of ἔργοις ἀγαθοῖς being carried over to the relative pronoun οἷς which modifies it. The case ending of the relative pronoun would normally be governed by the syntax of the clause it is in. See, for example, Eadie (pp. 158-159), O'Brien, (p. 181, fn. 115). A number of translations also follow this option. See, for example, NASB, NIV, NJB, NRSV, TEV. This is how it is expressed in the display.

The aorist active indicative προητοίμασεν "he prepared beforehand" clearly refers to an event which occurred at some unspecified time before an individual believer's salvation. It is sufficient here to say "God has already prepared" or "God had planned".

The clause ἵνα ἐν αὐτοῖς περιπατήσωμεν "in order that we might walk in them" indicates God's purpose in preparing the good works. The verb περιπατέω "walk" contains the idea of a consistent, habitual way of life. God's purpose is that believers should habitually do those good deeds which he has prepared for them to do.

The consistency of this way of life is expressed in the display in the propositionalisation of ἔργοις ἀγαθοῖς "good works". The verb "do" is used in the display to render περιπατήσωμεν "we might walk" and the ἵνα clause is rendered as an infinitive.

BOUNDARIES AND COHERENCE

See the section on Intent and Macrostructure of 2:1–10 for the initial boundary and the section on Boundaries and Coherence for 2:1–10 for the final boundary.

PROMINENCE AND THEME

The 2:8–10 paragraph consists of a CONCLUSION and its grounds. Since both components are integral to expository paragraph structure, the nuclear elements of both are included in the theme statement, along with nuclear elements of their amplification units.

Note that, even though "through faith" is not forefronted as "by grace" is, yet it is integral to the theme of the paragraph: that salvation is by God's action alone and not by human efforts.

SUBDIVISION CONSTITUENT 2:11–22: (Expository Section: Nucleus₂ of 2:1–22)

THEME: God brought you Gentiles, along with Jewish believers, into his spiritual family by uniting you spiritually with Christ, so that now you all share the same blessings and form one church. Through Christ's death, both Jewish and Gentile believers are at peace with God and one another, which is evidenced by the fact that all believers, whether Jew or Gentile, may approach God freely, by means of the Holy Spirit.

MACROSTRUCTURE	CONTENTS
CONCLUSION₁	2:11–13 Formerly, you were spiritually separated from Christ and not part of God's spiritual family, but now you are spiritually united with Christ and are part of God's family.
grounds	2:14–18 This [2:11–13] is based on the fact that Christ himself has caused believers, both Jews and Gentiles, to be at peace with God and with one another. He did this by dying on the cross, with the result that the regulations of the Jewish law were made ineffective. The validity of this peace is evidenced by the fact that all believers are able to approach God by means of the Holy Spirit.
CONCLUSION₂	2:19–22 So then, you Gentile believers are no longer excluded from God's blessings, but share in them equally with the Jewish believers, and together with them, form one church.

INTENT AND MACROSTRUCTURE

This unit consists of CONCLUSION₁ (2:11–13) and CONCLUSION₂ (2:19–22) and a grounds component (2:14–18) which supports both CONCLUSIONS. The unit is, therefore, expository. Paul sets out how God, through Christ, has united Jewish and Gentile believers into one church and has reconciled them all to himself. Paul wants to convince the Ephesian believers that both Jewish and Gentile believers have received great blessings, since they were united as one body, the church. In particular, he wants to prepare them so that they will respond positively to the exhortations in the second part of his letter. He uses the imperative μνημονεύετε "remember/think-about" to emphasise the importance of what he has to say. This imperative serves as a prominence orienter, rather than as an exhortation intended to affect some specific behaviour.

BOUNDARIES AND COHERENCE

For the initial boundary of this unit, see the section on Boundaries and Coherence for 2:1–10. For the final boundary, see the section on Boundaries and Coherence for 2:1–22.

There is strong coherence between the three paragraphs which make up this unit. As has been stated before, they focus on the reconciliation of Gentile believers with Jewish believers and the fact that, as members of God's family, they share in the blessings of his chosen people, those who believe in Christ. References to Christ as the agent of this reconciliation occur in almost every verse and are evidence for the coherence.

There is a tail-head link between the first two paragraphs of the cluster, 2:11–13 and 2:14–18, that is, 2:13 ends with a reference to τοῦ Χριστοῦ "of Christ" and 2:14 begins with the personal pronoun αὐτός "he", which also refers to Christ.

There is also a link between the second and third paragraphs of the cluster, 2:14–18 and 2:19–22, in that there is a reference to τὸν πατέρα "the Father" at the end of 2:18 and 2:19 refers to οἰκεῖοι τοῦ θεοῦ "members of the family of God".

PROMINENCE AND THEME

In a CONCLUSION-grounds unit, both constituents are integral to the theme. So the theme of this paragraph cluster is drawn from both CONCLUSIONS and their grounds.

SECTION CONSTITUENT 2:11-13
(Expository Paragraph: Conclusion₁ of 2:11-22)

THEME: Formerly, you were spiritually separated from Christ and not part of God's spiritual family, but now you are spiritually united with Christ and are part of God's family.

RELATIONAL STRUCTURE	CONTENTS
prominence orienter — description of 'you' — NUCLEUS	2:11a You were born Gentiles.
amplification — 'Jews'	2:11b You are those who are *derogatorily* called *"those who are uncircumcised"* by *the Jews*,
description	2:11c who call *themselves "those who are circumcised"*, *though* they are *merely* circumcised physically by men.
'you'	2:11d You should constantly remember/think-about *these things* [2:12-13]:
contrast — GENERIC	2:12a Formerly, you were *spiritually* separated from Christ,
specific₁	2:12b you were excluded from *God's chosen* people, Israel,
specific₂	2:12c and you did not share/participate-in the things which God promised in his covenants.
specific₃	2:12d You had no hope *that God would save you*,
specific₄	2:12e and you *did* not *know* God while *you lived* in this world.
reason	2:13a But now, *because* you *are spiritually united* with Christ Jesus,
NUCLEUS — RESULT — RESULT	2:13b you who once were *spiritually* separated *from God* have been brought into *his spiritual family by him* [God],
means	2:13c by means of Christ's *shedding* his blood *for you when he died*.

INTENT AND STRUCTURE

In this expository paragraph, Paul reminds the Gentile believers at Ephesus of their state before their conversion and of what they have now become through Christ. He urges them to remember these things (μνημονεύετε "remember"), since he wants to influence the way that they think about these matters in order that they will respond positively to the exhortations in chapters 4-6. Although μνημονεύετε "remember" is an imperative, it does not indicate that the paragraph is hortatory since "remember" is functioning as a prominence orienter.

NOTES

2:11a You were born Gentiles. This verse begins with διό, which is generally glossed as "therefore". Here, it indicates a transition to a new aspect of the subject matter, though Paul first repeats ideas in 2:11-12 that were presented in 2:1-3.

Most commentators consider διό to indicate a relationship back to 2:1-10. See, for example, Ellicott (p. 36), Hendriksen (pp. 128-129), Meyer (p. 376). Paul wants the Ephesians to recall their former state and to compare it with their present state, in order that they might fully appreciate what God has done for them through Christ.

However, on the section level (how 2:11-22 relates to 2:1-10), it is likely that this relationship is best understood as co-ordinate. See the section on Intent and Macrostructure for 2:1-22 for reasons why this is the best analysis. Because of the parallel semantic structure of 2:1-10 and 2:11-22, διό is not translated in the display.

Here, and in 2:11b, the referent of ὑμεῖς "you" is identified as τὰ ἔθνη ἐν σαρκί "the nations/Gentiles in (the) flesh", with the τὰ ἔθνη being taken as in apposition with ὑμεῖς. In most versions, ἔθνη is translated "Gentiles" throughout the letter. An alternative is to use "non-Jews".

The phrase ἐν σαρκί "in (the) flesh", in this context, can be understood in two ways:

1. Literally. It refers to the flesh of the human body. The evidence that they are Gentiles is in their physical bodies in that they have not been circumcised. See, for example, Eadie (p. 161), Ellicott (p. 37), Hodge (p. 125).
2. Figuratively. It refers to the fact of their birth into Gentile families. See, for example, Bratcher and Nida (p. 51), Candlish (p. 59).

The first option is true. The focus in this paragraph, however, is on the fact that they were born Gentiles and nothing can change that. They cannot become ethnically Jewish. What has changed is their spiritual nature and their relationship to God and his church.

2:11b You are those who are *derogatorily* called "*those who are* uncircumcised" by *the Jews*, This further describes "the Gentiles". The οἱ λεγόμενοι "the ones being called" refers to ὑμεῖς "you".

The term ἀκροβυστία "uncircumcision" rarely occurs in the New Testament apart from in Paul's letters. It is a collective epithet used by the Jews as a term of contempt for the heathen world, "those who are uncircumcised". In the display, it is made explicit that it is the Jews who use this expression to refer to the Gentiles. The fact that the Jews used this as a term of insult is important, so the adverb "derogatorily" is used in the display.

2:11c who call *themselves* "*those who are* circumcised", *though* they are *merely* circumcised physically by men. The term περιτομή "circumcision" is a collective epithet which refers to the Jews and the fact that circumcision is the physical sign which marks them as God's chosen people. It contrasts with ἀκροβυστία "uncircumcised", which refers to the Gentiles.

The phrase ἐν σαρκί "in (the) flesh" is used here of the Jews as was used of the Gentiles in 2:11a. Here, however, Paul adds χειροποιήτου "made by hands" to emphasise that circumcision is a physical rite, not a spiritual one, and that human beings are the agents of the action rather than God.

Many Jews simply valued circumcision as a physical sign marking them as God's chosen people, and ignored the spiritual aspect. The expression "in the flesh made by hands" seems to imply a negative evaluation in this context. See, for example, Eadie (pp. 161-162), Hodge (p. 125), Hendriksen (p. 129). The word "*merely*", in the display, is an attempt to express the ineffectual nature of the physical sign without the accompanying spiritual aspect.

2:11d You should constantly remember/think-about *these things* [2:12-13]: The present imperative μνημονεύετε "remember, think about" provides an orienter for the content of 2:12-13. In the display, the verb is qualified by the adverb "constantly" to make clear the implicit meaning of the present tense, that this was something Paul wanted the Ephesians to continue doing.

The imperative is followed by ὅτι "that". The ὅτι "that" is repeated at the beginning of 2:12. After the appositional phrases describing the Gentiles (2:11a–c), Paul proceeds with the points he wants them to remember. Paul uses ὅτι this second time to state his further thoughts on the subject, this time in non-subordinated grammatical form.

2:12 This verse describes the Ephesians' condition before they trusted in Christ as Saviour. It contrasts with 2:13, in which their present state, ἐν Χριστῷ Ἰησοῦ "in Christ Jesus", is described. The introductory phrase τῷ καιρῷ ἐκείνῳ "at that time" parallels the ποτέ "formerly" of 2:11.

This verse contains five clauses, describing this former state of the Ephesians:

"without Christ" (2:12a)
"excluded from the commonwealth of Israel" (2:12b)
"strangers to the covenants of promise" (2:12c)
"without hope" (2:12d)
"without God" (2:12e)

There has been much discussion about how these clauses relate to one another. The following are the three main options suggested in the commentaries:

1. They are five separate predicates. See, for example, Hendriksen (pp. 129-131).
2. The first predicate, "without Christ" (2:12a), is explained by the four predicates (2:12b-e) that follow. See, for example, Ellicott (p. 37), Meyer (p. 377).
3. The first predicate, "without Christ" (2:12a), is the cause of the pre-Christian state of the Ephesians. The other four predicates (2:12b-

e) express the effects or results of being in this state. See, for example, Eadie (p. 163).

All three options make good sense. However, the second option is followed in the display.

Following this choice, the generic nucleus of this propositional cluster is ἦτε τῷ καιρῷ ἐκείνῳ χωρὶς Χριστοῦ "you were at that time without Christ" (2:12a). In the rest of the verse, 2:12b-e, are specific aspects of being without Christ.

2:12a Formerly you were *spiritually* separated from Christ, The phrase τῷ καιρῷ ἐκείνῳ "at that time" refers to the time before the Ephesians were converted. This is expressed, in the display, as "formerly".

The preposition χωρίς followed by a genitive means "without, apart from, far from, separated from". Here, χωρὶς Χριστοῦ "without Christ" contrasts with ἐν Χριστῷ Ἰησοῦ "in Christ Jesus" in 2:13.

In 1:4, Paul made it clear that the Ephesian believers had been included by God among his chosen people since "before the foundation of the earth". So, this separation from Christ must refer to their personal experience of him before their conversion. More specifically, it could refer to the fact that:

1. They did not have that personal relationship and knowledge of Christ which they now have because they are united with him spiritually. See, for example, Hendriksen (p. 129), Hodge (p. 126).
2. They were "without the promise of Christ", that is, as the promised Messiah. See, for example, Eadie (pp. 163-164), Lincoln (pp. 136-137).

The separation is clearly spiritual separation. So, in the display, this is expressed as "you were *spiritually* separated from Christ". This includes both options.

2:12b you were excluded from *God's chosen people, Israel*, The form of the verb here is the perfect passive participle ἀπηλλοτριωμένοι "having been alienated/excluded from". The agent of the alienation is not expressed. It could be God or they themselves ("they excluded themselves"). However, this is not the focus. Rather Paul focusses on that from which they are alienated, i.e. τῆς πολιτείας τοῦ Ἰσραήλ "the commonwealth/citizenship of Israel".

In the New Testament, the noun πολιτεία "citizenship" only occurs here and in Acts 22:28. In the Acts passage, it clearly means "citizenship". In Ephesians, however, its meaning seems to be spiritual and religious, not political, since it is closely related to the following clause ξένοι τῶν διαθηκῶν τῆς ἐπαγγελίας "strangers of the covenants of the promise", a clear reference to God's promise of the Messiah, redemption, salvation by grace, etc. Those who make up this πολιτεία, therefore, are God's chosen people. Some translation possibilities are to use a phrase such as "God's chosen people" in conjunction with the proper name, "Israel". See, for example, TEV: "you...did not belong to God's chosen people".

Some commentators suggest that ἀπηλλοτριωμένοι "having been excluded" implies that the Gentiles had initially belonged to "God's chosen people" and were later excluded. See, for example, Ellicott (p. 38), Braune (p. 90). This would mean that the first covenant God made (Gen. 9:8-17) was with the whole of humanity, not just Abraham and his descendants. The Gentiles, therefore, were exiles from what should have been theirs, and their calling into the church of Christ was the restoration of their privileges. In this context, however, this does not seem to be relevant to Paul's focus on their state when they were outside the people of God contrasted with their state now when they *are* people of God.

2:12c and you did not share/participate-in the things which God promised in his covenants. The genitive construction τῶν διαθηκῶν τῆς ἐπαγγελίας "the covenants of the promise" is a genitive of content, i.e. the covenants referred to contain the promise. See, for example, Eadie (pp. 165-166), Ellicott (p. 38), Hodge (p. 127), Stott (p. 95).

Most commentators agree that the covenants referred to are the one made with Abraham (Genesis 12:3; 22:18) and those made with his descendants to ratify the first one (Genesis 26:3-4; 28:13-14). The content of the promise itself is the coming of the Messiah and the blessings that will follow.

The Greek term ξένος "strange, foreign", in this context, means,

> [A]n entity that is unacquainted with someth[ing], w[ith] gen[itive] τινός *strange to someth[ing]*, estranged fr[om] it, unacquainted w[ith] it, without interest in it (BDAG, p. 684.1b).

Before their conversion, the Gentiles were not part of God's chosen people. So they did not share in what God had promised in the covenants he had made with his people.

2:12d You had no hope *that God would save you,* The noun ἐλπίδα "hope, expectation, prospect" is forefronted in the Greek text for emphasis. The "hope" referred to is the hope of salvation and eternal life. Before their conversion, the Gentiles had no hope of this because they did not share in the covenants of promise. The object of the hope, *"that God would save you"*, is made explicit in the display.

2:12e and you *did* **not** *know* **God while** *you lived* **in this world.** This is the only time the word ἄθεοι "without God" occurs in the New Testament. There are two possible meanings:

1. They were ignorant of God. See, for example, Lloyd-Jones (p. 173), Stott (p. 96).
2. They had been forsaken by God. See, for example, Eadie (pp. 167-168), Ellicott (p. 39), Hodge (p. 128), Meyer (p. 380).

The first option has the best support and so is represented in the display.

There are two ways to understand the term ὁ κόσμος "the world" in this verse:

1. It refers to the physical universe, it does not focus on moral connotations. See, for example, Scott (pp. 169-170).
2. It refers to the world as a system that is in opposition to God and is, therefore, evil. See, for example, Eadie (pp. 168-169), Hendriksen (p. 131), Lincoln (pp. 137-138).

Either option is possible in the context. In the display, it is expressed neutrally as "in this world".

Another point for discussion is the relationship of this phrase to the rest of the verse. Again there are two possibilities:

1. It relates to both ἐλπίδα μὴ ἔχοντες "not having hope" and ἄθεοι "without God".
2. It only relates to ἄθεοι "without God".

The second option has better commentary support. See, for example, Alford (p. 96), Ellicott (p. 39), Hodge (p. 128), Meyer (p. 380).

2:13a But now, *because* **you** *are spiritually united* **with Christ Jesus,** The initial νυνὶ δέ "but now" introduces a sharp contrast with ποτέ "formerly" (2:11) and τῷ καιρῷ ἐκείνῳ "at that time" (2:12). Paul turns from describing the former state of the Ephesians to describing their present spiritual condition.

The phrase ἐν Χριστῷ Ἰησοῦ "in Christ Jesus" is forefronted in the Greek text for emphasis. It contrasts with χωρὶς Χριστοῦ "without Christ" in 2:12. See the note on 1:3 for more discussion on the phrase ἐν Χριστῷ Ἰησοῦ "in Christ Jesus".

The phrase possibly gives the reason for the verb phrase ἐγενήθητε ἐγγύς "you have been brought near" in 2:13b. See, for example, Hodge (p. 128), Meyer (p. 381).

2:13b you who once were *spiritually* **separated** *from God* **have been brought into** *his spiritual family by him* **[God],** The participial clause ὑμεῖς οἵ ποτε ὄντες μακράν "you who once were afar off" describes the Ephesians (the ὑμεῖς "you") before their conversion.

Both μακράν "afar" and its antonym ἐγγύς "near" can be understood literally or figuratively. In the times of the Old Testament, the Gentile nations were geographically distant from God's temple in Jerusalem. This physical distance became symbolic of spiritual distance, that is, Israel, as God's chosen people, had a close spiritual relationship with God, but the Gentiles were spiritually unrelated to him. Here, in Ephesians 2:13, the words have a figurative sense, as they do in 2:17 where they also occur.

In this context, the figurative meaning of "you became near" is "you have been brought into God's spiritual family". Previously, the Ephesian Gentiles were outside the covenant relationship with God. Now, having trusted in Christ, they are part of God's family.

An alternative way to express 2:13b from that used in the display would be "you who once did not know *God* have come to know *him*".

2:13c by means of Christ's *shedding* **his blood** *for you when he died.* The phrase τῷ αἵματι τοῦ Χριστοῦ "the blood of Christ", as in 1:7, stands for Christ's sacrificial death on the cross. Although "blood" is a metonymy for death, the reference to the shedding of Christ's blood is kept in the display, because it is such an important theme/concept in Scripture. The phrase *"when he died"* is included to clarify the meaning.

The ἐν at the beginning of the phrase ἐν τῷ αἵματι τοῦ Χριστοῦ "by the blood of Christ" indicates a means relationship. It is by means of Christ's death that the Gentiles have been brought into the spiritual family of God.

BOUNDARIES AND COHERENCE

For the initial boundary, see the section on Intent and Macrostructure for 2:1–22.

The paragraph 2:11–13 forms a unit because it makes up the content of the orienter μνημονεύετε "remember" (2:11a). In conjunction with this, throughout the paragraph, Paul uses second person plural pronouns, in contrast to first person plural pronouns in 2:10 and 2:14.

This is a paragraph of contrasts. Paul contrasts the former condition of the Gentiles (ποτέ "once, formerly" [2:11], τῷ καιρῷ ἐκείνῳ "at that time" [2:12]) with their state now (νυνί "now" [2:13]). He also uses contrastive sets of vocabulary to describe these two conditions:

Formerly, they were:

> χωρὶς Χριστοῦ "without Christ" (2:12)
> ἀπηλλοτριωμένοι "alienated" (2:12)
> ξένοι "strangers" (2:12)
> ἐλπίδα μὴ ἔχοντες "without hope" (2:12)
> ἄθεοι "without God" (2:12)
> μακράν "afar" (2:13)

Now, they are:

> ἐν Χριστῷ Ἰησοῦ "in Christ Jesus" (2:13)
> ἐγγὺς ἐν τῷ αἵματι τοῦ Χριστοῦ "near by means of the blood of Christ" (2:13)

PROMINENCE AND THEME

In a contrastive paragraph, both parts of the contrast are integral to the theme, and so are included in the theme statement.

SECTION CONSTITUENT 2:14–18
(Expository Paragraph: Grounds of 2:11–13 and 19–22)

THEME: Christ himself has caused believers, both Jews and Gentiles, to be at peace with God and with one another. He did this by dying on the cross, with the result that the regulations of the Jewish law were made ineffective. The validity of this peace is evidenced by the fact that all believers are able to approach God by means of the Holy Spirit.

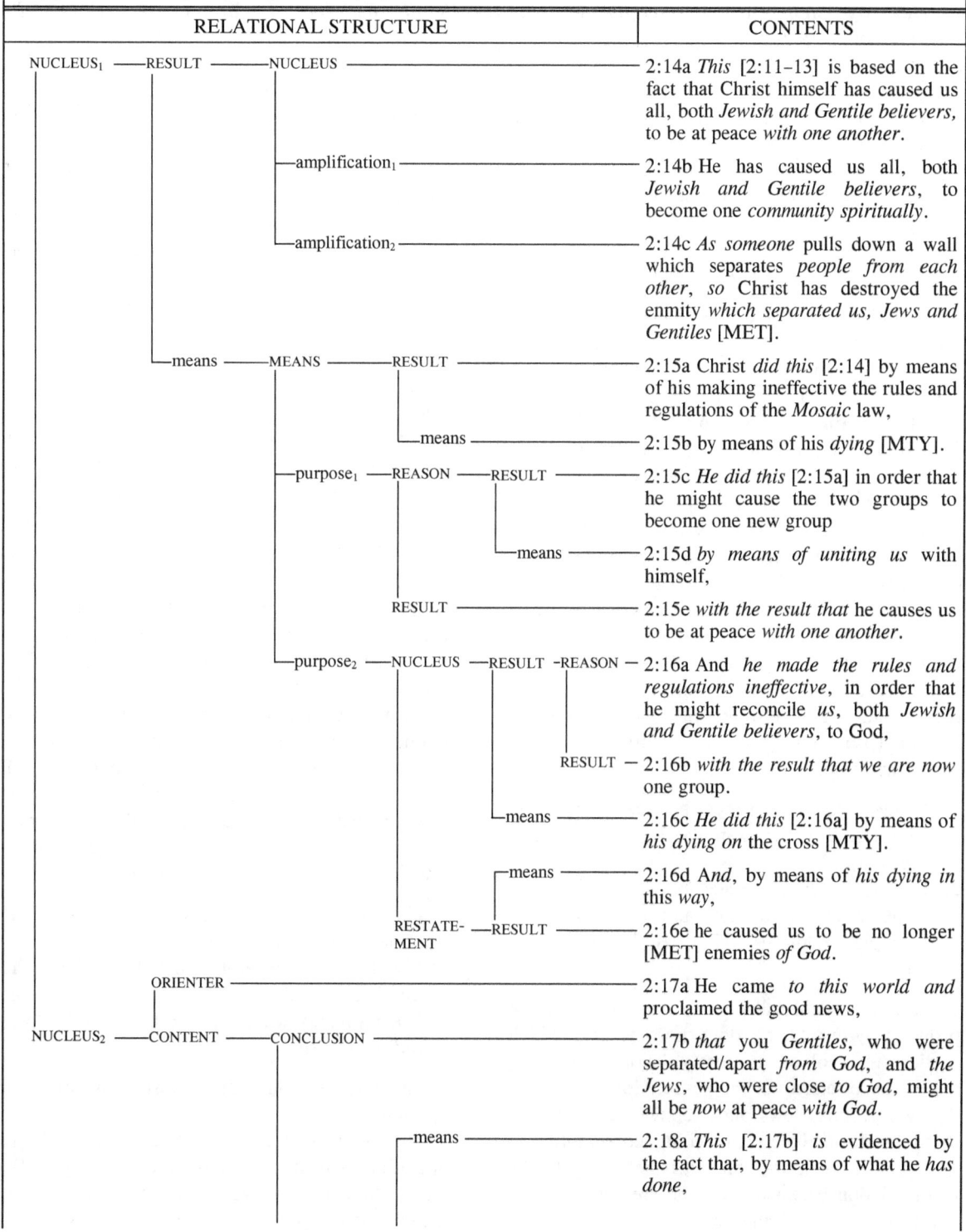

└ GROUNDS ── RESULT ─────────────── 2:18b we all, *Jews and Gentiles*, are able to approach *God* the Father, by *means of the* one *Holy* Spirit.

INTENT AND STRUCTURE

This expository paragraph provides the grounds for paragraphs 2:11-13 and 2:19-22. Paul wants believers, whether Jew or Gentile, to understand that God, through Christ, has reconciled them to himself and to each other. On the basis of this, they belong to one church, they have access to God through the Holy Spirit and they share in the many blessings he has for his people.

NOTES

2:14a ***This*** **[2:11-13]** **is based on the fact that** The initial γάρ "for" introduces the grounds for the statement made in 2:13, the nucleus of that paragraph, and so for the paragraph as a whole.

Christ himself has caused us all, both *Jewish and Gentile believers*, to be at peace with one another. Paul now switches from using the Ephesians as subject of the verbs, as he has been doing in 2:11-13, to using Christ as subject in 2:14a. This is clearly shown by the reference to Christ (αὐτός "he") at the beginning of the verse. He is the one who causes people to be at peace with one another.

The word εἰρήνη "peace" occurs four times in this paragraph. However, it is not clear what reconciliation Paul is referring to here. There is no consensus among commentators. There are two possibilities:

1. It may refer to peace between Jews and Gentiles. See, for example, Lincoln (p. 140), Meyer (p. 382).
2. It may refer to peace between Jews and Gentiles and also man and God. See, for example, Eadie (p. 171), Hodge (pp. 130-131).

Although Paul talks about "our peace", the pronoun ἡμῶν "our" does not indicate which parties are involved. It merely denotes that "we" are the beneficiaries of the peace. However, since the two groups, Jews and Gentiles, are referred to in the immediately preceding context (2:11-13), it is more likely that he is referring to the reconciliation between Jews and Gentiles to form one community, the church.

2:14b He has caused us all, both *Jewish and Gentile believers*, to become one *community spiritually*. The relative pronoun ὁ "who" in the clause ὁ ποιήσας τὰ ἀμφότερα ἕν "who having made both one" refers to Christ. In the display, the pronoun "he" is used, since it clearly refers to Christ in the context. This proposition (2:14b) and 2:14c explain the statement Αὐτός...ἐστιν ἡ εἰρήνη ἡμῶν "He is our peace" (2:14a). The two propositions (2:14b-c) are represented in the display as amplification₁ and amplification₂ of 2:14a.

The phrase τὰ ἀμφότερα "the both" refers to the Jews and the Gentiles. This is made explicit in the display.

The word ἕν "one" means "one people" or "one community" in a spiritual sense, since it is as believers that these two groups form one community, the church, not as different races forming a new race or nation. They are united by their relationship to God and the privileges entailed by that.

2:14c *As someone* pulls down a wall which separates *people from each other, so* Christ has destroyed the enmity *which separated us, Jews and Gentiles*. This constituent is related to what precedes by καί "and". It continues the explanation begun in 2:14b of how Jewish and Gentile believers have become one community.

The genitive construction τὸ μεσότοιχον τοῦ φραγμοῦ "the dividing wall of the fence" is clearly metaphorical. The combination of the two nouns describes a wall which was erected to separate or protect. This could refer to:

1. The wall in the temple which separated the court of the Jews from that of the Gentiles.
2. The law that separated the Jews from the Gentiles.
3. The animosity which existed between the Jews and the Gentiles.

The third option seems most appropriate in the context.

The noun τὴν ἔχθραν "the enmity" is in apposition to τὸ μεσότοιχον "the dividing wall", that is, this partition represents the enmity that existed between the two groups.

In 2:14c, both the figure ("pulls down a wall which separates") and the non-figurative meaning ("has destroyed the enmity *which separated*") are presented. "Christ" is the agent here, carried over from 2:14a–b.

2:15 The statement "Christ is our peace" (2:14a) was amplified in 2:14b–c. Now Paul goes on to describe the means by which this has been achieved, that is, by removing the cause of the enmity: τὸν νόμον τῶν ἐντολῶν ἐν δόγμασιν "the law of the commandments in decrees".

The phrase ἐν τῇ σαρκὶ αὐτοῦ "in his flesh" can be connected to its context in two ways:

1. It is connected to the following aorist participle καταργήσας "having abolished" (2:15). See, for example, Eadie (pp. 174–175), Hendriksen (p. 134), Hodge (p. 133), Hoehner (p. 374), Lincoln (pp. 141–142), O'Brien (p. 196), Stott (p. 100).
2. It is connected with one of the preceding participles in 2:14: ποιήσας "having made" or λύσας "having broken down" (2:14). See, for example, Bratcher and Nida (p. 56).

Although some versions follow the second option (e.g. NCV, NRSV, REB, TEV), most commentators follow the first option. So this is followed in the display.

Note that ἐν τῇ σαρκὶ αὐτοῦ "in his flesh" actually occurs at the end of 2:14 in some Greek texts. Many versions, as does the display, place it in 2:15, because it connects better with the following text.

In 2:14, Paul stated that Christ had destroyed the enmity that existed between Jews and Gentiles and has united them spiritually. He now goes on, in 2:15, to say how this has been achieved: By his death, Christ satisfied all the demands of the Jewish/Mosaic law, and so purchased salvation for humanity. In satisfying the demands of the law, he made ineffective the rules and regulations of the law which had been the cause of the enmity between Jews and Gentiles.

2:15a Christ *did this* [2:14] by means of his making ineffective the rules and regulations of the *Mosaic* law, The Greek verb καταργέω means "to make ineffective, invalid, nullify". It is translated as "abolish" in most versions. The form of the verb here, aorist active participle, indicates the possibility of a means relationship with 2:14.

It is not clear what exactly Paul is referring to by τὸν νόμον τῶν ἐντολῶν ἐν δόγμασιν "the law of the commandments in decrees".

The word νόμος "law" itself can refer to:

1. The law recorded in the first five books of the Old Testament, the Torah. These are the laws which God gave to Moses for the Israelites.
2. The law of God in its widest sense (Hodge, p. 134). This is a law that applies to Jew and Gentile alike.

The first option has the better commentary support, and so is followed in these notes.

One reason for selecting option 1 above is that most commentators agree that the whole phrase τὸν νόμον τῶν ἐντολῶν ἐν δόγμασιν "the law of the commandments in decrees" refers to the Mosaic law.

However, the Mosaic law has two parts and commentators do not agree as to which part Paul means here. There are two possibilities:

1. It is limited to the ceremonial law. See, for example, Calvin (p. 151), Eadie (p. 177), Hendriksen (pp. 134–135), Lloyd-Jones (pp. 208–210).
2. It includes both the ceremonial and the moral law. See, for example, Alford (pp. 97–98), Ellicott (p. 41), Hodge (pp. 134–135), Braune (p. 93), Meyer (p. 384).

The Jewish law contained many detailed rules, regulations and ceremonies which the Jews emphasised, such as circumcision, dietary regulations and ritual cleansing. (See the parallel passage in Col. 2:11, 16–21.) The keeping of these laws set the Jews apart from the Gentiles and caused division between them and the Gentiles.

However, it seems that both aspects of the law are involved here. The difficulty with this view is that while Jesus clearly καταργήσας "abolished, made ineffective" the ceremonial aspects of the law, he did not abolish the moral law. Stott resolves this seeming anomaly,

> Jesus certainly did not abolish the moral law as a standard of behaviour...; but he did abolish it as a way of salvation.... To sum up, Jesus abolished both the regulations of the ceremonial law and the condemnation of the moral law. Both were divisive. Both were put aside by the cross (pp. 100–101).

2:15b by means of his *dying*. The phrase ἐν τῇ σαρκὶ αὐτοῦ "in his flesh" is a metonymy, in which "his flesh" stands for the most contextually significant event in Christ's earthly life, namely, his sacrificial death on the cross. See, for example, Alford (p. 97), Eadie (p. 178), Ellicott (p. 41), Hendriksen (p. 134), Hodge (p. 136), Stott (p. 100). This interpretation is supported by the occurrence of ἐν τῷ αἵματι τοῦ Χριστοῦ "by the blood of Christ" (2:13) and διὰ τοῦ σταυροῦ "by means of the cross" (2:16), where Christ's death is said to be the means of reconciling the Jewish and Gentile believers.

2:15c–16d The conjunction ἵνα "in order that" introduces two purpose clauses dependent upon 2:15a–b. These two purposes are expressed by the two parallel propositional clusters, 2:15c–e and 2:16a–e.

2:15c *He did this* **[2:15a] in order that he might cause the two groups to become one new group** Christ is the agent of the aorist subjunctive κτίσῃ "he might create, make". The object τοὺς δύο "the two" refers to τὰ ἀμφότερα "the both" in 2:14, i.e. the Jewish and the Gentile believers.

Most commentators consider that the expression ἕνα καινὸν ἄνθρωπον "one new person" refers collectively to all the believers, whether Jew or Gentile, who make up the church. The union of these two previously antagonistic groups refers to the joining of two different peoples to form a single entity. This "new people" is "new" in that both Jewish and Gentile believers have become one spiritually.

2:15d *by means of uniting us* **with himself,** The pronoun αὐτῷ "him, himself" refers back to Christ, last mentioned by name in 2:13. The ἐν in the expression ἐν αὐτῷ "in himself" refers to the means by which Jewish and Gentile believers became one community/unit, the church. It is by means of their relationship with Christ that they have become one.

2:15e *with the result that* **he causes us to be at peace** *with one another.* Most commentators consider that the participial phrase ποιῶν εἰρήνην "making peace" indicates the result of κτίσῃ ἐν αὐτῷ εἰς ἕνα καινὸν ἄνθρωπον "that he might create in himself one new person" (2:15c). See, for example, Ellicott (p. 41), Hodge (p. 137), Lloyd-Jones (p. 213), Meyer (p. 387).

The peace referred to in this context is generally taken to refer to that between Jews and Gentiles. See, for example, Calvin (p. 151), Eadie (p. 179), Hodge (p. 137), Lloyd-Jones (p. 211), Meyer (pp. 386–387).

2:16a And *he made the rules and regulations ineffective* **in order that he might reconcile** *us,* **both** *Jewish and Gentile believers,* **to God,** The conjunction καί "and", together with the subjunctive verb ἀποκαταλλάξῃ "he might reconcile", indicates a second purpose dependent on 2:15a and relating to the ἵνα "in order that" in 2:15c. As in the previous purpose clause, Christ is the agent and τοὺς ἀμφοτέρους "the both" refers to the two groups, Jews and Gentiles.

2:16b *with the result that we are now* **one group.** The phrase ἐν ἑνὶ σώματι "in one body" can be understood in two ways:

1. It refers to the fact that the church is the "one new person", as mentioned in 2:15, made up of Jews and Gentiles. The phrase then refers to the church as a body of believers. The natural opposition between "the-two/both" and "the one body" is emphasised, as it was in the preceding verses, along with the contrast between "the near" and "the far off".
2. It refers to Christ's own body. In this case, it means that Christ would reconcile both Jews and Gentiles to God by his death on the cross.

The first option is preferred by most commentators. The phrase ἑνὶ σώματι "one body" then can be equated with ἕνα καινὸν ἄνθρωπον "one new person" in 2:15 (i.e. the Jewish and Gentile believers united in one group, which is the church). See also 1:22–23; 3:6; 4:4; 5:23, 30. It is, therefore, the option followed in the display.

2:16c *He did this* **[2:16a] by means of** *his dying on* **the cross.** In the phrase διὰ τοῦ σταυροῦ "through the cross", διά "through" indicates the means of the reconciliation. "The cross" is a metonymy which represents the event of Christ's dying on the cross. This is the event which reconciles all believers to God.

2:16d *And,* **by means of** *his dying in* **this** *way,* The phrase ἐν αὐτῷ "in himself/it" at the end of 2:16 may refer to Christ or to the cross. In either case, it is Christ's death which is in view.

2:16e he caused us to be no longer enemies *of* **God.** The expression ἀποκτείνας τὴν ἔχθραν "having killed the enmity" is a metaphor. The verb ἀποκτείνω "to kill" is used in the sense of terminating something, bringing something to an end, just as the death of Christ on the cross brought his mortal life to an end. In this context, it is "enmity" that is terminated. The enmity may refer to:

1. The enmity between Jews and Gentiles. See, for example, Calvin (p. 152), Eadie (p. 183), Ellicott (p. 42), Meyer (p. 389).
2. The enmity between human beings and God. See, for example, Alford (p. 98), Hodge (p. 141), Hoehner (p. 383), Lincoln (pp. 144–146), Lloyd-Jones (p. 231), O'Brien (p. 201), Stott (p. 102).

Both views are possible. However, in this context, the second option is the more appropriate. In 2:14–15, Paul talked about the removal of the enmity between Jewish and Gentile believers through Christ's death. In 2:16, the focus changes to the reconciliation between believers, both Jewish and Gentile, to God, i.e. the removal of the enmity between them and God.

The parallel passage in Colossians 1:20–22 also supports the second option. There the peace referred to is clearly that between God and men.

The aorist active participle ἀποκτείνας "having killed" denotes an action that occurs at the same time as that of the main verb, "to reconcile" (2:16a), or occurs prior to the action of this main verb. Here, it seems that the event is seen in positive terms ("reconcile") in 2:16a and in negative terms in 2:16e ("bring to an end the enmity"). To quote Hodge,

> Reconciliation involves the removal of enmity; the reconciliation is to God, therefore the enmity is that which subsisted between God and man—the peace announced in consequence of this reconciliation, verse 17, is peace with God; it consists in the liberty of access to him spoken of in verse 18 (p 141).

The use of ἀποκτείνω "kill" may also allude to the death of Christ, as following σταυρός "cross" in the previous clause. In some translations, it may be difficult to keep the connection that the one who "killed" the enmity did so by offering himself to be killed.

The non-figurative meaning of the metaphor "killed" in this verse part has been expressed in the display rather than expressing the figure itself.

2:17 There are different ways to understand the initial καί "and" at the beginning of 2:17:

1. It indicates "a summary or conclusion of 2:14–16" (Graham, p. 173). Some versions indicate this by the use of "so". See, for example, NRSV, REB, TEV.
2. It indicates an addition relationship. In this unit further information is given concerning the theme of the paragraph, Αὐτὸς γάρ ἐστιν ἡ εἰρήνη ἡμῶν "For he is our peace" (2:14).

The second option fits the context best. Paul has stated that Christ brought about peace between Jew and Gentile (2:14). He then explained the means by which this was brought about (2:15–16). Then in (2:17) he adds a further fact: that Christ proclaimed this good news about peace. No time frame is given, so it is best to translate this "addition" clause generically without specific reference to chronological time. This has been done in the display.

2:17a He came *to this world and* proclaimed the good news, The words ἐλθὼν εὐηγγελίσατο "having come, he proclaimed the good news" function as an orienter for the content of what Christ proclaimed (2:17b–18b).

The verb ἐλθών "having come" implies a location or destination. It may be necessary in some languages to supply this, for example by saying "to this world" or "to this earth". There is some discussion about what event this "coming" refers to, but the consensus is that it refers to Christ's coming after his resurrection, both in person and in his Spirit. In translation, it is best to leave the statement as general as possible.

2:17b *that* you Gentiles, who were separated/apart *from God,* and the Jews, who were close *to God,* might all be *now* at peace *with God.* As previously, εἰρήνη "peace" could refer to:

1. peace between Jews and Gentiles
2. peace between human beings and God
3. both the above options

In 2:18, Paul goes on to say ἔχομεν τὴν προσαγωγὴν οἱ ἀμφότεροι ἐν ἑνὶ πνεύματι πρὸς τὸν πατέρα "we both have access by one Spirit to the Father". So, at this point, peace between human beings and God seems to be the focus. Both those who were "far off" and those who were "near", that is, both Gentiles and Jews, are now at peace with God.

See the notes on 2:13 for discussion on τοῖς μακράν "the ones far off" and τοῖς ἐγγύς "the ones near".

2:18a *This* [2:17b] *is* evidenced by the fact that, The conjunction ὅτι "because/that" may indicate one of the following:

1. The ὅτι functions to indicate reason or evidence. It introduces proof or evidence for the previous statement: that the message of the gospel of peace has been offered to both Jews and Gentiles. See, for example, Eadie (p. 186), Hodge (p. 143), Meyer (p. 391).
2. The ὅτι functions to indicate the content of a speech word (εὐηγγελίσατο "he proclaimed"). It introduces the content of the gospel of peace, that is, both Jews and Gentiles have access in one Spirit to the Father. See, for example, Lenski (p. 446).

The second option is the simpler. However, as most commentators support the first option, it is better to follow it. Hodge says,

> The proof that peace has thus been obtained for both is, that both have equally free access to God (p. 143).

by means of what he *has done*, The preposition διά "through" signals a means proposition. The pronoun αὐτοῦ "him" refers to Christ. It is by means of what Christ has done that we have access to the Father. See the notes on "by the blood of Christ" (2:13), "in his flesh" (2:15), "through the cross" (2:16).

2:18b we all, *Jewish and Gentile believers*, are able to approach *God* the Father, by *means of the* one Holy Spirit. Both Jewish and Gentile believers are indicated by οἱ ἀμφότεροι "the both", as throughout this unit.

In the New Testament, the word προσαγωγή "approach, access" is only used three times: here, in 3:12 and in Romans 5:2. All believers are free to approach God by the same means. This is highlighted by the contrast between οἱ ἀμφότεροι "the both" and ἑνί "one" in their juxtaposition (οἱ ἀμφότεροι ἐν ἑνὶ πνεύματι "the both in one spirit/Spirit").

In the expression ἐν ἑνὶ πνεύματι "in one spirit/Spirit", the preposition ἐν is best understood as instrument, "by (means of)". In some languages, a verb or verbal noun will be needed. Bratcher and Nida (p. 60) suggest as a possibility "we are able by the one Spirit's help to come into the presence of the Father". Other possibilities are "by means of depending upon", "by means of relying upon".

The consensus here is that πνεύματι "spirit/Spirit" refers to the Holy Spirit. See, for example, Alford (p. 99), Calvin (p. 154), Eadie (p. 188), Hodge (p. 146), Meyer (p. 391), Stott (p. 103). This is followed in the display.

BOUNDARIES AND COHERENCE

For the initial boundary of the 2:14-18 paragraph, see the section on Boundaries and Coherence for 2:11-13. The verse 2:19 begins a new sentence in the Greek text with ἄρα οὖν "therefore", a connector that is sometimes found at the beginning of higher level units (e.g. Rom. 5:18; 8:12).

There is strong lexical coherence in this paragraph due to:

1. The frequent references to εἰρήνη "peace" (2:14, 15, 17).
2. The frequent references to making "both/two" become "one" (ἀμφότεροι "both" [2:14, 16, 18], δύο "two" [2:15], ἕν "one" [2:14, 15, 16, 18]).
3. The references to removing enmity (2:14, 16) and to reconciliation (2:16).

PROMINENCE AND THEME

The 2:14-18 paragraph consists of two NUCLEI. The second NUCLEUS repeats features of the theme of the first NUCLEUS. However, the CONCLUSION proposition of the second NUCLEUS is supported by a significant grounds: "we are all now at peace with God since both Jews and Gentiles are able to approach the Father through Christ and the Holy Spirit". This grounds, therefore, is included in the theme statement.

SECTION CONSTITUENT 2:19–22:
(Expository Paragraph: Conclusion₂ of 2:11–22)

THEME: So then, you Gentile believers are no longer excluded from God's blessings, but share in them equally with the Jewish believers, and together with them, form one church.

RELATIONAL STRUCTURE	CONTENTS
POSITIVE — negative	2:19a Therefore, you are no longer *excluded from God's people, as* foreigners and strangers *are excluded from the people they are staying among* [MET].
— amplification	2:19b But instead, along with all God's people, you have become citizens *of the country of which he is king*. You have become members of the family of *which* God *is the Father* [MET].
NUCLEUS₁	2:20a *God* has built you up *to form his church*. The apostles and prophets *who teach the word of God are like* the foundation *of the building* [MET].
NUCLEUS₂	2:20b Christ Jesus himself is *the most important part of the church, just as* the cornerstone *is the most important part of a building* [MET].
NUCLEUS₃	2:21 *God is continually causing* all you *who are united with Christ to* grow/mature *together spiritually, in order that you become a church which is dedicated to the Lord Jesus Christ, just as people might* put together the different parts of a building to become a temple dedicated to the Lord *Jesus Christ* [MET].
NUCLEUS₄ — MEANS — NUCLEUS	2:22a And you *Gentiles who are united* with Christ are also *being added to the church*,
— comparison	2:22b *just as parts of* a building are added to the building [MET],
— purpose	2:22c in order that God *might be present in the church* by means of *his Holy* Spirit, *just as he* is present in a temple [MET].

INTENT AND STRUCTURE

In this paragraph, Paul uses three figures of speech to demonstrate to the Ephesian believers their privileged position as members of the body of believers made up of both Jews and Gentiles. He describes them as being fellow-citizens of God's kingdom, members of God's family and part of God's temple. Although this is an expository paragraph, it has expressive overtones as Paul tries to help the Ephesians appreciate their privileges.

NOTES

2:19a Therefore, Most commentators agree that the joint conjunctions ἄρα οὖν at the beginning of 2:19 have an inferential function and may be translated as "as-a-result/therefore". They introduce a result or conclusion based on the previous section. See, for example, Eadie (p. 189), Ellicott (p. 43), Hodge (p. 147), Meyer (p. 391), O'Brien (p. 210, fn. 224), Stott (p. 104).

you are no longer *excluded from God's people, as* foreigners and strangers *are excluded from the people they are staying among*. This is a metaphor and, in the display, the point of comparison is made explicit. The present state of the Gentile believers whom Paul is addressing is described in negative terms here. In 1:19b. Paul uses positive terms.

Both ξένοι and πάροικοι have been translated as "strangers", "foreigners", "aliens" in various versions. Most commentators consider that:

1. ξένοι is a general term for referring to people of another ethnic group or country.
2. πάροικοι, more specifically, refers to resident aliens, people living more or less

permanently in a foreign country, but who are not full citizens of that country.

The important component of meaning in both words is that these people were outsiders who did not enjoy the privileges of being citizens of the country in which they were living. In this context, it means that, at one time, the Ephesian believers did not belong to God's people. They were excluded from the privileges enjoyed by God's people, just as "foreigners" and "aliens" do not enjoy the privileges enjoyed by a true citizen of a country.

2:19b But instead, The conjunction ἀλλά "but" introduces the positive side of the negative-positive metaphorical statement occurring in 2:19a–b. The Ephesian believers are described as συμπολῖται τῶν ἁγίων "fellow-citizens with the saints" and οἰκεῖοι τοῦ θεοῦ "members of the household of God". These two terms contrast with the terms ξένοι "strangers" and πάροικοι "aliens" in 2:19a. The display makes the non-figurative meaning explicit in both 2:19a and 2:19b.

along with all God's people, The term ἅγιοι "saints" refers to all believers, whether Jew or Gentile.

you have become citizens *of the country of which he is king.* All believers are regarded as being πολῖται "citizens" of the kingdom of God. Here, the term συμπολῖται "fellow-citizens" is used. It emphasises that Gentile believers and Jewish believers are both equal citizens of God's kingdom. This connects with the expression "the commonwealth of Israel" in 2:12.

The point of comparison is that all believers, whatever their background, have the rights and privileges of their citizenship of God's kingdom, just as the citizens of an earthly country have the rights and privileges granted by that country.

You have become members of the family of which God *is the Father.* The phrase οἰκεῖοι τοῦ θεοῦ "members of the household of God" is a further metaphor to describe the state of the Gentile believers. They are not only citizens of God's kingdom, but also members of his family.

2:20–22 The rest of this paragraph contains an extended metaphor relating to building. Paul compares the body of believers, to which the Gentile believers also belong, as a building under construction. It has a foundation and a cornerstone, and parts are continually being added to it. The building is a temple consecrated to the Lord Jesus Christ where God is present through his Spirit.

The points of similarity between this illustration and its topic, the church, need to be stated non-figuratively in the display. The relevant points are the following:

1. The stones, or parts of the building, which are being continually added, represent individual believers, including Gentile believers.
2. The foundations of the building represent the apostles and prophets or what they taught.
3. The chief cornerstone of the building represents Jesus Christ.
4. The building is a temple where God is present by his Spirit. It represents the body of believers, the church, which is indwelt by the Holy Spirit.

2:20a *God* **has built you up** *to form his church.* **The apostles and prophets** *who teach the word of God are like* **the foundation** *of the building.* The genitive construction τῷ θεμελίῳ τῶν ἀποστόλων καὶ προφητῶν "the foundation of the apostles and prophets" can be understood in several ways:

1. It is a genitive of apposition, i.e. the foundation consists of the apostles and prophets. See, for example, Best (p. 279), Hodge (pp. 148–150), Hoehner (pp. 398–399), O'Brien (p. 213, fn. 242). Lincoln expresses this as follows,

   > The apostles and prophets are foundational in the sense of being primary and authoritative recipients and proclaimers of revelation.... [They had] a foundational role as those to whom the mystery of Christ was made known in order that it might be proclaimed to the Gentiles (p.153).

2. It is not the apostles and prophets themselves who are the foundation, but the teaching of Christ which they proclaimed. See, for example, Lloyd-Jones (p. 352), Stott (p. 107).

The first option has the best commentary support. While the second option is also true, Paul here speaks of personal beings as symbolised by the various parts of the building. So it seems best to follow option 1.

2:20b Christ Jesus himself is *the most important part of the church, just as* **the cornerstone** *is the most important part of a building.* The Greek word ἀκρογωνιαῖος occurs only here and in 1 Peter 2:6. It is used figuratively in both cases to refer to Christ Jesus. The exact function (and, therefore, translation) of ἀκρογωνιαῖος is debated. Some suggestions are:

1. It refers to the stone that holds together both the walls and the foundation.
2. It refers to the stone with which everything else is lined up.
3. It refers to the stone that holds the whole weight of a building.
4. It refers to the stone that holds the whole structure together.

What is clear is that this stone is the most important stone in the building, vital to the stability of the whole structure. This then is the main point of comparison and needs to be made explicit in the display.

2:21-22 These two verses consist of two parallel relative clauses. The first of these, 2:21, focusses on the growth of the church in general and has the following elements:

ἐν ᾧ "in whom"
πᾶσα οἰκοδομή "(the) whole building"
συναρμολογουμένη αὔξει "being fitted together grows"
εἰς ναὸν ἅγιον "into a holy temple"
ἐν κυρίῳ "in (the) Lord"

The second one, 2:22, focusses on the specific place of the Gentile believers in that growth and has the elements:

ἐν ᾧ "in whom"
ὑμεῖς "you"
συνοικοδομεῖσθε "being built together"
εἰς κατοικητήριον τοῦ θεοῦ "into a dwelling place of God"
ἐν πνεύματι "in (the) Spirit"

2:21 In this verse, Paul continues the metaphor of a building. He describes the structure progressing as the different parts are added to it.

Paul uses this metaphor to represent the growth of the church as a body of believers, united with Christ Jesus. Individual believers are gradually being added to God's people, and God is present among them.

***God is continually causing* all you *who are united* with Christ *to* grow/mature *together spiritually*,** The word πᾶσα "whole, every, all" modifies the noun οἰκοδομή "building". In this context, it could mean:

1. "Whole". Paul is speaking of one building, which would represent the universal church.

See, for example, Alford (p. 101), Eadie (p. 200), Ellicott (pp. 45-46), Hendriksen (p. 143, fn. 77), Hodge (p. 151).

2. "Every". Paul is speaking of a number of buildings, each of which would represent a local congregation within the universal church. See, for example, Meyer (p. 396), Salmond (pp. 300-301).

The consensus is that πᾶσα οἰκοδομή means "(the) whole building". This seems appropriate in this context, since Paul's object is to describe the one temple in which both Jewish and Gentile believers are united in Christ and, in which, God dwells by his Spirit. A further support for this interpretation is that, in 2:20, only one building is referred to, with "(one) foundation" and "(one) cornerstone".

In the phrase ἐν ᾧ πᾶσα οἰκοδομή συναρμολογουμένη "in whom (the) whole building being fitted together", the relative pronoun ᾧ refers to Christ, and the metaphor of being "fitted together in Christ" describes the growth of the church, both in size and development, as those who are united to Christ are added to it and themselves grow in spiritual maturity.

Both the participle συναρμολογουμένη "being fitted together" and the indicative αὔξει "grows" are in the present tense. This indicates that the action is continuous.

in order that you become a church which is dedicated to the Lord Jesus Christ, This display rendering is the non-figurative meaning of the metaphor εἰς ναὸν ἅγιον ἐν κυρίῳ "into a holy temple in (the) Lord".

The result of the construction is ναὸν ἅγιον "a holy temple". Here it symbolises the church. The adjective ἅγιον "holy" is rendered as "dedicated" in the display.

The phrase ἐν κυρίῳ "in (the) Lord" is generally regarded as being attached to ναὸν ἅγιον "holy temple" and to refer to Christ.

***just as people might* put together the different parts of a building to become a temple dedicated to the Lord *Jesus Christ*.** This is the figurative part of the metaphorical πᾶσα οἰκοδομή συναρμολογουμένη...εἰς ναὸν ἅγιον ἐν κυρίῳ "(the) whole building being fitted together...into a holy temple in (the) Lord".

2:22a-b And you *Gentiles who are united* with Christ are also *being added to the church, just as parts of* a building are added to the building, Paul addresses the Gentile believers directly, using καὶ ὑμεῖς "you also", and goes on to explain their place in the spiritual building he has been describing: that they too are being built together as part of the temple and that God is present among them.

The pronoun ᾧ "him" refers back to κυρίῳ "(the) Lord" at the end of 2:21 and Χριστοῦ Ἰησοῦ "Christ Jesus" in 2:20. So 2:22 is parallel to 2:21. The phrase ἐν ᾧ "in him", then, has the same meaning "united with Christ".

The verb συνοικοδομεῖσθε "you are built together" (2:22) has a similar meaning and reference to συναρμολογουμένη "being fitted together" in 2:21.

2:22c in order that God *might be present in the church* by means of *his Holy* Spirit, *just as he* is present in a temple. The expression εἰς κατοικητήριον τοῦ θεοῦ "into a dwelling place of God" (2:22c) is parallel to εἰς ναὸν ἅγιον "into a holy temple" (2:21).

The genitive τοῦ θεοῦ "of God" indicates that God is the one who lives there. The preposition εἰς "into", in 2:22, indicates the goal or purpose that is in view, that is, a place where God lives/dwells.

The phrase ἐν πνεύματι "in spirit" can be understood in two ways:

1. It refers to the Holy Spirit.
2. It describes the building, i.e. it is "a spiritual building".

The majority of commentators support the first option. The Holy Spirit is the means by which God is present among his people.

BOUNDARIES AND COHERENCE

The initial boundary is marked by the joint conjunctions ἄρα οὖν "consequently/as-a-result, so then". Paul frequently uses this combination to mark progress in an argument or to introduce a conclusion based on previous reasoning. See, for example, Romans 5:18; 7:3, 25; 8:12; Galatians 6:10. So, in this paragraph, Paul sets out the consequences for the Gentiles of the reconciliation described in the previous verses.

For the final boundary, see the section on Boundaries and Coherence for 2:1–22.

Unit 2:19–22 is a single Greek sentence. The coherence for this unit lies principally in the extended metaphor of the building (2:20–22), which Paul uses to describe the church of which the Gentiles are now a part.

PROMINENCE AND THEME

The most prominent information in this paragraph is found in the two indicative verb forms in 2:19, οὐκέτι ἐστέ "you are no longer" and ἐστέ "you are", as well as their complements, which state in negative and positive terms the present position of the Gentiles as members of God's family. The theme statement is based on these.

DIVISION CONSTITUENT 3:1–13
(Expository Section: Authoritative grounds for 2:1–22)

THEME: I, Paul, am in prison because I serve Christ on the behalf of you Gentiles. God graciously appointed me to make known to you that Christ is the source of infinite blessings for you, as well as for Jewish believers. He also appointed me to make known to everyone how God accomplished what he had secretly planned, in order that, by means of establishing the church, he might now make known his infinitely wise plan to those beings who exercise power in the heavens.

MACROSTRUCTURE	CONTENTS
CONCLUSION (CLAIM)	3:1 I want you to know that it is because I serve Christ Jesus on the behalf of you Gentiles that I am in prison.
GROUNDS$_1$	3:2–7 God graciously appointed me to be responsible for preaching the gospel to you Gentiles. He revealed to me that he will bless you equally with the Jewish believers, and that you will, with them, belong to one church.
GROUNDS$_2$	3:8–13 God graciously appointed me to make known to the Gentiles that Christ is the source of infinite blessings for them, and to cause everyone to understand how God accomplished what he had secretly planned. God's purpose in this was that, by means of establishing the church, he might now make known his infinitely wise plan to those beings who exercise power in the heavens.

INTENT AND MACROSTRUCTURE

It seems likely that Paul was intending to pray for the Gentile believers in Ephesus at the beginning of this unit. He begins with an incomplete sentence, "For this reason, I, Paul, the prisoner of Christ Jesus for you Gentiles". He then breaks off and does not actually begin his prayer until 3:14. Instead, he talks about himself and describes the privileges which God has given to him: revealing to him the mystery that he goes on to explain in 3:2-6, and entrusting him with the ministry of preaching the gospel to the Gentiles (3:7-8).

The focus, in the three paragraphs which make up this unit, is Paul himself. He is someone whom God has chosen for a particular task and to whom God has given the authority to carry it out. The emphatic reference to "himself" in 3:1 serves as a basis for the account of his special ministry, which he explains in the following verses.

He addresses himself specifically to "you Gentiles", in order to explain his place in God's plan and purpose for them, and in order to strengthen his relationship with them.

Although this unit may be regarded as a digression within the prayer (resumed in 3:14), it also has many important thematic connections with the claims which Paul makes in chapter 2. In particular, Paul again speaks about the reconciliation of Jewish and Gentile believers as members of one church.

The unit functions as authoritative grounds for 2:1–22.

As well as having connections with what precedes, these verses lead into the prayer in 3:14–21. In presenting himself as someone who is suffering on their behalf (3:1 and 3:13), and as someone who prays for them (3:14), Paul prepares the Ephesian believers for the exhortations in chapters 4–6. He intends that his relationship with them will help to make the exhortations more acceptable to them.

BOUNDARIES AND COHERENCE

The initial boundary has been discussed in the section on Boundaries and Coherence for 2:1–22.

The initial boundary of the next unit is marked by the repetition of the expression τούτου χάριν "for this reason" in 3:14, which, with its occurrence in 3:1, brackets the digression in 3:1b–13.

This section is further marked as a unit by the rhetorical bracketing of 3:1 and 3:13, where Paul refers respectively to his being a "prisoner...on behalf of you Gentiles" and to his "suffering on behalf of you".

Also, there is parallelism between paragraphs 3:2–7 and 3:8–13: they both begin with references to Paul's ministry being "given" to him "by the grace of God".

A further unifying factor is the recurrence of a number of concepts, as follows:

"mystery" (3:3, 4, 5, 9)
"make-known/understand/reveal" (3:3, 4, 5, 8, 10)
"gift/give" (3:2, 7, 8)
"hidden/not-made-known" (3:5, 9)
"grace" (3:2, 7, 8)

The final boundary of this unit is marked by a change in genre from informative here to prayer in the next unit.

PROMINENCE AND THEME

As the CONCLUSION in a *grounds*-CONCLUSION relationship, 3:1 has natural prominence. However, the two paragraphs, 3:2–7 and 3:8–13, which provide the grounds for the claim made in 3:1, are marked for prominence in two ways:

1. By their length.
2. By the fact that they also serve to give force to Paul's prayer of 3:14–19 and the discourse of 2:1–22 and are not supportive of the claim in 3:1 alone.

The theme statement, therefore, is based on the CONCLUSION (3:1) and a summary of the two GROUNDS on which this CONCLUSION is based.

SECTION CONSTITUENT 3:1 (Propositional Cluster: Conclusion of 3:2-13)

THEME: I want you to know that it is because I serve Christ Jesus on the behalf of you Gentiles that I am in prison.

RELATIONAL STRUCTURE	CONTENTS
⌐nucleus₁ ───────────	3:1a Because *God has done all* this [2:1-22] *for you Gentiles*, I, Paul, *pray for you*.
└ NUCLEUS₂ ───────────	3:1b *But firstly, I want you to know* that it is because *I serve* Christ Jesus on behalf of you Gentiles *that* I am a prisoner.

INTENT AND STRUCTURE

Paul intends to pray for the Gentile believers in Ephesians, but, after his brief statement in 3:1, he digresses and gives an account of his calling and ministry on their behalf (3:2-13). In these opening words, he states his reason for praying for them (Τούτου χάριν "for this reason", 3:1a) and the reason for his imprisonment (3:1b). His purpose in stating these things is to strengthen his relationship with the Ephesian believers, so that what he will say later in the letter will be accepted by them.

NOTES

3:1a Because *God has done all* this [2:1-22] *for you Gentiles*, The phrase τούτου χάριν "for this reason", "because of this" relates Paul's intention to pray for the Gentile believers (3:1a) most likely to all of chapter 2. He wants to pray for them because he knows what they had been previously and what they have now become by God's grace.

I, Paul, The use of the proper name "Paul" with the free pronoun ἐγώ "I" is significant. Paul wants to establish his authority with the Ephesian believers.

His use of ὁ δέσμιος "prisoner" also draws attention to his imprisonment as part of his service to the Lord. He is presenting his credentials, so that what he will say to the Ephesians later in the letter will be accepted by them.

pray for you. Paul's incomplete sentence in the Greek is completed by the phrase "pray for you" in the display. Paul resumes his prayer in 3:14, after the digression of 3:2-13.

3:1b *But firstly, I want you to know* These words are supplied in the propositionalised text to indicate the semantic feature of the digression.

***that it is because I serve* Christ Jesus on behalf of you Gentiles *that* I am a prisoner.** It is not clear whether in the genitive phrase, ὁ δέσμιος τοῦ Χριστοῦ Ἰησοῦ "the prisoner of Christ Jesus", Paul is saying that:

1. Christ caused Paul's imprisonment.
2. It was something that occurred because Paul voluntarily served Christ.

Either makes sense here. The latter, however, is preferable in the context. The inclusion of the phrase ὑπὲρ ὑμῶν τῶν ἐθνῶν "on behalf of you Gentiles" suggests that Paul considered his imprisonment to be a consequence of his serving Christ, in particular, by preaching the gospel to the Gentiles.

The digression of 3:2-13 provides the grounds for Paul's statement in 3:1. So it supports this view.

God revealed the mystery to Paul that both Gentile and Jewish believers belong to one community and share the same blessings. He also gave Paul the privilege and responsibility to take the gospel to the Gentiles. On the basis of these claims of Paul, it is reasonable for Paul to say that it is because he serves Christ on behalf of the Gentiles that he is a prisoner (Hodge, p. 158).

BOUNDARIES AND COHERENCE

The initial boundary of this unit has been discussed in the section on Boundaries and Coherence for 3:1-13.

This unit consists only of a partial verse, which Paul then interrupts with his explanatory digression (3:2-13). The initial boundary of the next unit is marked by εἴ γε "surely", which introduces this digression. The prayer is resumed in 3:14, with Paul's statement κάμπτω τὰ γόνατά μου πρὸς τὸν πατέρα "I bow my knees before the Father" and the repetition of τούτου χάριν "for this reason". The event expressed in 3:14 as "I bow my knees" is expressed here in the display for 3:1 as "I...pray for you" to complete the sense of the intended sentence which he interrupted by his digression.

PROMINENCE AND THEME

In 3:2–13, Paul digresses from his brief introduction to the prayer. The second part of 3:1 relates directly to what he says in this digression. So NUCLEUS$_2$ is considered more prominent than the first nucleus and forms the theme statement.

SECTION CONSTITUENT 3:2–7 (Expository Paragraph: Grounds₁ for 3:1)

THEME: God graciously appointed me to be responsible for preaching the gospel to you Gentiles. He revealed to me that he will bless you equally with the Jewish believers, and that you will, with them, belong to one church.

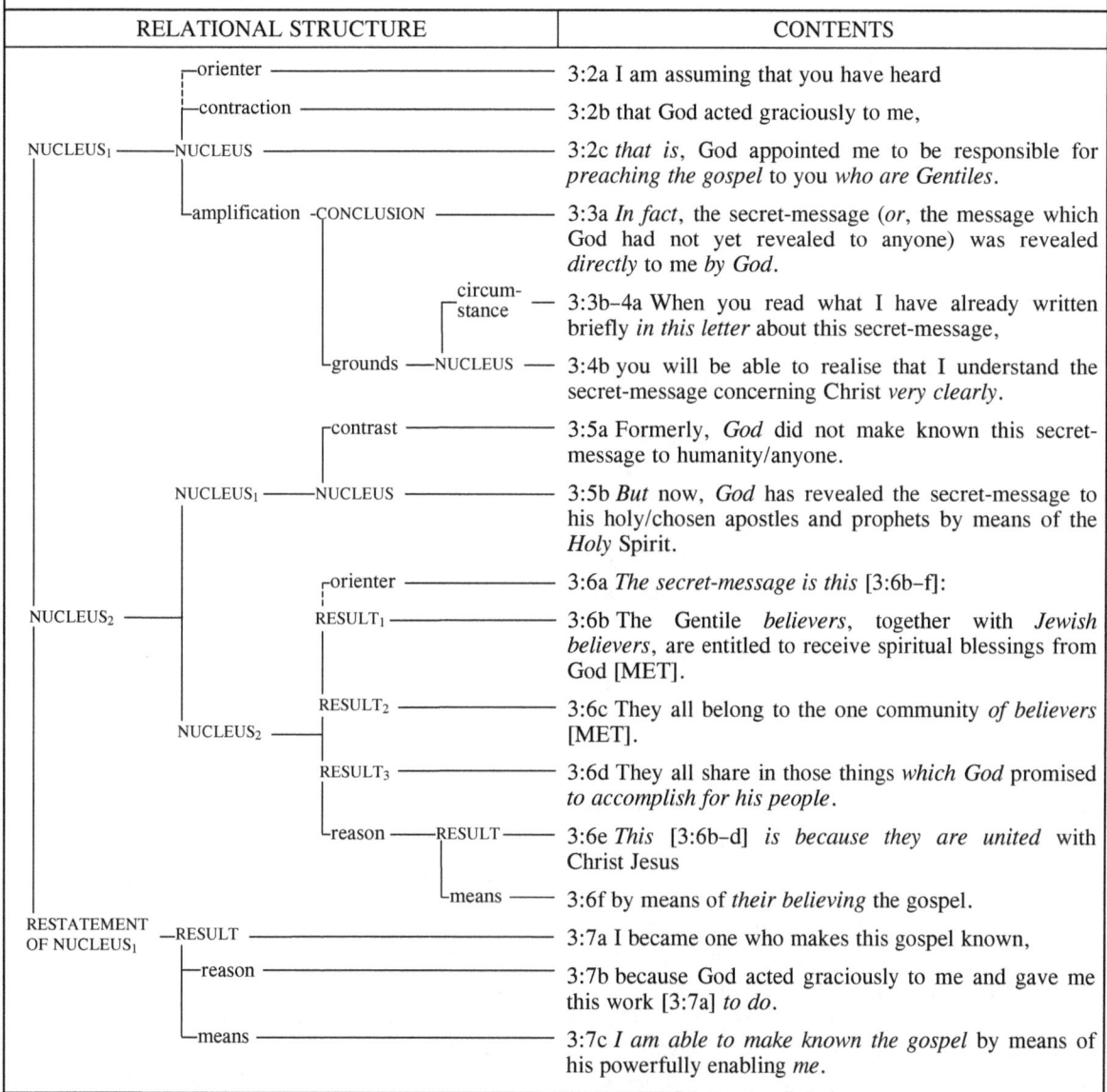

INTENT AND STRUCTURE

The 3:2–7 paragraph is co-ordinate with 3:8–13 and provides grounds for Paul's statement in 3:1, that it is because of his ministry to the Gentiles that he is a prisoner. This paragraph is completely expository, stating what God has revealed to him.

NOTES

3:2a I am assuming that you have heard The Greek εἴ γε "if indeed, inasmuch as" does not necessarily express doubt. It is often used where the thing spoken of is taken for granted. See 4:21; 2 Corinthians 5:3. In this context, it is generally accepted that it indicates that most of the Ephesians had already heard what Paul was going to tell them. Therefore, Paul was possibly using this to remind them of something they already knew.

This proposition provides an orienter for 3:2b–3a.

3:2b–c that God acted graciously to me, *that is*, God appointed me to be responsible for *preaching the gospel* to you *who are Gentiles*. The Greek used here, τὴν οἰκονομίαν τῆς χάριτος τοῦ θεοῦ τῆς δοθείσης μοι εἰς ὑμᾶς "the stewardship of the grace of God given to me for you", is similar to that used in Colossians 1:25. Callow notes, with regard to that verse,

> The word οἰκονομία 'stewardship' may refer to the role of administrator or supervisor, or it may be an abstract noun referring to the event of administrating or supervising (1983:100; 2002:64).

He also considers that it is best to take the noun "as an abstract noun representing the attribute 'responsible' associated with such tasks as administrating or supervising" (ibid.).

Here in Ephesians, as in Colossians, the Gentiles are the goal/destination of Paul's actions. This is clearly shown in 3:1. Paul is saying that he is responsible for the Gentiles.

The three Greek nouns δουλεῖα, διακονία, οἰκονομία all refer to "service" of some sort, but the service is of variable status.

The last-mentioned, οἰκονομία, refers to a high status, a highly responsible ministry. By contrast, διακονία, although also referring to ministry, refers to a ministry without the same level of responsibility or status in focus. The ministry represented by the noun δουλεῖα refers to a ministry with no responsibility or status at all.

Note that these are distinctive terms. In some contexts, the distinction is sharply maintained, but, in other contexts, the meanings will overlap.

In the parallel passage in Colossians 1:25, the genitive construction "the stewardship of God" means that God is the source of the stewardship. In that verse, Paul was saying, "I was appointed by God to be responsible towards you". Here in Ephesians 3:2, there is an additional genitive construction, "the stewardship *of the grace* of God". So it has to be decided what the verb "given" relates to. There are three possibilities:

1. It relates only to "grace".
2. It relates to the complete expression "stewardship of the grace of God".

In 3:7, Paul speaks about the "gift of God's grace which was given to me" and, in 3:8, he says "this grace was given, to preach to the Gentiles the unsearchable riches of Christ...".

These verses would seem to support the view that "given" relates only to "grace". Many commentators hold this view.

Alternatively, since οἰκονομία is the head noun, it would also make good sense to relate τῆς δοθείσης μοι εἰς ὑμᾶς to it, i.e. this responsible ministry was given to Paul to *exercise* on behalf of the Gentiles.

The relationship between God and "grace" is generally agreed to be that it is God who gives grace. There is some discussion, however, about what "grace" refers to here. It may refer to:

1. Paul's responsibility as apostle to the Gentiles.
2. The gift of grace that selected and qualified Paul for this responsibility.
3. The message about God's mercy to the Gentiles.

These possibilities are inextricably linked. God gave Paul grace, in the sense that God favoured Paul by giving him the ability to fulfil the responsibility which God had given, that of preaching to the Gentiles. God appointed him to do this in order that the Gentiles might be blessed.

This is the basis for the display, except that the part about the Gentiles being blessed is not expressed.

The statement "God acted graciously to me" might be regarded as generic, with 3:2c stating more specifically the way in which God acted graciously towards Paul. Alternatively, the two statements might be considered to be in a contraction-amplification relationship.

3:3a *In fact*, Most commentators consider that the particle ὅτι "that" introduces an explanation of 3:2. It is translated as "how", "that is", "namely". In some versions, it is not explicitly translated, but marked by the start of a new sentence. In the display, it is expressed as "In fact" and introduces an amplification of 3:2c.

the secret-message (*or*, the message which God had not yet revealed to anyone) See the note on μυστήριον in 1:9a.

was revealed *directly* to me *by God*. The abstract noun ἀποκάλυψιν "revelation" expresses the means by which the "secret-message" was made known to Paul. Other people did not teach him about this "secret-message". Rather, it was revealed to him directly by God. The word "*directly*" has been included in the display, in order to make clear that there was no human intervention.

God is the agent of "making known" and "revealing". However, since it is the "secret-message" that is in focus in these verses, rather than God himself, the passive form is retained in the display. The agent is expressed as *"by God"*. Also, since "made known" and "revealed" are synonymous, the redundancy is not kept in the display.

3:3b–4 In the display, 3:3b–4 is analysed as a grounds for 3:3a, since it provides specific evidence for the validity of the statement that the secret-message was revealed to Paul.

3:3b–4a When you read what I have already written briefly *in this letter* about this secret-message, This proposition represents καθὼς προέγραψα ἐν ὀλίγῳ "as I previously wrote in brief" (3:3b) and πρὸς ὃ...ἀναγινώσκοντες "as to which...(when/by) reading" (3:4a). The phrase "as I previously wrote in brief" could refer to two things:

1. Paul is referring to a previous letter or letters that he had written to the Ephesians. See, for example, Calvin (p. 158), Thompson (p. 54).
2. Paul is referring to various passages in this present letter, specifically 2:11–22. See, for example, Abbott (p. 79), Bratcher and Nida (p. 70), Hodge (p. 161).

The second option seems most appropriate here. What Paul has written about is "the secret-message".

The present participle ἀναγινώσκοντες "reading" may be understood in two ways:

1. It represents a temporal clause, to indicate that the action takes place at the same time as νοῆσαι "to realise/perceive" (3:4), i.e. "while reading you will realise".
2. It may signal the means by which the Ephesian believers will come to realise Paul's understanding of the secret-message, i.e. "by reading you will realise".

Either makes good sense. In the display, the first option is followed. The two actions are regarded as simultaneous, with "reading" stating the circumstance in which the "realising" takes place.

3:4b you will be able to realise that I understand...*very clearly* It is difficult to express the abstract noun σύνεσις "insight, under-standing" as an event. One possibility might be, "I understand...*very clearly*".

the secret-message concerning Christ Commentators discuss how the two nouns in the genitive construction τῷ μυστηρίῳ τοῦ Χριστοῦ "the mystery of Christ" are related. There are two possibilities:

1. It is a genitive of apposition, i.e. Christ is the mystery. See, for example, Candlish (p. 69), Ellicott (p. 50).
2. It is an objective genitive, i.e. the mystery is about Christ. See, for example, Abbott (p. 80), Eadie (p. 215).
3. The mystery is attained through Christ. See Best (p. 304).

Best states,

> The uniting of Jew and Gentile can be described as the mystery of Christ because it is through him that it is attained, for both Jew and Gentile are now in the one body of Christ.

In 3:6, Paul will give the content of the mystery, that is, that the Gentile believers, together with the Jewish believers, are one community and will receive the same spiritual blessings in Christ. In the display, therefore, τῷ μυστηρίῳ τοῦ Χριστοῦ "the mystery of Christ" has been expressed, following option 2, as "the secret-message concerning Christ" since, on the basis of the details in 3:6, this would be more inclusive than the other options above.

3:5 Grammatically the relative pronoun ὅ "which", at the beginning of 3:5, introduces a subordinate construction. However, in this context, it also signals a shift to the next aspect of the topic.

3:5a–b These are three contrastive statements concerning the secret-message, as can be seen clearly from the contrastive words occurring in them:

"formerly" (3:5a) contrasts with "now" (3:5b)

"not made known" (3:5a) contrasts with "revealed" (3:5b)

"not to anyone" (3:5a) contrasts with "to his holy apostles and prophets" (3:5b)

In other words, in the past God had not fully revealed the secret-message (3:5a), but *now*, he has revealed this message to his holy apostles and prophets.

The two temporal expressions, ἑτέραις γενεαῖς "in other generations, formerly" and νῦν "now" are forefronted in the Greek to emphasise the contrast.

3:5a Formerly, In the Greek, the phrase used here, ἑτέραις γενεαῖς "in other generations, formerly", is a general expression referring to sometime in the past.

***God* did not make known this secret-message** God is the implicit agent of οὐκ ἐγνωρίσθη "was not made known".

The major question here is what the relative pronoun ὅ "which" refers to. There are three possibilities:

1. It refers to τὸ μυστήριον "the mystery" in 3:3.
2. It refers to τῷ μυστηρίῳ τοῦ Χριστοῦ "the mystery of Christ" in 3:4.
3. It refers to both.

Most commentators agree that it refers to both, since "the mystery of Christ" (the whole gospel revealed to people) includes the more limited idea of 3:3, i.e. the part of the gospel revealed first to Paul. It is unlikely that the meaning of μυστήριον should vary in three consecutive verses, 3:3, 3:4, 3:5, without a significant marker for the difference.

The mystery is the mystery of redemption in Christ. In particular, in this letter, the mystery refers to the fact that Gentile believers are equal participants with Jewish believers in sharing blessings in Christ. Hendriksen (p. 153, fn. 82) compares "the mystery of Christ" here with "this mystery among the Gentiles, which is Christ in you, the hope of glory" in Colossians 1:27, where it clearly refers to the inclusion of the Gentiles in the blessings. The meaning would be the same here.

to humanity/anyone. Most commentators agree that the expression υἱοὶ τῶν ἀνθρώπων "sons of men" simply means "people" or "humanity".

3:5b *But* now, *God* has revealed the secret-message In the Greek, this proposition is introduced by ὡς "as" which indicates a comparison. However, in this context, the comparison is better analysed as a threefold contrast, as set out in the note on 3:5a–b. In the display, therefore, "*But*" is used as an alternative to ὡς "as".

to his holy/chosen apostles and prophets It is generally agreed that "holy" modifies both "apostles" and "prophets".

Some commentators suggest that, since the Greek ἅγιος "holy" can apply to all God's people in some contexts it needs extra significance here. Some versions translate it as "dedicated" or "consecrated". See, for example, JBP, NEB. Also, see Hodge (pp. 163–164).

The possessive pronoun "his" may refer to either God or Christ. Most commentators refer it to God. This is supported by the fact that God is probably the agent of "reveal".

by means of the *Holy* Spirit. The Greek simply says ἐν πνεύματι "in/by spirit", but it is generally agreed that "spirit", in this context, refers to the Holy Spirit. He is the means by which the revelation just mentioned was made, i.e. "God revealed the secret-message by means of the Holy Spirit" or "God caused the Holy Spirit to reveal the secret-message".

3:6a *The secret-message is this* [3:6b–f]: In 3:6, Paul specifies the content of the secret-message referred to in the preceding verses. It is introduced in the display by an orienter, "*The secret-message is this* [3:6b–f]".

3:6b–d There are three terms used in this verse to describe the blessings received by the Gentile believers:

συγκληρονόμα "joint-heirs"
σύσσωμα "joint-body"
συμμέτοχα "joint-sharers"

Commentators do not agree whether these three terms are nearly synonymous or express different ideas. However, a distinction can be made in that σύσσωμα "joint-body" refers to an entity which is united together, while συγκληρονόμα "joint-heirs" and συμμέτοχα "joint-sharers" refer to the members of this entity in reference to the common blessings they share.

While there are distinctions, the use of three words with the συν- prefix emphasises aspects of unity that are true for all believers because they are united in Christ.

Each of these three aspects (3:6b–d) reflects statements in other sections of the letter. See the notes on 3:6b, c, d.

3:6b The Gentile *believers*, Most versions translate τὰ ἔθνη "the nations" as "the Gentiles" here. They also agree that the infinitive εἶναι "to be", which introduces this verse, specifies the content of "the secret-message".

together with Jewish believers, Here, as in 3:6c and 3:6d, Paul uses a compound adjective with the prefix συν- "together with" to make it clear that he is referring to both Gentiles and Jewish believers. The adjective here is συγκληρονόμα which functions as a substantive, "inheritors together with".

are entitled to receive spiritual blessings from God. The word συγκληρονόμα is related to the noun κληρονομία "inheritance" which Paul used in 1:14 and 1:18. It reminds the Ephesians that they have a privileged position as part of God's chosen people.

In this context, the concept of "inheritance" is used figuratively, i.e. the inheritance consists of all the benefits of salvation. Gentile believers have the same rights and privileges as Jewish believers. The emphasis here is possibly on their entitlement to these privileges while, in 3:6d, the emphasis is on the actual participation in the blessings they receive.

It is difficult to express 3:6b propositionally, without giving the sense that the benefits that believers receive are material goods such as money or property. In the display, "spiritual blessings" is used in order to avoid this potential problem.

3:6c They all belong to the one community *of believers*, As with συγκληρονόμα in 3:6b, σύσσωμα "belonging to the same body" is another figurative expression. The metaphor that the church is Christ's body also occurs in 1:23; 2:16; 4:4, 16. The Gentile believers belong to this body as do the Jewish believers.

3:6d They all share in those things *which God promised to accomplish for his people*. In the Greek here, Paul uses the third adjective with a συν- prefix, συμμέτοχα τῆς ἐπαγγελίας "sharers together of the promise". God is the agent in the event represented by the abstract noun "promise" (i.e. "God promised"). Again, Paul is explaining that the Gentile believers, together with the Jewish believers, share in everything which God promised to believers. This contrasts with the previous state of the Gentiles, described in 2:12, as "strangers to the covenants of promise".

It is generally considered that Paul is here referring specifically to the promise of salvation. Since this involves action on the part of God it is expressed as "those things *which God* promised *to accomplish for his people*".

3:6e-f This [3:6b-d] is because they are united with Christ Jesus by means of *their believing* the gospel. Many commentators agree that both ἐν Χριστῷ Ἰησοῦ "in Christ Jesus" and διὰ τοῦ εὐαγγελίου "through the gospel" are attached to all three adjectives, συγκληρονόμα, σύσσωμα and συμμέτοχα in this verse, and not just τῆς ἐπαγγελίας "of the promise".

The cluster of propositions in 3:6e-f provides a reason for 3:6b-d. The Gentile believers are fellow-heirs, members of the same body and partakers of the promise, "*because they are united* with Christ Jesus". Their union with Christ is accomplished through the gospel, more precisely, "by means of *their believing* the gospel".

3:7a I became one who makes this gospel known, This verse begins with οὗ ἐγενήθην διάκονος "of which I became a minister/servant". The relative pronoun οὗ "of which" refers back to τοῦ εὐαγγελίου "the gospel" in 3:6.

In this context, the noun διάκονος "minister, servant" refers to someone whose work is to make known the gospel. In the display, therefore, this is expressed as "one who makes this gospel known".

3:7b because God acted graciously to me and gave me this work [3:7a] *to do*. The Greek expression here is κατὰ τὴν δωρεὰν τῆς χάριτος τοῦ θεοῦ τῆς δοθείσης μοι "according to the gift of God's grace which was given to me". There are two ways to understand the preposition κατά followed by a noun in the accusative case, as here:

1. It denotes a standard or norm and may be translated "in accordance with, in conformity with". The majority of commentaries support this option and it is also followed in NASB, NET, NRSV.

2. The relationship is one of means. See, for example, NIV, "I became a servant of this gospel *by* the gift of God's grace..." (italics mine). Most English versions seem to follow this option. See, for example, NCV, NLT, REB, TEV.

3. The relationship is one of reason. BDAG comments on the use of κατά for this relationship as follows,

Oft[en] the norm is at the same time the reason, so that *in accordance with* and *because of* are merged (p. 512.B5aδ).

This would seem to be appropriate in this context, especially when a verbal expression of "grace" is used.

There is also some discussion about the relationship between the nouns in the genitive construction τὴν δωρεὰν τῆς χάριτος "the gift of the grace". There are two options:

1. It is a genitive of apposition. In this case, "grace" itself is the gift.
2. The noun χάριτος "grace" may qualify τὴν δωρεάν "the gift". So the genitive expression would mean "the gracious gift". In this case, the genitive would describe the manner in which God gave the gift.

Whichever is preferred, the gift referred to is Paul's appointment to be the apostle to the Gentiles.

Here, Paul says two things about his ministry:

1. It is a free gift from God.
2. It involved the exercise of divine power.

It is the first of these which is represented by proposition 3:7b. The agent is God, since he is the one who gave the gift, and the gift is that he has chosen to appoint Paul to make known the gospel to the Gentiles.

As has been pointed out in earlier references to "grace", this abstract noun is difficult to represent propositionally. Here, it is expressed as "God acted graciously to me". The expression "gave me this work [3:7a] *to do*" then expresses the nature of the gift which Paul received.

3:7c *I am able to make known the gospel* by means of his powerfully enabling *me* In the phrase κατὰ τὴν ἐνέργειαν τῆς δυνάμεως αὐτοῦ "according to the working of his power", Paul again uses κατά followed by a noun in the accusative case, τὴν ἐνέργειαν "the working". There is the same disagreement among commentators about whether it indicates correspondence or means. The majority of versions follow the latter and this is followed in the display. This agrees with 1:19 and 3:20 where similar expressions occur.

The genitive construction τὴν ἐνέργειαν τῆς δυνάμεως αὐτοῦ "the working of his power" refers to God's working in and through Paul. This power enables Paul to perform the task to which God appointed him. It is the same power referred to in 1:19-20, the power which raised Christ from the dead.

Again, God is the agent. The event is ἐνέργειαν "working", and the abstract noun δυνάμεως "power" qualifies the event, i.e. "God worked powerfully". Since this refers to God's power working in Paul, this is expressed in the display as "his powerfully enabling me".

Most commentators consider that this second prepositional phrase in 3:7, κατὰ τὴν ἐνέργειαν τῆς δυνάμεως αὐτοῦ "according to the working of his power", is connected to the immediately preceding participle δοθείσης in the phrase τῆς δοθείσης μοι "[the gift of God's grace] having been given to me". Paul is then saying that it is by means of exercising his power that God gave Paul the ministry that he had prepared for him and, by means of that same power, God enables him to fulfil the responsibility which he has been given. Enablement is at least partially in focus here as a component of the gift since it is the appropriate result of the exercising of God's power. In propositionalising, this can be expressed by supplying, "*I am able to make known the gospel*" at the beginning of 3:7c, i.e. "*I am able to make known the gospel* by means of his powerfully enabling *me*".

BOUNDARIES AND COHERENCE

The initial boundary has been discussed in the section on Boundaries and Coherence for 3:1.

The final boundary is problematic. There are two suggestions:

1. It should be after 3:6. This is supported by the following points:

   a. The words διὰ τοῦ εὐαγγελίου "through the gospel" which end 3:6 and the relative pronoun οὗ "of which" (referring to "the gospel") which begins 3:7 could be functioning as a paragraph-connective tail-head link.

   b. There is formal parallelism between 3:2 and 3:7, with a reference to "ministry", which is a "gift of grace". These terms would then start both paragraphs.

   c. The subject matter of the two paragraphs 3:2-6 and 3:7-13 (which provide the grounds for 3:1) is different. In the first of these, the theme is concerned with "the mystery *revealed to* me". In the latter, the theme is concerned with "the message *proclaimed by* me".

2. It should be after 3:7. This is supported by the following points:

   a. 3:7 begins with the relative pronoun οὗ, referring to τοῦ εὐαγγελίου in 3:6. So, grammatically, this clause is dependent on the previous verse. Paul does clearly make such breaks elsewhere, e.g. Colossians 1:13 (Callow, 1983:44-45; 2002:23-24). However, this is not the most common pattern in Greek or in Paul's writings. This supports a paragraph break after 3:7, rather than before it.

   b. There are the following parallels between 3:8 and 3:2:

   ἐδόθη "was given" (3:8) parallels δοθείσης "given" (3:2)

   ἡ χάρις αὕτη "this grace" (3:8) parallels τῆς χάριτος τοῦ θεοῦ "the grace of God" (3:2)

   ἐμοί "to me" (3:8) parallels μοι "to me" (3:2)

This would support the analysis of 3:2 and 3:8 each beginning paragraphs.

In view of the stronger grammatical evidence for the second alternative, this is the analysis which is followed in the display.

PROMINENCE AND THEME

At the highest level this paragraph consists of two conjoined NUCLEI, as well as a restatement of the first NUCLEUS. The first NUCLEUS is 3:2-4. The second is 3:5-6. The first deals with the revelation of the secret-message to Paul, while the second deals with the content of the secret-message. Then in 3:7, Paul restates the information in 3:2-4. Since NUCLEUS$_1$ and NUCLEUS$_2$ are equally prominent, the theme statement for the paragraph is based on a summary of both units.

SECTION CONSTITUENT 3:8–13 (Expository Paragraph: Grounds₂ for 3:1)

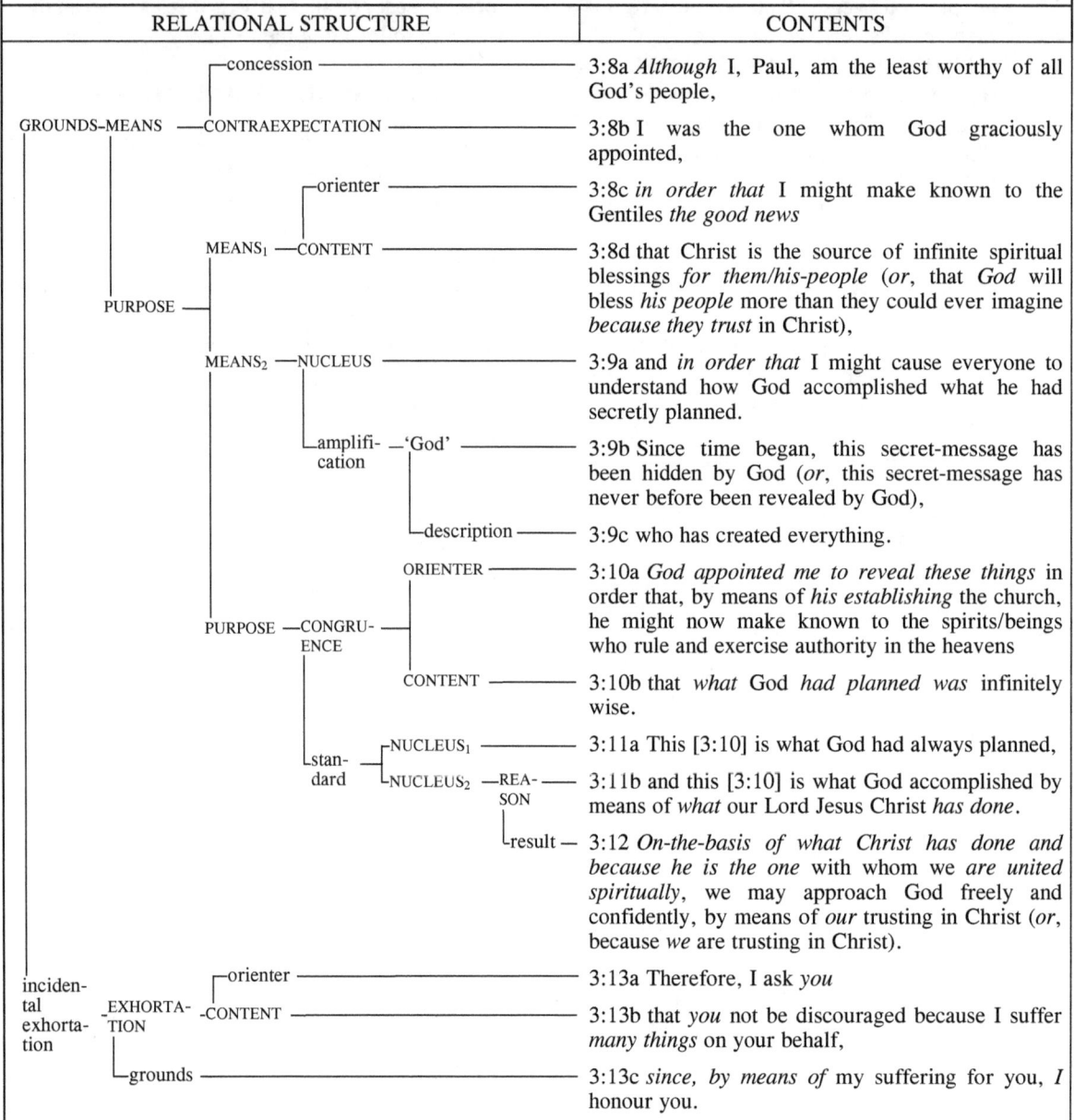

INTENT AND STRUCTURE

As with paragraph 3:2–7, Paul's intention in this paragraph is to encourage the Ephesian believers to accept what he says about what God has done and is doing for them (chapters 1 and 2) and to respond positively to his exhortations in chapters 4–6.

These verses are basically expository, but have expressive overtones, for example, in 3:8 where Paul refers to himself as τῷ ἐλαχιστοτέρῳ πάντων ἁγίων "less than the least of all the saints", and in 3:13 where he refers to ταῖς θλίψεσίν μου ὑπὲρ ὑμῶν "my afflictions on behalf of you". By these personal references, he hopes to strengthen his relationship with the Ephesian believers.

Structurally, this paragraph consists of five propositional clusters: 3:8a–b; 3:8c–d; 3:9; 3:10–12; 3:13. The first of these is in a MEANS-PURPOSE relationship with the second and third one. These, in turn, are in a MEANS-PURPOSE relationship with the fourth. The first four together make up the GROUNDS for the final cluster, 3:13, which is an *incidental exhortation*. It is not part of the thematic focus of the paragraph. See the note on 3:13.

NOTES

3:8 In this verse, Paul begins to expand what he said in the preceding verse about his appointment by God to bring the gospel to the Gentiles. There is a close connection between this verse and 3:7.

3:8a *Although* I, Paul, am the least worthy of all God's people, Propositions 3:8a–b provide the MEANS for 3:8c–12.

The pronoun ἐμοί "to me" is forefronted in the Greek text maintaining Paul's reference to himself and at this point intending to focus even more attention on himself. The use of the longer form ἐμοί would add to this focus. According to BDAG, p. 275, "In the oblique cases the longer forms ἐμοῦ, ἐμοί, ἐμέ are used as a rule where the main emphasis lies on the pron[oun]".

The noun ἁγίων "saints" refers to all believers, i.e. all those "called to be saints". See also 1 Corinthians 1:2; Romans 1:7.

The adjective ἐλαχιστοτέρῳ "less than the least" is a comparative formed from a superlative. It expresses Paul's sense of complete unworthiness. It is generally agreed that this sense of unworthiness stems from his previous persecution of the church. See 1 Corinthians 15:9, where he calls himself the "least of all the apostles, not fit to be called an apostle, because I persecuted the church of God". The exaggeration here in Eph. 3:8 can be expressed as "the least worthy".

3:8b I was the one whom God graciously appointed, It is generally agreed that the referent of ἡ χάρις αὕτη "this grace" is τὴν δωρεὰν τῆς χάριτος τοῦ θεοῦ "the gift of the grace of God" in 3:7.

In the English versions, χάρις "grace" here is translated as, for example:

"I was chosen for this *special joy*" (NLT)
"God was *kind* and chose me" (CEV)
"To me...he has granted *the privilege* of..." (REB)
"God gave me this *gift*" (NCV)

(italics mine in each quotation to indicate the specific translation for "grace").

In many versions, however, the word "grace" is retained. The sense of God's special favour being conferred on Paul and Paul's own sense of privilege need to be conveyed here. In the display, this is expressed as "I was the one whom God graciously appointed". In conjunction with 3:8a, which stresses Paul's unworthiness to be chosen for this task, the use of the qualifying adverb "graciously" provides part of the meaning, although it fails to convey the full sense.

The focus that Paul places on himself is shown in the display as "I was the one" in initial position.

The relationship between 3:8a and 3:8b is one of concession-contraexpectation. It would be against expectation for someone so unworthy to be entrusted by God with such an important task as making the gospel known to the Gentiles.

3:8c *in order that* I might make known to the Gentiles *the good news* "To the Gentiles" is forefronted in the Greek text for emphasis. That Paul should make the gospel known *to the Gentiles* is the purpose for which God chose and appointed Paul (3:8b).

3:8d that Christ is the source of infinite spiritual blessings *for them/his-people* (*or,* that God will bless *his people* more than they could ever imagine *because they trust* in Christ), In the genitive construction, τὸ ἀνεξιχνίαστον πλοῦτος τοῦ Χριστοῦ "the unsearchable riches of Christ", clearly the "riches" are spiritual and not material. The riches are all the spiritual blessings available to believers through Christ. In translating this expression, care must be taken to avoid the sense of "riches" being material wealth.

In order to bring out the relevance of this statement to the Gentiles, it seems necessary to express not only the spiritual richness and perfection of Christ, but also the sense that the blessings which flow from Christ's nature are available to all his people and, therefore, to them.

The adjective ἀνεξιχνίαστος literally means "not to be tracked out". In this context, it is translated in various ways, e.g. "unsearchable" (NIV), "infinite" (TEV), "unfathomable" (REB), "incalculable" (Phillips). It refers to something which is impossible for a human mind to understand.

It is difficult to express the sense of this genitive construction without using an abstract noun like "blessings". If such a noun can be used, then, "Christ is the source of infinite spiritual blessings *for his people*" might represent the meaning.

If not, another possibility would be, "*God* will bless *his people* more than they could ever imagine *because they trust* in Christ". Or for the final reason clause, "*because of what* Christ *has done for them*".

3:9a and *in order that* I might cause everyone to understand how God accomplished what he had secretly planned. The initial καί "and" may signal one of the following:

1. Co-ordination, i.e. the two infinitives, εὐαγγελίσασθαι "to proclaim" (3:8) and φωτίσαι, "to give light to" (3:9), are co-ordinate, with the latter stating a second aspect of God's appointed work for Paul.
2. A generic-specific relationship, with φωτίσαι stating one specific aspect of preaching to the Gentiles.

The majority of the commentaries favour the first alternative. This makes good sense. As Stott points out,

> ...the thought shifts from the content of the message (good news) [3:8] to the condition of those to whom it is proclaimed (in the darkness of ignorance) [3:9] (p. 121).

The verb φωτίζω literally means "give light to, illuminate". But here, as in 1:18, it is used figuratively to mean "cause something to be fully known", "reveal something" or "enlighten someone spiritually". In 2 Corinthians 4:4, Paul speaks about "the light of the gospel". This light was knowledge and so "to illuminate" means to teach. In the display, this has been expressed as "cause to understand".

There are two possible manuscript readings here:

1. Many manuscripts have πάντας "all" following the verb as direct object, i.e. "to enlighten *all* people".
2. Other manuscripts do not have πάντας "all". The expression τίς ἡ οἰκονομία is then the object of φωτίσαι, i.e. "to reveal what is the plan...".

In fact, the general sense is very much the same with either reading, since the people enlightened are at least implicit in the context.

If the word "all" is included (i.e. the first option is followed), a further decision must be made as to whom it refers. There are two possibilities:

a. It refers to "all the Gentiles".
b. It refers to "all-people/everyone", both Jews and Gentiles.

As 3:10 speaks about the wideness of the proclamation, the option b, "everyone", seems more likely and so has been followed in the display.

If πάντας is not included (i.e. option 2 is followed), "people", or a similar word, will need to be provided in languages where a direct or indirect object is obligatory to complete the case frame (i.e. indicating the people enlightened, in this context).

Most commentators consider οἰκονομία in the phrase ἡ οἰκονομία τοῦ μυστηρίου to mean "plan, arrangement", the phrase literally meaning "the plan of the mystery". It is also generally agreed that God is the intended agent as author of this plan. What is being referred to is the accomplishment of God's secret plan, i.e. how the content of the secret-message was put into effect by God.

3:9b-c The rest of 3:9 is an amplification of 3:9a.

3:9b Since time began, this secret-message has been hidden by God (*or*, this secret-message has never before been revealed by God), The Greek phrase ἀπὸ τῶν αἰώνων literally means "from the ages". Since ἀπό, with a time reference, usually means "from the start of, since", the sense of the phrase here is probably "ever since there were any ages", "since time began".

In some languages, it might not be possible to say that time began. So it may be necessary to find an alternative way to express this, e.g. "this secret-message has never before been revealed by God".

The phrase ἐν τῷ θεῷ can mean either "in God" (most commentaries and versions) or "by God" (see Louw and Nida 90.6, and the discussion on this subject in Bratcher and Nida, p. 78). God retained the secret-message in his own thinking, causing it to remain concealed from humanity. In either case, God is the agent, the one effecting the concealment.

3:9c who has created everything. The phrase τῷ τὰ πάντα κτίσαντι "the one all (things) having created" is generally regarded as being in apposition to "God" (3:9b), i.e. a comment on, or description of, him. However, commentators do discuss its implications. The most straightforward implication is that, as the Creator, God has a plan for what he has made. Part of that plan is the redemption of humanity. At various moments in history, he chooses to reveal details of this plan, first to the Jews and now to the Gentiles.

The additional words, "through Jesus Christ", are found in *The Greek New Testament according to the Majority Text*. However, they are omitted in most modern versions. It is not given as a variant reading in UBSGNT, although Metzger mentions it in *A Textual Commentary on the Greek New Testament* (p. 535).

3:10a *God appointed me to reveal these things* in order that, There is general agreement that the initial ἵνα "in order that" indicates purpose, rather than result. It may relate back in one of three ways:

1. It relates back to εὐαγγελίσασθαι "to proclaim" (3:8) and φωτίσαι "to give light to" (3:9), but also includes the idea that this was by God's grace, i.e. God had given Paul the grace to preach and to enlighten, in order that.... See, for example, Hodge (pp. 172-173), Lincoln (p. 185).
2. It relates back to the mystery that was hidden (3:9), i.e. the mystery was hidden in order that.... See, for example, REB, TEV.
3. It relates back to the immediately preceding participle, κτίσαντι "having created", i.e. God created all things in order that....

The third option is the least likely, since the participle κτίσαντι is in a relative clause. Option 1 seems to make the best sense.

The infinitives, "to make known" (3:8) and "to enlighten" (3:9), express the main idea in the clauses in which they occur. Therefore, 3:10a–b relates back to the infinitives in 3:8 and 3:9, giving the purpose of both, and bringing to a conclusion this portion of the paragraph. Paul is speaking about his call to apostleship, and the grace given to him to reveal the plan of God to all people, in order that, through the church, God's wisdom might be made known to "the powers in the heavens". This is a final purpose of the revelation of the mystery.

by means of *his establishing* the church, Paul simply says διὰ τῆς ἐκκλησίας "through/by-means-of the church" without being more specific. Therefore, there is no indication as to whether it refers to,

1. The church's existence as a body of Jewish and Gentile believers reconciled to Christ.
2. What the church does in proclaiming the gospel.

However, the first alternative seems more appropriate since only Paul is referred to as proclaiming the gospel in this context. That Jewish and Gentile believers make up one redeemed body is more remarkable than the Church's proclaiming the gospel. God makes known his wisdom by the very act of bringing the church into existence. The church, drawn from many different nations, but united in Christ, living in love and unity will demonstrate God's wisdom to those "who rule and exercise authority in the heavens".

he might now make known There are two interwoven discussion points here. Firstly, who the agent in the passive verb γνωρισθῇ "might be made known" should be. Secondly, how this agency affects the prepositional phrase διὰ τῆς ἐκκλησίας "through/by-means-of the church".

There are three main views:

1. It is the church itself which makes known the many-sided wisdom of God to "the powers in the heavenlies". See, for example, Eadie (pp. 232, 234).
2. It is Paul who does so by the agency of the church. See, for example, Hodge (pp. 172-173).
3. It is God who is the agent in this event. He works out his purpose by means of the church. This is the majority view. See, for example, Best (p. 322), Lenski (p. 481), O'Brien (p. 248).

Although Paul is active in preaching the gospel and revealing how God's hidden purpose is being put into effect, ultimately it is only God who can enable people to know the complexity and variety of his own wisdom. It seems best, then, to follow the majority view, and so "he" referring to God is stated as the agent of "make known" in the display.

The temporal adverb νῦν "now" and the verb γνωρισθῇ "might be made known" contrast with "from the beginning" and "having been hidden" in 3:9.

to the spirits/beings who rule and exercise authority in the heavens In the Greek, the words used here are ἀρχαί "rulers, authorities" and ἐξουσίαι "authorities". See the notes on 1:21, where these terms also occur. The terms also occur in 6:12.

The main point of discussion here is what kind of beings are being referred to. There are three possibilities:

1. They refer to "good" spiritual beings, that is, those who are subject to God. See, for example, Bratcher and Nida (p. 78), Hendriksen (pp. 158-159).
2. They refer to "evil" spiritual beings, that is, Satan and his angels/demons. See, for example, Lincoln (pp. 185-186).
3. They refer to all spiritual beings, good and evil. See, for example, Hoehner (p. 460), O'Brien (pp. 246-247), Stott (pp. 124-125).

The expression "rulers and authorities" itself is neutral. It is normally the context which determines whether they are good or bad.

However, there is nothing in this immediate context to indicate which type is being referred to here. The expression ἐν τοῖς ἐπουρανίοις "in the heavenlies" describes the place where both good and evil spirit beings live, and implies that they both attempt to influence human beings. In 6:12, the expression clearly refers to evil spirit beings. However, in this context, as in 1:21, there is no way to be certain whether good or evil beings is referred to. So it is best to use a neutral term such as "spirits/beings who rule and exercise power/authority in the heavens".

See the notes on 1:3 for ἐν τοῖς ἐπουρανίοις "in the heavenlies". This expression also occurs in 1:20; 2:6 and 6:12.

3:10b that *what* God *had planned was* infinitely wise. The genitive phrase ἡ πολυποίκιλος σοφία τοῦ θεοῦ "the many-sided wisdom of God" provides the content of "might be made known" (3:10a).

The compound adjective πολυποίκιλος "manifold" occurs only here in the New Testament, although the simple form ποίκιλος "varied, many, several" occurs elsewhere. Here it emphasises the diversity and greatness of God's wisdom.

In the context, this wisdom refers to the content of the wisdom. It may be expressed propositionally as, "*what* God *had planned was* infinitely wise" or "God *was* infinitely wise *in what he had planned*".

3:11a This [3:10] is what God had always planned, How the preposition κατά "according to" relates to the rest of the verse needs to be considered. Commentators suggest two possibilities:

1. It relates back to ἡ σοφία τοῦ θεοῦ "the wisdom of God" (3:10b) and means that what God in his wisdom had planned was in conformity with his eternal purpose.
2. It relates back to γνωρισθῇ "might be made known" (3:10a) and indicates that the revelation of what God in his wisdom had planned was in conformity with his eternal purpose.

The latter makes better sense. It recalls 1:5 and 1:11. See the notes on those verses. This would indicate a relation of standard-CONGRUENCE with 3:10.

The genitive construction πρόθεσιν τῶν αἰώνων "the purpose of the ages" is generally regarded as defining the relation of time to God's purpose, i.e. τῶν αἰώνων is equivalent to the adjective "eternal", and the whole construction can be translated "the eternal purpose". The one who "purposes/plans" is God.

3:11b and this [3:10] is what God accomplished by means of *what* our Lord Jesus Christ *has done*. The relative pronoun ἥν "which" at the beginning of 3:11b refers back to "purpose/plan" (3:11a), which, in turn, refers back to 3:10. However, the whole relative clause ἥν ἐποίησεν ἐν τῷ Χριστῷ Ἰησοῦ τῷ κυρίῳ ἡμῶν "which he formed/accomplished in Christ Jesus our Lord" may have one of two meanings in this context. This will depend on the sense which the verb ποιέω "do, make" is understood. The whole relative clause, therefore, may mean:

1. The purpose which God formed/planned in Christ Jesus our Lord.
2. The purpose which God accomplished/carried-out in Christ Jesus our Lord.

The commentators are divided about this, but the second alternative is more appropriate in the context, for the following reasons:

a. When Paul uses the verb ποιέω elsewhere in Ephesians, he means "accomplishing" a purpose. See 2:3, 14, 15; 3:20; 6:6, 8, 9.

b. The reference to ἐν τῷ Χριστῷ Ἰησοῦ τῷ κυρίῳ ἡμῶν "in Christ Jesus our Lord" suggests the "accomplishment" of God's plan in Christ's sacrificial death for humanity, not simply its formation.
c. The parallel expression in 1:11 relates to God "accomplishing" his purpose.

God is the agent in the accomplishment of his plan, but the phrase "in Christ Jesus our Lord" indicates that it was in the person and work of Christ that God's plan was accomplished. This is expressed in the display as "by means of *what* Christ Jesus our Lord *has done*".

3:12 On-the-basis of what Christ has done and because he is the one with whom we *are united spiritually,* It is difficult to pinpoint how 3:12 relates to what precedes. Paul has been speaking on a wider scale about causing God's infinite wisdom to be made known to all people and all angelic powers. Now, the focus returns to Paul and the Ephesian believers and what Christ has done for them all personally.

Paul's train of thought seems to be: since it is through what Christ has done that all these things have been accomplished, those who are united with Christ spiritually and trust in him, can be sure that God will accept them. This is reminiscent of 2:18, "for through him we have access...to the Father".

The phrase ἐν ᾧ "in whom" refers back to "Christ Jesus our Lord" in 3:11 and, as in chapters 1 and 2, means "united with Christ Jesus our Lord" in the spiritual sense. In this context the phrase ἐν ᾧ also represents a reason, i.e. *because* Christ is the one with whom we are united spiritually, we have freedom of access to God. The "we" here is, of course, inclusive.

we may approach God freely and confidently, Semantically, there is only one event in this part of the verse, ἔχομεν...προσαγωγήν "we have access", freely translated as "we may approach *God/God's-presence*". The noun προσαγωγήν "access" is used especially when the one being approached is of high rank. In this verse, God is the one who is being approached.

The first discussion point among commentators is how the noun παρρησίαν "boldness" relates to the main event ἔχομεν...προσαγωγήν "we have access". There are two possibilities:

1. The nouns, "boldness" and "access", form a doublet (hendiadys) which means "have-access/can-approach with boldness".
2. The nouns, "boldness" and "access", are separate concepts, i.e. "we are bold" and "we have access". The commentators who support this option do so mainly because they follow Greek manuscripts which have the definite article before both words.

The variant reading with the article before both words is not mentioned in the UBSGNT, though it appears in the *The Greek New Testament according to the Majority Text*. In the first option, παρρησίαν "boldness" semantically qualifies the main event "approach" and may be expressed as an adverb "boldly, confidently, freely". It refers to a confident attitude in which someone who is reconciled to God can approach him. This is very appropriate in the context.

The second discussion point is how the phrase ἐν πεποιθήσει "in confidence" qualifies προσαγωγή "access". Here there is general agreement that it also qualifies the main event, strengthening the idea of the believer being able to approach God freely and confidently.

by means of *our* trusting in Christ (*or, because we are trusting in Christ*). In the genitive construction διὰ τῆς πίστεως αὐτοῦ "through the faith of him", it is clear that αὐτοῦ "of him" refers to Christ.

The relationship between the noun τῆς πίστεως "the faith" and the pronoun αὐτοῦ "of him" may be understood in two ways:

1. It is an objective genitive, that is, Christ is the *object* of faith. Therefore, the meaning is "through faith in him".
2. It is a subjective genitive, that is, Christ is the *subject* of faith. Therefore, "faith" is used in the sense of "faithfulness", i.e. "because of his faithfulness".

Option 1 has the greater commentary support.
The preposition διά "through" may signal:

1. A means relationship. Here this would refer to the means by which we have access to God, i.e. by means of faith in Christ.
2. A reason relationship. Here this would refer to the reason that we have access to God, i.e. because of our faith in Christ.

The majority of commentators choose means here. But this may well be a place where there is no real difference between reason and means. In some languages words indicating reason would be natural here.

3:13 This cluster of propositions consists of an EXHORTATION with its orienter (3:13a), its CONTENT (3:13b) and the grounds for the exhortation (3:13c).

The relationship between this cluster and what precedes is difficult to establish. There are two main possibilities.

1. 3:13 provides a conclusion (in the form of a request) to 3:12, "since we have freedom to approach God through Christ, I ask...".
2. 3:13 provides a conclusion (in the form of a request) to the digression started in 3:2, "since God has appointed me to this task I ask you not to be discouraged because I suffer on your behalf".

Although it is possible grammatically to connect this verse with 3:12, it is less likely as it would then be connected to a secondary thought. Therefore, the second option seems to be the most appropriate. It brings us back to the wider and more prominent reference to Paul's commission to the Gentiles and, hence, his being prisoner of Jesus Christ on their behalf.

Normally exhortations (here, a request) are naturally prominent. However, here the exhortation is of secondary importance to the GROUNDS (3:8–12), since the function of the paragraph, along with the preceding paragraph (3:2–7), is to provide the grounds for Paul's statement in 3:1, that he is a prisoner of Jesus Christ on their behalf.

An alternative analysis of this verse (though not pursued in the notes that follow on 3:13a–d) is,

> 3:13a I ask *you* 13b that *although* I suffer *many things* on your behalf, 13c you *should* not become discouraged *because this is so,* 13d *but* you *should regard yourselves/the-church as* being honoured by this [3:13b].

In this alternative analysis, propositions 3:13b and 3:13c–d are regarded as being in a concession-CONTRAEXPECTATION relationship, 3:13c being a negative exhortation, "you *should* not become discouraged *because this is so*", and 3:13d a positive one, "*regard yourselves as* being honoured by this". The "this" refer to "that I suffer on your behalf".

3:13a Therefore, I ask *you* The versions indicate varying degrees of urgency in their translation of the verb αἰτοῦμαι: "I desire", "I ask", "I beg", "I pray". It is also possible to represent the request by some such word as "please", e.g. "please do not be discouraged".

In the Greek text there is nothing in this verse to indicate to whom Paul is making his request. The verse simply continues with "not to lose heart in the afflictions of me, on behalf of you", which does not indicate who is not to lose heart. There are three possibilities:

1. Paul is asking *God* not to let *the Ephesians* lose heart.
2. Paul is asking *the Ephesians* not to lose heart.
3. Paul is asking *God* that he, *Paul*, should not lose heart.

There is nothing in the context which suggests that God is the one to whom the request is being made and Paul mentions nowhere else that he personally is discouraged. So option 2 seems the most likely and is supported by the majority of commentators. It is in keeping with the tenor of the passage that Paul should refer to the possibility of their losing heart. Furthermore, what follows, "which is your glory", can be seen as a motivation for them not to lose heart. Therefore, option 2 is followed in the display.

3:13b that *you* not be discouraged because I suffer *many things* on your behalf, The abstract noun θλίψις "oppression, affliction" may refer to distress brought on by either outward circumstances or spiritual affliction. Here, it is the former. The event represented here is "to suffer" or "to be afflicted" and the phrase ταῖς θλίψεσίν μου "the afflictions of me" refers to what Paul is suffering physically as a prisoner.

The relationship indicated by the ἐν "in" in the phrase ἐν ταῖς θλίψεσίν μου "in my afflictions" may be:

1. The circumstances in which the Ephesians might have become discouraged, i.e. "when I [Paul] am suffering".
2. The reason-for/cause-of the Ephesians' possible discouragement, i.e. "because I [Paul] am suffering".

The latter alternative is followed in the display since it makes good sense in the context and is followed in most versions.

The phrase ὑπὲρ ὑμῶν "on your behalf" continues the focus of the phrase ὑπὲρ ὑμῶν ἐθνῶν "on behalf of you Gentiles" (3:1) and the εἰς ὑμᾶς "for you" (3:2). It ends this section by recalling the close relationship between Paul and the Ephesians.

3:13c *since, by means of* my suffering for you, *I* honour you. The feminine singular relative pronoun ἥτις "which" in the expression ἥτις ἐστὶν δόξα ὑμῶν "which is your glory" may refer to:

1. The feminine plural ταῖς θλίψεσίν μου "my afflictions", i.e. "the afflictions, instead of being a discouragement to you, are a glory to you".
2. The infinitival expression μὴ ἐγκακεῖν "not despair", i.e. "not despairing is a glory to you".

The first option is the majority view and makes the better sense. Paul did not want the Ephesians to consider the afflictions which he suffered because of his ministry to them as a disgrace to them and, therefore, a discouragement. Rather, he wanted them to understand that they were "a glory/honour". This is because they, the Gentiles, and their inclusion in the church, are proof of Paul's successful labours.

Therefore, "which" refers to "I suffer for your benefit" (3:13b). It has the force of an explanatory or motivational grounds, i.e. "do not become discouraged by my sufferings, since they are your glory".

It is generally agreed that δόξα ὑμῶν "your glory" refers to some present benefit to the church, rather than the final glorification of the church. It demonstrates the value placed on the church by Paul and, ultimately, by God.

Thus the clause "which is your glory" provides a grounds for 3:13a–b. It is the basis for Paul's exhortation to the Ephesians not to become discouraged.

BOUNDARIES AND COHERENCE

See the sections on Boundaries and Coherence for 3:2–7 and 3:1–13.

PROMINENCE AND THEME

In this paragraph, Paul develops the theme introduced in the final verse of the preceding paragraph (3:7), i.e. his appointment by God to make known the riches of the gospel to the Gentiles.

Normally an exhortation is naturally prominent. However, here it is the GROUNDS (3:8–12) which is prominent, since it develops the main theme of 3:1–13, Paul's commission to the Gentiles. The theme statement, therefore, is based on the nuclear GROUNDS unit.

This nuclear unit consists of a MEANS followed by two propositional clusters denoting PURPOSE. These two act as the MEANS FOR 3:10–12, which is the final PURPOSE.

SUBPART CONSTITUENT 3:14–21 (Expressive Section: Response to 2:1–3:13)

THEME: I pray that the Holy Spirit may empower you, that you may experience Christ's infinite love and that God may cause you to be perfect, just as he is perfect. May he be glorified through the church and through Christ Jesus forever. Amen.

MACROSTRUCTURE	CONTENTS
NUCLEUS₁ (Prayer)	3:14–19 I pray that God may empower you by means of his Holy Spirit, and that you may be able to understand and experience how greatly Christ loves us, and that God may cause you to be perfect, just as he is perfect.
NUCLEUS₂ (Responsive Doxology)	3:20–21 May our infinite God be glorified through the church and through Christ Jesus forever. Amen.

INTENT AND MACROSTRUCTURE

The 3:14–21 constituent provides a RESPONSE to 2:1–3:13, which is the NUCLEUS of the first half of the BODY of the letter to the Ephesians. It might even be regarded as a RESPONSE to everything which precedes it in the BODY, 1:3–3:13. It consists of an intercessory prayer (3:14–19) and a doxology (3:20–21). They are co-ordinate, connected by δέ (3:20), which typically begins a doxology, probably because of its distinctive formulaic nature, style and semantic content (cf. Rom. 16:25–27; Phil. 4:20; 1 Tim. 1:17).

At 3:20, Paul turns from praying to God on behalf of the Ephesian believers (3:14–19), to praising God (3:20–21), in response to references to God's power and perfection in his prayer. Whereas δέ normally occurs between co-ordinate units, i.e. units which do not have a cause-effect relation between them, here a cause-effect relation is quite evident semantically. This is a situation where a choice is possible between two different types of relationships. Since the co-ordinate relation appears to be the primary one, the labelling in the display is NUCLEUS₁, NUCLEUS₂, but the latter is further labelled "Responsive Doxology".

Probably Paul was intending to begin praying in 3:1, but he digressed in order to give an account of his calling and ministry (3:2–13). He resumes the prayer in 3:14.

In both the prayer and the doxology, Paul's intent is to enable the Ephesians to understand the greatness of God's power working on their behalf and the possibility of being "filled with all the fulness of God" (3:19).

He shows his concern and love for them by praying for them. This should encourage them to join him in his outburst of praise in 3:20–21 and then to respond positively to his exhortations in 4:1–6:20.

The paragraph 3:20–21 also provides motivational information which acts as a basis for the exhortations in 4:1–6:20. See the Intent and Structure note for 3:20–21.

The BODY began in 1:3 with Paul's praising God for the many blessings God has lavished on believers. The first half ends with this further expression of praise.

Consisting as it does of a prayer and a doxology, this is an expressive unit. However, as is the case with the prayer of 1:15–23, it has strong expository characteristics, as Paul brings to the attention of the Ephesians the extent of God's power and how it affects them as individuals and the church as a body.

BOUNDARIES AND COHERENCE

The initial boundary has been discussed in the section on Boundaries and Coherence for 3:1–13. The final boundary has been discussed in the section on Boundaries and Coherence for 1:3–3:21.

Both the paragraphs which make up this unit focus on God's power working in the lives of believers (3:16, 20), and on his glory (3:16, 21).

PROMINENCE AND THEME

Since the prayer and the doxology are co-ordinate NUCLEI, the theme statement for 3:14–21 is based on prominent elements of both.

SECTION CONSTITUENT 3:14–19
(Expressive Paragraph: Nucleus₁ of 3:14–21 [Prayer])

THEME: I pray that God may empower you by means of his Holy Spirit, and that you may be able to understand and experience how greatly Christ loves us, and that God may cause you to be perfect, just as he is perfect.

RELATIONAL STRUCTURE	CONTENTS
ORIENTER — 'Father'	3:14 Because *God has done all* this [2:1-22] *for you Gentiles*, I kneel *and pray* [MTY] to *God our* Father.
— description	3:15 *He is the one* who is the Father of the whole family *of believers* which is in heaven and which is on earth.
CONTENT₁ — MEANS	3:16a *I pray* that God may empower you with his own divine power (*or*, to the extent of his own divine power) by means of his *Holy* Spirit,
— purpose — NUCLEUS	3:16b in order that you become strong in your hearts and in your minds,
amplification — RESULT	3:17a *that is*, that Christ may always be in your hearts (*or*, may always be with you spiritually),
means	3:17b by means of your believing *in him*.
— reason	3:17c *I pray* that, because you love *Christ* steadfastly and faithfully,
CONTENT₂ — RESULT — NUCLEUS	3:18 you may be able, together with all *other* believers, to comprehend how greatly Christ loves *us/his-people* [MET],
amplification — CONTRA-EXPECTATION	3:19a and that you may be able to know/experience how greatly Christ loves *us*,
concession	3:19b *even though* it is impossible to understand fully how much he loves *us*.
CONTENT₃ — CONGRUENCE	3:19c *I pray* that *God may cause* you to be perfect,
standard	3:19d just as he is perfect.

INTENT AND STRUCTURE

In this paragraph, Paul resumes the prayer which he began in 3:1 in response to the discourse of 2:1–22. In the intercession of 3:14–19, he shows his concern for the Ephesians by praying for them. This serves to validate his exhortations to them in chapters 4–6.

This paragraph consists of a prayer which is a restatement and development of the prayer of 1:15–23. In the former, having praised God for all the blessings believers have received through Christ, Paul prays that they might be enabled to understand the extent of these blessings. Here, he prays that God's wonderful plan of salvation, which he has been explaining to them, might be fulfilled in their experience, that they might understand and experience God's enabling power and love, and be "filled to all the fulness of God".

Commentators suggest several different analyses of the structure of this paragraph. Their suggestions depend on how many petitions they recognise in 3:16–19. This varies from one to five, according to the following considerations:

1. Whether the pairs of infinitives are separate petitions or not:

   κραταιωθῆναι "to be strengthened" (3:16)
   κατοικῆσαι "to dwell" (3:17)
   καταλαβέσθαι "to comprehend" (3:18)
   γνῶναί "to know" (3:19)

2. Whether the expression "being rooted and grounded in love" (3:17) supports 3:17, 3:18 or is itself a separate petition. It would then make the fifth petition.

The best support is for either three or four petitions.

If there are three petitions, they would be as follows (see Kopesec, pp. 40–41; also O'Brien, pp. 256, 260, 265):

1st Petition:
ἵνα subjunctive...infinitive...infinitive (16, 17) [SSA display CONTENT₁]:
ἵνα δῷ "that he may grant"...κραταιωθῆναι "to be strengthened"...κατοικῆσαι "to dwell"

2nd Petition:
ἵνα subjunctive infinitive...infinitive (18, 19a) [display CONTENT₂]:
ἵνα ἐξισχύσητε "that you may be able" καταλαβέσθαι "to comprehend"... γνῶναί "to know"

3rd Petition:
ἵνα subjunctive (19b) [display CONTENT₃]:
ἵνα πληρωθῆτε "that you may be filled"

If there are four petitions, they are linked to the key words "strength", "love", "knowledge" and "fulness". See, for example, Stott (p. 134). The first three petitions build up to a climax with the final, i.e. that believers might be "filled to all the fulness of God".

The display follows the analysis of three petitions.

NOTES

3:14 Because *God has done all* **this [2:1–22]** *for you Gentiles,* The majority view is followed here, i.e. this is a repetition of the τούτου χάριν in 3:1 and τούτου refers back to the same material as there.

I kneel *and pray* Literally, the Greek means "I bend my knees", i.e. actually kneeling in prayer. Figuratively, the posture of prayer is being used for the act of prayer itself. It also may indicate the humility of the one praying. Most versions include the posture adopted for prayer, i.e. kneeling, and the act of praying. See REB "I kneel in prayer", JB "I pray, kneeling", JBP "I fall on my knees...and pray".

to *God our* **Father.** Some manuscripts have in addition, "of our Lord Jesus Christ", but most versions and commentators omit this, since it is not found in the oldest manuscripts. UBSGNT gives the shorter reading a B rating, i.e. it has been considered to be almost certain. However, if a translation in the dominant language in the area follows the longer reading, it may be better to maintain this in the translation. In either case, it is a good idea to include a footnote with the alternative reading.

3:15 *He is the one* **who is the Father of the whole family** *of believers* **which is in heaven and which is on earth.** The ἐξ οὗ "of whom" refers to τὸν πατέρα "the Father" in 3:14, the one from whom the believers take their name.

The word πατριά is a collective term for the descendants of the same father, immediate or remote. In Luke 2:4, the same word is used for "the family of David" and, in Acts 3:25, for "all the families of the earth". These are the only other occurrences of the word in the New Testament.

Here, there is probably a play on words in the Greek between πατήρ "father" in the preceding verse and πατριά "family/fatherhood" in this verse, showing that the latter derives from the former. It is usually not possible to keep this play on words in translation, although some English versions attempt to do so by using "fatherhood" rather than "family", cf. "the Father *(from whom all fatherhood...derives its name)*" JBP (italics mine).

Here, πᾶσα πατριά has two possible meanings:

1. "Every family". In this case, Paul is referring to God as the universal Father of all living creatures. See TEV, REB, NRSV.
2. "The whole family". In this case, Paul is referring to those who are redeemed, the whole family of believers. See KJV, NIV.

The first alternative uses πᾶσα in its more common sense "all, every" (Greek has another word ὅλη which means "whole"). The phrase ἐν οὐρανοῖς καὶ ἐπὶ γῆς "in heaven and on earth" then would refer to groups of people on earth and angels in heaven.

However, the second alternative seems the more appropriate in the context. The main thrust of the paragraph is God as the spiritual Father, not God the Creator. Also, the focus in these chapters as a whole is on the union of believers both Jewish and Gentile in one body/family, the church. The phrase ἐν οὐρανοῖς καὶ ἐπὶ γῆς "in heaven and on earth" would refer to those believers who are in heaven and those who are still here on earth.

There is some discussion about the meaning of ἐξ οὗ...ὀνομάζεται "from whom...is named". Whether πᾶσα πατριά is understood as "every family" or "the whole family", the one to whom they owe their existence is God. So they "derive their name from him". A further option put forward by commentators is that ὀνομάζεται in this context means the same as "is constituted" or "exists". The basis for this sense of the word is that "name" frequently stands for identity or character. He is the one from whom the existence of the whole family in heaven and on earth comes and so is its Father. This is the meaning represented in the display.

3:16a–17b This propositional cluster expresses the content of the first petition of Paul's prayer. The initial ἵνα "that" introduces it.

3:16a *I pray* This is not present in the Greek text of 3:16a but is understood and is, therefore, made explicit in the display.

that God may empower you The agent of δῷ "he may give" is God. The object of the verb is the aorist passive infinitive κραταιωθῆναι "to be strengthened". This subjunctive verb+infinitive construction is, in effect, a causative, which could be rendered as "empower". This then is how it is propositionalised in the display.

with his own divine power (*or*, to the extent of his own divine power) The phrase κατὰ τὸ πλοῦτος τῆς δόξης αὐτοῦ "according to the riches of the glory of him" defines δῷ "he may give" more closely.

In a similar passage in Colossians 1:11, Paul refers to the Colossians as being strengthened κατὰ τὸ κράτος τῆς δόξης αὐτοῦ "according to the might of the glory of him". A type of comparison is involved, with the divine might providing the standard by which their being strengthened is to be measured. Callow (2002:28; cf. 1983:52) suggests that "the limit of the strengthening is set by God's might; in other words, there is no measurable limit". He expresses this as "to the extent of the mighty power".

Here, the phrase could be expressed as "to the extent of the riches of his glory". But what does this mean? "Glory" is a difficult concept to express, referring, as it does, to the absolute perfection of the character of God in all its aspects. Possibly, in this context, since it is manifested in his power to give spiritual strength to the Ephesian believers, it could be expressed as "with his own divine power" or "to the extent of his own divine power".

by means of his *Holy* Spirit, The preposition διά "through" indicates the means by which God empowers them, i.e. by means of his Holy Spirit.

3:16b in order that This proposition is in a purpose relation with 3:16a which provides the MEANS for it.

you become strong See the note on 3:16a.

in your hearts and in your minds, What is being stated is that the strengthening referred to is an inner, spiritual strengthening and not a strengthening of the body. Since it is difficult to translate "spiritual" or "spiritually" in some languages, the sense might be expressed in the display as "become strong in your hearts and minds" in order to express the inward nature of the strengthening.

3:17a *that is*, that Christ may always be in your hearts (*or*, may always be with you spiritually), There are a number of different analyses with regard to the relationship indicated by the infinitive κατοικῆσαι "to dwell" in the clause κατοικῆσαι τὸν Χριστὸν διὰ τῆς πίστεως ἐν ταῖς καρδίαις ὑμῶν "that Christ may dwell in your hearts by faith" and the preceding context. The two which have the greatest support are as follows:

1. This clause is grammatically co-ordinate to the previous infinitive κραταιωθῆναι "to be strengthened" and the clause it governs, but semantically it is a definition or amplification of that clause.
2. This clause gives the purpose of the previous infinitive κραταιωθῆναι "to be strengthened".

The two options are equally possible in the context.

There are a number of parallels between 3:16b and 3:17a–b, for example, the "indwelling of Christ in the heart" is equated with "being strengthened through the Spirit in the inner person". This would seem to favour the first option.

However, although these two clauses are parallel and closely related, they are still significantly different in sense. This would seem to favour the second option.

Romans 8:9, 10 makes it clear that when believers have the Spirit within themselves they have Christ within themselves. It can be said, therefore, that Christ's indwelling of the believer is not something additional to the strengthening, but is a further definition of it and so, in the display, the first option is followed, with 3:17a–b providing an amplification of 3:16b. See, for example, Best (p. 341), Hodge (p. 183), O'Brien (p. 258), Stott (pp. 134–135).

The aorist infinitive κατοικῆσαι "to dwell" means "to live in a place in an established or settled manner". This contrasts with the verb παροικέω "to inhabit (a place) as a stranger". Paul has used the related noun πάροικος in 2:19 in the sense of "an alien", someone who is not permanently settled in a place. Here Paul says that Christ takes up permanent residence in the believer's heart and mind and being, therefore, he is a lasting power and influence in the believer's life. The aorist tense here carries the meaning of something that happens at a point in time and lasts forever. This might be indicated by "come to be", i.e. "Christ may come to be in your heart always".

3:17b by means of your believing *in him*. The prepositional phrase διὰ τῆς πίστεως "through faith" states the means by which Christ is present in a believer's heart.

3:17c *I pray* that, because you love *Christ* steadfastly and faithfully, The relationship of the two participles ἐρριζωμένοι "having been rooted" and τεθεμελιωμένοι "having been grounded" to the surrounding text is unclear. There are two main possibilities:

1. They are connected to the preceding infinitive clause or clauses in 3:16b and 3:17a.
2. They are connected to the following ἵνα "that, in order that" clause in 3:18.

Both options have certain grammatical problems.

In the first option, this clause is linked with what precedes. However, the nominative forms of the two perfect passive participles, ἐρριζωμένοι "having been rooted" and τεθεμελιωμένοι "having been grounded" must then be regarded as irregular, since they do not agree with the genitive ὑμῶν "you" in 3:17.

In the second option, the problem is that this clause precedes the introductory ἵνα. However, such an order is found elsewhere. See Acts 19:4 and Galatians 2:10 for examples of clauses where other elements precede the ἵνα (Hendriksen, p. 172, fn. 95; Hoehner, p. 483). See Intent and Structure for 3:14–19 for more support for this analysis. A good number of translations follow this alternative, e.g. KJV, NASB, NIV, NJB, REB, TEV. This analysis is followed in the display.

These two participles then may be regarded in a number of ways:

1. They express the grounds upon or circumstance in which the action of the following ἵνα clause takes place. This would then mean, "having been rooted and grounded in love in order that you may have strength to comprehend...".
2. They may express a command or prayer, i.e. "be rooted and grounded in love in order that..." or "I pray that you may be rooted and grounded in love in order that...". In TEV the last-mentioned is followed, "I pray that you may have your roots and foundation in love...". In the wider context of prayer, this is certainly possible. Bratcher and Nida (p. 86) consider that, although grammatically these two participles function to describe the condition of the Ephesians, it is perfectly in keeping with the use of the participle elsewhere in the New Testament to regard them as expressing a wish or command.
3. If ἵνα is understood to introduce a further petition of the prayer, it makes good sense for this clause to provide the reason for 3:18, i.e. "because you love Christ steadfastly and faithfully you may be able to comprehend...". This is a necessary prerequisite to their being able to understand the love God has for them. See the notes on 3:18.

Whether the relationship is means-purpose or reason-result depends upon what is considered to be in focus in this context. If Paul is presenting "being rooted and grounded in love" as something which the Ephesian believers have already attained then reason would be more appropriate. If he is presenting it as something they still need to work towards, then it may be means. In the display, it is represented as reason-RESULT. The whole propositional cluster (3:17c–19b) relates back to 3:14–15 and is the second petition. See the notes in the section on Intent and Structure.

This construction (3:17c) containing two perfect passive participles, "having been rooted" and "having been grounded", is subordinate to the main clause of 3:18, with its aorist subjunctive and infinitive, ἐξισχύσητε καταλαβέσθαι "you may have strength to comprehend". The two participles indicate an event in the past, that has present implications. They describe a state in which the Ephesian believers already are and in which they continue to be. This state is presupposed (by Paul), in order that they "may comprehend" (3:18).

As in Colossians 2:7 and 1 Corinthians 3:9, Paul uses two seemingly different metaphors here: one connected with a tree, the other with a building. They are both generally regarded as dead metaphors and indicate qualities of firmness and stability. In the display, they are expressed as "steadfastly and faithfully".

In the Greek, the two participles are preceded by ἐν ἀγάπῃ "in love", thus putting the emphasis on the abstract noun "love". It is not clear which "love" is referred to here. It may be the Ephesians' love for God, Christ or other people, or it may be God's love for them.

It is difficult to represent this expression non-figuratively. What does it mean for people to be "firm and stable in love"? Probably the sense is that the basis of their lives should be love, i.e. the basis of everything they think and do should be love, the love in question being their love for Christ and, hence, for other people. In the display, I have thought it sufficient to state "you love *Christ* steadfastly and faithfully", since love for others should be inherent in this and flow from it.

3:18 you may be able, The initial ἵνα in 3:18 introduces the second petition of the prayer, which consists of the propositional cluster 3:17c–19b.

The verb ἐξισχύσητε "be strong enough, be in a position" may also be translated as "be able". It does not represent an event or action in itself.

together with all *other* believers, The σύν "with" indicates "together with others". The Ephesians were to be accompanied in their understanding by "all the saints". This has been expressed as "together with all *other* believers", in order to make clear that the Ephesians are members of the church, along with all those who believe in Christ.

to comprehend In the Greek text, ἐξισχύσητε "you may be strong enough, be able" is followed by an aorist middle infinitive, καταλαβέσθαι "to seize, win, attain, make one's own". Here, the sense is "to understand, comprehend", followed by the direct object, "what is the breadth, etc.".

how greatly Christ loves *us/his-people*, Note that, in the Greek text, the noun ἀγάπην "love" does not occur until 3:19. Paul puts another verb first (γνῶναι "to know") before he mentions "love", which is the implied nuclear concept of the direct object of the first verb and the grammatical direct object of the second.

Most commentators agree that the dimensions described here refer to Christ's love for us, his people. Although other possibilities are suggested, in the context, specifically the following verse, with its explicit reference to the "love of Christ", it seems most appropriate to regard Christ's love as the referent here.

This description recalls the architectural figure of chapter 2. However, Paul does not intend there to be a separate meaning to each dimension. He mentions all four dimensions in order to emphasise the infinite nature of the love described. Compare this with 1:19; 2:7; 3:8. Paul likes to use such superlatives. In the display, a non-figurative expression is used to convey the enormous extent of Christ's love, but, in some languages, there may be idiomatic or figurative ways to express this.

3:19a and that you may be able to know/experience The particle τε "and" indicates a close relationship between the two clauses 3:18 and 3:19a. However, there are two possible relationships:

1. The aorist active infinitive γνῶναι "to know, experience" is parallel to καταλαβέσθαι "to comprehend" in 3:18 and both complete the thought of "be strong/able", i.e. "that you may be able to comprehend" and "that you may be able to know/experience".
2. The aorist active infinitive γνῶναι "to know, experience" may semantically be a restatement of "to comprehend" in 3:18, i.e. "to comprehend what is the breadth..." ("that is, to know the love...").

In order to decide which option is the most likely, the two verbs καταλαβέσθαι (3:18) and γνῶναι (3:19a) need to be compared and a decision made about them:

1. whether they both refer to intellectual knowledge;
2. whether they both refer to experiential knowledge;
3. whether καταλαβέσθαι refers to intellectual knowledge and γνῶναι to experiential knowledge.

It seems that the greatest support is for the third option. A number of commentators clearly consider καταλαβέσθαι to refer to the intellectual aspect of understanding something. For example, Lloyd-Jones states,

> The word means 'to take a firm mental grasp' of a thing, or 'to lay hold of something with the mind'. It describes the process of grasping mentally an idea or a truth.... The emphasis is upon the fact that it is a mental process, it is something done with the mind (p. 230).

The verb γνῶναι is generally regarded as referring to gaining knowledge by direct, personal experience.

The relationship between 3:18 and 3:19a, then, is best regarded as one of addition or, possibly, amplification, rather than equivalence.

how greatly Christ loves *us*, The relationship of the nouns in the genitive construction τὴν...ἀγάπην τοῦ Χριστοῦ "the love of Christ" is that Christ is the agent, "Christ loves us". The phrase is the object of "to know/experience".

3:19b *even though* it is impossible to understand fully how much he loves *us*. The phrase τὴν ὑπερβάλλουσαν τῆς γνώσεως "the surpassing of knowledge" qualifies "the love of Christ". This is a typically paradoxical statement of Paul's—to know the unknowable. It emphasises the superlative and infinite nature of Christ's love for believers. No matter how much a believer knows and experiences that love, there will always be more to know. This has been expressed by a clause of concession.

Paul also uses the verb ὑπερβάλλω "go beyond, surpass, outdo" in 1:19 and 2:7. See the notes on 1:19.

3:19c–d *I pray* that *God may cause* you to be perfect, just as he is perfect. There are a number of possibilities as to the connection indicated by the initial ἵνα of this clause. It may signal:

1. Another petition within the prayer.
2. The culminating, climactic purpose of all that goes before, from 3:16–19b.
3. The purpose of knowing the love of Christ (3:18–19a).

This was discussed earlier when considering the structure of the paragraph and the first of these is followed in the display. See the section on Intent and Structure.

Paul uses the verb πληρόω "fill" and the noun πλήρωμα "fulness" a number of times in this letter. See also 1:10, 23; 4:10, 13; 5:18.

The genitive construction, "the fulness of God", may be:

1. A subjective genitive. It then refers to all that which fills God and makes him perfect.
2. An objective genitive. It then refers to all the blessings that God bestows on believers, so that they become more like him.

The majority of commentators support the first of these, i.e. the fulness of God is his excellence or perfection. See also the parallel passages in Colossians 2:9 and Matthew 5:48. It seems fitting that God's excellence or perfection is the sense here, as in 4:13 where this meaning is also expressed in relation to Christ, the "measure of the stature of the fulness of Christ". See also Romans 8:29, "to be conformed to the image of Christ".

In the clause ἵνα πληρωθῆτε εἰς πᾶν τὸ πλήρωμα τοῦ θεοῦ "that you may be filled to all the fulness of God", the preposition εἰς probably indicates goal. Paul is praying that the Ephesian believers may attain to a standard or reach a goal: "all the fulness of God", i.e. his perfection. In effect, he is praying that they may be perfect, just as God is perfect. Paul wants the Ephesians to be filled with the spiritual perfection of God, the very nature of God.

The verb πληρωθῆτε "you may be filled" is generally understood to be a divine passive indicating that God is agent. Propositionally, the full clause is expressed as "that *God may cause* you to be perfect, just as he is perfect".

BOUNDARIES AND COHERENCE

The initial boundary has been discussed in the section on Boundaries and Coherence for 3:1–13.

The final boundary occurs at the end of 3:19 as is evident by the commencement of the doxology in 3:20.

The unity of this paragraph consists in its being a prayer. Also, throughout, there is second person plural (audience) orientation:

"that God may grant *you*" (3:16)
"in *your* hearts" (3:17)
"that *you* might be enabled" (3:18)
"that *you* might be filled" (3:19)

In the following doxology (3:20–21), no forms of "you" occur.

PROMINENCE AND THEME

The content of this prayer corresponds in many ways with the prayer of 1:15-19, restating the need for spiritual knowledge and enlightenment, which can only come through God working powerfully in the hearts and minds of believers.

God is prominent as the agent in this prayer, the one who enables the believers to increase in their knowledge of him. This is evident in such expressions as:

> "that *he* may grant you, according to the riches of *his* glory" (3:16)
> "through *his* Spirit" (3:16)

The power of God at work in the hearts and lives of believers is prominent in this paragraph, as it is throughout this whole section of Ephesians, (chapters 1-3).

Prominence is also given to "love" in this paragraph. When it first occurs, in 3:17, it is forefronted, then it is focussed upon in the following verse by the use of terms which are all-encompassing, namely, "breadth and length and height and depth". Finally, in 3:19, "the love of Christ which surpasses knowledge" is referred to, along with the ultimate goal of spiritual maturity.

The theme statement of this unit, therefore, is based on these prominent semantic features as found in CONTENTS$_{1,2,3}$.

The significance of God's power and Christ's love, in relation to the development of spiritual maturity, are brought out in this prayer. These are important in preparing the Ephesians for Paul's exhortations in the following chapters.

SECTION CONSTITUENT 3:20-21
(Expressive Paragraph: Nucleus₂ of 3:14-21 [Responsive Doxology])

THEME: May our infinite God be glorified through the church and through Christ Jesus forever. Amen.

RELATIONAL STRUCTURE	CONTENTS
reason — CONGRUENCE	3:20a God is able to do infinitely greater *deeds* than anything we might ask him to do and infinitely greater *deeds* than anything we might think he can do
standard	3:20b according to *his* power which works within us (*or*, by means of *his* power working within us).
EXPRESSIVE RESULT	3:21 *May God be* glorified through the church and through Christ Jesus forever and ever. Amen.

INTENT AND STRUCTURE

This unit is a doxology in response to the prayer of 3:14-19. It also brings to a conclusion the first half of the letter. It is Paul's response to the unlimited power of God, about which he has been writing in the preceding chapters, and to the knowledge that this same power is still working in, and on behalf of, believers.

As a doxology, it is an expressive paragraph. In the semantic propositionalisation in the display, it consists of a reason (3:20) and an expressive RESULT (3:21). Paul's response is one of praise to God. His intention is to encourage his fellow-believers to join him in this and, at the same time, strengthen his bond with them.

In the Greek text, this doxology follows the usual pattern of doxologies in the New Testament:

> First, the one who is to receive the praise is introduced in a dative construction, here, τῷ...δυναμένῳ... "to the one...being able..." with the connector δέ following the article in its regular postpositive position (3:20).
>
> Next, there is the characteristic absence of a copulative verb.
>
> This is followed by the occurrence of one or more praise words, here, ἡ δόξα "glory, praise".
>
> The doxology concludes with a prepositional phrase referring to the eternal endurance of the praise, here, εἰς τὰς γενεὰς τοῦ αἰῶνος τῶν αἰώνων, ἀμήν "throughout all generations forever and ever, Amen" (3:21).

For other doxologies, see Romans 16:25-27; Philippians 4:20; 1 Timothy 1:17.

These verses also provide motivational concepts which act as a basis for the appeals in 4:1-6:20. The doxology acts as a conclusion to all the information in the first three chapters which supports Paul's exhortation to holy living in the second half of his letter. It picks up some of the ideas put forward in the preceding chapters, such as, the greatness of God's power and his ability to answer prayer beyond our expectations. It links back to the expression of praise in 1:15-23 and helps to redirect attention to the source of that power, which the Ephesians need in order to live as Paul will exhort them to live in the following chapters.

NOTES

3:20 The initial δέ introduces the change from prayer to doxology. Paul has been praying to God in 3:14-19. Now he turns to praising God for what he has done and can do for believers. The focus of the paragraph is on God and his mighty power.

3:20a-b This cluster of propositions describes God's infinite ability to bless his people. It is this situation to which Paul responds in 3:21.

3:20a God is able to do infinitely greater *deeds* than anything we might ask him to do and infinitely greater *deeds* than anything we might think he can do In some languages, it may be necessary to begin this paragraph with a proposition such as "*Let us praise God*", in order to make clear the expressive nature of the paragraph.

In the Greek, Paul uses two superlative expressions in order to express God's incomprehensible power: ὑπὲρ πάντα "beyond all (things)" and ὑπερεκπερισσοῦ "superabundantly". Even these terms are insufficient to express the nature of God's power and so is the expression used in the display. In translation, it will be necessary to use the strongest expressions possible in order to communicate the limitless nature of God's power.

3:20b according to *his* power which works within us (*or,* by means of *his* power working within us). The Greek phrase κατὰ τὴν δύναμιν τὴν ἐνεργουμένην ἐν ἡμῖν "according to the power working in us" brings us back to an important theme of this section of the letter, the mighty power of God. See 1:19, 21; 3:7, 16.

The preposition κατά "according to", followed by a noun in the accusative case, can be understood in two ways:

1. It means "by" and signals the relation of means or instrument. The verse then means that the same divine power which raised Christ from the dead is effective in the hearts and minds of believers, through the Holy Spirit.
2. It means "in accordance with". That is, God's doing such mighty things is "in accordance with" his power, i.e. his unlimited power is the only measure of what he can do.

Louw and Nida support the second option. In their entry for κατά (89.8), they suggest that this usage of the preposition indicates a relation involving a correspondence or similarity of process. If this analysis is followed, 3:20b would provide a standard for 3:20a, which would be in a relation of CONGRUENCE with it. The proposition would be "according to *his* power that works within us".

Paul then adds a description of that power, implying that it is that same power which raised Christ from the dead that is at work in us.

3:21 *May* God *be* glorified through the church and through Christ Jesus There is no explicit verb here. There are two possibilities:

1. The optative "be" is implied, i.e. "to him (be) glory".
2. The indicative "is" is implied, i.e. "to him (is) glory".

The first option has the better support.

The αὐτῷ "to him" refers to God. It repeats the reference of τῷ δυναμένῳ "to him who is able" in 3:20.

The word δόξα "glory", in this context, could mean:

1. "Praise", i.e. "Let us praise God in the church and in Christ Jesus".
2. The manifestation of God's glory and power, i.e. "May God's glory and power manifest itself in the church and in Christ Jesus".
3. Both these ideas.

This is a formalised "doxology" and such a construction generally functions to praise God. It also occurs at the end of a highly emotive passage, where praise would be natural. Therefore, the first option is the most likely, i.e. δόξα here has to do with praising God.

However, in this verse, ἡ δόξα is modified not only by ἐν τῇ ἐκκλησίᾳ "in the church", but also by καὶ ἐν Χριστῷ Ἰησοῦ "and in Christ Jesus". The addition of such phrases constrains its meaning from a general sense of praise to a more specific one. The very existence of the church, with Christ as its head, manifests God's glory. This has been made clear in the first three chapters. Now Paul asks the Ephesians to join with him in praising God forever by manifesting his glory in their lives, in union with Christ Jesus (or, together with Christ Jesus), the head of the church.

Most of the commentaries support the view that the two occurrences of ἐν "in" in the phrase αὐτῷ ἡ δόξα ἐν τῇ ἐκκλησίᾳ καὶ ἐν Χριστῷ Ἰησοῦ "to him glory in the church and in Christ Jesus" are similar in meaning. Each has local significance and refers to the sphere in which God's glory is acknowledged. As Hoehner states,

> God is to be glorified in the church because his power and splendor are displayed there and he is glorified in Christ Jesus because Christ's work, which pleased the Father, made the church possible (p. 495).

This is appropriate in the context of this letter, in which the unity of the church under the headship of Christ is such a prominent theme. However, ἐν is expressed as "through" in the display since "in" tends to be ambiguous and more abstract.

forever and ever. Amen. The Greek εἰς πάσας τὰς γενεὰς τοῦ αἰῶνος τῶν αἰώνων is literally "to all the generations of the age of the ages". It is another example of Paul using intensive constructions in order to emphasise what he is saying. The expressions would correspond with such phrases as "forevermore" or "forever and ever".

BOUNDARIES AND COHERENCE

Grammatically, this unit consists of a single sentence in Greek.

The use of vocabulary connected with "power" gives coherence:

δυναμένῳ "being able"
δύναμιν "power"
ἐνεργουμένην "working"

Expressions such as ὑπὲρ πάντα "beyond all (things)" and τοῦ αἰῶνος αἰώνων "the age of the ages" help to enhance this idea.

PROMINENCE AND THEME

Since the EXPRESSIVE RESULT is the most naturally prominent unit, it forms the basis of the theme statement. But the reason is represented by the term "infinite" in "infinite God".

PART CONSTITUENT 4:1–6:20 (Hortatory Subpart: Nucleus of 1:3–6:20)

THEME: Behave as God's people should. Use the spiritual gifts which Christ has given to each of you to ensure that the church becomes completely united and spiritually mature. Do not behave in an evil way or disobey God, but imitate him, letting your lives be characterised by love for one another. By so doing, evil will be exposed and the truth revealed. Behave wisely, be controlled completely by the Holy Spirit and submit yourselves to one another. At all times, rely wholeheartedly on the Lord Jesus Christ to strengthen you. Make use of every spiritual resource which God provides for you, in order to successfully resist the devil and all his powerful evil spirits. Persevere in prayer for all God's people.

MACROSTRUCTURE	CONTENTS
HORTATORY NUCLEUS₁	4:1–6:9 Behave as God's people should. Use the spiritual gifts which Christ has given to each of you to ensure that the church becomes completely united and spiritually mature. Do not behave in an evil way, but be good to one another. Do not disobey God, but imitate him. Specifically, let your lives be characterised by love for one another. Live righteous lives, since, by doing so, evil is exposed and the truth is revealed. Behave wisely, be controlled completely by the Holy Spirit and submit yourselves to one another.
HORTATORY NUCLEUS₂ (Climax)	6:10–20 At all times, rely wholeheartedly on the Lord Jesus Christ to strengthen you. Make use of every spiritual resource which God provides for you, in order to successfully resist the devil and all his powerful evil spirits. At the same time, persevere in prayer to God for all his people.

INTENT AND MACROSTRUCTURE

The 4:1–6:20 subpart of the BODY of the epistle is hortatory. Paul used the first subpart of the BODY (1:3–3:21) to remind the Ephesians about the many blessings they have received from God, and about the fact that they are all, both Jewish and Gentile believers, part of God's purpose in forming his church and for bringing all things under the headship of Christ. This provides the grounds for the exhortations of this second part of the letter. It consists of two HORTATORY NUCLEI, 4:1–6:9 and 6:10–20.

In 4:1–6:9, Paul's intention is to motivate the Ephesian believers to behave in a way that shows that they are truly God's people (4:1). He urges them to use the spiritual gifts God has given them, in order to live righteous lives characterised by unity and love, so that the church might be completely united and spiritually mature under the headship of Christ.

In the final exhortations of 6:10–20, Paul's intention is to encourage the Ephesian believers to use the resources God has made available to them as they try to respond to the exhortations of 4:1–6:9. He refers to these resources in the context of the wider struggle between the forces of good and evil. He wants them to resolutely resist Satan and all evil powers, using every spiritual resource which God has supplied. In effect, Paul is stating the means by which the Ephesians can live as God wants them to live, and in a way by which they can defeat evil. He uses the extended metaphor of a soldier's armour to enumerate these resources (6:13–17). He finishes the unit by emphasising the necessity for them to persevere in prayer at all times (6:18–20).

BOUNDARIES AND COHERENCE

The initial boundary of this division is clearly marked by the following features:

1. The ἀμήν at the end of the doxology (3:21) which brings the first part of the epistle to a close.
2. The change from expressive to hortatory genre, signalled by the use of the first person singular verb παρακαλῶ "I urge, exhort" and the second person plural ὑμᾶς "you", referring to those addressed in the epistle (4:1).
3. The use of ἐγώ "I", with the descriptive phrase ὁ δέσμιος ἐν κυρίῳ "the prisoner in (the) Lord" (4:1).
4. The conjunction οὖν "therefore", in its function of relating higher-level parts together in a grounds-EXHORTATION relationship (4:1).

The final boundary of this unit coincides with the final boundary of the BODY. See the section on the BODY.

The following features mark the cohesion and coherence of unit 4:1–6:20.

1. The thematic use of the verb περιπατέω in the figurative sense of "live, behave, conduct oneself" (4:1, 17; 5:2, 8, 15).
2. References throughout the unit to the church and to moral conduct.
3. A high proportion of imperative verbs.

PROMINENCE AND THEME

Since this unit is composed of HORTATORY NUCLEI of equal natural prominence, a summary of each of these NUCLEI is included in the theme statement, seeking to keep the main points, but, at the same time, to avoid repetition. At lower levels, the repetition of these items would mark them as prominent, but, at this high level, their accumulative repetition is unnecessary.

SUBPART CONSTITUENT 4:1–6:9 (Hortatory Division: Nucleus₁ of 4:1–6:20)

THEME: Behave as God's people should. Use the spiritual gifts which Christ has given to each of you to ensure that the church becomes completely united and spiritually mature. Do not behave in an evil way, but be good to one another. Do not disobey God, but imitate him. Specifically, let your lives be characterised by love for one another. Live righteous lives, since, by doing so, evil is exposed and the truth is revealed. Behave wisely, be completely controlled by the Holy Spirit and submit yourselves to one another.

¶MACROSTRUCTURE	CONTENTS
Hortatory Nucleus₁	4:1–16 Behave in a way that shows that you are God's people. Do all you can to ensure that the church remains united. Christ has given different spiritual gifts to each of God's people, in order that they might minister to each other and that, by this means, the church might become completely united and spiritually mature.
Hortatory Nucleus₂	4:17–32 You have learnt that you must behave in a manner which is consistent with your new, godly character. Therefore, stop doing those immoral things which unbelievers do and which are harmful to one another. Rather, act appropriately towards one another.
Hortatory Nucleus₃	5:1–6 Imitate God. Specifically, let everything you do be done because you love one another. Do not let anyone persuade you to disobey God and live immoral lives, since God will punish those people who habitually disobey him.
Hortatory Nucleus₄	5:7–14 Live righteous lives, as those who are in the light should. By doing so, expose the evil deeds which evil people do, since, by living righteously, the truth is revealed to ungodly people.
Hortatory Nucleus₅	5:15–6:9 Be very careful that you behave wisely, that you be controlled completely by the Holy Spirit, and that you submit yourselves to one another. Wives, submit yourselves to your husbands. Husbands, love your wives. Children, obey your parents. Fathers, bring up your children well. Slaves, obey your earthly masters. Masters, treat your slaves well.

INTENT AND MACROSTRUCTURE

The 4:1–6:9 unit consists of five HORTATORY NUCLEI (4:1–16; 4:17–32; 5:1–6; 5:7–14; 5:15–6:9).

In this hortatory unit, Paul's intention is to motivate the Ephesians to behave in a way that is fitting for those who are God's people. A generic exhortation to this effect is made in 4:1. This is followed by other, more specific, exhortations which deal with various aspects of living such a life.

BOUNDARIES AND COHERENCE

The initial boundary of this unit is discussed in the section on Boundaries and Coherence for 1:3–6:20.

The final boundary is marked by the start of a new section at 6:10. This is signalled by τοῦ λοιποῦ "finally, for the rest", as Paul turns from the list of specific exhortations linked to ἀξίως περιπατῆσαι "walk worthily" (4:1), to make a final short series of exhortations (6:10–20) related to the means by which believers will be enabled to accomplish those things which Paul has exhorted them to do in the five previous sections of 4:1–6:9.

There is also a change of semantic domain, from that of "right attitudes" between slaves and masters to that of "warfare", and a change of participants from "slaves" and "masters" to a more general second person plural.

The cohesion of the 4:1–6:9 unit is largely due to the many imperative and subjunctive verbs which Paul uses throughout the unit. In particular, the occurrence of the verb περιπατέω "walk" in each of the five hortatory units along with the conjunction οὖν "therefore" adds to this cohesion.

PROMINENCE AND THEME

Since the individual constituents of division 4:1–6:9 are in a co-ordinate relation, the theme statement is based on a summary of them all.

DIVISION CONSTITUENT 4:1–16 (Hortatory Section: Nucleus₁ of 4:1–6:9)

THEME: Behave in a way that shows that you are God's people. Do all you can to ensure that the church remains united. Christ has given different spiritual gifts to each of God's people, in order that they might minister to each other and that, by this means, the church might become completely united and spiritually mature.

MACROSTRUCTURE	CONTENTS
HORTATORY NUCLEUS	4:1–6 Behave in a way that shows that you are God's people. Do all you can to ensure that you remain united with one another, since there is one church, one Holy Spirit, one Lord Jesus Christ and one God.
└─motivational grounds	4:7–16 Christ has given different spiritual gifts to each one in his church, in order that the church might remain united and become spiritually mature.

INTENT AND MACROSTRUCTURE

Section 4:1–16 constitutes the first *hortatory* section of this division of the epistle. It consists of two paragraphs.

The first, 4:1–6, contains the EXHORTATIONS of the section.

The second paragraph, 4:7–16, is expository. It provides the motivational grounds for the HORTATORY NUCLEUS in 4:1–6. Paul wants the Ephesians each to use their spiritual gifts to benefit the whole church, in order to maintain its unity and to encourage its progress towards full maturity. Although paragraph 4:7–16 is expository, it is also mitigated hortatory in nature in the sense that it draws the attention of the Ephesians to the fact that God has given them these gifts to be used in the church.

Paul exhorts them to make every effort to preserve the unity of the church. Then, in order to motivate them to respond positively to his exhortation, he goes on to speak about the diversity of spiritual gifts given to believers by Christ. These gifts should be used to maintain unity and to enable the church to become spiritually mature.

The theme of unity was prominent in the first part of this epistle (1:3–3:21). In 1:10, Paul stated that God's primary objective in sending Christ into the world was to unite all things in Christ. Chapter 2 is concerned with the unity in Christ of all believers, whether Jewish or Gentile, and 3:5–6 speaks of this unity as "the mystery" now revealed.

Now, in the second part of the letter, Paul focusses on the need to maintain this unity. As Lloyd-Jones says,

> ...it is inevitable that when [Paul] comes to the particulars of the Christian walk and life, the preservation of this unity must be mentioned first. ...it is what displays God's glory above everything else (p. 35).

BOUNDARIES AND COHERENCE

The initial boundary has been discussed in the section on Boundaries and Coherence for 4:1–6:20.

The final boundary is marked by the following features:

1. There is a contrast of subject matter. Unit 4:1–16 deals with the fostering of unity and the growth of spiritual maturity in the church. The following unit, 4:17–32, concentrates on the contrast between the former, pagan way of life and the new way of life in Christ.
2. The οὖν...περιπατεῖν "walk therefore" in 4:17, which may have either inferential or resumptive force.
3. The double orienter λέγω καὶ μαρτύρομαι "I say and insist/testify" in 4:17 is emphatic and marks a new start, introducing all the admonitions which follow.

The relational coherence between the two paragraphs making up this unit is shown in the display above.

There is lexical cohesion (resulting in coherence) in the use of vocabulary from the semantic field of "unity":

ἑνότης "unity" (4:3, 13)
εἷς "one" (4:4 [three times], 4:5 [three times], 4:6)
πᾶς "all, every" (4:2, 6, 13, 15, 16)
τὸ σῶμα "the (one) body" (4:4, 12, 16)
σύνδεσμος "that which binds...together" (4:3)
συναρμολογέω "fit/join together" (4:16)

συμβιβάζω "bring together, unite" (4:16)

PROMINENCE AND THEME

As is usual in a section, the theme statement is based on the paragraph theme of the NUCLEUS (4:1-6) of the section and either the whole paragraph theme of the grounds (4:7-16) or the parts of it that are prominent enough to be included. The whole theme of the grounds units is included here since each of its parts is highly prominent.

SECTION CONSTITUENT 4:1–6 (Hortatory Paragraph: Nucleus of 4:1–16)

THEME: Behave in a way that shows that you are God's people. Do all you can to ensure that you remain united with one another, since there is one church, one Holy Spirit, one Lord Jesus Christ and one God.

RELATIONAL STRUCTURE	CONTENTS
orienter	4:1a Based on all this [1:3–3:21], I, who am a prisoner because *I serve* the Lord *Jesus Christ*, urge you, whom *God* has called *to be his people, as follows*:
GENERIC EXHORTATION	4:1b Behave as God's people should.
specific exhortation₁ (means)	4:2a Always be humble and always be considerate of one another.
specific exhortation₂ (means) — NUCLEUS	4:2b Be patient with one another,
amplification — RESULT	4:2c *that is*, you should be tolerant towards one another,
reason	4:2d because you love one another.
grounds	4:3a The *Holy* Spirit has caused you to be united with one another.
SPECIFIC EXHORTATION₃ (RESULT) — EXHORTATION RESULT	4:3b *Therefore*, do all you can to ensure that you remain united with one another,
means	4:3c by means of living peacefully with one another [MET].
NUCLEUS₁	4:4a *There is* one body, *that is*, one church [MET],
NUCLEUS₂ — NUCLEUS	4:4b and *there is* one *Holy* Spirit,
comparison — RESULT	4:4c just as also each one of you hopes for the same thing,
reason	4:4d because *God* has called you *to be his people*.
NUCLEUS₃ — NUCLEUS	4:5a *There is* one Lord *Jesus Christ*.
amplification₁	4:5b *It is in the Lord Jesus Christ* alone *that we all* believe.
amplification₂	4:5c *It is in his name* alone *that we* are baptised.
NUCLEUS₄ — 'God'	4:6a *There is* one God.
description₁	4:6b He *is* the *spiritual* Father of all *his-people/believers*.
description₂	4:6c He *rules* over all *his people*.
description₃	4:6d He *empowers/sustains* all *his people*.
description₄	4:6e He *is present spiritually* in *the hearts of* all *his people*.

(Left bracket groupings: EXHORTATION — grounds)

INTENT AND STRUCTURE

This paragraph consists of a hortatory unit (4:1–3) and a grounds unit (4:4–6). Paul's purpose is to motivate the believers to live in such a way that their lives will show that God has chosen them to be his people. They can best do this by living in unity and peace with each other (4:1–3). He makes a series of statements (4:4–6) about "oneness", with respect to the church, the Holy Spirit, the Lord (Jesus), God, baptism, hope and faith, in order to encourage them to take action to maintain "oneness", i.e. unity among themselves.

NOTES

4:1 Prominence is given to Paul as the agent of the orienter παρακαλῶ "I urge/insist", by the use of the free pronoun ἐγώ "I" and the description ὁ δέσμιος ἐν κυρίῳ "the prisoner in (the) Lord". This latter reference, in conjunction with οὖν, recalls 3:1–13, which served to validate Paul's authority and continues to do so here, though it is perhaps not as significant to the theme as it was there.

4:1a Based on all this [1:3–3:21], I, who am a prisoner because *I serve* the Lord *Jesus Christ*, urge you, whom *God* has called *to be his people, as follows*: The conjunction οὖν, normally translated as "therefore", relates the hortatory part of the BODY (4:1–6:20) to the expressive and expository part (1:3–3:21). It seems best to translate οὖν here as "Based on all this [1:3–3:21]".

Proposition 4:1a serves as orienter for the CONTENT of 4:1b–3.

The phrase ὁ δέσμιος ἐν κυρίῳ "the prisoner in (the) Lord" means "I am a prisoner because *I serve* the Lord *Jesus Christ*". See the note on 3:1 also.

The repetition of cognate words, as here, τῆς κλήσεως ἧς ἐκλήθητε "the calling with which you were called", is common in Greek, but is not idiomatic in English. It represents the event "*God called you to be his people*". The verb "call" is not used in its primary sense here, but in the sense of "called successfully", i.e. they had been "called, invited" by the preaching of the gospel and had responded by believing the gospel. It might be preferable, in some languages, to use the verb "chosen".

4:1b Behave as God's people should. As in 2:2 and 2:10, the verb περιπατέω "walk" is used figuratively here to mean "live, behave, conduct oneself". See also 4:17; 5:2, 8, 15.

It is difficult to express the sense of the adverb ἀξίως "worthily, suitably" in this context. The idea is, as people whom God has called to belong to his family of believers, they should live in obedience to his will and in gratitude for the many blessings they have received from him. Possible renderings are: "Conduct-yourselves/behave as God's people should" or "in a way that shows that you are God's people".

4:2–3 In this cluster of propositions, Paul presents a number of qualities which should characterise the life of a believer. These qualities, mentioned in 4:2, are appropriate to the command in 4:3, all having to do with Christian fellowship: humility, meekness, patience, tolerance, love. By cultivating them, the unity of the church will be maintained.

Therefore, there is a means-result relationship between 4:2 and 4:3b. See, for example, Lenski (pp. 507–508), O'Brien (p. 276).

However, since grammatically verses 4:2–3 depend on the imperatival construction in 4:1 and can be seen as specific exhortations in relation to it, it seems best to label the relationship within 4:1b–3b as generic-specific. However, the final specific exhortation is considered prominent because of this underlying means-result relationship. Also it is supported by the expansive grounds of 4:4–6.

4:2a Always be humble and always be considerate of one another. Moore (p. 48) considers the two abstract nouns ταπεινοφροσύνης "humility" and πραΰτητος "meekness" to be a near-synonymous doublet.

However, a number of the commentators (Hendriksen, p. 183; Lincoln, pp. 235–236; O'Brien, pp. 276–277; Stott, pp. 148–149) make a distinction between the two nouns, as follows:

1. The first noun ταπεινοφροσύνη "humility" refers to "the humble recognition of the worth and value of other people" (Stott, p. 148) or "the ability to count others as better than oneself" (Lincoln, p. 236, referring to Phil. 2:3).
2. The second noun πραΰτης "meekness" "involves the courtesy, considerateness, and "willingness to waive one's rights...seeking the common good without being concerned for personal reputation or gain" (Lincoln, p. 236).

Most commentators consider that the adjective πάσης "all" qualifies both nouns, i.e. "with all humility and all meekness" denoting the highest degree of both humility and meekness. This may be expressed as "very", with the two abstract nouns represented by adverbs or adjectives, according to whether the sense is expressed by an imperative such as "behave..." or a stative verb such as "be...": "behave very humbly and meekly" or "be very humble and meek". Alternatively, it might be expressed as "always", indicating completeness. The latter option is followed in this analysis.

4:2b Be patient with one another, The next quality mentioned is μακροθυμία "forbearance, patience towards others". This third abstract noun is introduced with a second μετά "with", as were the two preceding nouns. It is generally agreed that this prepositional phrase is parallel with the preceding μετά prepositional phrase, adding another quality to the first two qualities.

4:2c *that is,* you should be tolerant towards one another, Commentators disagree about how the nominative participle ἀνεχόμενοι "enduring, bearing with, putting up with" connects with the rest of the verse and what its function is:

1. It further defines the phrase μετὰ μακροθυμίας "with patience" (4:2b). So, for example, Lincoln (p. 236) says that the whole clause, ἀνεχόμενοι ἀλλήλων ἐν ἀγάπῃ "bearing with one another in love", is "an amplification of what is meant by patience". See also O'Brien (p. 278), Ellicott (p. 65), Lenski (pp. 507–508).
2. It forms a natural pair with "patience" and is the fourth quality in a list of five which culminates in "love" (Stott, p. 149).

Most commentators favour the first option. The main point to observe in translation is that all the qualities listed in 4:2 emphasise attitudes conducive to sustaining the unity referred to in 4:3.

4:2d because you love one another. Most commentators agree that the phrase ἐν ἀγάπῃ "in love" is attached only to the preceding participial clause ἀνεχόμενοι ἀλλήλων "being tolerant towards one another", not all four of the preceding qualities.

However, there is no consensus as to the relationship indicated by the preposition ἐν. The main possibilities are:

1. It signals a reason for 4:2c. See. for example, Hodge who states,

   [The phrase] ἀνεχόμενοι ἀλλήλων ἐν ἀγάπῃ...means *restraining yourselves in reference to each other in love*. Let love induce you to be forbearing towards each other (p. 200).

   See also Candlish (p. 83), O'Brien (p. 278, fn. 25).

2. It signals a means relation with 4:2c. See, for example, Lincoln, who states,

   Here in Ephesians 4:2 love is seen as the only means of Christian forbearance (p. 236).

   See also Lenski (p. 508).

Both options seem equally possible, since the qualities listed are so intimately related to one another, and the difference in meaning between "because you love one another" and "by means of loving one another" is slight. In the display, it is expressed as a reason relationship, taking the view that tolerance arises from Christian love. Paul prayed, in 3:17, that the Ephesian believers might be "rooted and grounded in love". See also 4:15, 16. Here in 4:2, tolerance, and probably the other qualities listed, are the result of believers loving one another.

4:3a The *Holy* Spirit has caused you to be united with one another. Most commentators agree that the spirit referred to here in the genitive construction τὴν ἑνότητα τοῦ πνεύματος "the unity of the spirit" is the Holy Spirit. He is the one who brings about true unity in the church. The event represented by the genitive construction is expressed in the display by using the verbal phrase "caused...to be united" and by making clear who the participants are.

The event referred to here is a completed action. The Holy Spirit has already provided the unity between the believers in Ephesus. This is made clear in 4:3b where they are urged to "*maintain* the unity of the Spirit". Since this proposition represents a past action, it may be analysed as providing the grounds for 4:3b, i.e. on the basis that the Holy Spirit has united them, they should make sure that they maintain that unity.

4:3b *Therefore,* do all you can to ensure that you remain united with one another, The relationship between the participle σπουδάζοντες "making every effort" and the infinitive τηρεῖν "to keep, preserve", may be translated as means-purpose in some languages, for example, "Do whatever you can in order that you may remain united to one another". In other languages, it may be better translated as an auxiliary followed by a verb.

It is τὴν ἑνότητα τοῦ πνεύματος "the unity of the Spirit" which is to be maintained. The participle, σπουδάζοντες "making every effort", has the force of an imperative and, being in the present tense, refers to continuous action.

The abstract noun τὴν ἑνότητα "unity" represents the state of being united and the verb τηρεῖν "keep" semantically qualifies the time aspect of the unity. This has been re-expressed as "remain united" (4:3b).

Since σπουδάζοντες τηρεῖν τὴν ἑνότητα "doing all you can to maintain the unity" functions as a command, following the command in 4:1, 4:3b is analysed as the nucleus of 4:3a–c. And 4:3b is also nuclear to the whole paragraph (4:1–6) since it is an exhortation for maintaining ἑνότητα "unity" which is the theme of 4:1–16. It is, therefore, represented as SPECIFIC EXHORTATION₃ in relation to 4:1b, which is a GENERIC EXHORTATION.

4:3c by means of living peacefully with one another. Once again, with ἐν τῷ συνδέσμῳ τῆς εἰρήνης "in the bond of peace" there is a need to transfer abstract nouns into a verbal phrase. Here the abstract noun εἰρήνη "peace" represents the event "live peacefully (with)" or "live at peace (with)". The noun σύνδεσμος "that which binds something together, that which unites" is used figuratively here.

In this genitive construction, most commentators agree that the genitive τῆς εἰρήνης "of the peace" is in apposition to συνδέσμῳ "bond". See, for example, Eadie (pp. 271-272), Ellicott (p. 66), Hendriksen (p. 185). Peace *is* the bond by which unity is to be preserved. In the metaphor, "bond" is the figurative image and "peace" is its non-figurative meaning. Since "bond" is an abstract noun and an abstract concept here and is in apposition to "peace", it is difficult to propositionalise the event by only using verbs. So the figure "bond" is not represented explicitly in the display.

The majority view seems to be that ἐν in the expression ἐν τῷ συνδέσμῳ τῆς εἰρήνης "in the bond of peace" indicates the means whereby "the unity of the Spirit" is to be preserved. The Ephesian believers are to maintain unity within the church by living peacefully with one another. See, for example, Hodge (p. 201), Lloyd-Jones (p. 45), Stott (p. 152).

4:4-6 In these verses, Paul turns from exhortation to exposition as he introduces grounds for the exhortations of 4:1b-3.

There is no connecting particle to relate 4:4 to 4:1-3. In addition, there is also no verb in the Greek text of these verses, just a list of characteristics that are foundational/fundamental to the unity of the church. They are represented in the display by four propositional clusters (4:4a, 4:4b-d, 4:5a-c, 4:6a-e), in which the church, the Holy Spirit, the Lord Jesus Christ and God the Father are respectively central.

4:4a *There is* one body, *that is, one church*, The Greek has merely ἕν σῶμα "one body". This is a live metaphor, as can be seen from 1 Corinthians 12 and other passages and, therefore, should be retained. It refers to the universal church and may be expressed as "one body, that is, one church" or "one group of believers". The implied verb "to be" has been made explicit as "there is...". An alternative rendering would be: "We are all one body, that is, one church".

4:4b and *there is* one *Holy* Spirit, The Greek has just καὶ ἓν πνεῦμα "and one spirit", but commentators agree that it refers to the Holy Spirit.

4:4c-d just as also each one of you hopes for the same thing, because *God* has called you *to be his people*. Moore (p. 48) regards ἐκλήθητε...τῆς κλήσεως ὑμῶν "you were called...of your call" as being a repetitive doublet (verb-noun). This use of the verb and cognate noun provides an important link with 4:1 where a similar expression is used. See the notes on 4:1.

In the double genitive phrase μιᾷ ἐλπίδι τῆς κλήσεως ὑμῶν "one hope of the calling of you", "the calling" is the same as that referred to in 1:18 and 4:1, i.e. God has called you to be his people.

Also, "the hope" is the same as that referred to in 1:18. It is a confident expectation based on the promise of God. The object of "the hope" is not stated in the Greek text, but, for better understanding, a generic object should be supplied in any verbal representation of the abstract noun phrase. This is especially important since the object of the hope is integral to the meaning in this context, that is, believers are hoping in the same thing.

This double genitive construction represents two events semantically:

1. You hope for the same thing.
2. *God* called you *to be his people*.

The relationship between these two events, "the hope" and "the calling" is one of reason-result. It is because God has called the Ephesian believers to be his people that they have this hope. As his people, they can be sure that he will fulfil his promises to them.

In the Greek. the propositional cluster 4:4c-d is introduced by καθὼς καί "just as also". Commentators discuss the relationship which this signals. The most likely relationship here is either comparison or cause. The phrase καθὼς καί occurs elsewhere in Ephesians—in 1:4 and 4:32 it is considered to be causal. In 4:17, it is considered to be comparative. The causal relationship would be: We know that there is only one body and one Spirit dwelling within us all since we were all called with/to the one hope of our calling. But 4:4-6 is not a unit in which Paul lays out logical argument for units *within itself* but a stating of the truths of the gospel. It is not a matter of one supporting another, but of each one adding to the force of the argument for unity.

The relationship with 4:4a–b, therefore, is regarded as being one of comparison.

4:5 This second set of three marks of unity centres on the Lord Jesus Christ. As Scott says,

> It is better to take the whole sentence as expressive of a single fundamental fact: 'one Lord in whom we all believe and in whose name we have been baptized' (p. 204).

The NUCLEUS of this cluster of propositions is 4:5a, with 4:5b and 4:5c providing further information as to the equality of relationship all believers have with "the one Lord" of 4:5a.

4:5a *There is* **one Lord** *Jesus Christ*. Most commentators agree that εἷς κύριος "one Lord" here refers to the Lord Jesus Christ, in view of the references to the other two members of the Trinity, ἓν πνεῦμα "one Spirit" (4:4) and εἷς θεὸς καὶ πατὴρ πάντων "one God and Father of all" (4:6).

4:5b *It is in the Lord Jesus Christ* **alone** *that we all* **believe**. The Greek only says μία πίστις "one faith". There are several ways to understand this:

1. "Faith" is here used in an objective sense and refers to a corpus of truth, what is believed. See, for example, Best (pp. 368-369), Lenski (p. 512), Lincoln (p. 240), O'Brien (p. 283).
2. "Faith" is used here in a subjective sense and refers to "faith" or "trust" in Christ, i.e. the act of believing. See, for example, Candlish (p. 84), Eadie (p. 275), Hendriksen (pp. 186-187), Hoehner (pp. 516-517).
3. "Faith" here includes both senses. See, for example, Hodge (p. 208).

Hendriksen suggests that in this context the subjective sense is preferable. He says "one faith" refers to

> true and genuine trust—by means of which we embrace the *one* Lord Jesus Christ.... The fact that *faith* is mentioned immediately after *Lord* and is immediately followed by *baptism*, all in one very short sentence, would seem to indicate that the triad is a closely knit unit (p. 187).

All three possibilities make good sense and, in reality, both objective and subjective senses are interdependent, since belief in the person of Christ also means acceptance of, and trust in, that corpus of truth which he taught.

In the display, the subjective sense is represented as "*it is in the Lord Jesus Christ* alone *that we all* believe".

If the objective sense is preferred then it might be represented as "*what we all* believe *about the Lord Jesus Christ is* the same".

4:5c *It is in his name* **alone** *that we are* **baptised**. In the Greek there are just two words, ἓν βάπτισμα "one baptism". Most commentators agree that this refers to water baptism. Since Paul is concerned with the unity of believers in these verses, this symbolic, public demonstration of a believer's faith in Christ is significant, since it is something in which every converted person participated.

This might be expressed as "*it is in Christ's name* alone *that we* are baptised" or, possibly, "*it is to demonstrate this* [4:5b] alone *that we* are baptised".

4:6 This propositional cluster consists of a NUCLEUS (4:6a) followed by further description of "the one God" (4:6a) in 4:6b–e.

4:6a–b *There is* **one God**. He *is* the *spiritual* **Father** *of all his-people/believers*. The term, πατήρ "Father" (referring to God) can be understood in two ways:

1. The "spiritual Father", i.e. the "Father of everyone who believes" or the "Father of all his people".
2. The "universal Father", i.e. the "Father of everyone", the one who created everything.

Since the theme of these verses is the unity of God's people, the first option is the most likely in the context.

4:6c He **rules** *over all his people*. The Greek simply says ὁ ἐπὶ πάντων "the [one] over all". The commentators suggest two possible referents for πάντων "all" in this verse:

1. It refers to all humanity.
2. It refers only to the church.

The second option is the majority view, i.e. it refers only to the church. This seems appropriate in the context for several reasons:

a. Paul is writing *to* believers and *about* the church, not to and about the world in general.
b. One of Paul's themes is the unity of the church.
c. In 4:7, Paul talks about the gifts given to "every one of us", which could only apply to believers. It is unlikely that Paul would change referent so suddenly without some overt signal.

The sense of the whole phrase ὁ ἐπὶ πάντων "the [one] over all", therefore, is "the God who rules over his people".

4:6d He empowers/sustains all *his people.* The Greek text here is simply διὰ πάντων "through all". Commentators discuss the sense in which God is "through all". The two main suggestions they make are:

1. It means that God works through believers. They are his instruments, working out his purposes. See Candlish, p. 84.
2. It means that God pervades all believers, empowering and sustaining them.

For example, Abbott says,

> διὰ πάντων expresses a relation to the whole body, through the whole of which the influence and power of God are diffused. It is a sustaining and working presence (p. 109).

Lloyd-Jones (p. 140) expresses the same idea by saying that God is "energetic" in all his people, i.e. it is God's power and energy which sustains the church. In 1:19–20, Paul says,

> ...how very great is his power at work in us who believe. This power working in us is the same as the mighty strength which he used when he raised Christ from death... (TEV).

This also supports option two. So, in the display, this is expressed by using the verbs "empowers/sustains".

4:6e He *is present spiritually* **in** *the hearts of* **all** *his people.* Most commentators consider that the phrase ἐν πᾶσιν "in all" means that God is present spiritually in the hearts of his people in the person of the Holy Spirit.

BOUNDARIES AND COHERENCE

The initial boundary coincides with that of the division, 4:1–6:20, and has been discussed in the section on Boundaries and Coherence there. It might be possible to posit a boundary between 4:1 and 4:2, since 4:1 appears to be a generic exhortation, with the following exhortations in 4:2–6:9 being in a specific relation to it on a higher level, but it is doubtful that Paul had in mind a break between 4:1 and 4:2 when he wrote the letter.

Grammatically, these verses are dependent on the verb περιπατῆσαι "to walk" in 4:1. Structurally, the use of asyndeton to relate clauses is a distinctive feature of 4:1–6.

The following factors contribute to the cohesion of the paragraph:

1. Seven occurrences of εἷς "one", five occurrences of πᾶς "all"
2. References to the three persons of the Trinity

The beginning of the next unit 4:7–16 is marked by the δέ in 4:7. It signals the introduction of a new aspect of Paul's current theme. The focus shifts from the Christian community as a whole to the individual believers and their contribution to the unity and spiritual growth of the whole community. See Ἑνὶ... ἑκάστῳ ἡμῶν "to each one of us" (4:7).

PROMINENCE AND THEME

The recurrence of εἷς "one" and πᾶς "all" in these verses gives prominence to the idea of unity as the theme of this unit.

The GENERIC EXHORTATION of 4:1b is naturally prominent. SPECIFIC EXHORTATION₃ in 4:3 is regarded as being marked prominent, since, although specific exhortations₁&₂ of 4:2 are hortatory in themselves they also semantically support 4:3. Also 4:3 is supported by the motivational grounds of 4:4–6. The theme statement, therefore, is based on 4:1b and 4:3b, the latter being nuclear to propositional cluster 4:3a–c, and also on the NUCLEI of the grounds (4:4a–6e).

SECTION CONSTITUENT 4:7–16 (Expository Paragraph: Grounds for 4:1–6)

THEME: Christ has given different spiritual gifts to each one in his church, in order that the church might remain united and become spiritually mature.

RELATIONAL STRUCTURE	CONTENTS
GENERIC — CONCLUSION	4:7 Christ has freely given a spiritual gift to each one of us, in accordance with what he has chosen to give,
grounds — orienter	4:8a as it is written *in the following Scripture*,
grounds — NUCLEUS	4:8b "When he ascended to the-highest-place/heaven, he was victorious over his enemies *and* he gave gifts to people".
contraction — orienter	4:9a "He ascended" must imply
contraction — CONTENT	4:9b that he had also previously descended to the earth [RHQ].
explanatory amplification — NUCLEUS — MEANS	4:10a Christ who descended is also the one who ascended to the most exalted position in heaven,
PURPOSE	4:10b in order that he might exercise his power throughout the universe.
MEANS — SPECIFIC	4:11 He gave/appointed some people to be apostles. He appointed some people to be prophets. He appointed some people to be evangelists. He appointed some people to be pastors/leaders and teachers.
means — means	4:12a *Christ did this* [4:7, 11] *in order that they* [those in 4:11] *might prepare/equip God's people*
means — PURPOSE	4:12b to minister *to one another*,
means — INTERMEDIATE PURPOSE	4:12c in order that the church of Christ might become *spiritually* mature,
PURPOSE — NUCLEUS — ULTIMATE PURPOSE — NUCLEUS₁ — NUCLEUS₁	4:13a so that, finally, all we *believers* are completely united by means of believing in the Son of God
NUCLEUS₂	4:13b and we are all completely united by means of fully knowing the Son of God
NUCLEUS₂ — NUCLEUS	4:13c *and* we all *individually and as a church* become fully mature spiritually [MET],
EQUIVALENT	4:13d *that is*, we all become completely conformed to Christ, who is perfect.
negative — NUCLEUS	4:14a *That is to say*, we will no longer be *spiritually* immature like children are immature [MET].
amplification₁	4:14b We will no longer be completely unstable about what we believe, like a wave of the sea *is unstable, because it* is blown about and carried here and there by the wind [MET].
amplification₂	4:14c We will no longer be influenced by people who teach what is false, *that is*, by people who scheme cleverly/unscrupulously, in order to deceive *us/people*.

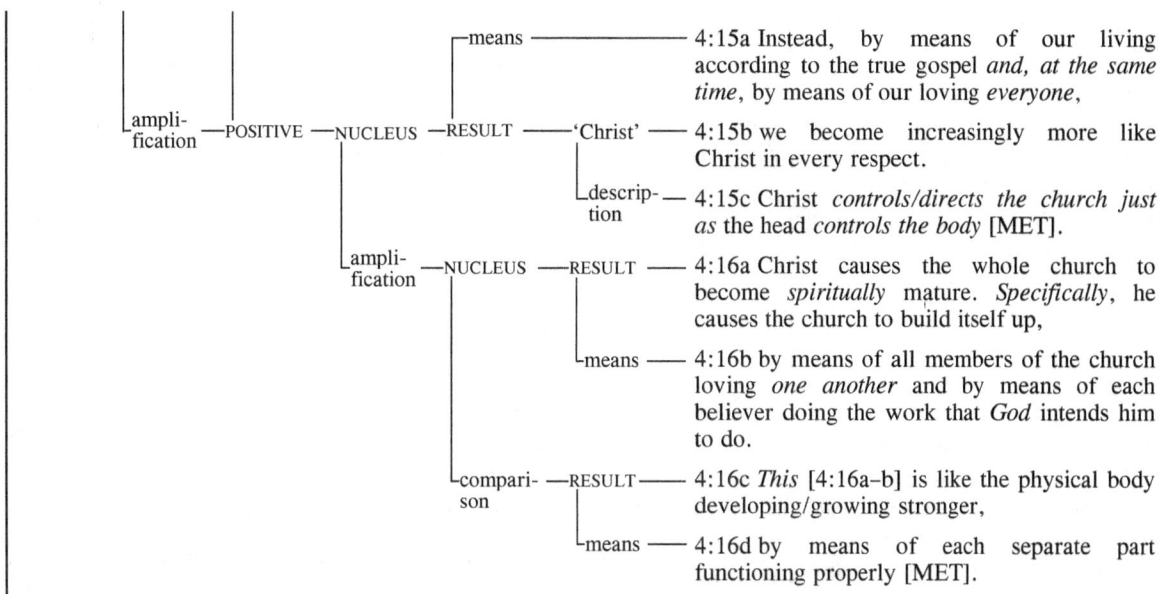

INTENT AND STRUCTURE

Paragraph 4:7-16 is an amplification of paragraph 4:1-6 and, at the same time, provides motivational and enabling information for the exhortations of 4:7-16 that believers should do all they can to maintain unity in the church.

In 4:7-11, the focus is on the variety of gifts which Christ has given to individual believers in the church. In 4:12-16, the purpose for which these gifts have been given is in focus, i.e. the development of a spiritually mature and united church.

NOTES

4:7 The initial δέ here may indicate several relations:

1. A participant switch to the members of the church as individuals.
2. A change from one aspect of a subject to another aspect of the same subject.
3. A contrast between two subjects.

Although there is a contrast between the unity referred to in 4:4-6 and the diversity referred to in 4:7-16 (option three), it is clear that the subject being dealt with in 4:7-16 is related very closely to the one which Paul was discussing in 4:1-6. He continues, in 4:7-16, with the subject of the unity of the church, but now goes on to deal with a different aspect of that subject (option two). Having emphasised those matters in which believers should all be the same, he now deals with matters in which there will be differences, as each believer fulfils the role ascribed to him by Christ, using the spiritual gifts he has received for the benefit of all.

A number of translations indicate the transition simply by beginning a new paragraph, e.g. JBP, TEV.

4:7 Christ has freely given a spiritual gift to each one of us, In the Greek text, Paul uses the noun ἡ χάρις "the grace". However, here he is not referring to God's grace in the sense of 2:8, i.e. the "grace" by which we have been saved. Rather, ἡ χάρις "grace" in this verse needs to be something that can be given (the full phrase used in the verse is ἐδόθη ἡ χάρις "grace was given"). Therefore, in this context, ἡ χάρις "the grace" is probably equivalent to χάρισμα "gift", the term Paul uses in 1 Corinthians 12:4 and Romans 12:6.

Paul is concerned, in this section of his letter, with the unity of the church and how the church should function in order to maintain that unity and become spiritually mature. Verse 4:11, in particular, illustrates that Paul's theme is the grace given to each member of God's church, which enables each one to make their own particular contribution to the spiritual growth of the body of Christ.

The Greek phrase ἐδόθη ἡ χάρις "grace was given" is difficult to propositionalise, since, in the expression "give a gift", "gift" most naturally refers to a material gift. In order to avoid this misunderstanding, the adjective "spiritual" is used in the display to qualify the noun "gift".

The agent of the passive verb "was given" is Christ, as the context makes clear.

in accordance with what he has chosen to give, The preposition κατά "according to" in the phrase κατὰ τὸ μέτρον τῆς δωρεᾶς τοῦ Χριστοῦ "according to the measure of the gift of Christ" indicates the standard against which the quantity of grace given can be measured. That standard is "according to what Christ has chosen to give".

The relationship between the three nouns in the genitive construction τὸ μέτρον τῆς δωρεᾶς τοῦ Χριστοῦ "the measure of the gift of Christ" is that "Christ" is the one who gives and he gives a certain amount of grace to each believer, i.e. he gives as much as he chooses to give. The specific details of the giving of these spiritual gifts is dealt with in 4:11, where Paul enumerates the various tasks to which Christ has appointed individuals in the church.

4:8-10 The διό "therefore" introduces the proof of what Paul says in 4:7, i.e. we know that Christ gave gifts, since the Scriptures say so.

Although the primary meaning of διό is "therefore", most commentators consider that here it introduces the grounds for 4:7. Commentators consider the Old Testament quotation in 4:8 chronologically as prior and logically as evidential grounds for the validity of the statement in 4:7.

In 4:8, Paul cites Psalm 68:18, while, in 4:9-10, he comments on the significance of the verse. In the Old Testament context, the reference is to the *Lord God* (the Hebrew text has YAHWEH). Here Paul uses it to refer to the *Lord Jesus Christ*.

4:8a as it is written *in the following Scripture*, The Greek has simply λέγει "he/it says", i.e. Paul does not make the subject of "says" explicit. There are two options:

1. The subject is "God".
2. The subject is "Scripture".

Although it is God who speaks in the Scriptures, since the Old Testament quotation refers to God as "you", it is preferable to follow the second option, i.e. to consider "Scripture" as the subject of λέγει. The verb is then equivalent to γέγραπται "it is written", the more usual expression used in the New Testament when an Old Testament quotation is being referred to. So it is acceptable to translate λέγει in the same way as γέγραπται is translated elsewhere. Another possibility is to translate it as "*Scripture* says", especially if it is natural in a language to use "say" with "books" as agents of the speaking.

This proposition provides an orienter for the rest of the verse.

4:8b "When he ascended to the-highest-place/heaven, Commentators discuss whether the Greek ἀναβὰς εἰς ὕψος "having ascended to (the) height" referred, in the the original psalm, to,

1. God, going up to heaven.
2. God, entering into the temple on Mt. Zion.
3. The king of Israel, entering the temple on Mt. Zion after a literal victory.

They agree, however, that Paul applies it to Christ's ascension to heaven, forty days after his resurrection. In the display, the pronoun "he" is retained, since this is an Old Testament quotation.

he was victorious over his enemies The Greek ᾐχμαλώτευσεν αἰχμαλωσίαν "he led captivity captive" is a translation of a figurative Hebrew expression describing the victory parade of a triumphant conqueror.

Regarding Paul's use of the text, commentators do not agree about who the people are that Christ leads in his procession. There are two views:

1. Most commentators consider that he is leading his enemies, those whom he has conquered and are now his prisoners. In this context, these prisoners would be the principalities and powers opposed to him whom Paul refers to elsewhere. See, for example, Alford (pp. 115–116), Hodge (p. 214), Lloyd-Jones (p. 153), Stott (p. 157).
2. Other commentators consider that he is leading his own people in triumph, after his victory over death. See, for example, Foulkes (p. 123), Hendriksen (p. 191).

Most commentators argue for the first option and that is what is followed in this analysis.

***and* he gave gifts to people".** This part of the verse in the New Testament Greek text differs from the original psalm in both the Hebrew and the LXX texts. There is no obvious reason for this difference. It may be because Paul was quoting from a different version of the Old Testament than we have now or because he wanted to make it appropriate to the point he wished to make here. The translator should follow what Paul says here in the Greek text and not make it agree with the original psalm.

When he died on the cross, rose again and ascended to heaven, Christ defeated Satan, sin and death, all the powers of evil. As the victor, he has the right to give gifts to his people, whom he has freed from these powers. Unlike a triumphant conqueror who gives *material* gifts to his people, it is *spiritual* gifts that Christ gives to his people.

4:9-10 Paul now explains the quotation in 4:8. He concentrates, in particular, on ἀναβάς "having ascended". This propositional cluster (4:9-10) is an explanatory amplification of 4:8b.

The principle of unity is emphasised by the fact that Christ is the only one who dispenses these spiritual gifts.

In 4:9, Paul uses a rhetorical question to introduce the topic of what "he ascended" means. If Christ ascended, then he must previously have descended, since his place is in heaven, cf. John 3:13.

4:9a "He ascended" must imply The Greek is τὸ δὲ Ἀνέβη τί ἐστιν εἰ μή "he ascended what is it except...". The δέ introduces another aspect of the topic under discussion. It is translated as "now" (connective "now" rather than temporal "now") in some versions and omitted in others. The use of τί "what" signals that the form in Greek is a question. In this verse it is a rhetorical question. In the display, a positive statement, "must imply", has been used. This provides an orienter for the next clause.

4:9b that he had also previously descended to the earth. In this clause, ὅτι κατέβη εἰς τὰ κατώτερα μέρη τῆς γῆς "that he descended into the lower parts of the earth", most of the discussion centres on the relationship between the nouns in the genitive construction τὰ κατώτερα μέρη τῆς γῆς "the lower parts of the earth". It may refer to:

1. The region lower than the surface of the earth, specifically, to hades, the place of the dead. See, for example, Bratcher and Nida (pp. 99-100), Ellicott (p. 71), Lenski (pp. 521-522).
2. The earth. It is a genitive of apposition: "the lower parts, namely, the earth". See, for example, Eadie (p. 293), Hodge (pp. 220-

221), Lincoln (p. 245), O'Brien (p. 294, fn. 84), Stott (p. 158).

The second option seems the more appropriate in the context, since, as Lincoln says,

> [T]he contrast in these verses appears to be between an ascent to heaven and descent from heaven, while the descent involved in the traditional view of a descent into Hades is not so much from heaven but from earth to the underworld or the realm of the dead (p. 245).

Following the second option, the "descent" may refer to two things:

1. Christ's incarnation
2. His coming in the Spirit at Pentecost.

Most of the commentators consider the first option to be the correct one, i.e. that the "descent" refers to Christ's incarnation. See, for example, Hendriksen (pp. 192-193, fn.111), Hodge (pp. 220-221), O'Brien (p. 296), Stott (p. 158). This is, therefore, the view followed in the display.

As the heavens are "the higher parts", so the earth is "the lower parts". Paul is, therefore, asserting that it is the work which the Lord Jesus did when he was here on earth that elevates him to the position in which he, as head of the church, is the one who gives gifts to the believers, cf. 1:19-23.

There is another issue with this verse. Some Greek manuscripts (and, therefore, English versions) have the word πρῶτον "first, previously" immediately after the verb κατέβη "he descended". See, for example, KJV, NAB. The UBS text and most versions, however, omit it.

It is, however, included in the display to make the chronological order clear.

4:10a-b This propositional cluster is an amplification of 4:9. Christ continues to be the subject of the verbs. This verse is considered to be more prominent than 4:9 because of its focus on the exalted position of Christ.

4:10a Christ who descended is also the one who ascended to the most exalted position in heaven, The Greek says ὁ καταβὰς αὐτός ἐστιν καὶ ὁ ἀναβάς, literally "the one descending is *himself* also the one ascending". The use of αὐτός "himself" emphasises that it was the same person who ascended as descended and that that person was Christ. See the note on 4:9b.

The meaning of ὑπεράνω πάντων τῶν οὐρανῶν "far above all the heavens" is that Christ is exalted above the whole universe in rank and power. All things are subject to him. His position is as exalted and supreme as that of God the Father, with whom he shares authority. This has been expressed, in the display, as "the most exalted position in heaven", since this is the position of authority and power.

4:10b in order that he might exercise his power throughout the universe. The ἵνα "in order that" indicates the purpose of Christ's ascending to the most exalted position in the universe.

However, the meaning of πληρώσῃ τὰ πάντα "he might fill all (things)" is not clear. There are two main views:

1. Christ ascended in order to fill the universe with his presence. More specifically, Christ ascended to exercise his sovereign power and authority throughout the universe. See, for example, Eadie (pp. 296-297), Ellicott (p. 72), Hodge (p. 221), Meyer (p. 452), O'Brien (pp. 296-297).
2. Christ, in his incarnation and ascension, perfectly completed all that God required in uniting all things in himself. See, for example, Robinson (p. 96), Scott (p. 209).

The first option has most support. For example, Hodge says,

> It is not of the ubiquity of Christ's body of which the apostle speaks,...but of the universal presence and power of the ascended Son of God. It is God clothed in our nature, who now exercises this universal dominion; and, therefore, the apostle may well say of Christ, as the incarnate God, that he gives gifts unto men (p. 222).

This view is, therefore, followed in the display. As a result of Christ's ascension, he now dispenses the gifts which he has carried: salvation and all that it includes, and the services of those who proclaim it, such as apostles, evangelists, etc. Paul goes on in 4:11 to list some of these gifts.

4:11 This cluster of propositions is in a specific relationship with 4:7. The label SPECIFIC is in upper case letters because 4:11 is marked prominent by its direct relationship as MEANS to the PURPOSE unit of 4:12-16.

4:11a-d He gave/appointed some people to be The Greek pronoun αὐτός "he" refers to Christ.

In most versions, the verb ἔδωκεν is translated "he gave" or "gave gifts" (JB, KJV, NEB, NIV, NLT), and this is supported by the majority of commentaries. See, for example, Alford (p. 117), Eadie (pp. 297-298), Ellicott (pp. 69, 72), Hendriksen (p. 195), Hodge (p. 222). In TEV (1976, 1992) it is translated,

> It was he who 'gave gifts to people'; he appointed some to be apostles....

Both senses of the Greek verb δίδωμι "give, appoint" are given in the display. In some languages it may be better to use "appoint" if the use of "give" would result in a collocational clash. Christ appointed men to various roles in the church. However, since all of 4:7-11 revolves around the words "give" and "gifts" in the Greek and, in some languages, "give" is appropriate for the idea of "appoint", the alternative "give" may be preferred. In fact, the relationship between giving gifts and appointing people to these positions may be obscured in translation if some way is not found to maintain the correspondence which the use of "give" has in both places in the Greek text.

apostles. The key biblical term ἀπόστολος "apostle" has several meanings, two of which are appropriate here:

1. It refers only to the original twelve disciples and Paul: those whom Jesus commissioned and sent out to proclaim the gospel, and to establish and build up his church. See, for example, Ellicott (pp. 72-73), Hendriksen (p. 196), Hodge (p. 223), O'Brien (pp. 297-298, fn. 100, 101).
2. It refers to a wider circle of men; they may not have been directly commissioned by Jesus and may not have witnessed his resurrection, but they still ministered to the early church. This would include believers like Barnabas, Apollos and Titus. See, for example, Hoehner (p. 541), Meyer (p. 453).

There is no consensus as to which alternative Paul meant here. However, in 2:20 and 3:5, Paul referred to both "apostles" and "prophets" as playing a foundational role in the church. Also, as O'Brien says about "apostle",

> The term is also used by Paul on occasion in a nontechnical sense to signify a 'messenger' of the churches (2 Cor. 8:22-23; Phil. 2:25). However, the overwhelming number of instances in his letters are to 'apostles' in a technical sense who were called and sent by Christ (p. 84).

In view of this it may be preferable to understand the term in its more restricted sense.

prophets. The term προφήτης "prophet" may refer to:

1. Old Testament prophets, for example, Isaiah, Jeremiah.
2. New Testament prophets, for example, Agabus (Acts 21:10).

There is greater support for the latter in the commentaries. New Testament prophets were people in the early church to whom God spoke directly on different occasions, and who then spoke this inspired message to the local church.

evangelists. The Greek noun εὐαγγελιστής "evangelist" is only used here, in Acts 21:8 (referring to Philip) and 2 Timothy 4:5 (referring to the work Paul is urging Timothy to do). Most commentators believe that an evangelist was someone sent out from the church to proclaim the message of salvation to those outside the church.

Although there was some overlap between the functions fulfilled by apostles, prophets and evangelists, it can be said,

> [T]he evangelists would win converts to the faith, the apostles would establish churches, and the prophets would fill in needed revelation for the perfection of the saints (Hoehner, p. 543).

pastors/leaders and teachers. There is some debate as to whether the designation ποιμένας καὶ διδασκάλους (literally, "shepherds and teachers") indicates:

1. One group of people: those who both "shepherded" and taught believers.
2. Two groups of people: those who "shepherded" believers (i.e. cared and watched over them) and those who taught believers.

Most commentators consider that only one group is referred to here, referring to people who have the gift of both being a "shepherd" and a teacher within the church. This view is supported grammatically by Paul's use of the particle δέ with each of προφήτας and εὐαγγελιστάς, but only one with ποιμένας καὶ διδασκάλους.

The Greek ποιμήν "shepherd" is used figuratively of someone who exercises leadership in the church. The function of leadership is stressed by many commentators.

Some equate this function with a modern-day pastor of a local congregation. Most English versions do translate as "pastors". The sense of caring for and nurturing the church most likely remained as a component of meaning of the word ποιμήν "shepherd". See Acts 20:28 and Lincoln (p. 251).

4:12 The initial πρός "for" indicates Christ's purpose in giving certain believers the gifts referred to in the preceding verses.

The main point for discussion in this verse is the relationship between the three prepositional phrases, introduced respectively by πρός, εἰς and εἰς. The following are some of the possibilities commentators suggest:

1. The three prepositional phrases are parallel/co-ordinate. Each phrase contains a distinct purpose. Each is related independently to ἔδωκεν "he gave" in 4:11. See, for example, Lincoln (p. 253).
2. The three prepositional phrases are successive. The sentence as a whole depends on ἔδωκεν "he gave" (4:11), but each phrase depends on the preceding one, with the third providing the climax and expressing the ultimate object of the giving. See, for example, Best (pp. 398–399), Lenski (p. 530), Hoehner (pp. 548–549), O'Brien (pp. 302–303).
3. The first phrase is the ultimate end, with the second and third being co-ordinate and depending on ἔδωκεν "he gave" (4:11). See, for example, Eadie (p. 308), Ellicott (p. 74), Hodge (pp. 229–230).

In making a choice between these options, the following points need to be considered:

a. Paul changes the preposition, using πρός before the first phrase and εἰς before the other two phrases, so that it is unlikely that they are simply co-ordinate.
b. The first and last phrases are similar, referring to τῶν ἁγίων "the saints" and τὸ σῶμα τοῦ Χριστοῦ "the body of Christ". This seems to indicate that the second phrase is dependent on the first to define who is doing ἔργον διακονίας the "work of ministry".

The display is based on the second option: each prepositional phrase providing the means for the following phrase. From the first two purposes (4:12a and 4:12b), Paul moves to the intermediate purpose (4:12c) and then on to the ultimate purpose in 4:13a–b.

If this analysis is followed the building up of the body of Christ is the responsibility of all believers and not just a select group. As O'Brien says,

> [T]he letter as a whole has emphasized Christ's riches being received by *all* the saints (1:3-19; 3:20), while the immediate context of vv. 7-16 is framed by an insistence at the beginning of the paragraph that each believer was given 'grace' (v. 7), and at its conclusion that the *whole* body is growing from the head as *each part* (v. 16) does its work (p. 303).

4:12a *Christ did this* [4:7, 11] In order to avoid an overly long sentence, a new sentence is started here in the display. A short generic clause has been added in the display to link 4:12-16 to 4:7-11.

in order that *they* [those in 4:11] might prepare/equip This proposition is the purpose related most directly to 4:11. However, it is also the purpose for all 4:7-11 and it provides the means for 4:12b.

The Greek noun καταρτισμός literally means, "the setting of a bone", but, more generally, "restoration". In this context, it has the sense of "equip" for service, although "training, discipline" is another possible meaning (BDAG, p. 526).

Most commentators agree that the people referred to in 4:11 are the agents in this clause. It is their ministry that equips.

God's people The Greek term τῶν ἁγίων "the saints, the holy ones" refers to believers in general, that is, the whole body of Christ, the church. It is translated in the display as "God's people" to emphasise the aspect of the word ἅγιος "holy" meaning that believers are dedicated to God.

4:12b to minister *to one another*, The preposition εἰς "to" introduces the purpose of 4:12a. Even though normally we would represent purpose in the propositionalisation with "in order that", here it is represented by "to" so as to avoid being too repetitious in this string of four purpose constituents.

In the genitive construction ἔργον διακονίας "the work of ministry", διακονία may refer to two possibilities:

1. An official/recognised ministry in the church, i.e. as an apostle, prophet, etc. See, for example, Hodge (p. 228) and Meyer, who says,

    διακονία, where the context is speaking of those engaged in the service of the church, always denotes the *official* service (p. 455).

2. Christian ministry in general, i.e. something which all believers are equipped to do. See, for example, Hoehner (p. 550) and Hendriksen, who remarks,

    > The important lesson taught here is that not only apostles, prophets, evangelists, and those who are called "pastors and teachers," but the entire church should be engaged in spiritual labor. ...it is the task of the officers of the church to equip the church for these tasks (p. 198).

The context seems to support the second option, i.e. that Christian service in general is referred to here. In this chapter, Paul is emphasising both the unity of the church and its diversity, and the part that each one has to play in maintaining the unity. The wider reference then, of believers ministering to one another, would be more appropriate.

4:12c in order that the church of Christ might become *spiritually* mature, This proposition is in a purpose relation with 4:12b which provides its means.

The Greek here is εἰς οἰκοδομὴν τοῦ σώματος τοῦ Χριστοῦ "for building up of the body of Christ". See the note on 4:12b for εἰς.

The οἰκοδομήν "building up" is not a live metaphor. It simply means helping the church to grow and develop spiritually.

4:13 The conjunction μέχρι "until" introduces a description of the final goal or ultimate purpose of building up the church. According to Lincoln (p. 255), it has "both a prospective and a final force". Believers are to carry out their ministry in order that the church might achieve its goal, and they are to do so *until* that goal is reached. See also Candlish (pp. 90-91), Hodge (p. 230), O'Brien (p. 305).

It is not clear whether:

1. This verse connects with the immediately preceding prepositional phrase εἰς οἰκοδομὴν τοῦ σώματος τοῦ Χριστοῦ "for building up of the body of Christ" (4:12).
2. This verse connects with ἔδωκεν "he gave" (4:11).

There is no consensus among commentators as to which is preferred. In the display, 4:13 is shown as the ULTIMATE PURPOSE of 4:12 and the PURPOSE of 4:11.

This final goal is described in three prepositional phrases (in 4:13a–b, 13c, 13d), each introduced by εἰς "to". Commentators differ in how they understand the connection between these phrases. The following possibilities are suggested:

1. The three prepositional phrases are parallel/co-ordinate, each one depending on the verb καταντήσωμεν "we arrive at, attain to". See, for example, Bratcher and Nida (p. 103), Lincoln (p. 255), Robinson (p. 183).
2. The second prepositional phrase explains or builds upon the first and the third prepositional phrase explains or builds upon the second. See, for example, Hodge (pp. 233-234), Hoehner (p. 553), Lenski (p. 533).
3. The first two prepositional phrases are parallel/co-ordinate with each other and the third prepositional phrase more specifically defines the second. See, for example, Candlish (p. 91), O'Brien (pp. 306-307).

The third option is followed in the display.

4:13a so that, finally, all we *believers* are completely united by means of believing in the Son of God "All we *believers*" in the display represents οἱ πάντες "all", as well as the first person plural ending on the verb καταντήσωμεν. This probably refers to τῶν ἁγίων "the saints" in 4:12a and τοῦ σώματος τοῦ Χριστοῦ "the body of Christ" in 4:12b, i.e. the church, all believers, among whom Paul is including himself.

The verb καταντάω literally means "to come to, arrive at". Here it is used figuratively and means "to attain to something". In this case, what is to be attained is expressed by two genitive phrases: τὴν ἑνότητα τῆς πίστεως "the unity of the faith" and τῆς ἐπιγνώσεως τοῦ υἱοῦ τοῦ θεοῦ "the knowledge of the Son of God" (4:13a-b).

The idea of unity is represented in the display as "are completely united". An alternative would be "are like one".

Commentators differ in how they understand the genitive phrase τοῦ υἱοῦ τοῦ θεοῦ "of the Son of God" to relate to other parts of the verse. The suggestions are:

1. It is in a genitival relationship with only τῆς ἐπιγνώσεως "the knowledge" (4:13b). See, for example, Lincoln (p. 256), O'Brien (p. 306, fn.139).
2. It is in a genitival relationship with both τῆς πίστεως "the faith" (4:13a) and τῆς ἐπιγνώσεως "the knowledge" (4:13b). See, for example, Eadie (p. 310), Ellicott (p. 75), Hodge (p. 232), Lenski (p. 534).

Most commentators follow the second option and so it is followed in the display. The object of both τῆς πίστεως "the faith" and τῆς ἐπιγνώσεως "the knowledge" is τοῦ υἱοῦ τοῦ θεοῦ "the Son of God". So the full expression in 3:13a is τὴν ἑνότητα τῆς πίστεως...τοῦ υἱοῦ τοῦ θεοῦ "the unity of the faith...of the Son of God".

Commentators differ in how they understand τῆς πίστεως "the faith" here. There are two possibilities:

1. It refers to "that which is believed", i.e. doctrine. See, for example, Best (p. 400), Hoehner (p. 553), Lincoln (p. 255), O'Brien (p. 306).
2. It refers to the act of believing. See, for example, Candlish (p. 91), Eadie (pp. 310-311), Lenski (pp. 533-534), Robinson (pp. 182-183).

The second option is followed in the display because "this passage is not about diverse doctrines and heresies, but about the unity of believers" (Bratcher and Nida, p. 103). It is by means of believing in the Son of God that the believers are united.

4:13b and we are all completely united by means of fully knowing the Son of God Most commentators understand the καί "and" here as introducing an addition relation.

There are two ways to understand the genitive phrase τῆς ἐπιγνώσεως τοῦ υἱοῦ τοῦ θεοῦ "the knowledge of the Son of God":

1. It refers to what believers know about the Son of God, i.e. doctrine. See, for example, Eadie (p. 311), O'Brien (p. 306).
2. It refers to how fully believers know Christ in a personal, experiential way. See, for example, Bratcher and Nida (p. 103), Foulkes (pp. 129-130).

The Greek noun ἐπίγνωσις "knowledge" used here is a strong word which has the sense of "experiential knowledge" or "full knowledge", rather than simply knowing *about* someone. It, therefore, does not refer just to doctrine about Christ (option one). It is true, personal, experiential knowledge of Christ himself (option two), i.e. "to know perfectly, fully". See also 3:18-19. As "faith...of the Son of God" was the means of unity in 4:13a, so here, "knowledge of the Son of God" is a means of unity.

4:13c *and* we all *individually and as a church* become fully mature spiritually, The Greek here εἰς ἄνδρα τέλειον "to a mature man" is also dependent on καταντήσωμεν "we attain to" and is parallel to 4:13a-b. It is further explained by 4:13d, εἰς μέτρον ἡλικίας τοῦ πληρώματος τοῦ Χριστοῦ "to the measure of the stature of the fulness of Christ". It also contrasts with νήπιοι "infants" (4:14).

The main point for discussion in the commentaries is about who the word ἀνήρ "man" refers to here. There are two possibilities:

1. It refers to believers as individuals. See, for example, Mitton (p. 154), TEV.
2. It refers to the church as a corporate body. See Best (pp. 401, 403), Eadie (p. 313), Hoehner (p. 555), Lincoln (p. 256), O'Brien (p. 307).

Most commentators support the second option, i.e. that ἀνὴρ τέλειος "a mature man" is a metaphorical reference to the church as it attains spiritual maturity. The figure is of an adult, a fully developed, mature man. This "mature man" represents the church, with Christ the head, and believers as members of the body.

The immediate context also supports the second option since there is an apparent movement from the varied service of individuals (4:11), to "the body of Christ" (4:12), to "we all", "unity" and "the mature man" (4:13). In 4:13, Paul's focus appears to be on God's people collectively, as a unit. In the wider context, this option would agree with Paul's use of the expression "the one new man" (εἷς καινὸς ἄνθρωπος) in 2:15 to refer to Jewish and Gentile believers united as one church.

In this analysis, therefore, the "mature man" is understood to refer to the growth towards maturity of the church as a whole. However, this growth depends on the maturing of individuals who make up the church. So the two meanings are inextricably connected. The display, therefore, contains both meanings.

The meaning is expressed non-figuratively in the display, with the adverb "spiritually" qualifying the verb "become...mature".

The use of "fully" to further qualify the verb distinguishes this proposition from 4:12c, in which the event is viewed as an intended purpose, i.e. the goal to be worked towards now. Here it is viewed more as the final purpose realised. In the display, 4:12c is labelled as INTERMEDIATE PURPOSE and 4:13a-d as ULTIMATE PURPOSE.

4:13d *that is,* we all become completely conformed to Christ, who is perfect. Here εἰς introduces the third εἰς prepositional phrase in this verse. It is in apposition to 4:13c, further explaining it. Constituent 4:13d refers to the standard of perfection for the church, i.e. complete conformity to Christ.

The Greek expression τοῦ πληρώματος τοῦ Χριστοῦ "the fulness of Christ" recalls 3:19 "the fulness of God". The latter refers to God's perfection. See the notes on 3:19.

In the genitive construction μέτρον ἡλικίας τοῦ πληρώματος τοῦ Χριστοῦ "the measure of the stature of the fulness of Christ", "fulness" may be considered a characteristic of "stature", i.e perfection. In turn μέτρον "measure" is the standard to which the church should attain: the standard of perfection—complete conformity to Christ. In other words, the church is to become perfect, as Christ is perfect, which entails each individual member's conforming to that standard of perfection.

4:14 The initial ἵνα "so that" may indicate a number of relationships. The two main possibilities are:

1. It describes an intermediate purpose in attaining the goal of 4:13. See, for example, Eadie (p. 315).
2. It further explains what the attainment of 4:13 means. See, for example, Ellicott (p. 76).

There is no consensus among the commentators. However, it seems best to understand verses 14 and 15 as amplificatory to verse 13, stating, first in negative terms (v. 14) and then in positive terms (v. 15), those things that should be evident in the lives of believers as they progress towards their ultimate goal of being perfect.

4:14a *That is to say,* we will no longer be *spiritually* immature like children are immature. The Greek μηκέτι ὦμεν νήπιοι "no more we may be infants" contrasts with ἄνδρα τέλειον "a mature/full-grown man" in 4:13. The metaphor compares the spiritual immaturity of a believer at an early stage of spiritual growth with the immature nature and attitudes of a child. Paul goes on to amplify this in 4:14b-c.

4:14b We will no longer be completely unstable about what we believe, like a wave of the sea *is unstable, because it* is blown about and carried here and there by the wind. Paul uses a further metaphor here to explain the immaturity referred to in 4:14a. This is a live metaphor, so both the figure and its non-figurative meaning are stated in the display.

Anything immature believers hear, whether true or false, easily influences them. They, therefore, are constantly changing their mind about what they believe. They are not stable/consistent in their beliefs, just as waves are not stable when the wind blows them about. One of the principal elements of the perfection described in 4:13 is the ability to discern what is true and remain stable in those beliefs. Cf. James 1:6 and Hebrews 13:9.

Moore (p. 48) considers κλυδωνιζόμενοι "be tossed here and there by waves" and περιφερόμενοι "be carried about here and there" as a doublet. If this analysis is followed then perhaps "completely unstable/inconsistent" might be used to express the sense.

4:14c We will no longer be influenced by people who teach what is false, The phrase ἐν τῇ κυβείᾳ τῶν ἀνθρώπων "in the cunning of men" further explains 4:14a.

The word κυβεία "cunning" originally referred to games played with dice. As such games often involved trickery/cheating, the word, therefore, came to refer to trickery, cunning.

The complete genitive phrase ἐν τῇ κυβείᾳ τῶν ἀνθρώπων "in the cunning of men" has the sense of "men who practise cunning, men who behave in a cunning way". In this context, it refers to false teachers. Immature believers are easily drawn away from the truth by such people, i.e. they are "influenced by (*or* susceptible to) men who teach what is false".

***that is,* by people who scheme cleverly/ unscrupulously, in order to deceive *us/people*.** The phrase ἐν πανουργίᾳ πρὸς τὴν μεθοδείαν τῆς πλάνης "in cleverness unto the craftiness/ scheming of error" is parallel with, and explanatory of, ἐν τῇ κυβείᾳ τῶν ἀνθρώπων "in the cunning of men" in the first part of 4:14c.

The initial ἐν "in" introduces a restatement and explanation of the previous clause. The πρός "to" introduces the purpose of men's πανουργία "cleverness". In the New Testament the noun πανουργία "cleverness" occurs five times, Luke 20:23; 1 Corinthians 3:19; 2 Corinthians 4:2; 11:3 and here, always in a pejorative sense, referring to unscrupulous conduct. In this context, it is regarded as semantically qualifying μεθοδείαν "scheming", i.e. "men craftily/ cleverly scheme".

The genitive construction τὴν μεθοδείαν τῆς πλάνης "the scheming of error" has the sense of someone scheming in order to deceive other people. The word πλάνης "error" states a quality of this scheming, i.e. it is "deceitful". In the display, this is expressed as "scheming in order to deceive people".

4:15 The first word in this verse is ἀληθεύοντες "doing/speaking the truth". This contrasts with the final words of 4:14, τὴν μεθοδείαν τῆς πλάνης "the craftiness of error". The δέ marks the switch from the negative statements in 4:14 to this series of positive statements concerning how believers should live. Those who belong to the church are to build up one another, so that the church as an entity will be spiritually strong.

4:15a Instead, by means of our living according to the true gospel The Greek verb ἀληθεύοντες literally means "truthing". While it can merely mean "speaking the truth", it does have a wider reference. This includes speaking, but also includes the attitude and behaviour, i.e. "doing/living the truth". In translation, therefore, it is preferable to use an expression that communicates this wider sense.

In 4:14, Paul stated that believers should not be spiritually immature and deceived by those who teach false doctrines. Now he encourages them to live according to the truth. In this context, "truth" refers to the truth expressed by God in the gospel.

The present participle ἀληθεύοντες "truthing" signals a means relationship with the main verb in the verse, αὐξήσωμεν "we may grow". By means of living according to the truth, we will mature as individual believers and the church will mature as an entity. This is expressed as "by means of our living according to the true gospel" in the display.

and, at the same time,* by means of our loving *everyone, Most commentators agree that the phrase ἐν ἀγάπῃ "in love" is connected to the participle ἀληθεύοντες.

It is difficult to express the abstract noun "love" as a verb in this context. The fact that love must accompany any expression of the truth, in both deeds and words, makes it especially difficult. Possibly, the phrase "at the same time" might be used to convey the idea that living according to the truth and loving everyone must go hand in hand.

4:15b we become increasingly more like Christ in every respect. It is generally agreed that αὐξήσωμεν εἰς αὐτὸν..., Χριστός "we may grow into him..., Christ" relates back to ἵνα in 4:14a. See the discussion in note 4:14 regarding understanding that ἵνα as introducing an amplification of 4:13 rather than purpose. Here in 4:15, the positive statement of that amplification contrasts with the negative statement of it in 4:14.

It is clear that αὐτόν refers to "Christ", who is referred to explicitly at the end of the verse.

There are two ways to understand the whole phrase εἰς αὐτόν "into him":

1. It means "united with him".
2. It indicates that Christ is the goal to which we should attain, that we may grow increasingly to be like him.

The latter is the more appropriate in the context of 4:13.

4:15c–16d Paul returns to the recurring figure of Christ as the head and the church as the body. See also 1:23 and 3:6. As the head controls and directs every activity of the body, so Christ controls and directs his church. It can only become spiritually mature if the believers are obedient to Christ's control and direction.

4:15c Christ *controls/directs the church just as the head controls the body*. The Greek simply states ὅς ἐστιν ἡ κεφαλή "who is the head". It is a description of Christ. Since this is a live metaphor, it is expressed in the display as a simile, which makes explicit that Christ is like the head of a body and the church is like the body itself. The point of comparison between Christ and the head is that Christ controls and directs the church just like a head controls and directs a body.

Some commentators suggest that Χριστός is in an emphatic position. It is good to keep this emphasis in translation. It might be expressed as "It is he, Christ, who...".

4:16 The initial ἐξ οὗ "from whom" refers to Χριστός "Christ" in 4:15. The relationship of 4:16 to 4:15b-c is one of amplification, i.e. it explains further the function of Christ as head of the church. In Colossians 2:19, Paul uses a similar metaphor to describe the spiritual development of the church.

The verse in Greek is ἐξ οὗ πᾶν τὸ σῶμα συναρμολογούμενον καὶ συμβιβαζόμενον διὰ πάσης ἁφῆς τῆς ἐπιχορηγίας κατ' ἐνέργειαν ἐν μέτρῳ ἑνὸς ἑκάστου μέρους τὴν αὔξησιν τοῦ σώματος ποιεῖται εἰς οἰκοδομὴν ἑαυτοῦ ἐν ἀγάπῃ literally "from whom all the body being fitly joined together and being united through every joint of supply according to the working in measure of each individual part makes/causes the growth of the body unto the building of itself in love". As this order is hard to understand, it has been re-ordered in the display. As for the relationship of the parts of the metaphor, the non-figurative meaning is expressed in 4:16a–b and the figure in 4:16c–d.

Because the Greek syntax is complicated, commentators discuss both the relations between the clauses and the meaning of terms used.

Despite these discussions, the main outline of the verse is quite straightforward. The subject of the clause is πᾶν τὸ σῶμα "the whole body". The main verb is ποιεῖται "makes". The object of the verb is τὴν αὔξησιν τοῦ σώματος "the growth of the body".

4:16a Christ causes the whole church to become *spiritually* mature. The prepositional phrase ἐξ οὗ "of/from whom" indicates the source or cause of all progress and development in the church. It refers back to Χριστός "Christ" in 4:15. He causes growth in the church.

In the basic structure of the verse, πᾶν τὸ σῶμα...τὴν αὔξησιν τοῦ σώματος ποιεῖται "the whole body...makes/causes the growth of the body", σῶμα is again used to represent "the church". The main verb, ποιεῖται "makes", has σῶμα (i.e. "the church") as subject, but, since Christ is the source of its power, "Christ causes the whole church to become *spiritually* mature" is used in the display to express the sense non-figuratively. The figurative representation is given in 4:16c–d.

***Specifically*, he causes the church to build itself up,** In the Greek text, this clause is near the end of the verse. Most commentators agree that the εἰς "to/for" indicates intended result or purpose. The purpose of spiritual growth in the church is οἰκοδομὴν ἑαυτοῦ "the building up of itself". This recalls chapter 2, where building metaphors are also used. In particular, it fits with 2:21, where both οἰκοδομή and συναρμολογέω "being fitly joined together" are used of the church, as they are here.

However, although εἰς οἰκοδομὴν ἑαυτοῦ "for the building up of itself" may indicate purpose in the Greek text, the idea of "building itself up" is similar to τὴν αὔξησιν...ποιεῖται "makes/causes the growth" (rendered as "to become *spiritually* mature" in the first part of display 4:16a). An alternative analysis, therefore, is that εἰς οἰκοδομήν restates "Christ causes the whole church to become *spiritually* mature". In the display, this relationship is expressed as "specifically", indicating that "building itself up" is a specific way in which the church becomes spiritually mature.

Each believer works to strengthen the church as a whole. As each believer becomes stronger spiritually, so the church is strengthened.

There is some combination of metaphors, it seems, of the growth of the body and of building construction. Some commentators focus more on the building metaphor, taking it to mean the completion or perfection of the church. Others focus on the strengthening of the church. In fact, there is little difference.

4:16b by means of all members of the church loving *one another* The paragraph 4:7–16 finishes with the prepositional phrase ἐν ἀγάπῃ "in love". In the Greek text this immediately follows εἰς οἰκοδομὴν ἑαυτοῦ "for the building up of itself". Most commentators consider that the phrase is connected to the noun οἰκοδομήν "building up". This view is followed in the display.

This is the third time this phrase has been used in this chapter. See also 4:2 and 4:15. It indicates the importance of love in preserving the unity of the church despite the differences between individual believers.

The preposition ἐν may indicate one of two things:

1. That love is the means by which the body builds itself up.
2. That it is the sphere or element within which the body builds itself up.

The first option seems to be the more applicable in the context, taking into account also 4:2 and 4:15. In each case, the phrase describes the loving attitude which should exist between believers as they interact, which strengthens the church as a whole.

Since "love" is an abstract noun which needs to be re-expressed in the display as an event, the participants in that event must be stated. As this section deals with the unity of the church and the contribution which each believer makes to the spiritual development of the church as a whole, the love refers to the believers' love for one another.

and by means of each believer doing the work that *God* intends him to do. This proposition is co-ordinate with the preceding one and provides a further means for 4:16a.

Moore (p. 48) considers that the two participles, συναρμολογούμενον "being fitly joined together" and συμβιβαζόμενον "brought together, united" are a near-synonymous doublet. Here, in conjunction with πάσης ἁφῆς τῆς ἐπιχορηγίας "every joint of supply/support", they refer to the way in which all the different parts of the body fit together so that they support one another and function efficiently in the way that God intended. Paul uses this metaphor to describe the way in which individual believers should use the gifts referred to in 4:7 and 4:11 to perform the tasks which God has allotted them. In this way the church as a whole will function effectively and become spiritually mature.

The Greek κατ' ἐνέργειαν ἐν μέτρῳ ἑνὸς ἑκάστου μέρους "according to the working in measure of each individual part" means that every believer has a particular contribution to make to the spiritual development of the church, just as the various parts of the body perform different functions in order that the body develops physically.

This statement is similar to that in 4:7, "to each one of us has grace been given according to the measure of the gift of Christ". Each believer receives sufficient life and energy to enable him to fulfil his particular function in the church.

4:16c–d *This* [4:16a–b] is like the physical body developing/growing stronger, by means of each separate part functioning properly. This is the figurative statement corresponding to 4:16a–b.

BOUNDARIES AND COHERENCE

For discussion of the initial boundary, see the section on Boundaries and Coherence for 4:1–6.

The final boundary coincides with the final boundary of 4:1–16. It is marked by an accumulation of features. See the section on Boundaries and Coherence for 4:1–16.

Lexically these verses form two main clusters, (4:7-11 and 4:12-16). The first cluster (4:7-11) is centred on the semantic domain of "giving":

ἐδόθη "was given" (4:7)
δωρεᾶς "gift" (4:7)
ἔδωκεν δόματα "he gave gifts" (4:8)
ἔδωκεν "he gave" (4:11)

Also, within this cluster, in 4:8-10, there are a number of references to "ascending" and "descending". As Kopesec points out,

> [T]he common denominator between these two domains [ascending and descending] is Christ. Paul is pointing out that the one who gives the gifts is Christ, who descended and again ascended to a place of power (p. 71).

The second cluster (4:12-16) is centred around the domains of "maturity" and "the body". Those terms having to do with "maturity" are:

τὸν καταρτισμόν "the equipping" (4:12)
καταντήσωμεν "we attain" (4:13)
ἄνδρα τέλειον "complete/perfect man" (4:13)
μηκέτι...νήπιοι "no longer...infants" (4:14)
αὐξήσωμεν "we may grow" (4:15)
αὔξησιν "growth" (4:16)
οἰκοδομήν "building up" (4:16)

The terms having to do with "the body" are:

ἡλικίας "stature" (4:13)
ἡ κεφαλή "the head" (4:15)
σῶμα "body" (4:12, 16)
ἁφῆς "joint" (4:16)

In the second cluster, the concept of "unity" is also important. The terms having to do with "unity" are:

τὴν ἑνότητα "the unity" (4:13)
πᾶν τὸ σῶμα συναρμολογούμενον καὶ συμβιβαζόμενον "the whole body being fitted together and being brought together" (4:16).

The focus of the first cluster (4:7-11) is the different gifts which Christ gives to believers. The focus of the second cluster (4:12-16) is the purpose of these gifts, i.e. to build up the church, the body of Christ.

The relationship between the two clusters is signalled by πρός "for" (4:12). This indicates that the immediate purpose of 4:7-11 follows. A further link is μέχρι "until" (4:13) which signals the ultimate purpose of 4:7-11.

PROMINENCE AND THEME

Within the propositional cluster 4:7-11, 4:7 is prominent as a GENERIC nucleus and, along with its SPECIFIC, 4:11, functions as the MEANS for 4:12-16. Both the GENERIC and SPECIFIC nuclei are supported by the grounds of 4:8-10.

Within the cluster 4:12-16, 4:13 is prominent. In a means-purpose relationship, the means proposition is usually prominent. However, here the PURPOSE construction has marked prominence, with the conjunction μέχρι "until" signalling the ultimate purpose of all that precedes in 4:7-11. The PURPOSE is also further developed by the propositional cluster 4:14-16 which provides an amplification of 4:13 in both negative and positive terms.

The nuclear units of the two propositional clusters, 4:7-11 and 4:12-16, are in a means-purpose relationship, and both are included in the theme statement, for reasons of natural and marked prominence respectively.

DIVISION CONSTITUENT 4:17-32 (Hortatory Section: Nucleus₂ of 4:1-6:9)

THEME: You have learnt that you must behave in a manner which is consistent with your new, godly character. Therefore, stop doing those immoral things which unbelievers do and which are harmful to one another. Rather, act appropriately towards one another.

MACROSTRUCTURE	CONTENTS
GENERIC HORTATORY NUCLEUS	4:17-19 You must no longer behave in the immoral manner in which unbelievers do.
SPECIFIC HORTATORY NUCLEUS — GROUNDS (mitigated hortatory)	4:20-24 You have learnt that you must behave in a manner which is consistent with your new, godly character.
SPECIFIC HORTATORY NUCLEUS — EXHORTATION	4:25-32 Therefore, stop doing those things which are harmful to one another. Rather, act appropriately towards one another.

INTENT AND MACROSTRUCTURE

This unit is essentially hortatory. This is signalled first by the use of the verbs λέγω καὶ μαρτύρομαι "I affirm and declare" in 4:17. They indicate the emphatic stating of an opinion or a desire (Louw and Nida 33:319). The second signal is the infinitive περιπατεῖν "to walk" which follows. As elsewhere in this letter it refers to behaviour or way of life.

Paragraph 4:25-32 has many imperative verbs. Paul urges the Ephesian believers to live lives which demonstrate the fact that they have become new creatures in Christ. Changes in thinking and attitudes should result in a change in behaviour. So, instead of living the immoral lives they used to live, they should now be living godly lives in obedience to what Christ taught.

The first paragraph, 4:17-19, is a GENERIC HORTATORY NUCLEUS.

The second paragraph, 4:20-24, functions as grounds for the third paragraph, 4:25-32. However, it also has a mitigated hortatory character.

The third paragraph is concerned with the specific details of a believer's everyday conduct. It comprises a series of specific EXHORTATIONS. It is therefore labelled as a SPECIFIC HORTATORY NUCLEUS.

Paul wanted the Ephesian believers to know that it is essential that they grasp the contrast between what they *had* been as pagans and what they now *are* as believers. This is set out in 4:17-19 and 4:20-24 respectively. The sharp contrast between the two is brought out by the emphatic ὑμεῖς δέ "But for *you*" which starts paragraph 4:20-24.

By these descriptions, Paul wants to motivate and encourage the Ephesian believers to respond to his appeal to live out in reality what they now are, new creatures in Christ.

BOUNDARIES AND COHERENCE

The initial boundary has been discussed in the section on Boundaries and Coherence for 4:1-16.

The final boundary is marked by the following features:

1. The conjunction οὖν with the commands Γίνεσθε...μιμηταί...καὶ περιπατεῖτε... "be imitators... and walk..." (5:1, 2) indicate the start of the next unit.
2. A change of subject matter. Paul focusses in this section on the change of behaviour which must result from the change in attitude from pagan to Christian. In 5:1, his focus changes to the living out of Christian love.
3. The form of περιπατεῖτε ἐν ἀγάπῃ καθὼς καὶ ὁ Χριστὸς ἠγάπησεν ὑμᾶς "walk in love as also Christ loved you" (5:2) is formally parallel to the closing section of 4:17-32 and so there is a tail-head link between the two units.

The coherence of this unit is centred round the contrastive descriptions of the pagan lifestyle they had followed in the past and their new Christian lifestyle which should spring from their new spiritual state. See 4:17, 22-24 (generic terms) and 4:25-32 (specific terms).

PROMINENCE AND THEME

HORTATORY NUCLEI are naturally prominent, therefore, elements of the two HORTATORY NUCLEI are incorporated into the theme statement.

At the same time, the GROUNDS is marked prominent by its mitigated hortatory character and the fact that two of its three nuclei are positive rather than negative. Therefore, it seems best to include a representation of the GROUNDS in the theme statement too.

SECTION CONSTITUENT 4:17-19
(Hortatory Paragraph: Generic Hortatory Nucleus of 4:17-32)

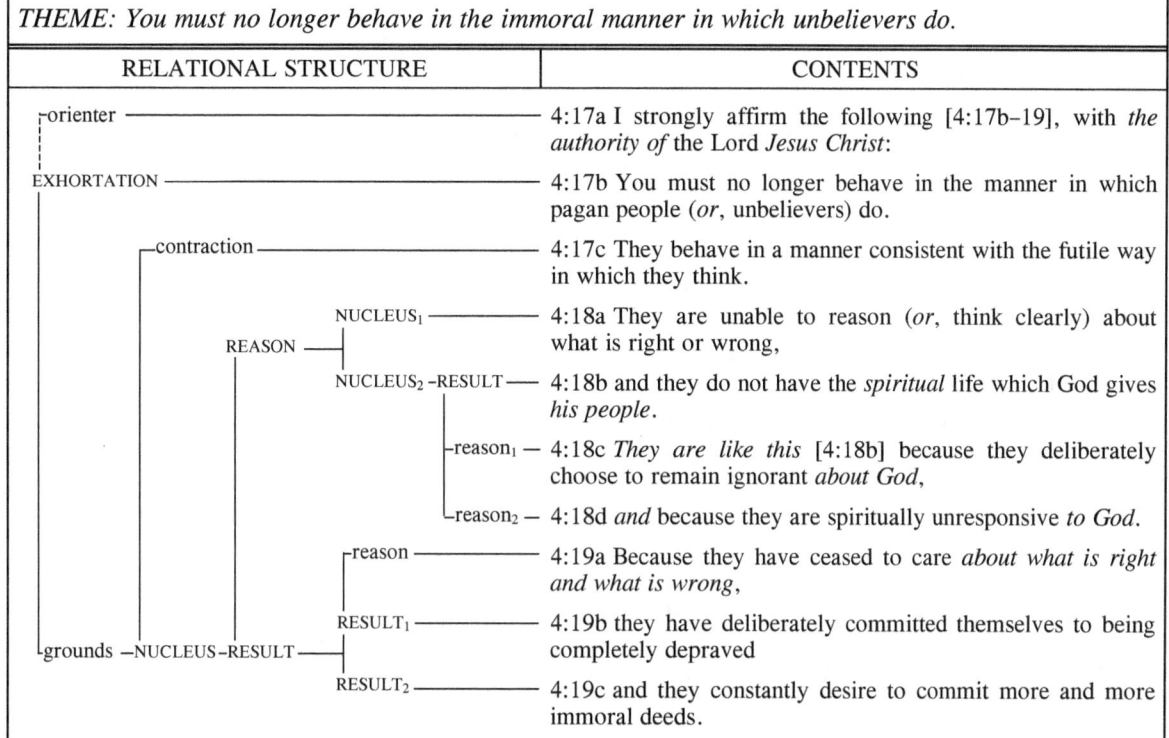

INTENT AND STRUCTURE

This is a hortatory paragraph. This is signalled by the use of λέγω καὶ μαρτύρομαι "I say and affirm/urge" and the infinitive περιπατεῖν "to walk". See the Intent and Macrostructure note on section 4:17-32. This paragraph consists of an EXHORTATION (4:17a-b) and a motivational grounds (4:17c-19) for that EXHORTATION. Paul wants the Ephesians to think about the immoral lifestyle followed by those who are not believers. He wants to give them strong motivational grounds for *not* behaving in the same way. The EXHORTATION, therefore, is a negative one, i.e. a prohibition.

NOTES

4:17 This paragraph opens with an emphatic statement, Τοῦτο οὖν λέγω καὶ μαρτύρομαι ἐν κυρίῳ "this, therefore, I say and affirm/urge in (the) Lord". This serves as orienter for 4:17b-19. The combination of οὖν "therefore", the two verbs λέγω "I say" and μαρτύρομαι "I affirm/urge" and ἐν κυρίῳ "in (the) Lord" give what Paul is going to say great authority and gives prominence to the words that are thus introduced (4:17b-19).

The οὖν "therefore" can have two functions:

1. It has an inferential focus, i.e. it signals what the response should be of those who accept what Paul stated in 4:1-16. See, for example, Hodge (p. 248), Lenski (p. 351) and Hendriksen, who states,

   > This "therefore" connects the present paragraph with all that has gone before in 4:1-16. "Because of your high calling, your duty to render service with a view to the building up of Christ's body, no longer conduct yourselves as do the Gentiles' (p. 209).

2. It has a resumptive function, i.e. it signals a resumption of the exhortation of 4:1-3. See, for example, Bruce (p. 90), Ellicott (p. 80), Lincoln (p. 276), Stott (p. 174).

Evidence for the resumptive function is the fact that the form of 4:17 is similar to that of 4:1. It states the implication of 4:1 in negative form, i.e. ἀξίως περιπατῆσαι τῆς κλήσεως ἧς ἐκλήθητε "walk worthy of the calling with which you were called" (4:1) implies μηκέτι ὑμᾶς περιπατεῖν, καθὼς καὶ τὰ ἔθνη περιπατεῖ "you must no longer walk as the Gentiles walk" (4:17).

There is good support for both views. In the display, it is represented as being resumptive and so no inferential conjunction, such as "therefore", is used.

4:17a I strongly affirm the following [4:17b-19], As mentioned in note 4:17, the combination of the two verbs of speaking, λέγω "I say" and μαρτύρομαι "I affirm, testify, urge", is forceful and emphatic. This needs to be brought out in the translation. NIV does so by saying, "I tell you this, and insist on it".

Another possibility might be to use a phrase which combines an adverb and a verb, such as "I strongly affirm", "I strongly insist", "I earnestly implore". This alternative is followed in the display.

Whatever is used should have a sense of authority and strength. It is not just a suggestion, but a strong plea or command.

The pronoun τοῦτο "this" looks forward to what Paul will say in 4:17b–19.

with *the authority of* the Lord *Jesus Christ*: The ἐν in the phrase ἐν κυρίῳ "in (the) Lord" makes it clear that it is Paul's position in Christ that is the source of his authority. Paul is speaking as someone who has authority as an apostle (1:1) and, in particular, as one chosen to take the gospel to the Gentiles (3:1–13). Because of this, he can speak on behalf of Christ and what he says carries the authority of Christ.

An alternative wording, avoiding the use of the noun "authority" would be "as one whom the Lord *Jesus Christ authorises to do so*".

4:17b You must no longer behave in the manner in which pagan people (*or,* unbelievers) do. This proposition is the only EXHORTATION of the paragraph and, therefore, the most nuclear unit.

The phrase μηκέτι ὑμᾶς περιπατεῖν functions as an exhortation here: "you must not walk" or "do not walk". As elsewhere in Ephesians, Paul uses the verb περιπατεῖν "to walk" in a figurative sense here to mean "live, behave, conduct oneself". It is further defined by καθὼς καὶ τὰ ἔθνη περιπατεῖ "as also the Gentiles walk".

The Greek noun phrase τὰ ἔθνη here refers to unbelievers, the heathen, pagans. Ethnically, those whom Paul is addressing were Gentiles, but they were no longer pagans. They were now believers, part of the body of Christ and, as such, were not to behave as they had done before they believed.

There is a textual issue here:

1. In some manuscripts, λοιπά occurs before ἔθνη (i.e. it would be translated as "other Gentiles/pagans").
2. Most modern English versions do not include it and it is not included as a variant reading in the UBS text.

4:17c–19 This cluster of propositions describes the immoral thoughts and attitudes of unbelievers and relates them to their immoral conduct. It provides motivational grounds for the exhortation of 4:17b.

4:17c They behave in a manner which is consistent with the futile way in which they think. An alternative would be, "The way in which they behave is determined by the futile way in which they think".

the...way in which they think The Greek word νοῦς "mind, attitude, way of thinking" refers to the whole mental and moral state/outlook.

futile The noun ματαιότης "emptiness, futility, purposelessness" is only used here and in Romans 8:20 and 2 Peter 2:18, although the adjective μάταιος "futile" is used elsewhere, e.g. 1 Peter 1:18.

The genitive phrase ἐν ματαιότητι τοῦ νοὸς αὐτῶν "in the futility of their minds" might be re-expressed as "they think in a futile manner". The sense is that their reasoning/thinking is worthless. It brings them to wrong conclusions, and so results in wrong actions.

4:18 The principle difficulty in this verse concerns the relationship between it and 4:17, as well as between the different propositions within it. For details on the many possibilities that commentators suggest, see Graham (pp. 349–355).

Verses 4:18–19 give further information about the spiritual and mental state of unbelievers and how it results in their immoral behaviour. Therefore, in the SSA, the propositional cluster 4:18–19 is analysed as more nuclear than 4:17c and the relationship is labelled in the display diagram as contraction-NUCLEUS.

Within that NUCLEUS, 4:18 and 4:19 are analysed as being in a reason-result relationship. The reason is considered marked as prominent because of the focus in the passage on the relationship between the unbelievers' spiritual and moral state and their behaviour.

4:18a They are unable to reason (*or*, think clearly) about what is right or wrong, The Greek noun διάνοια "mind, intelligence, understanding" refers to intelligence as opposed to feelings. It is an abstract noun representing the event "to think/reason".

The use of ἐσκοτωμένοι "having been darkened" here is figurative. In connection with διανοίᾳ, it describes the lack of spiritual and moral understanding of the unbelievers. Their ability to think about moral or spiritual issues has been adversely affected by sin. This contrasts with 1:18 where the spiritual enlightenment of believers is described.

There is some disagreement about which verb the participle ὄντες "being" should be connected to. There are two possibilities:

1. It is connected to the following verb ἀπηλλοτριωμένοι "alienated".
2. It is connected to the preceding verb ἐσκοτωμένοι "darkened".

In Colossians 1:21, there is a parallel expression, ὄντας ἀπηλλοτριωμένους "being alienated". However, most commentators, support the second option, i.e. it is connected to ἐσκοτωμένοι "darkened". So this option is followed in the display. Here the present participle ὄντες "being" along with the perfect tense of ἐσκοτωμένοι "darkened" serves to *emphasise* that this darkness is a present and continuing state.

4:18b and they do not have the *spiritual* life which God gives *his people*. The phrase ἀπηλλοτριωμένοι τῆς ζωῆς τοῦ θεοῦ "having been alienated from the life of God" recalls 2:12 where the pagan were described as "alienated from the commonwealth of Israel" and "without God in the world". As in 2:12, the fact that ἀπηλλοτριωμένοι "having been alienated" is in the perfect tense indicates that this is a present and continuing state. See also ἐσκοτωμένοι "having been darkened" (4:18a).

Most commentators agree that the genitive τῆς ζωῆς τοῦ θεοῦ "the life of God" is one of origin, i.e. it refers to the spiritual life which God gives to the believer through the indwelling of the Holy Spirit. See, for example, Eadie (p. 330), Ellicott (pp. 81–82), Hendriksen (pp. 209–210), Hodge (p. 252), Hoehner (p. 586), Lincoln (p. 277).

The phrase "having been alienated from the life of God" might be stated as "being without the spiritual life which God gives". Conversely, it might be stated as being "*spiritually* dead" (2:1). In the display, it is expressed as "they do not have the *spiritual* life which God gives *his people*".

Proposition 4:18b is analysed as being co-ordinate with 4:18a and the two NUCLEI provide a reason for 4:19b–c.

4:18c Commentators discuss the relationship between 4:18c and what precedes it. There are two options:

1. 4:18c provides a reason for both 4:18a and 4:18b.
2. 4:18c only provides a reason for 4:18b.

Most commentaries favour the second option, that is, 4:18c explains why unbelievers are alienated from "the life of God". See, for example, Ellicott (p. 82), Hodge (p. 254), Hoehner (p. 587), Lincoln (p. 278). In the display, the majority view is followed and 4:18c is shown in a reason relationship only with 4:18b.

4:18c–d These two clauses are both introduced by διά "because". Commentators debate the relationship between them. There are two options:

1. The relationship is co-ordinate.
2. 4:18d is subordinate to (the reason for) 4:18c.

There is no consensus among commentators as to which is correct. Both are possible. In the display, the clauses are regarded as co-ordinate and, therefore, both reasons for 4:18b.

4:18c They are like this [4:18b] because they deliberately choose to remain ignorant *about God*, The noun ἄγνοια "ignorance" is used only four times in the New Testament: Here; Acts 3:17; 17:30; 1 Peter 1:14. In each case the "ignorance" referred to is that of those who had been or were in a state of unbelief, i.e. they did not know the truth about God (or Christ). Therefore, this is the meaning represented in the display.

Some commentators note that the noun τὴν ἄγνοιαν "ignorance" is followed by the phrase τὴν οὖσαν ἐν αὐτοῖς "being in them". See, for example, Alford (p. 121), Bratcher and Nida (p. 111), Hoehner (p. 587), O'Brien (pp. 321–322). Therefore they suggest that Paul is referring to "ignorance" as a habitual and inherent condition in which there is an element of wilfulness, i.e. the unbelievers are unwilling to learn the truth, they refuse to know God. This idea of wilfulness, therefore, has been included in the proposition.

4:18d *and* because they are spiritually unresponsive *to God*. The noun πώρωσις, formed from πόος "hard skin", literally means "covering with a callous". It occurs three times in the New Testament: here; Mark 3:5; Romans 11:25 (the related verb πωρόω "harden" occurs in 2 Cor. 3:14). It is used figuratively of mental or moral hardening. Here, it refers to being insensitive, unresponsive, in a moral and spiritual sense. The unbelievers have become unresponsive to God's truth, "spiritually unresponsive *to God*".

As in 4:18c, some commentators consider that the idea of wilful stubbornness is present. See, for example, Bratcher and Nida (p. 111), Hendriksen (p. 210), Lincoln (p. 278). An alternative to the proposition in the display might be "because they stubbornly refuse to respond *to God*".

4:19 The cluster of propositions making up 4:19 indicates the behaviour of unbelievers which results from their spiritual condition (4:18). They are unable to reason, they are spiritually dead and they are spiritually ignorant and unresponsive. So, they are unable to restrain themselves from extremely immoral behaviour.

4:19a Because they have ceased to care *about what is right and what is wrong*, The οἵτινες "who" is an emphatic version of the simple relative pronoun. Here, as Lincoln (p. 278) proposes, it may have "the function of emphasising a characteristic quality which confirms a preceding statement". See also Hodge (p. 254), O'Brien (p. 322, fn. 203). It refers back to τὰ ἔθνη "the pagan" in 4:17-18, separating them out as a class: "they are the ones who…".

The verb ἀπηλγηκότες "having become callous, having ceased to care" describes the unbelievers' lack of spiritual responsiveness. Just as a calloused hand is insensitive to physical sensations, so their consciences are unresponsive to right and wrong. They are incapable of feeling shame for what they do and have ceased to care about what is right and what is wrong.

This clause (4:19a) indicates another reason for 4:19b-c. The unbelievers' moral and spiritual apathy causes them to abandon themselves to depravity.

4:19b they have deliberately committed themselves to being completely depraved The aorist active indicative παρέδωκαν "they have given over" is the main verb of this propositional cluster and so it is its grammatical nucleus. This proposition expresses RESULT₁ of 4:19a.

In the Greek text, the reflexive pronoun ἑαυτούς "themselves" is at the beginning of the clause and, therefore, is emphatic.

Paul says that the unbelievers have given *themselves* up to ἀσελγείᾳ "licentiousness, debauchery". Some commentators restrict the reference of this noun primarily to sexual sins, but others regard it as being more comprehensive and to refer to all sorts of unrestrained immoral behaviour.

An alternative way to express 4:18b would be: "they have deliberately chosen to behave in a completely immoral manner".

4:19c and they constantly desire to commit more and more immoral deeds. The phrase εἰς ἐργασίαν "for the practice" indicates a determined purpose to do something. As Alford (p. 122) says, "[a] conscious aim, not merely incidental result of the παραδοῦναι" (i.e. of the "giving over").

The noun ἀκαθαρσία refers to the type of actions they practise. It literally means "dirt, refuse", but when used figuratively, as here, it refers to immorality and, in particular, to sexual immorality/perversion. See also 5:3. In conjunction with πάσης "every", it refers to "every kind of immoral deed".

According to BDAG (p. 824), πλεονεξία has the basic idea of "the state of desiring to have more than one's due". It can, therefore, be translated as "greediness" or "covetousness".

The phrase ἐν πλεονεξίᾳ "with greediness/covetousness" can be connected to:

1. Both ἀσελγείᾳ "licentiousness" and ἀκαθαρσίας "uncleanness".
2. Only to ἀκαθαρσίας "uncleanness".

Most commentators connect it only with ἀκαθαρσίας.

The two vices of ἀκαθαρσία "uncleanness" and πλεονεξία "covetousness/greediness" also occur together elsewhere in the New Testament. See Ephesians 5:3, 5; Colossians 3:5; Romans 1:29; 1 Corinthians 5:10. Both words include the idea of a spirit of acquisition. A greedy person always wishes to have more than he has: of money, property, gratification of his desires. In this context, it has the sense "insatiable". These people "indulge themselves insatiably in every kind of immoral deed" or, as in the display, "they constantly desire to commit more and more immoral deeds".

BOUNDARIES AND COHERENCE

The initial boundary coincides with the initial boundary of the section 4:17-32.

The final boundary is marked by:

1. The contrasting subject matter of this paragraph and the one following: the way of life and the way of thinking of pagans (4:17-19) and the way of life and the way of thinking of believers (4:20-24). This contrast is marked by the conjunction δέ and the free pronoun ὑμεῖς "you" at the beginning of 4:20.
2. A change from the third person plural verb forms and pronouns that dominate 4:18-19 to the second person plural forms in 4:20-24.

The lexical cohesion and coherence of this paragraph consists in the use of vocabulary from the semantic domain of attitudes and thoughts, which shows the effect of warped thinking on the behaviour of the unbelievers. Such words are:

ματαιότητι τοῦ νοός "vanity of the mind" (4:17)

ἐσκοτωμένοι τῇ διανοίᾳ "darkened in the intellect" (4:18)

ἄγνοιαν "ignorance" (4:18)

πώρωσιν τῆς καρδίας "hardness of heart" (4:18)

ἀπηλγηκότες "having ceased to care" (4:19)

PROMINENCE AND THEME

Since the most important part of a hortatory paragraph is the EXHORTATION, 4:17b forms the major part of the theme statement here, especially because the full statement of the EXHORTATION in this paragraph contains features of the grounds: "in the immoral manner" of unbelievers.

SECTION CONSTITUENT 4:20–24
(Expository Paragraph [Mitigated Hortatory]: Motivational Grounds for 4:25–32)

THEME: *You have learnt that you must behave in a manner which is consistent with your new, godly character.*

RELATIONAL STRUCTURE	CONTENTS
orienter – POSITIVE – negative	4:20 But *what* **you** learnt *about* Christ is not consistent with *behaving like* this [4:17c–19].
NUCLEUS₁	4:21a I am sure that you heard *the message* about Christ,
NUCLEUS₂	4:21b and, *as people who are united* with him, you were taught the true message which *God makes known* in Jesus.
CONTENT (mitigated hortatory) — NUCLEUS₁ (negative) — 'former evil nature'	4:22a *You were taught at that time* that you must put-aside/renounce [MET] your former, *ungodly* nature.
description — NUCLEUS₁	4:22b This nature caused you to behave in the *evil* way you used to behave.
NUCLEUS₂ — RESULT	4:22c This nature was destroying you spiritually,
reason	4:22d because it was causing you to crave *that which is evil* and causing you to believe that this was good for you.
NUCLEUS₂ (positive)	4:23 *You were taught that* you must be made-new/transformed *by God* in the way that you think
NUCLEUS₃ (positive) — NUCLEUS	4:24a and you must acquire [MET] the new, godly nature which God created to be like himself,
amplification	4:24b *that is*, you must become truly upright and truly devout.

INTENT AND STRUCTURE

In the previous paragraph (4:17–19), Paul described how the Ephesian believers, before they believed in Christ, used to be like other unbelievers, and think and behave in the same ways that they do.

At the beginning of this paragraph (4:20–24), Paul uses an emphatic phrase, ὑμεῖς δὲ οὐχ οὕτως "but you not so", to introduce a contrast to the way the pagan act. The contrast is presented by reminding them about the instruction they had previously received concerning Christian character and behaviour. They had been taught that they should "put off" their former, ungodly nature, which had caused them to sin, and that they should "put on" the new, godly nature, which requires them to lead upright lives.

Paul wants to remind them about these things in order to motivate them to put into practice what they have learnt. He hopes that this will result in their accepting the exhortations he gives in 4:25–32.

The structure of this paragraph is somewhat complicated, although the general sense is reasonably clear. The relationship between the two major constituents of the paragraph, 4:20–21 and 4:22–24, is difficult to determine and depends largely upon the connection and force of the three infinitives which occur.

The three infinitives ἀποθέσθαι "to put off" (4:22), ἀνανεοῦσθαι "to be renewed" (4:23) and ἐνδύσασθαι "to put on" (4:24) may be regarded as follows:

1. They are equivalent to imperatives. Therefore, they carry on the main line of exhortation.
2. They provide the content of ἐδιδάχθητε "you were taught", i.e. "you were taught...that-you-must/how-to...". Therefore, they provide supportive rather than hortatory information. However, as Breeze points out:

> [this latter alternative] would not rule out the possibility that they also function as embedded mitigated exhortation reinforcing the command of v1 (p. 52).

The orienter would be "the truth Christ teaches is...". This would be in keeping with understanding the prepositional phrase ἐν τῷ Ἰησοῦ "in Jesus" as indicating Christ as the means, source or agent of "the truth". See Kopesec (p. 84).

If the infinitives in 4:22 and 4:24 are rendered as imperatives they represent fresh commands to the Ephesians. This being so, the command of 4:25 introduced by "therefore" does not make sense as following inferentially from the commands of 4:22 and 4:24, "Put off your old nature...and put on the new.... Therefore, put away falsehood". The sense is that, "because you did throw off your former self once and for all, you must now throw off all conduct which belonged to your old life" and behave in a way which is consistent with your new, godly nature (Stott, p. 183).

It seems best to regard the verses in which these infinitives occur (4:22-24) as explaining the content of the verb ἐδιδάχθητε "you were taught", which represents the POSITIVE half of the emphatic statement, which is made in 4:21. This has good support from the commentaries. See, for example, Best (p. 430), Ellicott (p. 84), Hendriksen (p. 213), Lincoln (pp. 283-284). The relationship, then, between 4:20-21 and 4:22-24 is that of orienter-CONTENT.

It is clear that the focus is upon these three infinitives. As in 4:17-19, the orienter is forceful and emphatic in order to draw attention to the CONTENT, which provides the theme of the passage: the believers' lives are to be characterised by godliness, in contrast to the ungodliness which had characterised them previously.

NOTES

4:20-21 The propositional cluster 4:20-21 provides an orienter for the content of 4:22-24. It consists of two statements concerning the Ephesian believers and their state, with reference to their knowledge of the behaviour required of them as believers. This is presented in negative terms (4:20) and positive terms (4:21).

The initial δέ "but" accompanied by the forefronted free pronoun ὑμεῖς "you (pl)" indicates (and emphasises) a switch of agents. After describing the ungodly behaviour of the pagan (4:17c-19), Paul now addresses the Ephesians directly again.

Also, prominence is given to Christ as the truth, by the forefronting of αὐτόν "him" and ἐν αὐτῷ "in him" (4:21), both referring to Christ.

4:20 But *what* you learnt *about* Christ is not consistent with *behaving like* this [4:17c-19]. The οὕτως "so" refers back to 4:17c-19, the manner of life of unbelievers. Here it is combined with οὐχ "not". So, most commentators consider that it forms a litotes equivalent to "entirely otherwise" or "completely opposite to". See, for example, Ellicott (p. 83), Hoehner (p. 593), Lenski (p. 560). It emphasises that it is impossible for the Ephesians to continue to live in the way described in 4:17c-19, because, as believers, they have now learnt different ways of thinking and behaving.

In this verse the Greek verb μανθάνω "to learn" is used in an unusual way, i.e. it has an animate direct object, τὸν Χριστόν "Christ". Normally, it would be used in phrases like "learn something", "learn about something/someone".

The commentators, therefore, discuss the meaning of "learn Christ". They suggest:

1. That "Christ" is a metonymy for teaching about Christ. See, for example, BDAG, μανθάνω, (p. 615.1), Bratcher and Nida (p. 112).
2. That "to learn Christ" extends the meaning to include both learning about Christ (Christian teaching) and to coming to know him as a person, Christ the Son of God. See, for example, Ellicott (p. 83), Hendriksen (p. 212), Hodge (p. 256), Meyer (p. 471), Stott (pp. 179-180).

Stott, like most commentators, argues for the second option. He says,

> Christ who is the substance of the teaching ('you learned Christ') is himself also the teacher ('you heard him') (p. 179).

In Galatians 1:16, 1 Corinthians 1:23, 2 Corinthians 1:19 and Philippians 1:15, Paul uses a similar phrase "to preach Christ" which means not only preaching about Christ, but also setting forth the very person of Christ. This would also support the second option. The knowledge of Christ that Ephesian believers have leads them to realise that they cannot behave in the manner described in 4:17-19, for Christ advocated entirely different behaviour.

However, following option one would tie in with the expression καθώς ἐστιν ἀλήθεια ἐν τῷ

Ἰησοῦ "as the truth is in Jesus" in 4:21, i.e. Christ is the manifestation/embodiment of the true message about himself or the source of this message.

The essential point here is that those who believe in Christ, acknowledge him for who he is and accept his teaching are required to abandon the sort of life described in 4:17-19 and accept/embrace the sort of life described in 4:22-24. The way in which unbelievers think and behave is not consistent with what the Ephesian believers have learnt about Christ.

The meaning of this clause might be expressed as "But *what* you learnt *about* Christ *by knowing him experientially is* not consistent with *behaving like* this [4:17c-19]". However, this might be difficult to translate in many languages, so an alternative is presented in the display, "But *what* you learnt *about* Christ is not consistent with *behaving like* this [4:17c-19]".

4:21 This verse provides the POSITIVE side of a negative-POSITIVE relation with 4:20.

Most commentators consider the clauses in which these two verbs occur to be included in "you learnt Christ" (4:20) or as explaining it more fully. See, for example, Ellicott (p. 83), O'Brien (p. 324).

4:21a I am sure that The εἴ γε "if indeed" at the beginning of the verse does not indicate doubt, but expresses and emphasises an assumption that what is said is true, i.e. "I am sure that" or "I assume that". See, for example, Eadie (p. 335), Hodge (p. 257), Lincoln (p. 280), O'Brien (p. 325). It is a way of reminding the Ephesians about the facts of their Christian experience.

you heard *the message* about Christ, The inclusion of a direct object (here a pronoun) to the verb ἠκούσατε "you heard" indicates that the verb means to "hear *about*" someone or something rather than hearing someone's words. In this context, therefore, it refers to their hearing about Christ in the gospel message. See also 1:13.

4:21b and, *as people who are united* with him, you were taught Most commentators regard the aorist verb ἐδιδάχθητε "you were taught" as referring to the teaching the Ephesians were given after their conversion by those specially equipped by Christ to do so.

Like the αὐτόν in the preceding clause, the phrase ἐν αὐτῷ "in him" is emphatic because it occurs before the verb. This may be understood as:

1. The manner in which they were taught.
2. The sphere in which they were taught.
3. Equivalent to "in their union with him".

The third option seems most appropriate in the context. It is also reflected in some English versions as follows (italics mine),

NCV ...*you are in him*, so you were taught the truth that is in Jesus.
REB ...were you not *as Christians* taught the truth as it is in Jesus?
TEV ...*as his followers* you were taught the truth that is in Jesus.

In the display, the clause is represented by "*as people who are united* with him you were taught".

the true message which God makes known in Jesus. In the clause καθώς ἐστιν ἀλήθεια ἐν τῷ Ἰησοῦ "as truth is in Jesus", the abstract noun ἀλήθεια refers to a quality: something is true. It is often used to refer to the content of Christian teaching (BDAG, p. 42.2b). Here, the sense may be that the truth is "embodied" or "manifested" in the person and life of Jesus. See John 14:6, where Jesus says, "I am...the truth".

With regard to the relationship indicated by καθώς "as" between ἐδιδάχθητε "you were taught" and ἐστιν ἀλήθεια ἐν τῷ Ἰησοῦ "as truth is in Jesus", commentators suggest the following options:

1. It has a causal sense, i.e. "in him you were taught since the true message is manifested in Jesus". See, for example, Best (p. 429), Hodge (pp. 257-259).
2. It indicates congruence in respect to manner or standard, i.e. "in him you were taught according to the truth which is in Jesus". See, for example, Alford (p. 123), Eadie (p. 337), Ellicott (p. 84), Lincoln (p. 283), O'Brien (p. 325).

Most commentators support the second option. The NIV translation, "in accordance with the truth that is in Jesus", agrees with this.

Other versions translate it as indicating a verb-direct object relationship, often referred to in commentaries as expressing the *content* of what is taught, i.e. "you were taught the truth that is in Jesus" (TEV, cf. NJB, NLT).

In this context, the difference between a congruence-standard relationship and a verb-direct object relationship is slight, since both refer to the same truth. In the display, it is represented as "you were taught the true message which *God makes known* in Jesus", a verb-direct object relationship.

4:22a-d The NUCLEUS of this propositional cluster is 4:22a, while 4:22b-d provide a description of the former, evil nature of the Ephesian believers and its effects.

4:22a *You were taught at that time* There are three infinitives in 4:22-24:

ἀποθέσθαι "to put off" (4:22)
ἀνανεοῦσθαι "to be renewed" (4:23)
ἐνδύσασθαι "to put on" (4:24)

Most commentators support the view that they are grammatically dependent on ἐδιδάχθητε "you were taught" (4:22a). The clauses in which they occur, therefore, explain the content of the teaching. See, for example, Ellicott (p. 84), Hodge (p. 260), Lenski (p. 562), Lincoln (pp. 283-284), O'Brien (p. 326).

The implicit information *"At that time"* helps clarify the fact that the instructions referred to in 4:22-24 are not new, but ones the Ephesians had also been taught in the past. They had already responded to them and become new creatures in Christ. See the section on Intent and Structure. However, there is truth in O'Brien's statement,

> [I]n this exhortatory context the three infinitives also seem to have an implied imperatival force, not in the sense that the readers are to repeat the event of putting off the old person and putting on the new, but in terms of their continuing to live out the implications of their mighty break with the past (p. 327).

that you must put-aside/renounce your former, *ungodly* nature. The aorist infinitive here ἀποθέσθαι "to put off, remove" contrasts with the aorist infinitive ἐνδύσασθαι "to put on" in 4:24. The non-figurative sense of the two verbs is "to remove (clothes)" and "to put on (clothes)". In these verses they are both used figuratively, though they may be considered dead metaphors.

In some languages, the use of either verb in the figurative sense may cause a collocational clash. In such languages, it may be necessary to remove the metaphor and translate the meaning of the verbs rather than the image, namely "to renounce/put-aside".

Here ἀποθέσθαι "to put off" is used with relation to τὸν παλαιὸν ἄνθρωπον "the old person/nature". REB translates the latter phrase as "that old human nature", RSV as "your old nature", NIV and TEV as "your old self". Paul uses the same figure in Colossians 3:8-10 and here, as in that passage, it refers to what they were in their former, pagan state.

In this context, the adjective παλαιόν "old" refers both to time and to nature, i.e. their "former, *ungodly* nature". The fact that their former nature was ungodly is made explicit in the display.

The non-figurative sense of the whole clause is "you must renounce (*or*, put aside) your former, *ungodly* nature".

4:22b This nature caused you to behave in the *evil* way you used to behave. In the Greek text, the clause κατὰ τὴν προτέραν ἀναστροφήν "in regard to the former behaviour" comes between the infinitive ἀποθέσθαι "to put off" and the direct object τὸν παλαιὸν ἄνθρωπον "the old nature".

This "former behaviour" clearly refers to the way the Ephesians used to behave before they became believers. This recalls 2:2-3, where the related verb ἀναστρέφω "behave" is used. A change in a person's nature must also involve a change in his way of life. He can no longer live as he used to do and as unbelievers still do.

Commentators regard the preposition κατά as used here in different ways:

1. It is connected to the infinitive ἀποθέσθαι "to put off", i.e. "put off, as concerns the former way of life, the old nature". See, for example, Eadie (pp. 338-339), Ellicott (p. 85), Hodge (p. 260).
2. It relates to the object, i.e. "Get rid of the old self which manifested itself in your former way of life" (Bratcher and Nida, pp. 113-114). TEV expresses this as "So get rid of your old self, which made you live as you used to".

All of these options make good sense and, semantically, there is little difference between them. Most of the commentators support the first option.

This proposition is NUCLEUS₁ of 4:22b-d, which is a description of the "former, *ungodly* nature".

4:22c-d This nature was destroying you spiritually, because it was causing you to crave

that which is evil **and causing you to believe that this was good for you.** The verb φθείρω means "to destroy, ruin, spoil". Here, the participle φθειρόμενον, which may be present passive or middle (i.e. "being destroyed" or "destroying itself"), indicates a continuous process and refers to moral and spiritual degeneration. Commentators discuss how the verb tense should be translated in this context:

1. Some commentators consider that the present tense should be understood in a way that represents the present tendency to corruption in the old nature, i.e. "which is being corrupted". See, for example, Abbott (p. 136), Ellicott (p. 85).
2. Others consider that it should be understood as indicating durative action in past time, i.e. "which was being corrupted". See, for example, Bratcher and Nida (p. 114), Foulkes (p. 137), Mitton (p. 164).

The second option seems most appropriate in the context, since what the Ephesians had been in the past is in focus here.

The clause τὸν φθειρόμενον κατὰ τὰς ἐπιθυμίας τῆς ἀπάτης "the one being corrupted according to the lusts of deceit" further describes τὸν παλαιὸν ἄνθρωπον "the old nature".

Both nouns in the genitive construction τὰς ἐπιθυμίας τῆς ἀπάτης "the lusts of deceit" are abstract nouns. The first noun, ἐπιθυμία "desire, craving" is a stronger word than "desire" in English. It indicates a strong and excessive desire. The second noun, ἀπάτης, means "deception, deceitfulness".

The two nouns represent the events "to desire/crave" something and "to deceive" someone. Most versions translate this as "deceitful desires/lusts". NRSV is more specific with its translation "deluded by its lusts". In the display, they are expressed as "causing you to crave *that which is evil* and causing you to believe that this was good for you".

The phrase τὰς ἐπιθυμίας τῆς ἀπάτης "the lusts of deceit" is preceded by the preposition κατά (the second in the verse). Here it most likely indicates causality, i.e. "because it was causing you to crave...". This would make good sense in the context, since it is the harmful desires referred to which are the cause of moral and spiritual destruction.

In the display, therefore, the two propositions in 4:22d provide the reason for the increasing spiritual deterioration (4:22c).

4:23 *You were taught that* **you must be made-new/transformed** *by God* **in the way that you think** The initial δέ marks the switch from the negative, the old life, to the positive, the new life they are to live.

The infinitive ἀνανεοῦσθαι "to be renewed", here, is dependent on ἐδιδάχθητε "you were taught" (4:21), as are the other two infinitives ἀποθέσθαι "to put off" (4:22) and ἐνδύσασθαι "to put on" (4:24). These two infinitives, ἀποθέσθαι "to put off" and ἐνδύσασθαι "to put on", are aorists. The infinitive here (4:23), ἀνανεοῦσθαι "to be renewed, be made new", is a present infinitive. Normally a present infinitive implies a continuous, repeated renewal, whereas an aorist indicates a "once for all" action.

The infinitive ἀνανεοῦσθαι "to be renewed", therefore, does not refer to the "once for all" renewal that comes when someone believes in Christ and "puts on the new nature". Rather, it is talking about the process of renewal as it continues through a believer's life. Paul reinforces this by the aorist in 4:24 to indicate decisive, "once for all" action.

The expression τῷ πνεύματι τοῦ νοὸς ὑμῶν "in/by the spirit of your mind" occurs only here in the New Testament. Therefore, commentators discuss its meaning. The first question is about τῷ πνεύματι "the spirit":

1. Some commentators consider that πνεῦμα refers to the Holy Spirit. See, for example, Candlish (p. 99), Ellicott (p. 86).
2. Others consider that πνεῦμα refers to the human spirit. See, for example, Abbott (p. 137), Alford (p. 124), Eadie (p. 341).

Most commentators support the second option.

There is no consensus among the commentators as to the distinction between πνεῦμα and νοῦς. However, most commentators agree that the entire genitive phrase, τῷ πνεύματι τοῦ νοὸς ὑμῶν "the spirit of your mind", refers to a person's innermost being which governs one's thoughts, emotions, attitudes, values. It recalls ἐν ματαιότητι τοῦ νοὸς αὐτῶν "in the futility of their minds" in 4:17.

The sense of this genitive construction is that the renewal is something deep and inward, which affects all of a person's thoughts and actions. It is also something continuous and progressive.

Meyer (pp. 475–476) suggests the sense "the spirit by which your νοῦς ['mind'] is governed". This approaches the essential part of the meaning.

An alternate expression of the sense is "be made-new/transformed in the way that you think". The latter is used in the display.

Also, since ἀνανεοῦσθαι "be renewed" is a passive form, the agent needs to be stated in the display. We have chosen to use "God" as the agent. "The Holy Spirit" or "God, by means of his Holy Spirit" could also be used.

4:24a and you must acquire the new, godly nature This infinitive, ἐνδύσασθαι "to put on", is third in the series within this paragraph.

The καί "and" which begins this verse relates it to 4:23 and indicates a co-ordinate relationship between the two verses.

This verb ἐνδύω "put on" is used in Ephesians 6:11, 14 and also in the parallel passage in Colossians 3:10. In each place it is used figuratively, just as ἀποθέσθαι "to put off" is used figuratively in 4:22. As with ἀποθέσθαι, this may be considered a dead metaphor and expressed non-figuratively.

Just as ἐνδύσασθαι "to put on" contrasts with ἀποθέσθαι "to put off", so this verse contains two other contrasts with the other parts of this paragraph:

- τὸν καινὸν ἄνθρωπον "the new nature" contrasts with τὸν παλαιὸν ἄνθρωπον "the old nature" (4:22)
- ἐν δικαιοσύνῃ καὶ ὁσιότητι τῆς ἀληθείας "in righteousness and holiness of the truth" with κατὰ τὰς ἐπιθυμίας τῆς ἀπάτης "according to deceitful lusts"
- κτισθέντα "created" with φθειρόμενον "being corrupted"

In discussing the parallel verse in Colossians 3:10a, Beekman (1974, pp. 3–13) represents "to put on" by "to acquire" and "the new person" as "new, good nature". "Acquire" is used in the display here, but "godly" is used instead of "good".

which God created to be like himself, The phrase τὸν κατὰ θεὸν κτισθέντα "the one created in accordance with God" has its parallel in Colossians 3:10: κατ' εἰκόνα τοῦ κτίσαντος αὐτόν "according to the image of the one who created him". The idea of κατὰ θεόν "in accordance with God" probably means "like God" or "in the image of God".

4:24b *that is,* **you must become truly upright and truly devout.** The phrase ἐν δικαιοσύνῃ καὶ ὁσιότητι τῆς ἀληθείας "in righteousness and holiness of the truth" is an amplification of 4:24a. It states the ways in which a believer with his new nature is like God, i.e. he should display God's characteristics of righteousness and holiness.

Most commentators consider τῆς ἀληθείας "of the truth" to be connected to both δικαιοσύνη "righteousness" and ὁσιότητι "holiness".

Commentators discuss the difference in meaning between δικαιοσύνη "righteousness" and ὁσιότης "holiness". Most commentators accept the distinction to be that δικαιοσύνη has regard to our relations to men and ὁσιότης to our relation to God. They therefore make a distinction between "integrity" and "piety". See, for example, Bratcher and Nida (p. 116), Hendriksen (pp. 214–215), Hodge (p. 265).

The two nouns, δικαιοσύνη and ὁσιότης, occur together in Luke 1:75, Titus 1:8 and 1 Thessalonians 2:10. In analysing the genitive construction δικαιοσύνῃ καὶ ὁσιότητι τῆς ἀληθείας "righteousness and holiness of the truth", the commentators discuss the type of genitive. It could be:

1. A genitive of origin (holiness and righteousness which arise from the truth). See, for example, Alford (p. 124), Bratcher and Nida (p. 116).
2. An adjectival genitive (true righteousness and holiness). Bruce sees this as a possibility here (p. 95, fn. 2).

Most of the commentaries regard it as a genitive of origin. Holiness and righteousness come from "the truth". The "truth", then, is the basis of a life of righteousness and holiness. This might be expressed as "you must live upright and devout lives which are based on the truth".

If the second option is followed, then the clause might be expressed as "you must become truly upright and truly devout".

As for the first option, commentators also differ in what they consider ἀλήθεια "truth" to refer to. There are three suggestions:

1. It refers to the truth as presented in the gospel. See, for example, Hodge (p. 266), Lenski (pp. 571–572).
2. It refers to that which is true and not deceptive, in contrast to ἀπάτης "deceitfulness" (4:22). See, for example, Eadie (p. 346).
3. It refers to God himself. See, for example, Alford (p. 124), O'Brien (p. 333).

All these views are valid and the meanings are similar. As O'Brien says,

> [God] is the truth. These qualities originate in him, are consistent with his character, and are ultimately real. In this sense it may be said that they are '*true* holiness and righteousness' (p. 333).

BOUNDARIES AND COHERENCE

For the initial boundary, see the section on Boundaries and Coherence for 4:17-19.

The final boundary is marked by the following features:

1. A further development of the theme occurs in 4:25-32. There Paul presents some specific principles and practices for daily living to be followed by those who have the new, godly nature (4:22-24).
2. A tail-head transition. Paragraph 4:20-24 contains a negative-positive contrast (put off the old life and put on the new life) and closes with the positive side, and 4:25-32 begins with a negative-positive contrast using the same negative verb "to put off" (ἀποτίθημι, 4:22, 25).
3. The conjunction διό "therefore" (4:25), which indicates the possibility of a new paragraph.

The fact that this paragraph is one sentence in the Greek is evidence for its cohesion. Other evidence for its cohesion includes the repeated second person plural reference:

1. The initial word of the paragraph is the free pronoun ὑμεῖς.
2. There are three finite verbs with second person plural suffixes:

    ἐμάθετε "you learnt" (4:20)
    ἠκούσατε "you heard" (4:20)
    ἐδιδάχθητε "you were taught" (4:21)

3. There are three infinitives with the second person plural subject ὑμᾶς:

    ἀποθέσθαι "to put off" (4:22)
    ἀνανεοῦσθαι "to be renewed" (4:23)
    ἐνδύσασθαι "to put on" (4:24)

3. The genitive pronoun ὑμῶν is used (4:23).

PROMINENCE AND THEME

The naturally prominent unit in this paragraph is the CONTENT (4:22-24) and, within that CONTENT, the two positive constituents (4:23-24). The theme statement, therefore, is based on these. "You have learnt" represents the verbs "learnt" and "were taught" in the orienter.

SECTION CONSTITUENT 4:25–32
(Hortatory Paragraph: Specific Hortatory Nucleus of 4:17–32)

THEME: Stop doing those things which are harmful to one another. Rather, act appropriately towards one another.

RELATIONAL STRUCTURE	CONTENTS
EXHORTATION₁ — EXHORTATION — negative	4:25a Therefore, no longer lie *to one another*.
— POSITIVE	4:25b *Rather*, speak truthfully to one another,
— grounds	4:25c since we all belong to *the one church, just as the different limbs are all parts of one human body* [MET].
EXHORTATION₂ — NUCLEUS	4:26a *If* you become angry, do not sin;
amplification — NUCLEUS₁	4:26b do not persist in being angry (*or, cease to be angry before the end of the day*),
NUCLEUS₂	4:27 and *in this way* [4:26b] do not allow the devil to influence you.
EXHORTATION₃ — negative	4:28a A person who has been stealing must steal no longer.
POSITIVE — MEANS	4:28b Instead, he should work hard and honestly with his own hands,
purpose	4:28c in order that he may have something to give to believers/people who are needy.
EXHORTATION₄ — NUCLEUS₁ — negative	4:29a Do not say anything which is offensive/unwholesome.
POSITIVE — MEANS	4:29b Rather, say only that which is suitable for edifying *people*,
purpose	4:29c in order that what you say may *spiritually* benefit those who hear it.
NUCLEUS₂ — EXHORTATION	4:30a And do not cause the Holy Spirit of God to grieve,
grounds – NUCLEUS	4:30b *since, by the Holy Spirit, God* confirmed that he will redeem you, on that day when he will *finally* redeem *all his people*.
comparison	4:30c *This* [4:30b] *is like when someone confirms that something belongs to him by* putting his seal *on it* [MET].
EXHORTATION₅	4:31 Never be resentful in any way. Never become angry in any way. Never shout *abusively at people*. Never slander *people*. Never behave maliciously in any other way.
EXHORTATION₆ — NUCLEUS₁	4:32a Rather, be kind to one another. Be compassionate to one another.
NUCLEUS₂ — EXHORTATION	4:32b Freely forgive one another,
grounds – RESULT	4:32c since God freely forgave you,
reason	4:32d because of *what* Christ *has done*.

INTENT AND STRUCTURE

The 4:25–32 paragraph is strongly hortatory in character. This is signalled by the eleven imperative verb forms which are used. The exhortations regarding the specific sins referred to and the virtues which should replace them are grouped together in the form of six hortatory units, labelled as EXHORTATIONS₁₋₆, in the display diagram. Paul wants the Ephesians to demonstrate their change of character by their everyday behaviour. So he now commands them to respond positively to what he said in 4:17–24.

The imperatives can all be related to the two basic ideas in the preceding paragraph (4:20–24), that the Ephesians should "put off the old nature" and "put on the new nature".

There is no indication that the issues addressed in this paragraph were particular problems among the believers at Ephesus. Paul's concern is for God's people to demonstrate their unity and love in a practical way, a concern which is clear from 4:1–16.

NOTES

4:25 The conjunction Διό "therefore" refers to 4:20–24 as the grounds for 4:25–32.

The first two clauses of this verse are matching negative-positive commands. In the display, this negative-positive feature has been maintained to show the emphasis of the original, i.e. the need to turn away from evil and lies and replace them with righteousness and truth.

In 4:25, 28, 29, Paul exhorts believers not only to abstain from doing evil but also to act positively for the benefit of others. This demonstrates the contrast between the old life and the new life.

4:25a Therefore, no longer lie *to one another*. As in 4:22, where ἀποθέσθαι "put off", was rendered in the display in its non-figurative sense of renouncing something, the same sense is followed here in translating the participial form of the same verb, ἀποθέμενοι. It refers to a radical change in behaviour.

The Greek term τὸ ψεῦδος "the falsehood" is a generic abstract noun, which represents any deceitful/untruthful action. It is not limited to a spoken lie. However, commentators disagree about what is referred to in this context. The suggestions are:

1. It refers to all dishonest dealings, whether actions or words. See, for example, Abbott (p. 139), Ellicott (p. 87).
2. It only refers to spoken lies. See, for example, Hodge (p. 267), Lincoln (p. 300), O'Brien (p. 337).

Either option makes good sense in the context of the previous paragraph. However, in view of the immediately following exhortation λαλεῖτε ἀλήθειαν "speak the truth", the focus here seems to be on *telling* a lie. This option is represented in the display.

4:25b *Rather*, speak truthfully to one another, Paul is quoting Zechariah 8:16.

The abstract noun ἀλήθεια "truth" represents the attribute of being "truthful" and is expressed in adverbial form "speak truthfully".

The Greek noun πλησίον "neighbour" may refer to:

1. Generally, "fellow-man". See, for example, Mitton (pp. 167–168).
2. Specifically, "fellow-believer". See, for example, Ellicott (pp. 87–88), Hendriksen (p. 217), Hodge (p. 268), Lincoln (p. 301), O'Brien (p. 338).

Most commentators support the second option. The immediately following clause, ὅτι ἐσμὲν ἀλλήλων μέλη "because we are members of one another" and the wider context of the mutual dependency of believers as members of the body of Christ (see 2:13–22; 3:6, 14, 15; 4:1–6, 16) supports this analysis. Lying is intrinsically wrong, but is particularly harmful between believers as it damages their unity, which is in focus here.

4:25c since we all belong to *the one church, just as the different* limbs are all parts *of one human body*. The conjunction ὅτι "since, because" introduces the grounds for telling the truth, i.e. union with one another through union with Christ. This recalls 4:12–16 and looks forward to 5:30.

The term μέλος "member, part, limb" is used figuratively here, as in 5:30. It refers to individual believers who together make up the church, which Paul frequently compares to the human body.

This is a live metaphor and the meaning is made explicit in the display by restating it as a simile and filling out the image.

The idea of the mutual dependency of believers is represented by this figure of the body. An alternate display rendering of the clause might be, "since we believers are all dependent upon one another, *just as the different* limbs which are all parts *of a human body are dependent upon one another*".

4:26a *If* you become angry, do not sin; This is a quotation from Psalm 4:4 (LXX). Commentators discuss how the imperative ὀργίζεσθε "be angry" should be understood and how it relates to μὴ ἁμαρτάνετε "do not sin".

Three possible relations are put forward:

1. The two verbs are co-ordinate. They are both commands, i.e. "Be angry and do not sin". See, for example, Eadie (pp. 348–349), Ellicott (p. 88). Righteous anger directed against evil people and evil deeds is not forbidden. There are references in Scripture to the anger of God and of Christ, e.g. Mark 3:5; John 2:13–17.
2. The two verbs are in a condition-consequence relationship, i.e. "If you become angry, do not sin". See, for example, Hodge (pp. 269–

270), Lincoln (p. 301), Stott (p. 185); also REB, TEV.

3. The two verbs are in a circumstance-nucleus relationship, i.e. "When you become angry, do not sin".
4. The two verbs are in a concession-contraexpectation relationship, i.e "Although you may become angry, nevertheless, do not sin". This analysis is based on a rare use of the imperative as a concessive clause (John 2:19), see BDF § 387.

Anger usually results in sin. Paul commands the Ephesians not to sin on those occasions when it may be justifiable to be angry. If the imperative "be angry" is used in translation, it may be necessary to make explicit that the anger spoken about here is righteous anger. The addition of an expression like "when it is justified" or "righteously" may be used to avoid the idea that all anger is permitted (which 4:31 contradicts). It may be possible, though, simply to say, "If (or, When) you become angry, do not sin", since "do not sin" obviously limits the anger.

4:26b do not persist in being angry (or, cease to be angry before the end of the day), There is no connecting word in the Greek text between 4:26a and 4:26b, but μηδέ "neither" (4:27) connects 4:27 with 4:26b. See the note on 4:27.

Even righteous anger, if indulged in for too long, may develop into unrighteous anger, a spirit of resentment, an unforgiving attitude. This is what Paul is warning the Ephesians against.

The word for anger used here, παροργισμός, is used nowhere else in the New Testament. So, based on the context, commentators suggest that it is this mood of settled anger which is referred to here. Therefore, "do not let the sun go down on your anger" may be expressed as, "cease to be angry before the end of the day". Alternatively, this sense might be expressed by "do not persist in being angry".

4:27 and *in this way* [4:26b] do not allow the devil to influence you. The conjunction μηδέ "and not, but not, nor" continues the preceding negation (4:26). The idea, therefore, is that any anger which is left unquenched and allowed to breed bitterness/resentment gives Satan an opportunity to influence a believer and augment these destructive feelings. See, for example, Hodge (p. 270), Eadie (pp. 349–350), Lenski (pp. 578–579).

The clause μηδὲ δίδοτε τόπον τῷ διαβόλῳ "do not give place to the devil" means "do not give opportunity/advantage to the devil". Believers should not allow the devil to influence them through their anger. The person who persists in anger, who cultivates a feeling of resentment, is open to such influence.

In translation, it may not be possible to use the verb "to give" with the noun "place" in the sense required here. It may need to be re-expressed as "do not allow the devil to influence you" or "do not let the devil exert his power over you".

The two clauses 4:26b and 4:27 are clearly connected. In the display, they are taken together as exhortations amplifying 4:26a. In effect, they explain how it is possible to be angry and yet not to sin.

The co-ordinate view is also acceptable, i.e. there are three warnings connected with being angry: "do not sin", "do not persist" and "do not allow the devil to influence you".

4:28 Here again we have the pattern of a negative command followed by a positive one. This is followed by a purpose clause which gives a motivation for carrying out these commands.

4:28a A person who has been stealing must steal no longer. The phrase ὁ κλέπτων "the (one) stealing" gives rise to a number of different interpretations in the commentaries. The two main ones are:

1. It simply refers to unlawfully taking property which belongs to someone else.
2. It has a wider meaning and includes all forms of obtaining something unjustly, e.g. cheating.

Both are relevant, but there is more support for the first option.

The main discussion, however, concerns the present participle in ὁ κλέπτων "the one stealing". The two options are:

1. It denotes action which precedes the action of the main verb in the phrase μηκέτι κλεπτέτω "no more let him steal". The emphasis is, therefore, on the *time* of the stealing. The force of the present participle then would be past durative or frequentative and might be translated by the imperfect tense, e.g. someone who "used to steal". See, for example, BDF, § 339 (3).

2. It denotes action rather than time, i.e. it is an action which is continuing and needs to stop. It is equivalent to a substantive, "the thief". See, for example, Ellicott (p. 90), Hoehner (p. 624), Lincoln (p. 303), O'Brien (p. 342).

Most commentaries support the second option, i.e. as expressed in NIV, "He who has been stealing must steal no longer".

4:28b Instead, he should work hard and honestly with his own hands, This is the positive half of the exhortation. It is introduced by μᾶλλον δέ "but rather, instead". The contrast is between stealing and working with one's own hands.

There are a number of textual variants in different manuscripts for this clause which UBSGNT has as ἐργαζόμενος ταῖς [ἰδίαις] χερσὶν τὸ ἀγαθόν, literally "working with [his own] hands the good (thing)". The variant readings are:

1. Omit ταῖς χερσίν "the hands".
2. Omit τὸ ἀγαθόν "the good (thing)".
3. Include ἰδίαις "(his) own" before χερσίν "hands".
4. Include αὐτοῦ "his" after χερσίν "hands".

In each case, the basic meaning remains the same. Paul is saying that no one should steal. Rather, each one should earn his living by his own efforts. In those languages where "with his hands" sounds unnatural, it could be omitted or its meaning translated in some natural way.

There are two verbs, κοπιάτω "let him work hard, strive" and ἐργαζόμενος "working", in this clause in Greek. The first is a present imperative form. The second is a present participle form. They can be translated in two ways:

1. As a synonymous doublet, i.e. "he should work hard". See, for example, Moore (p. 48).
2. As two separate verbs, i.e. "he should work hard and labour honestly". See, for example, Bratcher and Nida (p. 118), Foulkes (p. 142), Hoehner (pp. 625–626).

If the two verbs, κοπιάτω "work hard" and ἐργαζόμενος "working", are regarded as a doublet (option one), then the clause might also be expressed as "he should work hard and honestly with his own hands".

If these two verbs are not regarded as a doublet (option two), then the clause might be expressed as "he should work hard, that is, he should labour honestly with his own hands".

4:28c in order that he may have something to give to believers/people who are needy. The ἵνα "in order that" introduces the motivation/incentive for working hard. As well as the benefit of being able to take care of himself and his family, a believer should work in order to be able to share with those in the church who, for some reason, cannot work to support themselves.

The verb used here, μεταδιδόναι "to give, impart, share" may be used with respect to giving money or goods, or it may be used of giving spiritual benefits. Here, clearly, it is giving in a practical sense, i.e. giving money, food, etc. to those who lack these things.

There is some debate about whether τῷ χρείαν ἔχοντι "to him having need" refers to:

1. Fellow-believers who are in need.
2. Anyone who is in need, whether believer or not.

In the context of the mutual dependence of believers, the former is considered to be in focus, rather than the more general responsibility to give to any who are needy. As O'Brien says,

> Elsewhere Paul urges his readers to 'do good to all people'. But they do have a special responsibility to 'those of the household of faith' (Gal. 6:10) (p. 344, fn. 307).

See also Lincoln (p. 304).

4:29 This cluster of propositions provides NUCLEUS$_1$ of the EXHORTATION$_4$ unit.

4:29a Do not say anything which is offensive/unwholesome. The adjective σαπρός means, literally, "rotten, decayed, worn out". When used literally, for example, in Matthew 13:48; 12:33; Luke 6:43, it can be used to refer to rotten fruit or fish, etc. Used figuratively, as here, in relation to λόγος "word, speech", it means saying something that is "offensive, worthless, unwholesome".

4:29b Rather, say only that which is suitable for edifying *people*, As with the preceding admonitions, the negative command (4:29a) is now followed by a positive one (no verb actually occurs): εἴ τις ἀγαθὸς πρὸς οἰκοδομὴν τῆς χρείας "if any good for the edification/building-up of the need".

The clause is introduced by ἀλλά "but, rather" to mark the positive side of the negative-positive construction.

The adjective ἀγαθός "good" followed by the preposition πρός "to" means "suitable/ serviceable" for something. Bratcher and Nida (p. 119) suggest that the good language "is helpful, constructive, beneficial".

The preposition πρός "to" is followed by οἰκοδομήν "building up" and the genitive, τῆς χρείας "of the need", which refers to something that a person lacks but needs (BDAG, p. 1088.3).

The idea of spiritual strengthening is present in the use of οἰκοδομήν. This is a theme throughout the chapter, with οἰκοδομήν occurring also in 4:12 and 4:6. This view is well supported by commentators. See, for example, Eadie (p. 353), Hendriksen (p. 221).

Most commentators regard the genitive "οἰκοδομὴν τῆς χρείας "the edification/ building-up of the need" as an objective genitive. In the display, this objective genitive is expressed as, "that which is suitable for edifying *people*".

4:29c in order that what you say may *spiritually* benefit those who hear it. The initial ἵνα "in order to" introduces the purpose of 4:29b.

In this context, the abstract noun χάρις "grace" in the phrase δῷ χάριν "to give, impart grace" means "to confer spiritual benefit on someone". This might be expressed as "to benefit someone spiritually". The edifying words that are spoken (4:29b) are the source of these benefits and those receiving them are described as τοῖς ἀκούουσιν "those who hear".

4:30 Although the initial καί "and" may relate this cluster of propositions to all the preceding commands and prohibitions in 4:25-29, most of the commentators relate it to the immediately preceding injunctions in 4:29, especially the prohibition in 4:29a. See, for example, Eadie (p. 354), Ellicott (p. 91), Hodge (pp. 273-274), Meyer (p. 482), Stott (p. 189). Verse 4:30a strengthens the warning to guard against unwholesome talk. The conjunction καί "and" introduces NUCLEUS₂ in the cluster of propositions 4:29-30.

4:30a And do not cause the Holy Spirit of God to grieve, The negative imperative μὴ λυπεῖτε "do not grieve" in the clause μὴ λυπεῖτε τὸ πνεῦμα τὸ ἅγιον τοῦ θεοῦ "do not grieve the Holy Spirit of God" signals a further exhortation within the EXHORTATION₄ unit.

Special emphasis is placed on the adjective ἅγιον "holy" by its occurrence with the article following the noun.

4:30b-c This same figure of "being sealed" was used in chapter one (1:13). The presence of the Holy Spirit identifies a believer as someone who belongs to God. His presence makes that relationship secure.

4:30b *since,* by the Holy Spirit, *God* confirmed that he will redeem you, The clause is introduced by ἐν ᾧ "in/by whom" and is a motivational grounds for the exhortation of 4:30a.

The prepositional phrase ἐν ᾧ indicates that the Holy Spirit is the means/instrument of the "sealing". Since God makes a believer's salvation secure by means of his Holy Spirit, this is motivation not to grieve him.

The figure of "sealing something" is a live figure. Its non-figurative sense is expressed here in 4:30b. In translation, the figure, though not the non-figurative meaning of "confirming", may possibly be omitted here, especially if it has been stated in chapter one. Otherwise, it may be expressed as in 4:30c.

It is the presence of the Holy Spirit within a believer which identifies him as one who belongs to God and confirms his redemption.

on that day when he will *finally* redeem *all his people.* The phrase εἰς ἡμέραν ἀπολυτρώσεως "for/until the day of redemption" recalls 1:14 and the phrase there εἰς ἀπολύτρωσιν τῆς περιποιήσεως "until the redemption of the purchased possession". Ellicott (p. 92) suggests "the day on which the redemption will be fully realized". See also Hendriksen (p. 222), Lenski (p. 585), Lincoln (p. 307). It is the day on which Christ will return and finally claim those whom he has redeemed and marked as his own by the Holy Spirit.

4:30c *This* [4:30b] *is like when someone confirms that something belongs to him by* putting his seal *on it.* This proposition provides the figure of sealing.

4:31-32 These two verses read almost like a summary that concludes the exhortations against wronging our neighbour. As throughout this section, first the negative exhortations (4:31) are presented and then the positive exhortations (4:32).

4:31 The aorist passive third person imperative, ἀρθήτω "let (something) be put away, removed" applies to each sin listed in this verse. There should be no place in a believer's life for any of them. This series of negative exhortations (prohibitions) constitutes the EXHORTATION$_5$ unit.

Note that in the display, abstract nouns (e.g. "bitterness", "anger", "wrath") are changed into verb phrases, some of which include implicit objects of the verbs made explicit.

Never be resentful in any way. The Greek noun πικρία "bitterness" literally means "bitterness of taste". Here it is used figuratively and refers to the feelings of bitterness or resentfulness that someone has towards someone else.

The initial πᾶσα "all kinds of" relates to the first five sins referred to in this verse. The sixth sin κακία "evil" is qualified by πάσῃ, the dative form of πᾶσα.

Never become angry in any way. There is some discussion about the two nouns θυμός and ὀργή (both meaning "anger"):

1. They can be considered a doublet, i.e. "never become angry in any way". See, for example, BDAG, pp. 720.1 and 461.2.
2. They can be considered as having two different meanings. For example, some commentators suggest that θυμός is a sudden, violent outburst of anger, whereas ὀργή is a more settled form of anger. So it could be expressed as "never become angry and never become enraged". See, for example, Abbott (p. 144), Eadie (p. 358).

It seems preferable to regard this as a doublet. This is followed in the display.

Never shout *abusively at people*. The Greek noun κραυγή "shouting, clamour" is used with reference to loud, abusive, insulting language, to public and rowdy brawling. The component of abusiveness has been made explicit in the display.

Never slander *people*. The Greek noun βλασφημία "slander, defamation, blasphemy" means "to speak against someone in such a way as to harm or injure his or her reputation" (Louw and Nida 33.400).

Never behave maliciously in any other way. The Greek noun κακία is a general term for depravity or wickedness of any sort (cf. Acts 8:2; 1 Pet. 2:16) or sometimes, for ill-will or malignity in particular (cf. Rom. 1:29; Col. 3:8). In this context, the sense of "maliciousness" seems appropriate, as it is in the parallel passage, Colossians 3:8. In both passages, it follows closely on references to anger, which can readily lead to actions with malicious intent.

It is not clear whether the phrase σὺν πάσῃ κακίᾳ "with all malice" refers to:

1. A further vice to be added to the list.
2. A summary of all the previous terms.
3. A generic term to include any sins not already mentioned.

Most commentaries regard it either as a generic term (option three) or a summarising term (option two).

Option three seems likely as it seems that Paul wants to make sure that his list is all-inclusive. The phrase σὺν πάσῃ κακίᾳ "with all malice" then covers all other manifestations of evil intent not already referred to specifically in the rest of the verse. This is expressed in the display as "Never behave maliciously in any other way".

4:32 The initial δέ introduces a series of positive exhortations, following the negative ones in 4:31. This list parallels that in Colossians 3:12–13 quite closely, although there are differences. The three commands are co-ordinate and constitute the EXHORTATION$_6$ unit.

4:32a Rather, be kind to one another. Be compassionate to one another. Moore (p. 48) classifies χρηστοί "kind, loving, benevolent" and εὔσπλαγχνοι "tender-hearted, compassionate" as a near-synonymous doublet (borderline) and there seems very little difference in the two terms. However, since the accumulation of positive terms gives greater force to the exhortation to behave as befits God's people, two terms are used in the display, "kind" and "compassionate".

4:32b Freely forgive one another, The verb χαρίζομαι "to forgive" is not the usual word for forgiving sins (ἀφίημι). Rather it emphasises the gracious nature of the forgiveness. It is used in Jesus' parable of the two debtors in Luke 7:42. In the display, the quality of grace in relation to forgiveness is expressed by the use of the adverb "freely" to qualify the verb "forgive".

This verb χαρίζομαι "forgive" occurs twice in this verse, but the form changes from a present participle χαριζόμενοι "forgiving" to an aorist indicative ἐχαρίσατο "he forgave". Most commentators agree that the aorist form indicates that God forgave them once and for all in the past, while the present participle carries an imperative meaning and indicates that those he has forgiven should keep on forgiving one another.

In 4:32a, Paul uses εἰς ἀλλήλους "to one another", but here he uses the reflexive ἑαυτοῖς, which with the second person plural subject would normally mean "yourselves". The sense, however, is clearly "one another". He does the same in the Colossians passage (3:13). Callow considers that "the difference is probably to avoid an unacceptable repetition, rather than for some subtle distinction" (1983:186; 2002:127). Moule (p. 120) says, "In Col iii.13 it [ἑαυτοῖς] seems to be used as a synonym for the reciprocal ἀλλήλους".

4:32c since God freely forgave you, There is an issue concerning καθὼς καί "just as also" as to its sense or focus:

1. Its main sense is comparison here. This is the most common function of καθώς. It indicates a comparison between God's forgiving people and believers' forgiving each other. See, for example, Mitton (pp. 173-174).
2. Its main sense is causal here. Propositional cluster 4:32c-d provides the motivational grounds for the fulfilment of the injunction in 4:32b. They are to forgive one another since God has forgiven them. See, for example, BDAG (p. 494.3), Best (p. 464), Eadie (pp. 360-361).

O'Brien states,

> [It] has both comparative and causal force (cf. 5:2, 25, 29): what God has done 'in Christ' for believers, which has been so fully set forth in chapters 1-3, provides both the paradigm of and the grounds for their behaviour. Here God's forgiveness of them is the model of their forgiveness of one another (p. 352).

See also Lincoln (p. 310).

Most commentators support a motivational sense here. In the display, cluster 4:32c-d is presented as being motivational grounds for 4:32b. In translation, using a conjunction of comparison is certainly valid as long as it also carries a motivational sense in this context.

4:32d because of *what* Christ *has done*. The meaning of the phrase ἐν Χριστῷ "in Christ" here is difficult to express propositionally.

The commentators are divided as to the meaning of this phrase. The main suggestions are:

1. It signals cause, i.e. "because of Christ" or "because of *what* Christ *has done*". See CEV.
2. It signals means, i.e. "by means of *what* Christ *has done*". Bratcher and Nida (p. 121) mention this in connection with TEV's translation "through Christ". Calvin (p. 195) says, "[Paul] holds out the example of God, who has forgiven to us, through Christ, far more than any mortal man can forgive to his brethren".
3. It signals the sphere or condition of God's action, i.e. God acting "in Christ". See, for example, Hodge (p. 277), Hoehner (p. 641).

The last-mentioned has the greatest support among the commentaries. The meaning then would be that God, acting "in Christ", forgave you.

But it can be argued that since God acted "in Christ", in the sense that he sent Christ to die on behalf of sinners, it is as a result of what Christ has done that God forgives them. See also 1:7-12 and 2:4-10. The phrase ἐν Χριστῷ "in Christ", therefore, might be expressed as either reason (option one), "because of *what* Christ *has done*", or means (option two), "by means of *what* Christ *has done*".

In the display, it is expressed as the reason for God forgiving his people.

BOUNDARIES AND COHERENCE

For the initial boundary, see the section on Boundaries and Coherence for 4:20-24. For the final boundary, see the section on Boundaries and Coherence for 4:1-32. In addition, the rhetorical bracket of ἕκαστος μετὰ τοῦ πλησίον αὐτοῦ "each with his neighbour" and ἀλλήλων μέλη "members one of another" (4:25) and ἀλλήλους "one another" and ἑαυτοῖς "one another" (4:32) makes the boundaries even more clearly defined.

In 4:25-32, Paul turns from the general (4:17-24) to the specific. He now mentions specific sins which a believer must "put off" and the positive qualities which a believer must "put on", i.e. he is to replace the negative with the positive. The sins referred to are those which disrupt the unity of God's people, while the positive qualities enhance the unity and life of the community.

In the preceding paragraph (4:20-24), Paul reminds the Ephesians that they have put off the old nature and have put on the new nature, i.e. they have exchanged their former, evil nature for a good new nature.

The whole paragraph is characterised by vocabulary which brings to the fore the mutual dependence of believers and their individual responsibility. For example:

ἕκαστος μετὰ τοῦ πλησίον αὐτοῦ "each with his neighbour" (4:25)

ἀλλήλων μέλη "members of one another" (4:25)

ἵνα ἔχῃ μεταδιδόναι τῷ χρείαν ἔχοντι "in order that he may have (something) to give to the one having need" (4:28)

πρὸς οἰκοδομὴν τῆς χρείας "for building up according to need" (4:29)

δῷ χάριν τοῖς ἀκούουσιν "to give grace to those who hear" (4:29)

γίνεσθε...εἰς ἀλλήλους χρηστοί "be kind to one another" (4:32)

χαριζόμενοι ἑαυτοῖς "forgiving one another" (4:32)

PROMINENCE AND THEME

All the main elements of this paragraph are in an addition relationship, which means that no hortatory unit is more prominent than another in terms of natural prominence. However, the use of expressions such as those referred to in the Boundaries and Coherence note relating to the important issues of unity and mutual dependence of believers gives prominence to this motif. This mutual dependence is included in the theme statement in the phrase "one another".

The contrast between harmful and helpful behaviour is present both explicitly and implicitly in these verses. The theme statement, therefore, is a general statement based on the negative-positive contrast expressed in all the specific exhortations, i.e. that the Ephesians should avoid actions which may be harmful to their fellow-believers, and they should do things which will benefit them.

DIVISION CONSTITUENT 5:1–6 (Hortatory Paragraph: Nucleus₃ of 4:1–6:9)

THEME: Imitate God. Specifically, let everything you do be done because you love one another. Do not let anyone persuade you to disobey God and live immoral lives, since God will punish those people who habitually disobey him.

RELATIONAL STRUCTURE	CONTENTS
NUCLEUS₁ — GENERIC POSITIVE EXHORTATION — EXHORTATION	5:1a Imitate God,
└ grounds	5:1b since you *are* his *spiritual* children whom he loves [MET].
SPECIFIC POSITIVE EXHORTATION — CONGRUENCE	5:2a *Specifically*, let everything you do be done because you love *one another*,
└ standard — REASON	5:2b just as Christ also loved us,
└ result — NUCLEUS	5:2c and, *as a result*, he willingly chose to die on our behalf.
└ amplification	5:2d He offered himself to God *just as people offer* a sweet-smelling animal sacrifice *to God to please him* [MET].
NUCLEUS₂ — SPECIFIC NEGATIVE EXHORTATIONS — NUCLEUS₁ — EXHORTATION₁	5:3a But do not commit any kind of sexually immoral or indecent act,
EXHORTATION₂	5:3b and do not desire more of anything than you need.
EXHORTATION₃	5:3c Indeed, do not even mention these things [5:3a–b],
└ grounds	5:3d since it is not fitting that God's people *should do such things* [5:3a–b].
NUCLEUS₂ — NEGATIVE — EXHORTATION₁	5:4a Do not talk obscenely,
EXHORTATION₂	5:4b do not talk foolishly,
EXHORTATION₃	5:4c and do not use vulgar language,
└ grounds	5:4d *since* it is not fitting *that God's people should speak in this way* [5:4a–c].
POSITIVE	5:4e Rather, thank *God*.
grounds (warning) — NUCLEUS₁ — prominence orienter	5:5a *Do not do like that* [5:3–4c], since you may be sure
NUCLEUS₁	5:5b that no sexually immoral person nor indecent person will be among those people over whom Christ and God rule.
NUCLEUS₂ — CONCLUSION	5:5c Nor will any greedy person be among those people over whom Christ and God rule,
└ grounds	5:5d since a greedy person substitutes material things for God.
NUCLEUS₂ — PROMINENCE MARKING EXHORTATION	5:6a Do not let anyone deceive you by means of misleading words,
GROUNDS — RESULT	5:6b since God will punish [MTY] those people who habitually disobey him,
└ reason	5:6c because they sin in these very ways [5:3–5].

INTENT AND STRUCTURE

The two imperative verb forms γίνεσθε ...μιμηταὶ τοῦ θεοῦ "be...imitators of God" and περιπατεῖτε ἐν ἀγάπῃ "walk in love" (5:1, 2) signal immediately and clearly that the 5:1-6 paragraph is hortatory. It consists of three units:

1. A GENERIC POSITIVE EXHORTATION (5:1a) and grounds (5:1b).
2. A SPECIFIC POSITIVE EXHORTATION (5:2a) having a CONGRUENCE-standard relationship with 5:2b-d, which could also be seen as having a function of motivational grounds for loving. See, for example, Hodge (p. 277), Lincoln (p. 310), O'Brien (p. 352).
3. A series of SPECIFIC NEGATIVE EXHORTATIONS ending with a positive one (5:3-4) with a warning grounds (5:5-6) for these exhortations.

Paul wants the Ephesians to live lives which are characterised by obeying God and loving one another, rather than disobeying God and behaving in immoral ways.

NOTES

5:1 The initial οὖν marks the start of a new unit and progression in the hortatory material. So the link is not inferential, and need not be translated as "therefore".

5:1a Imitate God, In the Greek the noun μιμηταί "imitators" is used. In this context, the focus is on the event "imitating God". Therefore, it is not necessary to translate in the nominal form, which includes the component of the doers of the event, especially in languages where that form is not natural.

5:1b since you *are* his *spiritual* children whom he loves. The comparative ὡς "as" points to the manner in which the believer is to imitate God. See, for example, BDAG, p. 1104.3aα. It also indicates a reason or motive for a believer to imitate God, i.e. Paul is reminding the Ephesian believers that they are God's children, whom he loves and, as such, they should try to be like him. O'Brien says,

> [The designation] is not simply a comparison between father and children, but signifies the basis on which this demand to be imitators is made (p. 352).

It seems best, therefore, to represent the clause as a motivational grounds for 5:1a.

The Greek noun τέκνα "children" is used figuratively here about believers' relationship with God. The adjective ἀγαπητά "loved" represents the event "(God) loves (someone)", specifically, in this context, that he loves believers. The expression τέκνα ἀγαπητά "beloved children" is part of a live metaphor which might be expressed as "*spiritual* children whom he loves".

5:2 The conjunction καί "and" relates verse 5:2 to 5:1. It introduces a specific way in which believers are to imitate God. The relationship between 5:2a and 5:2b-d is CONGRUENCE-standard.

5:2a *Specifically,* let everything you do be done because you love *one another*, The command περιπατεῖτε ἐν ἀγάπῃ "walk in love" provides an antithesis to the prohibitions in 5:3-6. As with all the occurrences of the verb περιπατεῖτε "walk" in Ephesians, it refers to how the Ephesians should behave.

5:2b-d The conjunction καθὼς καί "as also" could introduce:

1. A comparison/standard for 5:2a.
2. A grounds for 5:2a.
3. A combination of both relationships.

The latter seems to be the sense here. This is supported, for example, by O'Brien (p. 354, fn. 353) and Lincoln (p. 311). In the display, it is represented as a CONGRUENCE-standard relation, but EXHORTATION-grounds would also be appropriate.

5:2b just as Christ also loved us, The relationship between the two verbs ἠγάπησεν "he loved" and παρέδωκεν "he gave himself up" is one of reason-result. The first verb, ἠγάπησεν "he loved", is prominent, since love is thematic in this context. Thus, the nucleus of the cluster is ὁ Χριστὸς ἠγάπησεν ἡμᾶς "Christ loved us" (5:2b). It was because Christ loved us that he was willing to die for us.

5:2c and, *as a result,* **he willingly chose to die on our behalf.** The clause παρέδωκεν ἑαυτὸν ὑπὲρ ἡμῶν "he gave himself up for us" has the sense "he died for us" or "he allowed himself to be killed for us". However this is expressed, it is important that it should be made clear that it was a voluntary act: Christ chose to die, he died willingly.

The prepositional phrase ὑπὲρ ἡμῶν means "on our behalf" or "for our benefit/good".

5:2d He offered himself to God *just as people offer* **a sweet-smelling animal sacrifice** *to God to please him.* The Greek expression προσφορὰν καὶ θυσίαν τῷ θεῷ εἰς ὀσμὴν εὐωδίας literally means "an offering and a sacrifice to God for an odour of sweet smell".

The first point for discussion is the meaning of the two nouns προσφορά "offering" and θυσία "sacrifice". The suggestions are:

1. Whereas they both refer to the same event here, the words each have a separate component of meaning important to the context. For a general definition, BDAG, pp. 887.2 and 462.2αγ, says that προσφορά means "that which is brought as a voluntary expression", while θυσία means "that which is offered as a sacrifice".
2. The two terms form a generic-specific doublet, where θυσία explains προσφορά, i.e. anything presented to God was an offering (προσφορά), but a sacrifice (θυσία) was an offering that was killed.
3. Although there was a meaning difference between these two terms at one time, by the time the New Testament was written either could be used to refer to a sin offering.

In the display, the noun προσφορά "offering" is represented by the verbal phrase "offered himself".

The second question relating to προσφορά and θυσία is whether they are to be understood literally or figuratively. It is preferable to understand them literally, since Christ was actually killed, as the animal sacrifices were. He was the sacrifice. The focus is on his freely offering himself as a sacrifice to God. This is expressed in the form of a simile in the display (5:2d).

The phrase ὀσμὴν εὐωδίας "an odour of sweet smell" is a figurative expression which indicates the acceptability of the sacrifice to God. See Genesis 8:21; Leviticus 1:9, 13, 17, etc. Cf. Philippians 4:18. Its basis is the anthropomorphism that the smell of the smoke of offerings rose to the nostrils of God and was pleasing to him. The phrase "*to please him*" has been supplied in the display to express the non-figurative meaning.

The proposition 5:2d amplifies 5:2c, describing Christ's death in more detail.

5:3 The initial δέ along with the first vice, πορνεία "fornication", moves the discourse on from positive exhortation (i.e. ways in which Paul wanted the Ephesians to behave in love) to prohibition, (i.e. avoiding self-indulgent behaviour which, in contrast, demonstrates love for self).

The phrase μηδὲ ὀνομαζέσθω ἐν ὑμῖν "let it not be named among you", which occurs in 5:3, refers to the abstract nouns listed in both 5:3 and 5:4. In this context, the implication is that believers should not commit these sins nor should they talk about them. In the propositions for 5:3–4, therefore, both these aspects of behaviour are represented. Believers are urged not to commit these sins and also not even to talk about them.

5:3a But do not commit any kind of sexually immoral or indecent act, There is a question about the difference in meaning between πορνεία "fornication" and ἀκαθαρσία "impurity, indecency". There are two options:

1. Consider the two nouns to have different meanings here that need to be represented independently. The noun πορνεία generally refers to illicit sexual intercourse between men and women, while ἀκαθαρσία "impurity" may refer to a wide range of immoral activities, including illicit sex acts other than those defined by πορνεία. See, for example, Bratcher and Nida (p. 125), Calvin (p. 197), O'Brien (p. 359).
2. Consider that the meanings of the two nouns do not need to be represented independently. The use of two basically synonymous nouns is for emphasis. See, for example, JBP, NCV.

The order of the words in the Greek text is πορνεία...καὶ ἀκαθαρσία πᾶσα "fornication and all uncleanness". The adjective πᾶσα "all" refers to, in this context, "every kind of, all sorts of". A similar phrase ἀκαθαρσίας πάσης occurs in 4:19 where it refers to "every kind of immoral deed". In the present context of the immediately preceding πορνεία, which clearly refers to wrong sexual behaviour, it is possible to understand ἀκαθαρσία as also referring to sexual immorality of any sort, rather than any act which is morally wrong.

However, in 5:5, cognate nouns of both πορνεία and ἀκαθαρσία are used referring to people who commit those acts. So, instead of using only one term here with an emphatic modifier, it seems better to distinguish the two, for example: "commit any kind of sexually immoral or indecent act".

5:3b and do not desire more of anything than you need. Commentators discuss πλεονεξία "greed/covetousness", the third abstract noun in this series, and how it relates to the rest of 5:3–4. They suggest two possibilities:

1. It is a separate vice in the list. See, for example, Eadie (p. 370), O'Brien (p. 360).
2. It is a further definition of ἀκαθαρσία. Therefore, in this context, it means "inordinate affection" or "sensual indulgence". See, for example, Hendriksen (p. 228), Lincoln (pp. 279, 321–322), Stott (p. 197).

The basic meaning of the word is that of desiring more than one needs. This supports the first option and is how it is represented in the display.

5:3c Indeed, do not even mention these things [5:3a–b], In the Greek, the phrase μηδὲ ὀνομαζέσθω ἐν ὑμῖν "let it not be named among you" means that not only should believers avoid committing these sins, but they should also avoid thinking and talking about them, since this encourages people to indulge in them. See Hodge (p. 283), Lincoln (p. 322), O'Brien (p. 360). This same idea is repeated in 5:12, "it is shameful even to speak of what is done by them in secret".

The μηδὲ ὀνομαζέσθω is a very strong negative form and is expressed as "Indeed, do not even mention these things" in the display. This emphasises that there should be not the slightest hint that believers are involved in such vices, in either word or deed.

5:3d since it is not fitting that God's people *should do such things* [5:3a–b]. The conjunction καθώς introduces the grounds for Paul's exhortation to avoid such behaviour, i.e. it is not fitting for believers to be associated with anything sexually immoral since they are the Lord's people (ἁγίοις "holy ones").

5:4 The initial καί introduces a co-ordinate set of vices which believers should make every effort to avoid. The vices mentioned in 5:3a–b are connected with indulgent behaviour of different kinds. Here in 5:4, Paul concentrates on vices relating to speech.

As he did in 5:3, Paul uses a list of abstract nouns which need to be expressed by event propositions in the display. These nouns are grammatically parallel to those in 5:3, also functioning as subjects of the verb ὀνομαζέσθω "be named" in 5:3c.

5:4a Do not talk obscenely, The first of this series of abstract nouns, αἰσχρότης, literally means "ugliness, wickedness".

It can refer to morally hateful/obscene behaviour as well as speech.

However, as the other two abstract nouns in this list clearly refer to speech, it seems appropriate for αἰσχρότης to be understood in the same way.

The adjective αἰσχρός "ugly, shameful, base" (related to αἰσχρότης) is used in 5:12 in connection with speech (λέγειν "to speak"), as is a cognate αἰσχρολογία "evil speech" in Colossians 3:8.

Most commentators follow the view that it refers to speech here in 5:4a. This is followed in the display.

5:4b do not talk foolishly, The noun μωρολογία refers to "senseless, foolish, frivolous talk".

5:4c and do not use vulgar language, The use of the particle ἤ "or" here is regarded as being disjunctive, separating two related vices, μωρολογία and εὐτραπελία. The latter, εὐτραπελία, refers to "coarse jesting, buffoonery", i.e. 5:4b–c are saying that as well as avoiding conversation that is "frivolous", the Ephesians must also avoid conversation that is "coarse/vulgar". The distinctiveness of the two needs to be expressed in the translation.

5:4d *since* it is not fitting *that God's people should speak in this way* [5:4a–c]. The relative clause ἃ οὐκ ἀνῆκεν "which (things) are not fitting" parallels 5:3d, καθὼς πρέπει ἁγίοις "as is fitting for God's people". Here, as there, it provides a grounds for the immediately preceding commands. Note the difference in orientation of 5:3 and 5:4: In 5:3, *not* partaking in the vices is fitting for God's people, in 5:4 partaking in them is *not* fitting.

5:4e Rather, thank *God*. The strong adversative ἀλλὰ μᾶλλον "but rather" introduces a positive command, in contrast with the preceding prohibitions. Paul uses yet another abstract noun, εὐχαριστία "rendering of thanks, thanksgiving". This too needs to be expressed as an event. The implied recipient of the thanks is God. This needs to be made explicit in the event proposition. This call to thanksgiving and praise is reiterated in 5:20. See, also, Colossians 3:15-17.

Commentators discuss which of the preceding prohibitions 5:4e contrasts with:

1. It contrasts only with the prohibitions in 5:4a-c. This would mean that all the commands, positive and negative, in 5:4, concern speech. See, for example, Bruce (p. 103), Candlish (p. 105), Hoehner (p. 658), Scott (p. 227).
2. It contrasts with all six prohibitions in 5:3-4c. The contrast, then, would not only be between thanksgiving and vices of speech, but would also include the contrast between thanksgiving and the self-centred acquisitiveness which sexual immorality and greed exhibit. This view is further supported by the strong warnings in 5:5-6 for those who indulge in any of the vices prohibited in 5:3-4. Houlden says,

> Whereas sexual impurity and covetousness both express self-centred acquisitiveness, thanksgiving is the exact opposite, and so the antidote required; it is the recognition of God's generosity (p. 324).

In the display, 5:4e is linked with 5:4a-c because of the common thread of speech, but relating it to the whole of 5:3-4c also makes good sense.

5:5-6 The initial γάρ in 5:5 indicates the grounds supporting the exhortations (prohibitions) of 5:3 and 5:4. The grounds takes the form of a warning which consists of two nuclei, 5:5 and 5:6.

5:5a *Do not do like that* [5:3-4c], since you may be sure The phrase τοῦτο γὰρ ἴστε γινώσκοντες contains two verbs, ἴστε and γινώσκοντες, both meaning "know". The use of the two verbs is generally agreed to be for emphasis. Commentators do not agree about the mood of the verbal phrase that should be used in translation. There are two possibilities:

1. It should be translated as an indicative ("you are well aware", "it is certain").
2. It should be translated as an imperative ("be sure of this", "be certain").

There is not much difference between these two options. Whichever is chosen, Paul is drawing attention to the certainty of what follows in the rest of 5:5. See Hoehner (p. 659), O'Brien (p. 362).

This proposition provides a prominence orienter for the rest of the verse.

5:5b that no sexually immoral person nor indecent person The ὅτι introduces the content of prominence orienter 5:5a.

The πᾶς "every" indicates the all-embracing nature of the warning—there will be no exceptions to the consequences.

The vices represented here (5:5b-c) in πόρνος "fornicator, sexually immoral person", ἀκάθαρτος "unclean/indecent person", πλεονέκτης "covetous/greedy person" repeat those set out in 5:3. See the notes on that verse.

will be among those people over whom Christ and God rule. The clause οὐκ ἔχει κληρονομίαν ἐν τῇ βασιλείᾳ τοῦ Χριστοῦ καὶ θεοῦ "does not have an inheritance in the kingdom of Christ and of God" is difficult to propositionalise.

The noun κληρονομία "inheritance" is used elsewhere in Ephesians: 1:11, 14, 18. In these verses, it refers to the things which God promised believers: salvation, forgiveness, eternal life, etc. It is reasonable to assume that the meaning is similar here and Paul is saying that no one who commits the sins mentioned in the first part of 5:5b will be part of "the kingdom of Christ and of God".

Bratcher and Nida (p. 128) suggest that this can be expressed as "they will never be part of the people ruled by Christ and by God".

Commentators discuss the phrase τοῦ Χριστοῦ καὶ θεοῦ. They say that it can refer to:

1. One who is both Christ and God, i.e. Christ as God.
2. Two distinct persons of the Trinity, i.e. the Father and the Son.

Since this is the only occurrence of the expression in the New Testament there is no comparison possible with other usages. It could be argued that the lack of the definite article before θεοῦ "God" means it refers to one person. However, there is plenty of evidence elsewhere in the New Testament to show that the use of θεοῦ without the article is by no means unusual.

Therefore, the second option is followed in the display: Christ and God are represented as two distinct persons.

5:5c-d Nor will any greedy person be among those people over whom Christ and God rule, *since* a greedy person substitutes material things for God. In the Greek, 5:5d consists of the relative clause ὅ ἐστιν εἰδωλολάτρης "which/who is an idolater". Most commentators agree that this clause only qualifies πλεονέκτης "greedy person" (5:5c) and not all three preceding nouns (5:5b–c).

The relative clause may be translated in two ways:

1. "Such-a-person/Who is an idolater".
2. "That is, an idolater".

However, the meaning is the same.

In the parallel verse, Colossians 3:5, Paul refers to τὴν πλεονεξίαν ἥτις ἐστὶν εἰδωλολατρία "greed/covetousness which is idolatry". In relating this verse to Matthew 6:24, "You cannot serve God and Mammon", Callow says, "Another god has been, in effect, chosen, the god of material gain". It is not that a greedy person worships what he desires. Rather, he treats those things as more important than God. Callow expresses this idea propositionally as "you are substituting (material) things for God" (1983:176; 2002:120). This seems to be an appropriate analysis in this context also.

The relative clause (5:5d) is analysed as grounds for the preceding prohibition (5:5c). Paul is doing more than simply describing covetousness; he is also giving grounds why the Ephesian believers should avoid this particular sin.

5:6 This propositional cluster provides NUCLEUS₂ of the warning grounds 5:5–6.

5:6a Do not let anyone deceive you by means of misleading words, The phrase κενοῖς λόγοις "empty words" is figurative. The primary sense of κενός is "empty", so the phrase means that the words said have no value or worth; they are devoid of truth or wisdom. For example, such people who use κενοῖς λόγοις "empty words" might persuade the Ephesian believers that the sins referred to in 5:3–5 are not as serious in God's eyes as Paul says. They might, therefore, say that there is no reason for avoiding them. Such statements sound as if they are true, though they are not. In the display, the phrase "misleading words" is used.

This proposition gives prominence to the warning in 5:6b.

5:6b since God will punish those people who habitually disobey him, The γάρ introduces a grounds for the exhortation of 5:6a. The expression ἔρχεται ἡ ὀργὴ τοῦ θεοῦ "the wrath of God comes" is also used in Colossians 3:6 and 1 Thessalonians 1:10. It refers to the future day of judgement when God will reveal his anger in the punishment of sinners.

In this context, ἡ ὀργή "the wrath" is a metonymy for "punishment", the cause ("wrath") being put for the effect ("punishment"). The event represented is "God will punish". Paul here describes those who will be punished as τοὺς υἱοὺς τῆς ἀπειθείας "the sons of disobedience". This is a common Hebrew idiom which means "those characterised by disobedience". This expression is also used in Ephesians 2:2 and Colossians 3:6. It has been expressed in the display as "those people who habitually disobey him [God]".

5:6c because they sin in these very ways [5:3–5]. The clause initial διὰ ταῦτα "because of these (things)" refers to the sins listed in 5:3–5 and provides the reason why God will punish these disobedient people.

BOUNDARIES AND COHERENCE

The initial boundary has been discussed in the section on Boundaries and Coherence for 4:17–32. The principal boundary feature is the οὖν...περιπατεῖτε... "therefore...walk..." in 5:1–2, which indicates a continuation of the theme begun in 4:1 with ἀξίως περιπατῆσαι "walk worthily".

Evidence that a new paragraph begins at 5:7 is the occurrence of οὖν "therefore" at the beginning of 5:7 and περιπατεῖτε "walk" in 5:8. These again mark the introduction of another set of specifics of 4:1 and a change of topic from "love" in 5:1–6 to "light" in 5:7–14.

This final border is less agreed on, with different versions making a paragraph break:

between 5:2 and 5:3 (TEV, NIV, REB, RSV)
between 5:4 and 5:5 (JBP, LB)
between 5:5 and 5:6 (NCV, NET, TEV)
between 5:7 and 5:8 (CEV, NIV)
between 5:14 and 5:15 (NASB, RSV)

However, making use of the sequence of οὖν...περιπατεῖτε, it seems best to make the break between 5:6 and 5:7 (see Hoehner, p. 643).

The occurrence of μιμηταὶ τοῦ θεοῦ ὡς τέκνα ἀγαπητά "imitators of God as dear children" (5:1) contrasts with τοὺς υἱοὺς τῆς ἀπειθείας "the sons of disobedience" (5:6). These then form a rhetorical bracket for the paragraph.

There is predominantly second person plural orientation throughout the paragraph which also provides cohesion to the paragraph.

PROMINENCE AND THEME

The two positive exhortations (5:1a, 2a) are naturally prominent and are considered more prominent than the prohibitions (5:3 and 5:4). The first positive exhortation (5:1a) could be regarded as generic, in relation to the series of commands involving περιπατεῖτε in 5:2, 8, 15, which specify the characteristics necessary if a person is to imitate God.

The theme statement is based on the two positive exhortations as well as a summary of the prohibitions and their grounds, since these are given prominence by the detailed exposition in 5:3-6.

DIVISION CONSTITUENT 5:7–14 (Hortatory Paragraph: Nucleus₄ of 4:1–6:9)

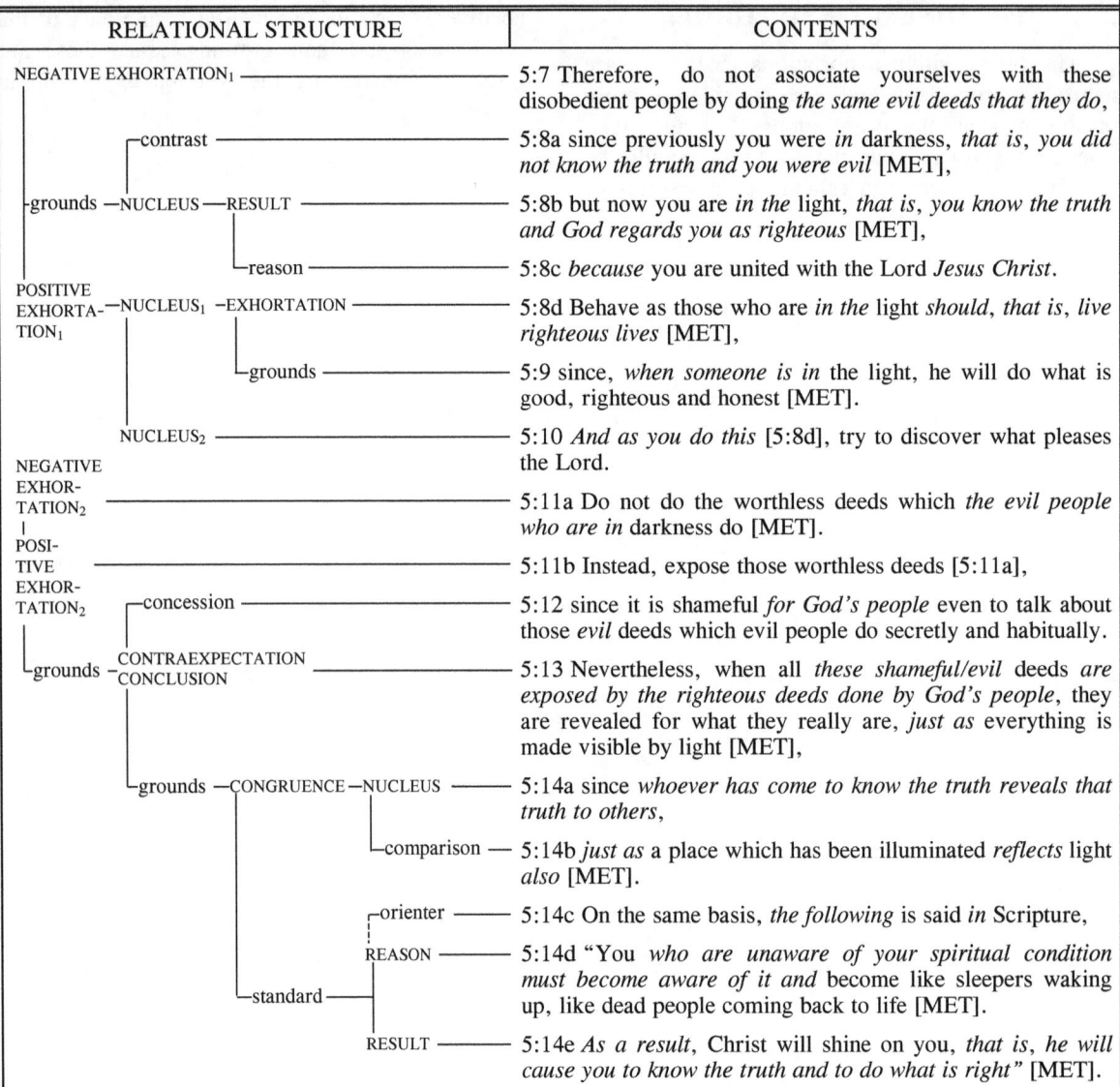

INTENT AND STRUCTURE

The imperative verb forms in 5:7–14 mark it as a hortatory paragraph. It consists of two units (5:7–10 and 5:11–14) which are regarded as co-ordinate nuclei within the paragraph, since they are both hortatory.

In the first unit (5:7–10), there is a NEGATIVE EXHORTATION₁ (5:7) and a grounds (5:8a–c) which supports both this NEGATIVE EXHORTATION₁ and the following POSITIVE EXHORTATION₁ (5:8d). And 5:8d is also supported by a further grounds (5:9). POSITIVE EXHORTATION₁ includes a second exhortation expressed by a participle in the Greek text (5:10).

The second unit (5:11–14) consists of NEGATIVE EXHORTATION₂ (5:11a) and POSITIVE EXHORTATION₂ (5:11b), but there is only one grounds (5:12–14).

This hortatory paragraph (5:7–14) is in response to Paul's statement in 5:6 about the wrath and punishment God will inflict upon those who live in disobedience to him. Paul wants the Ephesian believers to make sure that they avoid contact with these "children of disobedience" (5:6b), since they are now "children of light"

(5:8). As such, Paul says, they should show "the fruit of light" in their lives, which is "all that is good, righteous and honest" (5:9).

In order to motivate the Ephesians further, Paul wants to make them aware that their righteous lives will have a positive effect on those living sinful lives. Just as light dispels darkness, so their righteous lives can help to dispel the darkness of sin in the lives of those living sinfully, by revealing sin for what it really is. Some of these sinful people will then respond to the truth; as believers, their behaviour will change, as had happened to the Ephesian believers.

NOTES

5:7 Therefore, The initial οὖν "therefore" starts this new paragraph. It makes an inference from what Paul said in 5:5, i.e. since those who disobey God will experience his wrath, Paul is telling the Ephesians not to associate with them in doing the same evil deeds they do.

do not associate yourselves with these disobedient people by doing *the same evil deeds that they do,* In the New Testament, the Greek noun συμμέτοχος "sharer (in something) with (someone)" only occurs here and in Ephesians 3:6, although a verb with similar meaning, συγκοινωνέω "participate in", occurs in 5:11.

The consensus is that the pronoun αὐτῶν "them" refers to τοὺς υἱοὺς τῆς ἀπειθείας "the sons of disobedience" (5:6).

Commentators discuss what Paul is warning the Ephesians not to "share" with the unbelievers. There are two possibilities:

1. He is warning them against sharing in sins characteristic of these people, i.e. not to behave as these people do. See, for example, Eadie (p. 379), Ellicott (p. 97).
2. He is warning them both against sharing in sins characteristic of these people and sharing the punishment which will follow. See, for example, Hendriksen (p. 231), Hodge (pp. 288-289), Lincoln (p. 326), Stott (pp. 197-198).

The focus here is the behaviour of believers. Therefore, option one is more appropriate. Unit 5:8-11 (particularly, 5:11) supports this, where Paul urges the Ephesians "not to have fellowship with the unfruitful works of darkness".

Believers are to avoid those who do evil, in the sense that they should not get involved in these people's sins, i.e. they are not to commit the same sins, nor join them in activities which would encourage them [the Ephesian believers] to sin. It does not mean that they are to have no association with such people at all, since if this were so they would have no opportunity to present the truth of the gospel to them.

5:8a-c This is presented figuratively in terms of the contrast between darkness and light, with ποτε "once" and νῦν δέ "but now" indicating the time contrast between the two halves of the picture. A similar contrast was mentioned in 2:11, 13, contrasting the lives of the Gentiles before they trusted in Christ, with their present life in Christ. The figure here also recalls the "darkened minds" of 4:18 and the spiritual enlightenment referred to in 1:18.

This metaphor of "darkness" and "light" extends from 5:8 to 5:14, so the figure is regarded as a live metaphor. Other terms associated with "light" and "darkness" in these verses support the analysis that this is an extended metaphor, that "darkness" and "light" are being used as figures and do not refer to physical light and darkness. See the list of terms associated with this metaphor in the section on Boundaries and Coherence.

Since this is a live figure, the topic of the figure is indicated in the display, i.e. darkness represents ignorance and depravity, and light represents knowledge and purity. In the display, therefore, the figure is retained, but is accompanied by its non-figurative meaning.

5:8a since previously you were *in* **darkness,** *that is, you did not know the truth and you were evil,* The initial γάρ introduces a grounds for 5:7.

The Greek text here is ἦτε...σκότος "you were...darkness", and not "you were...*in* darkness". Paul is not describing to the Ephesians their surroundings, but the Ephesians themselves. In lives dominated by sin, they were bearers and instruments of darkness (BDAG, p. 932.4). In this context, σκότος "darkness" refers to religious or moral darkness, i.e. the state of people who live sinful and godless lives.

In order to give the non-figurative meaning of the metaphor, the Ephesians' spiritual condition (before they became believers) needs to be expressed. This will contrast with 5:8b, which describes their present state as believers.

It may be difficult for the metaphor of "darkness" and "light" to be understood as people *being* darkness or light. However, the idea of someone being *in* darkness or *in* light is perhaps clearer. So that is how they are expressed in the display. The non-figurative meaning here in 5:8a is made explicit as *"you did not know the truth and you were evil"*.

5:8b but now you are *in the* light, *that is, you know the truth and God regards you as righteous,* The νῦν δέ "but now" expresses the contrast between the spiritual darkness, in which the Ephesians used to live, and their new state of spiritual light.

The noun φῶς "light" is used figuratively here as σκότος was in 5:8a. It refers to the fact that believers, as the Ephesians are now, know and accept the truth about Christ and are considered righteous by God. This non-figurative meaning of the metaphor is made explicit in the display as *"you know the truth and God regards you as righteous"*.

This proposition contrasts with 5:8a.

5:8c *because* you are united with the Lord Jesus Christ. The prepositional phrase ἐν κυρίῳ "in (the) Lord", in this context, means the same as the more common expression "in Christ", i.e. "united with Christ".

Verse 5:8c gives the reason for 5:8b, i.e. why the Ephesian believers were able to change from "darkness" to "light". The phrase ἐν κυρίῳ can therefore be expressed as *"because you are united with the Lord Jesus Christ"*.

5:8d Behave as those who are *in the* light *should, that is, live righteous lives,* As a positive exhortation following the negative exhortation (prohibition) of 5:7, ὡς τέκνα φωτός περιπατεῖτε "walk as children of light" is prominent. The grounds for 5:8d are 5:8a–c. In 5:8a–c, Paul stated the Ephesians' former condition and what they are now. Since they are now "light in the Lord" (5:8b–c), Paul exhorts them to "walk as children of light". Their behaviour must now conform to their new identity as people who are "light", whom God has made righteous. As light and darkness cannot co-exist, so someone who has been made righteous cannot live a life devoted to doing what is evil.

The ὡς "as, like" indicates the manner, the way children of the light should walk. Their behaviour must be consistent with their new nature as those who know the truth.

The phrase τέκνα φωτός "children of light" is used in a similar way to "sons of disobedience" (5:6). It denotes people whose lives are characterised by light and, since "light" is used figuratively, those whose lives are characterised by righteousness.

5:9 since, The initial γάρ "for" introduces a brief statement to explain 5:8d, what it means to walk as a child of light. At the same time, it also acts as motivational grounds for 5:8d.

***when someone is in* the light, he will do what is good, righteous and honest.** The genitive phrase ὁ καρπὸς τοῦ φωτός "the fruit of the light" is a figure. It explains the way a believer's behaviour should change when he moves from "darkness" to "light". The "fruit" represents the moral qualities that should characterise his life. Paul goes on to list these:

ἀγαθωσύνη "goodness"
δικαιοσύνη "righteousness"
ἀλήθεια "truth"

The Greek term πάσῃ "all" has the sense of "every kind/form/aspect of" and qualifies all three abstract nouns, ἀγαθωσύνῃ, δικαιοσύνῃ and ἀληθείᾳ. These are qualities which characterise the behaviour of a believer. They may need to be expressed by adjectives or adverbs in translation.

Some manuscripts have ὁ καρπὸς τοῦ πνεύματος "the fruit of the Spirit" instead of ὁ καρπὸς τοῦ φωτός "the fruit of the light", but the latter reading is almost universally accepted by modern versions and commentators as the correct one. UBSGNT assigns φωτός "light" an A "certain" reading, but πνεύματος "Spirit" is accepted in *The Greek New Testament according to the Majority Text* and occurs in KJV.

5:10 *And as you do this* [5:8d], try to discover what pleases the Lord. This verse, in the Greek, is a participial clause related grammatically to the imperative περιπατεῖτε "walk" in 5:8.

The verb δοκιμάζω primarily means "put to the test, try, discover, prove", or "approve, commend by (successful) testing". It means testing someone/something in order to approve it as meeting a standard.

The participle δοκιμάζοντες can be understood as:

1. Having the force of an imperative, i.e. "Try to find out what is pleasing to the Lord" (NRSV).
2. Further defining what it means to walk as children of the light, i.e. "trying to learn what is pleasing to the Lord" (NASB).

The phrase τί ἐστιν εὐάρεστον τῷ κυρίῳ "what is pleasing to the Lord" is the grammatical object of δοκιμάζοντες. The sense is that, as the Ephesians consistently walk in the light, they will discover what is pleasing to the Lord and then behave accordingly.

Verse 5:17 has a similar thought, "understand what the will of the Lord is".

Commentators argue here about who τῷ κυρίῳ "the Lord" refers to:

1. It refers to the "Lord *God*".
2. It refers to the "Lord *Jesus Christ*".

Most commentators support the second option. However, there is no objective evidence to support either possibility. So, if possible, it is preferable to use the ambiguous "the Lord" in translation.

5:11-14 The conjunction καί "and" which occurs initially in 5:11 marks a co-ordinate relationship between the nuclei 5:11-14 and 5:7-10. The common topic, that believers should live as "children of light", confirms this relationship.

5:11 As in 5:7 and 5:8, Paul here uses a negative command followed by a positive one. Believers are to have nothing to do with any activities which are tainted by evil. Instead, they are to reveal such activities for what they are.

5:11a Do not do the worthless deeds which *the evil people who are in* darkness do. The imperative μὴ συγκοινωνεῖτε "do not participate in" refers to not participating in an activity, here not participating in τοῖς ἔργοις τοῖς ἀκάρποις τοῦ σκότους "the unfruitful works of darkness". The command not to participate in such actions might possibly be expressed simply as "Do not do...", "Have nothing to do with..." or "Avoid...".

The expression τοῖς ἔργοις τοῖς ἀκάρποις τοῦ σκότους "the unfruitful works of darkness" contrasts with ὁ καρπὸς τοῦ φωτός "the fruit of the light" in 5:9.

The adjective ἀκάρποις qualifies the noun τοῖς ἔργοις "the works". Its literal meaning is "unfruitful" but, in this figurative sense, it means "useless, futile, unproductive".

In 5:9, "the fruit of the light" is described as "every kind of goodness, righteousness and truth". The contrasting phrase here refers to actions which can only be evil because they result from a mind darkened by sin. Therefore, they do not benefit anyone. In the display, this is expressed as "the worthless deeds which *the evil people who are in* darkness do".

5:11b Instead, expose those worthless deeds [5:11a], The Greek expression μᾶλλον δὲ καί literally means "but rather even". A clearer way to translate it is "instead". This expression puts emphasis on the positive exhortation ἐλέγχετε "expose, reprove". Paul tells the Ephesians not just to abstain from the actions referred to in 5:11a. He exhorts then to go further and "expose" them.

The transitive verb ἐλέγχω has a range of meanings: "convict, reprove, discipline, expose". However, Paul has not made the direct object of the verb explicit. Most commentators understood it to be the evil deeds referred to in the previous clause, 5:11a. The passive form of the verb, ἐλεγχόμενα "being exposed", occurs in 5:13 with a neuter subject. This matches the case of the phrase "the deeds".

Therefore, it makes sense to understand the verb in the sense of "exposing" or "bringing to light" these deeds, rather than "convicting" or "rebuking" those engaged in such activities. Paul tells the Ephesian believers to make sure that these deeds do not remain hidden, instead they are to make sure other people know about them. This will help keep other believers from committing the same evil deeds.

5:12-13 The initial γάρ "for, since" introduces a grounds for both the positive and negative aspects of the exhortation in 5:11.

Paul tells the Ephesians to have nothing to do with "the unfruitful works of darkness". Rather, they are to expose those works, since this will show to people the true nature of those works.

5:12 since it is shameful *for God's people* even to talk about those *evil* deeds For "for, since", see the note on 5:12-13.

Commentators differ in their interpretation of the clause αἰσχρόν ἐστιν καὶ λέγειν "it is shameful even to talk about". They suggest:

1. It refers to a sense of shame felt by those who commit the sins referred to. See, for example, Lenski (p. 609).

2. It refers to a sense of shame felt by anyone who might speak about those sins. See, for example, Bratcher and Nida (p. 132), Ellicott (p. 99), Hendriksen (pp. 233-234), Lincoln (p. 330), O'Brien (p. 371).

The second option seems the most likely in the context: not only is doing the actions wrong, but even talking about them is shameful.

The conjunction καί functions as an adverb "even", which intensifies the statement in which it occurs (BDAG, p. 495.2b). Paul is contrasting "talking about" these evil deeds and "doing" them. Paul has already made it clear that it is sinful to *do* such things, but he says that *even talking about* them is bad.

In 5:13, Paul goes on to say that when these evil deeds are exposed, they are revealed for what they really are: evil. The implication is that exposing them is good.

So 5:12 may be understood to be in a concession relation with 5:13. The δέ in 5:13 has its adversative sense of "but, nevertheless". In turn, 5:13 is the grounds for the command to expose these worthless deeds (5:11b). Paul is telling the Ephesian believers to expose these worthless deeds since, when they are exposed, their true nature will be revealed by the light.

This concession is indicated by "*Nevertheless*" at the beginning of 5:13 in the display.

which evil people do secretly and habitually. In the phrase τὰ κρυφῇ γινόμενα ὑπ' αὐτῶν "the (things) being done by them in secret", the use of the present participle γινόμενα "being done" indicates the habitual nature of these deeds. This is represented in the display as "do...habitually".

The αὐτῶν "them" refers back to the τοὺς υἱοὺς τῆς ἀπειθείας "the sons of disobedience" in 5:6, those described in 5:11 whose works are described as being τοῦ σκότους "of the darkness". In the display, the phrase "evil people" is used.

The Greek adverb κρυφῇ "in secret, secretly" refers to the sins these "evil people" commit in private. The deeds themselves are referred to, in the display, as "those *evil* deeds".

5:13-14b In these verses, Paul explains what happens when the secret, evil deeds are exposed. The flow of the argument from 5:11 through 5:14b is not entirely clear. Commentators have many suggestions. Here only O'Brien is quoted:

The flow of the argument is from the exposure of the deeds of darkness (v. 11), through their illumination by the light (v. 13), to a focus on the light itself (v. 14). It appears, then, that the process by which darkness is transformed into light is being described (p. 372).

See also Hodge (pp. 292-295), Lincoln (p. 330), Robinson (p. 201).

5:13 Nevertheless, This verse is in a contra-expectation relationship with 5:12. See the note on 5:12.

when all *these shameful/evil* deeds *are exposed by the righteous deeds done by God's people*, they are revealed for what they really are, *just as* everything is made visible by light, There are a number of exegetical difficulties to be dealt with in this verse. These give rise to a variety of interpretations.

The first discussion point is about the referent of τὰ πάντα "all (things), anything". Commentators suggest:

1. It refers to τοῖς ἔργοις τοῖς ἀκάρποις τοῦ σκότους "the unfruitful works of darkness" (5:11).
2. It refers to τὰ κρυφῇ γινόμενα ὑπ' αὐτῶν "the (things) being done by them in secret" (5:12).
3. It refers to "all things" in general.

It seems best understood as referring to τὰ κρυφῇ γινόμενα ὑπ' αὐτῶν "the (things) being done by them in secret" (option two) since that is its nearest antecedent and collocates naturally with ἐλέγχω "to expose".

The second discussion point concerns the Greek phrase ὑπὸ τοῦ φωτός "by the light". Paul is talking about the effect of spiritual light, as he was in 5:8-9. Most commentators regard the phrase as metaphorical. However, they disagree about its reference. The three main suggestions are:

1. It refers to "Christ, his Word and his truth" Lenski (p. 610).
2. It refers to spiritual truth. See, for example, Hodge (p. 294).
3. It refers to the conduct of believers as "children of light". See, for example, Hendriksen (p. 234), Hoehner (p. 684), Lincoln (pp. 330-331).

As in 5:8-9, so here it might be understood to refer to "what is true/righteous".

The third discussion point is what the phrase ὑπὸ τοῦ φωτός "by the light" connects with. It may be:

1. With the preceding participle ἐλεγχόμενα "being exposed, reproved" i.e. "when they are exposed/reproved by the light". See, for example, Lenski (p. 610), Mitton (p. 185), Stott (p. 200).
2. With the following finite verb φανεροῦται: "is (are) manifested by the light". See, for example, Ellicott (p. 100), Hodge (p. 294), Lincoln (pp. 330-331), O'Brien (p. 372, fn. 55).

Most commentators support the second option, i.e. that ὑπὸ τοῦ φωτός "by the light" is connected with φανεροῦται "is (are) manifested". In the display, it is presented in this way.

This verb form φανεροῦται can be analysed as either middle or passive voice. The passive voice, "is (are) made manifest", seems most appropriate in the context.

Paul is saying that when the light, representing what is righteous, shines on these shameful deeds, it will reveal the true nature of the deeds. In the display, "the light" is expressed as "the righteous deeds *done by God's people*".

5:14a–b since *whoever has come to know the truth reveals that truth to others, just as* a place which has been illuminated *reflects* light *also*. This propositional cluster provides a grounds for 5:13. It is introduced by γάρ in the Greek text. In some translations and editions of the Greek text the verses are divided differently and this clause is included at the end of 5:13.

It is difficult to express the sense of each detail in this extended metaphor. As in 5:13, the verb φανερούμενον "making manifest" can be considered as middle or passive voice. Although there is support for both options, most commentators consider it to be in the passive voice ("which is made manifest, which is being revealed"). This would be in line with the analysis of the same verb in 5:13.

If the participle φανερούμενον is regarded as passive, "is being revealed", the clause may be understood as:

1. A statement of a general truth in support of the preceding specific statement in 5:13, i.e. "for everything that is revealed is light". In this context, the sense would be that the true nature of everything will be revealed since nothing can remain hidden when the light of truth shines. The shameful deeds referred to earlier will be seen for what they are when compared with the righteous deeds of believers. See, for example, Hendriksen (pp. 234-235), Lenski (p. 610).
2. A statement about the transforming power of light. The effect of light is that wherever it shines that place becomes light. It has a positive as well as a negative effect. As O'Brien says,

> Some abandon the darkness of sin and respond to the light so that they become light themselves.... The light thus has a twofold effect on the prevailing darkness: it makes visible and transforms (pp. 372-373).

This view is further supported by 5:8 which speaks of the transformation that had taken place in the lives of the Ephesian believers. When people see their evil deeds set alongside the righteous deeds of believers, they become aware of how wicked they are. See also Hodge (pp. 295-296), Lincoln (p. 331), Robinson (p. 201), Stott (p. 200).

The second option seems more appropriate in the context of 5:8 and the quotation in 5:14 Paul is about to use. The implication is that those who have come to know the truth and have been changed by that knowledge will reveal that truth to others. When they do so, there is the possibility that those to whom the truth is revealed will be changed also, just as a place which has been in darkness becomes illuminated when light shines on it.

These notes follow the second option. In the display, the metaphor is expressed as "*whoever has come to know the truth reveals that truth to others, just as* a place which has been illuminated *reflects* light *also*".

"*Just as*" (5:14b) introduces the image of the metaphor as a "comparison".

5:14c On the same basis, The conjunction διό which introduces this cluster of propositions is analysed here by most of the commentators as signalling a conclusion based on what precedes. However, its function appears to be the same as in 4:8, where it also occurs before λέγει "it says" introducing a quotation, as it does here. In 4:8, it has been analysed and presented in the display as introducing grounds or proof, as is done for that verse by the majority of commentators.

It is often the case in Scripture that a quotation will provide grounds for a statement made in the text. This is sometimes labelled as a "standard" to be conformed to, which is similar in function to grounds.

In analysing the use of διό in such contexts it may be that both the point being made and the quotation are thought of as proceeding from the same basis, as appears to be the case here. Hodge says about 5:14,

> Thus the passage is a confirmation of what is said in the preceding verse, viz., that every thing made manifest by the light, is light (p. 298).

In the display, therefore, it is represented by the phrase "on the same basis" and introduces the standard to which 5:14a–b conforms. The relationship between 5:14a–b and 5:14c–e is, therefore, shown as CONGRUENCE-standard.

***the following* is said *in* Scripture,** In the Greek we have simply λέγει "he/it says". Many versions translate this as the impersonal "it is said", indicating a quotation but without naming the source.

The origin of this quotation is unclear. It is possible that:

1. Paul was adapting an Old Testament passage.
2. Paul was quoting from an ancient liturgy.
2. Paul was quoting from an early Christian hymn.

Whatever the source, the quotation is something regarded authoritative by both Paul and the Ephesians.

Most commentators accept that the words come in some way from Scripture. They could be based on Isaiah 60:1 or a condensation of a number of Old Testament Scriptures, e.g. Isaiah 9:2; 26:19; 60:1.

Therefore, in the display, it is expressed as "*the following* is said *in* Scripture". Another possibility would be, "Scripture says".

If it is necessary to make explicit the personal agent of λέγει "he/it says" in translation, either God or the Holy Spirit is acceptable.

This proposition is an orienter, with the rest of the verse providing the content.

5:14d "You *who are unaware of your spiritual condition must become aware of it and* become like sleepers waking up, like dead people coming back to life. In the exhortation ἔγειρε, ὁ καθεύδων, καὶ ἀνάστα ἐκ τῶν νεκρῶν "Wake up, you who are sleeping, and rise up from the dead (ones)", it is unclear whom Paul considers to be ὁ καθεύδων "the one who is sleeping".

The commentators make two suggestions:

1. "The one who is sleeping" refers to an unbeliever. The term "sleep" is used as a euphemism for death (see 1 Thess. 5:10), and two of the verbs, ἔγειρε and ἀνάστα, are connected with resurrection, though ἔγειρε may also have reference to waking up. That is, "sleep" and "death" here symbolise spiritual death, the state of the soul apart from Christ. See, for example, Bruce (p. 108), Hodge (p. 298), Lenski (p. 611), O'Brien (p. 376), Scott (pp. 231–232), Stott (p. 201).
2. "The one who is sleeping" refers to a believer who is spiritually lethargic and unresponsive. Such a person has fallen back into sin and is living the way he used to do before he became a believer. See, for example, Candlish (pp. 108–109), Hoehner (p. 684), Lincoln (pp. 331–332).

Either alternative is a possible interpretation. However, in the context, it seems preferable to understand "the one who is sleeping" to refer to the unbeliever. This is consistent with other passages in Ephesians. In 2:1, 5, Paul describes unbelievers as being "dead in sins". Their conversion is described as being "made alive with Christ". Now in 5:14, "the one who is sleeping" is urged to "rise from among the dead ones".

Paul uses three metaphors here to express the idea of "turning to God":

1. Awakening from sleep (Ἔγειρε, ὁ καθεύδων "Wake up, O sleeper").
2. Being raised from the dead (ἀνάστα ἐκ τῶν νεκρῶν "rise up from the dead [ones]").
3. Coming out of darkness into light (ἐπιφαύσει σοι ὁ Χριστός "Christ will shine on you").

Since "darkness/light" is a live figure throughout this unit, it is likely that "sleep" and "death" are live figures also and so the figures should be kept in translation.

The expression ὁ καθεύδων "the sleeping one" may be expressed non-figuratively as "*you who are unaware of your spiritual condition*".

The clause ἔγειρε...καὶ ἀνάστα ἐκ τῶν νεκρῶν "Wake-up/Arise...and rise up from the dead (ones)" is a figurative description of spiritual resurrection. The state of the sinner is compared to death and his spiritual enlightenment to physical resurrection. This might be expressed as "becoming spiritually alive" or "becoming aware of your spiritual condition".

5:14e *As a result,* **Christ will shine on you,** *that is, he will cause you to know the truth and to do what is right"*. This clause is connected to those preceding it by καί "and" and is understood to indicate the next step in the metaphor. After an imperative, καί often introduces a result and this is the case here. When a person is made aware of his sinful state, the result will be that he becomes aware of the truth and begins to act in accordance with it.

Throughout this paragraph "light" has been equated with spiritual enlightenment, which should be demonstrated in righteous conduct. In this context, then, the expression ἐπιφαύσει σοι ὁ Χριστός "Christ will shine on you" refers to the fact that Christ "shines" on those who have become spiritually alive, i.e. he has continuing influence in the lives of believers.

BOUNDARIES AND COHERENCE

For the initial boundary of the 5:7-14 paragraph, see the section on Boundaries and Coherence for 5:1-6.

Evidence that 5:15 marks a new boundary is a further οὖν...περιπατεῖτε "therefore...walk" in that verse and a change of topic from "walking in light" to "walking in wisdom".

The main coherence feature in 5:7-14 is the metaphor of "light" and "darkness", the former representing the life of the righteous, lived in obedience to God, and the latter, the sinful life of unrighteous people.

The use of vocabulary belonging to the contrastive domains of φῶς "light" and σκότος "darkness" includes both figurative and non-figurative terms. The following belong to the semantic domain of "light":

φῶς "light" (5:8a, 8b, 9, 13)
ἀγαθωσύνῃ "goodness" (5:9)
δικαιοσύνῃ "righteousness" (5:9)
ἀληθείᾳ "truth" (5:9)
εὐάρεστον "well-pleasing" (5:10)
φανερόω "reveal" (5:13, 14)
ἐπιφαύσει "shine" (5:14)

The following belong to the semantic domain of "darkness":

σκότος "darkness" (5:8, 11)
ἀκάρποις "fruitless" (5:11)
κρυφῇ "hidden" (5:12)
αἰσχρόν "shameful" (5:12)
ὁ καθεύδων "the one sleeping" (5:14)
νεκρῶν "dead (ones)" (5:14)

Within the two propositional clusters, 5:7-10 and 5:11-14, there is relational cohesion in that in both there is a negative exhortation followed by a positive one. The conjunction δέ provides the link between the negative and positive exhortations in both cases, occurring in 5:8 and 5:11. In both clusters the exhortations are supported by grounds, each of which is introduced by γάρ (5:9, 12).

PROMINENCE AND THEME

In a hortatory paragraph, both the exhortation and the grounds are integral parts of the paragraph. Since there is natural prominence on the two positive exhortations, the theme for the 5:7-14 paragraph is based on them (5:8d and 5:11b), and a summary representation of the grounds of POSITIVE EXHORTATION$_2$. Motivational elements of the grounds for both NEGATIVE EXHORTATION$_1$ and POSITIVE EXHORTATION$_1$ are found in POSITIVE EXHORTATION$_1$ (5:8d), so those grounds are not otherwise represented in the theme statement.

DIVISION CONSTITUENT 5:15–6:9 (Hortatory Section: Nucleus₅ of 4:1–6:9)

THEME: Be very careful that you behave wisely, that you be controlled completely by the Holy Spirit, and that you submit yourselves to one another. Wives, submit yourselves to your husbands. Husbands, love your wives. Children, obey your parents. Fathers, bring up your children well. Slaves, obey your earthly masters. Masters, treat your slaves well.

MACROSTRUCTURE	CONTENTS
HORTATORY NUCLEUS₁	5:15–17 Be very careful that you behave wisely, that you make good use of your time and that you understand what the Lord wants you to do.
HORTATORY NUCLEUS₂	5:18–21 Let the Holy Spirit control and empower you completely at all times. Praise and thank God for everything. Submit yourselves to one another.
HORTATORY NUCLEUS₃	5:22–33 Wives, submit yourselves to your husbands in the same manner as you should submit yourselves to the Lord. Husbands, love your wives as Christ also loved the church.
HORTATORY NUCLEUS₄	6:1–4 Children, obey your parents since, as believers in the Lord Jesus Christ, it is right that you do so. Fathers, bring up your children well, by training them according to the teaching given by the Lord Jesus Christ.
HORTATORY NUCLEUS₅	6:5–9 Slaves, obey and serve your earthly masters wholeheartedly, since the Lord will reward each person for whatever good thing that person does. Masters, treat your slaves well, since you know that their Lord and yours deals with all people impartially.

INTENT AND MACROSTRUCTURE

This section (5:15–6:9) is the last in a series of five hortatory units which are each introduced by the verb "walk" and refer to behaviour. The preceding paragraphs have depicted the contrast there should be between the lifestyle of those who are believers in Christ and that of those who are outside of his church. Paul was outlining the new standards which God expects of his new society, the church.

In the previous unit, he did this by contrasting light and darkness. He begins this unit with the contrast between wisdom and foolishness. He urges the Ephesians to be careful how they "walk", that it should not be "as unwise but as wise". The importance of the exhortation is brought out by the use of the imperative βλέπετε "watch" and the adverb ἀκριβῶς "carefully" in relation with the phrase πῶς περιπατεῖτε "how you walk".

O'Brien says that the unit is thematically and structurally a well-knit unit, with each paragraph closely related to the one preceding it. He continues,

> There is an evident movement within the whole unit, and no sharp division should be made between each of the paragraphs (p. 378).

In this unit, Paul talks about how believers should behave with regards to closer relationship between individuals: within the family and household. He exhorts them "to be filled with the Spirit" (5:18), since this is the basis for their ability to carry out the rest of the exhortations that follow in Ephesians.

The first two paragraphs (5:15–17 and 5:18–21) consist of exhortations to the Ephesian believers in terms of general Christian living. Paul then goes on to speak about relationships within a believing household, between wives and husbands (5:22–33), children and parents/fathers (6:1–4), slaves and masters (6:5–9).

Verse 5:21 is problematic in how it relates to the surrounding verses and, therefore, to which paragraph it belongs. There are two possibilities:

1. It refers to what precedes. It, therefore, concludes the paragraph 5:18–21. See, for example, Bruce (p. 112), Ellicott (pp. 104–105), Hendriksen (p. 243, fn. 149), Lenski (p. 623).
2. It refers to what follows. It, therefore, begins the paragraph 5:21–23. See, for example, Hodge (p. 309), Lincoln (p. 352), Stott (p. 215).

It is difficult to decide on this boundary. Verse 5:21 clearly acts as a link between the two paragraphs, since it completes the thought of 5:18–20 about being filled with the Spirit. It also introduces a new topic, submission, which is developed in 5:22–6:9.

There are good arguments both grammatically and thematically on each side.

Looking at the verse in terms of grammar, it can be noted:

a. It is the last in a series of participles which depend upon the imperative verb "be filled" in 5:18. This suggests that 5:21 is part of the paragraph 5:18–20.
b. There is no verb form in 5:22, "being submissive" in 5:21 is clearly the predicate of 5:22. This suggests that 5:21 is part of the paragraph 5:22–33.

Looking at the verse in terms of theme, it can be noted:

a. To split the fifth participle (5:21) from the four preceding participles would lose "focus on submission as an essential mark of being filled with God's Spirit" (Snodgrass, p. 287). This suggests that 5:21 is part of the paragraph 5:18–20.
b. To begin a new paragraph at 5:22 "destroys the relationship to the theme of submission in v. 21" (O'Brien, p. 388). This suggests that 5:21 is part of the paragraph 5:22–23.

A further point in favour of considering 5:21 as starting the next paragraph is that words for "fear" in 5:21 (ἐν φόβῳ "in fear, reverence") and 5:33 (φοβῆται "fear, respect") form a rhetorical bracket which would mark this as a unit (Lincoln, p. 354; O'Brien, p. 388, fn. 110; pp. 436–437).

In modern versions, most place the paragraph break before 5:21. Some place it before 5:22, while others make 5:21 a separate paragraph.

In this analysis, 5:21 is considered to complete the preceding paragraph, 5:15–21. In this type of transition, the paragraph breaks are a case of imposing breaks for the purpose of fitting modern styles of organisation.

BOUNDARIES AND COHERENCE

The initial boundary of this section is clearly marked by the following features:

1. The imperative Βλέπετε "See" (5:15).
2. The conjunction οὖν "therefore" and the indicative verb περιπατεῖτε "you walk" introduce the fifth and last group of the series of exhortations which began in 4:1 and which relate to specific aspects of the conduct (walk) of believers.
3. A change of semantic domains, from the contrast between "light" and "darkness" to that between "wise" and "unwise".

The final boundary is marked by:

1. The term τοῦ λοιποῦ "for the rest" or "finally", "last of all", which begins a new unit at 6:10.
2. The imperative ἐνδυναμοῦσθε "be strong, be empowered" (6:10), addressed to all the believers, not any particular subgroup.
3. A change of semantic domain, from obedience, to an extended metaphor in which the believer is urged to stand firm and fight against Satan and all evil powers.

Vocabulary belonging to the semantic domains of "obedience", "love" and "reverence for Christ" contributes to the referential cohesion (and coherence) of this unit, as follows,

obedience:

ὑποτασσόμενοι "being subject" (5:21, 22)
κεφαλή "head" (5:23)
ὑποτάσσεται "is subject" (5:24)
φοβῆται "she respects" (5:33)
ὑπακούετε "obey" (6:1, 5)
τίμα "honour" (6:2)
φόβου "fear" (6:5)
δουλεύοντες "serving" (6:7)

love:

ἀγάπη "love" (5:25, 28, 33)
ἐκτρέφει "nourishes" (5:29)
θάλπει "cherishes" (5:29)
προσκολληθήσεται "will cleave to" (5:31)
εὐνοίας "goodwill" (6:7)

reverence for Christ:

τὸ θέλημα τοῦ κυρίου "the will of the Lord" (5:17)
τῷ κυρίῳ "to the Lord" (5:19)
ἐν ὀνόματι τοῦ κυρίου ἡμῶν Ἰησοῦ Χριστοῦ "in (the) name of our Lord Jesus Christ" (5:20)
ἐν φόβῳ Χριστοῦ "in the fear of Christ" (5:21)
ὡς τῷ κυρίῳ "as to the Lord" (5:22)

καθὼς καὶ ὁ Χριστός "as Christ also" (5:25, 29)
ἐν κυρίῳ "in (the) Lord" (6:1)
κυρίου "of (the) Lord" (6:4)
ὡς τῷ Χριστῷ "as unto Christ" (6:5)
ὡς δοῦλοι Χριστοῦ "as servants of Christ" (6:6)
ὑμῶν ὁ κύριός ἐστιν ἐν οὐρανοῖς "your Lord/Master who is in heaven" (6:9)

The theme of "reverence for Christ" is particularly important as a coherence factor. Everything that is commanded is to be done out of reverence for the Lord.

PROMINENCE AND THEME

This hortatory section of the epistle consists of five hortatory nuclei of equal prominence. The theme statement for the section, therefore, is a summary of the theme statements for these five nuclei.

SECTION CONSTITUENT 5:15–17 (Hortatory Paragraph: Nucleus₁ of 5:15–6:9)

THEME: Be very careful that you behave wisely, that you make good use of your time and that you understand what the Lord wants you to do.

RELATIONAL STRUCTURE	CONTENTS
GENERIC EXHORTATION	5:15a Therefore, be very careful how you behave.
SPECIFIC EXHORTATION₁ — negative	5:15b Do not behave as foolish/unwise people behave,
— POSITIVE	5:15c but behave as wise people behave.
SPECIFIC EXHORTATION₂ — EXHORTATION	5:16a Make good use of your time,
— grounds	5:16b since, in these days, *people* are extremely evil.
SPECIFIC EXHORTATION₃ — negative	5:17a In view of this [5:15–16], do not be foolish/ignorant,
— POSITIVE	5:17b but understand what the Lord wants *you to do*.

INTENT AND STRUCTURE

This 5:15–17 paragraph is hortatory. Paul is exhorting the Ephesians to be careful how they behave in their Christian life. Paul uses the key verb "walk" to remind the Ephesians of the implications of 4:1, where the theme of the second half of the epistle (the hortatory subpart of the BODY) was introduced ("Walk worthy of your calling"). This theme was repeated in 4:17; 5:2 and 5:8.

Paul wants the Ephesians to behave wisely, in accordance with the will of the Lord. They need to take care to do this because they are living among evil people. Their behaviour should be wise, in contrast with the foolish behaviour of the unbelievers.

Structurally, there is a generic exhortation, 5:15a, followed by two sets of negative-positive exhortations, 5:15b and 5:15c, and 5:17a and 5:17b. Each pair of exhortations has the same structure, μή...ἀλλά "not...but". There is also an exhortation-grounds relationship between 5:16a and 5:16b.

These exhortations focus on the contrast between the wise behaviour which should characterise believers, and the foolish behaviour which characterises the unbelievers among whom they live.

NOTES

5:15a Therefore, The four preceding hortatory sections have been introduced by either the conjunction οὖν (4:1, 17; 5:1) or διό (4:25). This occurrence of οὖν introduces the last hortatory section in the series.

The conjunction οὖν here can be understood in two ways:

1. It introduces a conclusion or summary based on the preceding exhortations concerning Christian behaviour. See, for example, Eadie (p. 391), O'Brien (p. 379).
2. It has a resumptive function. Paul continues to contrast the Christian behaviour with that of unbelievers. See, for example, Ellicott (p. 101), Hoehner (p. 690), Lenski (p. 613).

While οὖν may be analysed as resumptive in the sense that it introduces a new unit in the series, it also links the new exhortation with the previous verse(s), with respect to their providing supportive material for it. They have been exhorted to expose the evil deeds of others, *therefore*, they themselves should take care to behave wisely and not follow the example of those whose evil behaviour they expose. Living wisely is a further expression of how they are to live a life worthy of their calling (4:1).

be very careful how you behave. The imperative βλέπετε "look, see" is used here in the mental, not physical, sense, i.e. "to direct-one's-attention-to/consider something". The object of the verb is πῶς περιπατεῖτε "how you behave".

There is discussion about whether the adverb ἀκριβῶς "carefully" qualifies:

1. βλέπετε, i.e. "Look carefully, therefore, how you behave".
2. περιπατεῖτε, i.e. "Look, therefore, how carefully you behave". KJV has "See then that ye walk circumspectly".

Most versions follow the first alternative. so it is followed in the display.

The imperative βλέπετε "see, look" functions with ἀκριβῶς "carefully" as a prominence orienter, drawing attention to πῶς περιπατεῖτε "how you behave". It can be expressed as "be careful..." (NASB, NLT, NRSV), "be very careful" (NIV).

This clause provides a general exhortation to the Ephesian believers that they should be careful how they behave.

5:15b–c Do not behave as foolish/unwise people behave, but behave as wise people behave. In the Greek, there is no explicit verb. The text simply states μὴ ὡς ἄσοφοι ἀλλ' ὡς σοφοί "not as unwise but as wise", but the imperative περιπατεῖτε "walk, behave" is clearly to be understood. It is, therefore, included in the display without italics.

Paul now goes on to explain more fully how a believer should behave. He does this in a series of specific exhortations, beginning with 5:15b–c.

The contrast between ἄσοφοι "unwise" and σοφοί "wise" replaces the metaphor of "darkness" and "light" of the preceding paragraph (5:7-14). Those who are wise are those who know the truth, whose minds are no longer darkened by sin.

Lincoln points out, as do a number of commentators,

> To live as a wise person is not just to have knowledge but to have skill in living.... ...it is a living informed by an understanding of the will of the Lord (cf. v 17)... (p. 341).

5:16 This provides a second specific exhortation in relation to the generic exhortation of 5:15a. It consists of a present participial construction ἐξαγοραζόμενοι τὸν καιρόν "buying out the time". This exhorts believers to make the best use of their time.

5:16a Make good use of your time, The phrase ἐξαγοραζόμενοι τὸν καιρόν literally means "buying/redeeming the time". The same expression occurs in Colossians 4:5 in a similar context. Here, as in Colossians, the Greek noun καιρός "time" has the sense of "opportunity", referring to a particular occasion/time.

The participle ἐξαγοραζόμενοι "buying/redeeming" is used figuratively and means "making the most of" or "using to the full". Another way to express "redeeming the time" is "make good use of your time" or "use your time effectively".

If "every opportunity" is more natural to use in some languages, it may be necessary to specify what is involved in "every opportunity", e.g. "use every opportunity to do what is good".

Paul is telling the Ephesians to devote themselves eagerly to doing good and serving the Lord. In languages where "time" or "opportunity" cannot be used to express the meaning in this clause, translating with words describing eager devotion may be a possibility.

5:16b since, in these days, *people* are extremely evil. The conjunction ὅτι "because, since" introduces a grounds for 5:16a.

The phrase αἱ ἡμέραι πονηραί εἰσιν "the days are evil" is a metonymy, "days" representing what is done during those days, i.e. the evil deeds which people do during this time.

5:17 Following the pattern of this unit this exhortation is presented first in negative and then in positive terms.

5:17a In view of this [5:15-16], The initial διὰ τοῦτο "therefore, for this reason" may refer:

1. To 5:15-16. See, for example, Ellicott (p. 102), Hendriksen (p. 238), Hodge (p. 301).
2. Only to 5:16b. See, for example, Lenski (p. 615).

The first option has the greatest support, i.e. it refers to 5:15-16. As such, it resumes the exhortation of 5:15.

With respect to this verse being a restatement, O'Brien suggests that it further explains the general exhortation of 5:15, that those Paul is addressing should be careful how they live. However, he says,

> Although this exhortation is parallel to v. 15b (*not as unwise but as wise*), it is not simply a restatement of the former: there is a development of thought in v. 17 and a slightly different focus on the Lord's will (p. 383).

This would support the view that διὰ τοῦτο is resumptive. But at the same time 5:17 appears to build not only on the preceding exhortations but also inferentially on the preceding clause, "the days are evil". So διὰ τοῦτο is translated as "In view of this [5:15-16]" in the display.

do not be foolish/ignorant, The adjective ἄφρονες means "senseless, foolish". It describes someone who does not make use of the understanding he has. He is not stupid, but lacks discernment and so acts inappropriately. Hoehner (p. 696) suggests that the difference between ἄσοφος (5:15) and ἄφρων used here, is that ἄσοφος refers to someone who "lacks mental insight", while ἄφρων refers to someone who is "unable to apply knowledge practically".

5:17b but understand what the Lord wants *you to do*. This positive exhortation συνίετε τί τὸ θέλημα τοῦ κυρίου "understand what the will of the Lord (is)" recalls 5:10, δοκιμάζοντες τί ἐστιν εὐάρεστον τῷ κυρίῳ "trying to discover what is well-pleasing to the Lord".

The verb συνίημι "understand, comprehend, gain an insight into" is used of more than mere factual knowledge. It refers to moral understanding, to true, practical and spiritual wisdom.

The commentaries do not agree about the referent of τοῦ κυρίου "of the Lord" here. It could be:

1. God. See, for example, Mitton (p. 188), Stott (pp. 202-203).
2. Jesus Christ. See, for example, Hoehner (pp. 698-699), Lenski (pp. 616-617), Meyer (p. 505).

The first option seems more likely since the will of God is referred to unambiguously elsewhere in Ephesians (see 1:1, 5, 11; 6:6). However, if possible, the translator should leave it ambiguous. But, if it is necessary to make a choice, the Lord God is preferable.

The genitive construction τὸ θέλημα τοῦ κυρίου "the will of the Lord" needs to be expressed in verbal form in the display, e.g. "what the Lord wants *you to do*".

BOUNDARIES AND COHERENCE

The initial boundary has been discussed in the section on Boundaries and Coherence for 5:15-6:9.

The initial boundary of the next unit is marked in 5:18 by καί and the imperatival clauses μὴ μεθύσκεσθε οἴνῳ, ἐν ᾧ ἐστιν ἀσωτία, ἀλλὰ πληροῦσθε ἐν πνεύματι "do not be drunk with wine, in which there is wantonness, but be filled with the Spirit". This introduces a new topic, being filled with the Spirit.

In 5:15-17, there is lexical cohesion in the use of vocabulary belonging to the contrasting semantic domains of "foolishness" and "wisdom". In negative terms:

μὴ...ἄσοφοι "not...unwise" (5:15)
μὴ...ἄφρονες "not...foolish" (5:17)

In positive terms:

σοφοί "wise" (5:15)
συνίετε "understand" (5:17)

PROMINENCE AND THEME

The four positive exhortations in this paragraph (5:15a, 15c, 16a, 17b) are naturally prominent. The first of these is generic and the other three are specific in relation to it. The theme statement is based on the three specific exhortations and the prominence orienter "be very careful" from the generic exhortation (5:15a).

SECTION CONSTITUENT 5:18–21 (Hortatory Paragraph: Nucleus₂ of 5:15–6:9)

THEME: Let the Holy Spirit control and empower you completely at all times. Praise and thank God for everything. Submit yourselves to one another.

RELATIONAL STRUCTURE	CONTENTS
GENERIC EXHORTATION — negative — EXHORTATION	5:18a Do not become drunk with wine,
└ grounds	5:18b since *when a person is drunk it causes him* to become completely unrestrained in the way *he* behaves,
— POSITIVE	5:18c but instead, let the *Holy* Spirit control and empower you completely at all times [MET].
SPECIFIC EXHORTATION₁	5:19a Address one another by means of singing psalms and hymns and spiritual songs.
SPECIFIC EXHORTATION₂ — MEANS	5:19b Sing songs and psalms/hymns sincerely
└ purpose	5:19c *in order to praise* the Lord.
SPECIFIC EXHORTATION₃ — NUCLEUS	5:20a At all times thank God, who is *our* Father, for everything.
└ amplification — RESULT	5:20b *You are able to do this* [5:20a]
└ reason	5:20c as a result of *what* our Lord Jesus Christ *has done*.
SPECIFIC EXHORTATION₄ — EXHORTATION	5:21a Submit yourselves to one another
└ grounds	5:21b since you revere Christ.

INTENT AND STRUCTURE

This 5:18–21 paragraph begins with two present imperative verbs:

μὴ μεθύσκεσθε "do not become drunk"
πληροῦσθε "be filled"

They are in a negative-positive construction linked by ἀλλά "but" (5:18). The paragraph continues with a series of five present participles:

λαλοῦντες "speaking" (5:19)
ᾄδοντες "singing" (5:19)
ψάλλοντες "psalming" (5:19)
εὐχαριστοῦντες "giving thanks" (5:20)
ὑποτασσόμενοι "submitting" (5:21)

They depend on the preceding positive imperative "be filled". These participles may be understood as the expected results of being filled with the Holy Spirit. However, they also have an imperatival sense from their connection to the imperative πληροῦσθε "be filled".

Paul's primary concern here is to urge the Ephesians to live lives which are controlled continually by the Holy Spirit. There should be evidence of this in the harmonious nature of their relationship with the Lord (5:19, 20) and with other believers (5:19, 21). This then leads on to the exhortations (5:22–6:9) concerning specific relationships within Christian households.

NOTES

5:18 Most commentators consider that the initial καί indicates a transition from the preceding general exhortations in 5:15–17 to this more specific one.

5:18a Do not become drunk with wine, Commentators are unsure why Paul suddenly introduces this specific admonition. Perhaps he wants to warn the Ephesians to retain self-control even at the times of highest elation, such as those described in 5:19–20. Someone who understands the will of the Lord (5:17b) is unlikely to become intoxicated and unrestrained in his behaviour, but rather, he will be under the influence and restraint of the Holy Spirit.

It also is an example of contrast between foolish and wise behaviour. Lincoln expresses it:

> since traditionally drunkenness was associated with folly and the Spirit was seen as the mediator of wisdom (p. 347).

In other passages in Paul's letters, drunkenness and sobriety are associated with darkness and light, e.g. 1 Thessalonians 5:6–8. The introduction of the subject provides an opportunity to present the destructive effect of excessive drinking (5:18b) and the life-enhancing effect of being filled with the Holy Spirit (5:19–21).

The use of the present imperative form μὴ μεθύσκεσθε "do not get drunk" could mean that Paul is telling the Ephesians to stop an action that they were doing already, but it is more likely that he is warning them, in general, against excessive drinking, which was a problem in the early church, as passages such as 1 Timothy 3:3, 8 and Titus 1:7 indicate. The society in which they lived was marked by unrestrained behaviour resulting from drinking too much wine (1 Peter 4:3-4), so believers needed to be warned not be drawn into such behaviour. There would be a particular danger of this, since that is how many of them had behaved before their conversion.

5:18b since *when a person is drunk it causes him* to become completely unrestrained in the way *he* behaves, Proposition 5:18b provides the grounds for the exhortation of 5:18a.

The phrase ἐν ᾧ ἐστιν ἀσωτία "in which is wantonness" does not refer just to οἴνῳ "wine", but to the whole expression, μεθύσκεσθε οἴνῳ "be drunk with wine". The sense is causal: being drunk with wine causes reckless, senseless behaviour. The Greek word ἀσωτία is derived from ἄσωτος, "what cannot be saved". The word here, ἀσωτία, can refer to anything that brings about destruction, leads to utter ruin. Since it is an abstract noun, it needs to be expressed in the display by a verbal form such as "ruins/destroys *a person*", "*causes a person* to become completely unrestrained in the way *he* behaves".

5:18c but instead, let the *Holy* Spirit control and empower you completely at all times. The noun πνεύματι "spirit" in the expression, πληροῦσθε ἐν πνεύματι "be filled with the spirit/Spirit", refers to the Holy Spirit. This clause provides a positive exhortation in contrast with μὴ μεθύσκεσθε οἴνῳ "do not get drunk with wine" (5:18a).

The form of the verb πληροῦσθε "be filled" is present imperative, as is the verb μεθύσκεσθε "be drunk" in 5:18a. Here, as there, it indicates a continuous or a repeated experience or state. Many commentators consider it refers to a continuous state in which the Holy Spirit both controls and empowers the believer at all times. See, for example, O'Brien (pp. 392-393), Stott (p. 209). Lincoln (p. 348) refers to "an openness to and appropriation of the power of the Spirit" and to "the Spirit's mediation of the divine power and presence". He states that the Spirit is "the motivating force for their distinctive life of wise conduct and glad worship". In this same context other commentators speak of the Holy Spirit's transforming and changing or stimulating believers. In the display, therefore, to express the sense that the Holy Spirit should be an ever present and powerful force in the lives of believers, the exhortation is expressed as "let the Holy Spirit control and empower you completely at all times". The term "control" is used in the sense of guiding and directing rather than forcing or coercing.

This positive exhortation is naturally prominent and is the nucleus of the propositional configuration 5:18a–c.

5:19-21 These verses specify various ways in which the Holy Spirit's control and empowerment may be demonstrated in the lives of believers. This contrasts with the unrestrained and excessive actions of those drunk on wine (5:18a–b).

There are five present participles in 5:19-21. Commentators suggest various ways as to how they relate to each other and to the imperative clause πληροῦσθε ἐν πνεύματι "be filled with the Spirit". The main suggestions are:

1. These participles take an imperatival force from the initial imperative πληροῦσθε "be filled". See, for example, Bratcher and Nida (p. 135), Lenski (p. 619).
2. Paul is stating what will happen when a person is filled by the Holy Spirit and so these participles are describing the results of this filling. See Hoehner (p. 706), Lincoln (p. 345), O'Brien (p. 394). In support of this Hoehner states,

> participles of result are normally in the present tense and follow the main verb as here (p. 706).

In the context of this hortatory passage, it seems best to represent these participles as exhortations, but with an underlying relationship between them and the main verb of result-means: as a result of being filled by the Holy Spirit they should act as they are exhorted to in 5:19-21.

5:19a Address one another by means of singing psalms and hymns and spiritual songs. In the clause λαλοῦντες ἑαυτοῖς, it is generally agreed that ἑαυτοῖς has the reciprocal sense, i.e. "to one another", rather than "to yourselves", so that λαλοῦντες "speaking" does not refer to meditation, but to communication between people. The verb may be used in the sense of speaking or reciting the words of psalms, etc. It can also include singing, or antiphonal speech, where two groups speak responsively with each other.

The ἐν followed by the dative case has the sense of "by means of", i.e. believers should communicate with each other by means of using the words of psalms, etc. This parallels with the "teaching and admonishing one another" in Colossians 3:16.

Commentators discuss the three nouns ψαλμός "psalm", ὕμνος "hymn" and ᾠδή πνευματική "spiritual song". Their main point is what distinctions there might be between the three terms.

Although the three terms are not synonymous, it is unlikely that Paul was making precise distinctions here. The range of terms simply covers the range of songs sung by the Ephesian believers in praise of God.

On the parallel passage in Colossians 3:16, Callow (2002:134; cf. 1983:195) writes,

> While certainty is not possible, a good suggestion is to translate the word 'psalm' here as for any reference to an Old Testament psalm. The word 'song' here can be translated with a generic word for any song, and 'hymn' can be translated by the idea of praise, since this Greek word was used in the Septuagint to translate a Hebrew word meaning 'praise' (from the same verb as 'hallelujah'). In the light of modern experiences, 'spiritual songs' may mean songs given (immediately) by the Holy Spirit, and 'hymns' may have been longer-established compositions, perhaps ones that congregations shared. (Because there is no historical evidence for this, certainty is not possible.)

In translation it might be necessary to use the verb, e.g. to say "by means of *singing* hymns...", to complete the sense.

5:19b Sing songs and psalms/hymns sincerely
This part of the verse begins with two verbs ᾄδοντες καὶ ψάλλοντες which both have the meaning of "singing/making-music".

The second verb, ψάλλω, originally referred to plucking or playing a stringed instrument, but in the LXX it is frequently used to refer to singing, whether accompanied by an instrument or not. The consensus is that in this context, it should be understood as referring to singing. The two verbs therefore can be regarded as a doublet.

The phrase τῇ καρδίᾳ ὑμῶν "in your heart" qualifies both participles, ᾄδοντες "singing" and ψάλλοντες "singing/making music". This may refer to:

1. Hearty, enthusiastic singing.
2. Silent singing, within a person's heart.
3. The source of the singing is the heart. It is sincere, genuine.

The second option is least appropriate in this context as Paul is talking about the outward expression of the Holy Spirit.

Referring to the parallel passage in Colossians 3:16, Callow says,

> Both the Old Testament and the New Testament strongly condemn formal or outward religion, in which religious observances are adhered to while the heart is far from God (2002:134; cf. 1983:196).

This would support the third option above, since, if the heart is the source of what is said or sung, the singing or speaking will be sincere. In this context this sense seems to be the most appropriate and might be translated as "sincerely".

5:19c *in order to praise* the Lord. There is no clear evidence as to whether the dative phrase τῷ κυρίῳ "to the Lord":

1. Refers to the Lord God.
2. Refers to the Lord Jesus Christ.

The majority view favours the Lord Jesus Christ. If possible, it should be left ambiguous in translation, but, if a decision has to be made, we suggest that the majority view be followed.

The phrase indicates that the singing is directed towards the Lord.

In some languages, a literal translation of this phrase might suggest that the Lord himself was physically present. It may be preferable to express this phrase by a purpose proposition, as in the display, "*in order to praise* the Lord".

Commentators are divided about the relationship between the two participles ᾄδοντες "singing" and ψάλλοντες "singing/making music" and the participle λαλοῦντες "speaking" in 5:19a. They suggest:

1. They are co-ordinate with λαλοῦντες.
2. They are subordinate to λαλοῦντες.

According to O'Brien (p. 394) "the parallelism of this verse suggests that the two halves should be taken closely together". In this respect a number of commentators point out the use of cognate forms ψαλμοῖς "psalms" and ψάλλοντες "singing songs", ᾠδαῖς "songs" and ᾄδοντες "singing" in 5:19a and 5:19b. In view of this it may be argued that Paul "is not referring to two separate responses of speaking in songs (v. 19a) and singing (v. 19b), but is describing the same activity from different perspectives" (O'Brien, p. 394). The focus in 5:19a is on the mutual edification of believers and, in 5:19b-c, on the fact that this praise is directed towards the Lord. On this basis the participles in 5:19a and 5:19b should be regarded as co-ordinate with each other (O'Brien, p. 396; see also Ellicott, p. 104).

Lenski (pp. 620-621) maintains that these two participles are in a subordinate relation with λαλοῦντες (5:19a) and define it, i.e. λαλοῦντες "means: by singing with the voice and by playing on instruments". See also Hodge (pp. 304-305).

Either option is acceptable in the context. In the display, they are presented as co-ordinate, since there does not seem to be any particular prominence given to either of them. Each is then governed by the main imperative "be filled with the Spirit" (5:18c). As a result of being controlled by the Holy Spirit, they are to sing songs and psalms, and these should be directed towards edifying one another and towards praising the Lord.

5:20a At all times thank God, who is *our* Father, for everything. The participle εὐχαριστοῦντες "giving thanks" is co-ordinate with the preceding participles in 5:19 and is a further specific of 5:18c. It describes a third outcome of being completely controlled by the Holy Spirit, i.e. "being thankful to God".

The juxtaposition of πᾶς with one of its compound derivatives in the expression πάντοτε ὑπὲρ πάντων "always for every (thing)" serves to emphasise that thankfulness to God should pervade the believer's life.

There is some debate as to whether πάντων refers to:

1. Things which come from God and are clearly good.
2. Things in an all-inclusive sense, including the painful and the beneficial.

The all-embracing "everything" is not qualified in the display, in view of Scriptures such as Romans 8:28 where all things are said to work together for good for those who love God.

In the grammatical form of the phrase τῷ θεῷ καὶ πατρί "to the God and Father", the second noun describes the first (see Wallace, p. 271). The sense then is "God the Father". Most commentators agree that the meaning here is "God who is our Father", not just the Father of the Lord Jesus Christ.

5:20b-c *You are able do this* [5:20a] as a result of *what* our Lord Jesus Christ *has done*. It is difficult to express the meaning of the Greek phrase ἐν ὀνόματι τοῦ κυρίου ἡμῶν Ἰησοῦ Χριστοῦ "in (the) name of our Lord Jesus Christ" propositionally. In the commentaries, the main options seem to be:

1. Doing something in dependence on Christ and what he has done.
2. Doing something under Christ's authority.
3. Doing something with Christ's authority.

This is the only direct occasion in which Paul refers to thanks being offered in Jesus' name. However, elsewhere there are indirect references, e.g. Colossians 3:17, where it is offered δι' αὐτοῦ "through him".

Dependence on Christ and what he has done seems to be the most appropriate meaning in the context. In Scripture, a person's name often refers to what that person stands for and what he has accomplished. It is on the basis of who Christ is and what he has accomplished on our behalf that believers may approach God.

5:21 In the notes on Intent and Macrostructure for 5:15-6:9, there is a discussion as to whether 5:21 concludes 5:15-21 or begins 5:21-33. It is included in 5:15-21 in this analysis, but it provides a transition between this paragraph and 5:22-33. It concludes the list of specific exhortations relating to 5:18c, which at the same time represent the results of being controlled by the Holy Spirit.

5:21a Submit yourselves to one another The Greek verb ὑποτάσσω "subject/subordinate (someone/something to someone)" occurs also in 5:24 and in the parallel passage in Colossians 3:18. Callow suggests that it has the general sense of "to accept/recognize the authority of another" (1983:202; 2002:141). The participial clause ὑποτασσόμενοι ἀλλήλοις, therefore, has the sense "submit yourselves to one another". It provides the climax to the commands in 5:19-21.

5:21b since you revere Christ. Since φόβος "fear/reverence" is an abstract noun, ἐν φόβῳ Χριστοῦ "in reverence-to/fear-of Christ" needs to be expressed in the display by a clause such as "you revere Christ". The question among commentators is how much the element of "fear" should be present in a translation and understanding of this phrase.

On one hand, Best states,

> φόβος is a word with a wide range of meaning. Here it would be wrong to read into it any idea of 'terror'. It is instead a reverential fear which needs to be balanced by the motivation of love (Rom 12.1; 15.3f; 2 Cor 5.14; Eph 4.32; 5.2) (p. 518).

Most commentators also consider that, in this context, the sense is "reverence", "awe", "respect". O'Brien, however, criticizes many modern versions and says,

> [T]hese renderings are too soft to catch the nuance intended. 'Fear' is still the best translation. Although it does not convey the idea of 'terror' or 'intimidation' for those who are in Christ, it signifies a sense of awe in the presence of one who is Lord and coming Judge (p. 404).

Whether one agrees with O'Brien or not, in translation a term should be used which is strong enough to include some degree of awe or fear, possibly a term such as "revere", which has a sense of "deep respect".

The relationship between 5:21b and 5:21a, signalled by ἐν, is one of motivational grounds-EXHORTATION, i.e. the basis for subjecting themselves to one another is this reverence for Christ. This may be expressed as "since you revere Christ". See, for example, TEV, "because of your reverence for Christ".

BOUNDARIES AND COHERENCE

The initial boundary has been discussed in the section on Boundaries and Coherence for 5:15-17.

The final boundary is marked by a change from the general to the specific. In 5:15-21, Paul addresses "you (pl)". In 5:22, he addresses αἱ γυναῖκες "the wives" and then, in 5:25, οἱ ἄνδρες "the husbands".

An alternative analysis is for the participle ὑποτασσόμενοι "submitting yourselves" to be regarded as being joined to the following verses (5:22-5:33/6:9), serving to introduce the topic of mutual subjection in personal relationships among believers. While there are some modern versions that end the paragraph with 5:21 as in the display, most end it with 5:20. A few versions leave 5:21 to stand alone. Whichever analysis is preferred, the clause (5:21) forms a bridge between the general exhortations to believers and those to specific groups in 5:22-6:9. There is a full discussion of the relationship of 5:21 to its context under the section on Intent and Macrostructure for 5:15-6:9.

Within this paragraph, there is relational cohesion due to the series of participles:

λαλοῦντες "speaking"
ᾄδοντες "singing"
ψάλλοντες "making music"
εὐχαριστοῦντες "giving thanks"
ὑποτασσόμενοι "being subject"

These are all dependent on the imperative πληροῦσθε ἐν πνεύματι "be filled with the Spirit". The relationship can be seen as a generic means with specific results and with each participle having the force of a present imperative.

There is lexical coherence in that the vocabulary is predominantly from the semantic domain of "praise" and "worship" directed to the Lord. The exception to this is the final participial clause, "submitting yourselves to one another" (5:21a). Its connection with the preceding items is not clear. One possible line of thought might be that being drunk leads to lack of self-control (5:18), which in turn may result in disagreement. The control of the Holy Spirit leads to unity in worship (5:19) and thankfulness to the Lord (5:20), both of which are conducive to mutual respect (5:21) rather than drunken strife.

PROMINENCE AND THEME

In this hortatory paragraph the generic exhortation and the four specific exhortations are naturally prominent. The theme statement is based on the generic exhortation and a summary of the four specific ones.

SECTION CONSTITUENT 5:22–33 (Hortatory Paragraph: Nucleus₃ of 5:15–6:9)

THEME: Wives, submit yourselves to your husbands in the same manner as you should submit yourselves to the Lord. Husbands, love your wives as Christ also loved the church.

RELATIONAL STRUCTURE	CONTENTS
EXHOR- —CONGRUENCE ————————————————	5:22a Wives, submit yourselves to your husbands,
TATION₁ └standard ————————————————————	5:22b in the same manner as *you should submit yourselves* to the Lord *Jesus Christ*,
┌grounds -CONGRUENCE ————————————————	5:23a since a husband has authority over his wife,
│ for └standard —NUCLEUS —— NUCLEUS ———	5:23b just as Christ has authority over the church.
│ EXHOR- │ └compar- ————	5:23c *This* [5:23b] *is like* the head controls *the body* [MET].
│ TATION₁│ ison	
│ └amplification ————————————————	5:23d *Also*, Christ himself is the one who saves the church [MET].
│ ┌standard ————————————————————	5:24a Just as the church submits itself to Christ,
EXHORTA- │	
TION₁ ─CONGRUENCE —————————————————	5:24b wives must submit themselves to their husbands completely.
RESTATED │	
EXHOR- —NUCLEUS ———————————————————	5:25a Husbands, love your wives,
TATION₂ │	
└standard ──┬standard ──REASON ———	5:25b as Christ also loved the church,
└result ——MEANS ————	5:25c and *as a result* he willingly died on behalf of the church,
└pur- —MEANS —	5:26 in order that he might set apart *for himself* the church, *that is*, that he might cleanse/purify the church *from sin*, *symbolically*, by means of washing with water those who belong to the church *and, effectually*, by means of *making known* the gospel *to them*.
pose	
└pur- ———	5:27 Christ did this [5:25c–26] in order that he might present to himself a glorious church, *that is*, a church which is not morally flawed [MET] in any way, but which is perfectly holy/pure.
pose	
AMPLIFI-	
CATION ──CONGRUENCE —EXHORTATION ————	5:28a In the same manner [5:25b] also, a husband ought to love his wife as *he loves* his own body.
OF │	
EXHOR- │	
TATION₂ │	
├grounds₁ —CONCLUSION —————————	5:28b The husband who loves his wife loves himself.
│ └grounds —NUCLE- ———	5:29a This is shown by the fact that no one ever hated his own body, but rather, he nourishes his body and cares for it,
│ US	
│ └com- ————	5:29b–30 just as Christ also cares for the church because we are parts of the body of Christ [MET].
│ par-	
│ ison	
└grounds₂ —NUCLEUS ———————————	5:31 This [5:28–30] is in accordance with *the Scripture which says*, "A man shall leave his father and mother, and he shall be united to his wife, and the husband and the wife shall become *as* one body" [MET].
└evalu- — 'mys- ———	5:32a The secret-message which this *Scripture* [5:31] *expresses* is very important,
ation tery'	

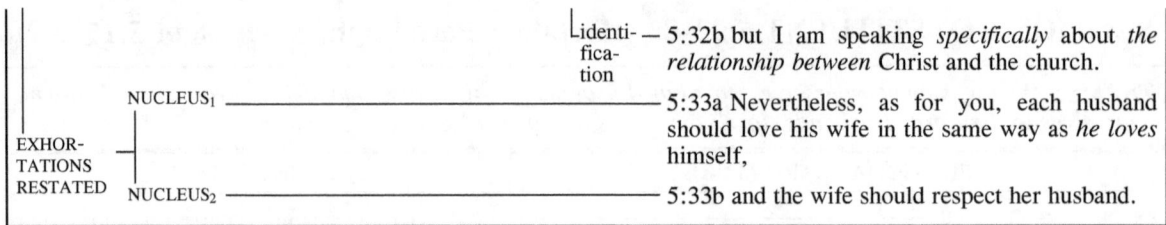

INTENT AND STRUCTURE

The 5:22-33 paragraph is hortatory. There are two EXHORTATIONS, each with its own grounds. However, the grounds for EXHORTATION₂ is in the form of a standard-CONGRUENCE relation with that exhortation. EXHORTATION₁ (5:22) is restated twice, in 5:24 and 5:33b. EXHORTATION₂ (5:25) is restated twice, in 5:28 (as its AMPLIFICATION) and 5:33a. Paul has made a general appeal to the Ephesians in 5:21, that they would submit themselves to one another, in the sense of a "voluntary yielding in love" (BDAG, p. 1042.1bβ). Now, he wants them to apply this, as individuals, to the various relationships they have with different people in their household. Firstly he discusses the relationship between a husband and wife.

NOTES

5:22a Wives, submit yourselves to your husbands, While *The Greek New Testament according to the Majority Text* has the imperative verb ὑποτάσσεσθε "submit" after ἀνδράσιν "husbands", the UBS committee considers the text without this verb as almost certain (B rating). With no verb stated, 5:22 is dependent on ὑποτασσόμενοι "submitting" in 5:21. The force of the verb is imperative. Therefore, there is no essential difference in meaning between the two readings. The commentators suggest that the verb means "to accept/recognise the authority of another". It is a voluntary subordination. The wife is to accept and respect the husband's position as head of the family.

5:22b in the same manner as *you should submit yourselves* to the Lord *Jesus Christ*, Loving and willing submission to Christ is the standard against which a wife's submission to her husband is to be measured.

5:23a–b since a husband has authority over his wife, just as Christ has authority over the church. The initial ὅτι "because, since" introduces a grounds for 5:22. As in 1:22–23 and 4:15, the figure of the head and the body in the statement ἀνήρ ἐστιν κεφαλὴ τῆς γυναικὸς ὡς καὶ ὁ Χριστὸς κεφαλὴ τῆς ἐκκλησίας "a man is head of the woman as also Christ is head of the church" expresses the authority Christ, the head, has over the church, the body. Here also it symbolises a husband's authority over his wife. The point of comparison ("has authority over") is expressed in the display.

5:23c *This* [5:23b] *is like* the head controls *the body*. This proposition states the figure and restates the point of comparison (here, "controls") of the metaphor.

5:23d Also, Christ himself is the one who saves the church. In the clause αὐτὸς σωτὴρ τοῦ σώματος "himself Saviour of the body", clearly, αὐτός refers to Christ and σώματος refers to the church. But it is not clear what relationship σωτήρ "saviour" refers to:

1. Does it refer only to the relationship between Christ and the church?
2. Is it also part of the analogy with the husband and wife, so that the husband is to be understood as being in some sense the "saviour" of his wife as Christ is the Saviour of the church?

The commentators discuss the issue as follows:

1. Some focus on how Christ's headship differs from that of the husband. They are alike in that both have authority, the one over the church and the other over his wife. They differ in that Christ is also the Saviour of the church, whereas the husband is *not* the saviour of his wife. In fact, the term σωτήρ "Saviour" in the New Testament always refers to Jesus or God and never to human beings. See, for example, Ellicott (pp.106–107), Hodge (pp. 313–314), Hoehner (pp. 742–743), Lenski (p 627), Lincoln (pp. 370–371), O'Brien (pp. 414–415).
2. Others focus on how the husband's headship parallels that of Christ. They both have authority, Christ over the church and the

husband over his wife. Christ has sacrificial concern for the salvation of the church, the husband should have sacrificial concern for the welfare of his wife. He is her preserver and protector in a general sense. See, for example, Hendriksen (p. 248), Robinson (p. 201).

This clause makes an emphatic statement about Christ, and it is his sacrifice that is in focus with respect to his relationship with the church. However, it is possible that Paul has the relationship between a husband and his wife in mind also. In 5:22-24, Paul's focus is on the submission of a wife to the authority of her husband. However, this clause αὐτὸς σωτὴρ τοῦ σώματος "himself Saviour of the body" may anticipate 5:25-32 with its exhortation for a husband to love his wife as Christ loved the church. In particular, it links to 5:25c, where reference is made to Christ being willing to die on behalf of the church.

So 5:23d probably contains a reference that the authority of a husband over his wife should be tempered with a self-sacrificing love based on the example of Christ.

This clause is regarded as an amplification of 5:23b, since its primary function is to give additional information about Christ's relationship to the church. It may also be understood, on a secondary level, as being additional information with respect to the standard set by Christ and to which a husband should aspire. In the display, this clause is rendered as "*Also*, Christ himself is the one who saves the church".

5:24a-b Just as the church submits itself to Christ, wives must submit themselves to their husbands completely. This verse is a restatement of 5:22, with the addition of ἐν παντί "in every (thing)": a wife should be submissive to her husband in all things, just as the church is to be submissive to Christ in all things.

There is some uncertainty as to the relationship signalled by the initial conjunction ἀλλά "but, then" with the material which precedes it. The possibilities are:

1. It is resumptive. Paul is continuing with his main line of thought from 5:23a-b, without further developing the thought of 5:23d. See, for example, Hendriksen (p. 249, fn. 154).
2. It has an adversative function and indicates a contrast with an implied statement derived from 5:23d, *Husbands cannot be the saviours of their wives as Christ is the Saviour of the church*, but/nevertheless the wives should be subject to their husbands as the church is subject to Christ. See, for example, Ellicott (p. 107), Hodge (p. 314), Lincoln (p. 372), O'Brien (pp. 415-416).

The decision is difficult. This is evident from the variety in the different English versions.

In this context, although 5:24a-b has an adversative relation with 5:23d, this is not in focus. Rather, Paul is restating the exhortation of 5:22 and reinforcing it by the addition of ἐν παντί "in every (thing)", as he prepares to move on to talk about the responsibilities of the husband to the wife in 5:25-33. This follows option one.

The phrase ἐν παντί "in every (thing)" might be expressed as "completely" or "at all times".

5:25-32 In this second major propositional cluster of the paragraph, Paul now addresses the husbands and exhorts them to love their wives as Christ loves the church. Paul gives three commands to Christian husbands to love their wives. In 5:25, he appeals to the example of Christ's love for the church and, in 5:28 and 5:31, he appeals to the Old Testament concept of marriage as "one body".

5:25a-b Husbands, love your wives, as Christ also loved the church, This exhortation to husbands to love their wives is the counterpart to the exhortation to wives to submit to their husbands (5:22-24).

The conjunction καθὼς καί "just as also" may indicate:

1. A comparison between a husband's love for his wife and the love shown by Christ for his church. See, for example, Hoehner (p. 748), Lenski (p. 630).
2. Both a comparison as in the first option *and* the grounds for the command to husbands to love their wives, i.e. it has both comparative and causal force. See, for example, Hodge (p. 315), Lincoln (p. 374), O'Brien (p. 419).

O'Brien states,

> [καθὼς καί] is part of the New Testament's 'conformity' pattern in which God or Christ's saving activity, especially Christ's sacrifice on the cross, is presented as a model of the lifestyle to which believers are to 'conform' (p. 419, fn. 234).

Models to which believers are to conform are labelled in SSAs as "standard" and conformity to them as "CONGRUENCE". They are a type of comparison, but in hortatory material may have a motivational grounds (causative) role, as here and in 5:2. In the display, therefore, 5:25b is shown as a supporting standard in a standard-CONGRUENCE relation with 5:25a and 5:28a. Christ's love for the church is the standard to which husbands should conform in their love for their wives.

5:25c and *as a result* he willingly died on behalf of the church, Here, καὶ ἑαυτὸν παρέδωκεν ὑπὲρ αὐτῆς "and gave himself up on behalf of her/it [the church]" recalls 5:2 καὶ παρέδωκεν ἑαυτὸν ὑπὲρ ἡμῶν "and gave himself up on behalf of us". As in 5:2, καί is analysed as signalling a result, "Christ loved the church, and *as a result* he willingly died on behalf of it". See the note on 5:2. It would also be possible to regard the καί as indicating a co-ordinate relationship with the preceding clause (5:25b).

5:26 The initial ἵνα "in order that" introduces the first of three clauses in 5:26 and 5:27 which give the purpose of Christ's death in relation to the church, i.e. the sanctification of the church. Some commentators suggest that Christ's desire to purify and save the church should be evident in the husband's love for his wife, but it is generally agreed that this is not in focus here and that these two verses apply solely to the union of Christ and the church.

The configuration of propositions in 5:26 represents the immediate purpose of 5:25c. It also provides the means for 5:27.

in order that he might set apart *for himself* the church, Although the general sense of these verses may be clear, there are some problems in clarifying the details.

The verb ἁγιάζω "sanctify" means "to cleanse", "to render morally pure", "to consecrate", "to regard as sacred" and, therefore, "to reverence". The commentaries seem to be divided about what the verb means here:

1. It refers to the church being set aside for God. See, for example, Calvin (p. 205), Hendriksen (p. 250), Hoehner (p. 751).
2. It refers to the moral or spiritual purification of the church. See, for example, Hodge (pp. 317–318).

The verb form used here, ἁγιάσῃ "he might sanctify" is an aorist subjunctive indicating a single, decisive event. This would fit best with the idea of "consecration", so that he might set apart the church for himself, to be wholly his. This supports the first option.

In the display, therefore, the event is expressed as "in order that he might set apart *for himself* the church".

***that is*, that he might cleanse/purify the church *from sin*,** The verb καθαρίζω "cleanse, purify" is used of moral and religious cleansing. When used symbolically, it can be used of ceremonial or ritual cleansing, cf. Acts 10:15; 11:9, or consecrating by cleansing, cf. Hebrews 9:22, 23. Otherwise it is used of ethical purification (2 Cor. 7:1; James 4:8) and freeing from the guilt of sin (Titus 2:14; Heb. 9:14; 1 John 1:7, 9). In the context of 5:27 possibly ethical purification is in focus.

Here, the aorist participle καθαρίσας "having cleansed" is used. Since it is aorist, commentators discuss the timing of this event. They suggest:

1. It describes an event which took place prior to the preceding subjunctive verb ἁγιάσῃ, i.e. that he might sanctify/set-apart the church *after* cleansing it. See, for example, Ellicott (p. 107), Hodge (p. 320), Stott (p. 227). This could also be understood as indicating a means, i.e. by means of having cleansed it.
2. It refers to an event which occurs at the same time as ἁγιάσῃ. It expresses the means by which, or the way in which, the sanctifying takes effect, i.e. by means of cleansing it. See, for example, Lincoln (p. 375), O'Brien (p. 422).
3. The participle καθαρίσας "having cleansed" explains ἁγιάσῃ "he might sanctify", or states another aspect of the same event: he might sanctify, that is, he might cleanse it from sin. See, for example, Hendriksen (pp. 250–251, fn. 156), Lenski (p. 632).

There is no conclusive evidence to support any of these options. The third option is represented in the display, with "that he might cleanse/purify the church *from sin*" being equivalent to, or explanatory of, the preceding proposition, "that he might set apart *for himself* the church".

***symbolically*, by means of washing with water those who belong to the church *and, effectually*, by means of *making known* the**

gospel *to them*. The clause τῷ λουτρῷ τοῦ ὕδατος ἐν ῥήματι "with the washing of water by (the) word" designates the means by which the cleansing takes place.

The meaning of the phrase τῷ λουτρῷ τοῦ ὕδατος "with the washing of water" is problematic. Most versions simply translate it as "the washing with/by water". It is generally agreed that this phrase refers to Christian baptism, the outward sign of cleansing from sin, of spiritual purification. So, in the display, the adverb "*symbolically*" is used to qualify the event "cleanse the church *from sin*...by means of washing with water".

The word ῥῆμα "word" is applied to the *spoken* word in the New Testament. In Paul's letters, it is used primarily for a word proceeding, directly or indirectly, from God. Commentators suggest different meanings in this context:

1. It refers to "the word of promise", i.e. the divine promise of forgiveness (Mark 16:16).
2. It refers to "the preached word/gospel". This would be supported by ῥῆμα θεοῦ "(the) word of God" in 6:17.
3. It refers to a word spoken at baptism by either the one being baptised or the one baptising him.

The second option seems the most likely here and so is followed in the display.

There is also discussion about how the phrase ἐν ῥήματι "by (the) word" connects with the context. There are three suggestions:

1. It connects with καθαρίσας τῷ λουτρῷ τοῦ ὕδατος "having cleansed with the washing of water", i.e. the cleansing was effected by the gospel's being made known.
2. It connects with ἁγιάσῃ "he might sanctify", i.e. sanctify/consecrate...by the word. See also John 17:17.
3. It connects with both expressions.

While the second option makes good sense, the distance of ἐν ῥήματι from ἁγιάσῃ is a problem.

Therefore, in the display, the first option is followed. The prepositional phrase ἐν ῥήματι "by (the) word", is expressed in a means construction with ἐν translated as: "by means of". "*Making known*" is supplied to make clear how "the word" is used in this context in accomplishing the cleansing.

The adverb *effectually* is used to qualify the event "cleanse the church *from sin*...by means of *making known* the gospel". This is done in order to express the fact that the event referred to is not symbolic but describes what has been effected by making known the gospel.

The point which should be made clear is that τῷ λουτρῷ τοῦ ὕδατος "with the washing of water" of itself does not make clean from sin, does not purify, but that it is an act which is symbolic of the spiritual cleansing effected by God through making known his word.

5:27 The initial ἵνα, as in 5:26, indicates purpose. The immediate purpose of Christ's giving himself for the church (5:25c) was to set the church apart for himself and to cleanse it (5:26). Now in 5:27 Paul states the ultimate purpose for which Christ died for the church: that he should present the church to himself, ἔνδοξον "glorious", μὴ ἔχουσαν σπίλον ἢ ῥυτίδα "not having spot nor wrinkle", ἁγία καὶ ἄμωμος "holy and unblemished". In effect, Paul is saying that the church should be completely holy.

Christ did this **[5:25c–26] in order that he might present to himself a glorious church,** In the clause ἵνα παραστήσῃ αὐτὸς ἑαυτῷ ἔνδοξον τὴν ἐκκλησίαν "in order that he might present the church to himself glorious", the pronoun αὐτός "he" refers back to Χριστός in 5:25 and ἑαυτῷ "to himself" must then also refer to Christ. Commentators discuss when this presentation takes place. There are two positions:

1. It refers to the present position of the church, sanctified by virtue of its union with Christ. See, for example, Lincoln (p. 377).
2. It refers to the time when the Lord returns in glory and the church will finally be as glorious and perfect as he is. See, for example, Ellicott (p. 108), Lenski (p. 635), Hodge (pp. 330–331), Stott (p. 228).

The latter option has the best support among commentators.

***that is*, a church which is not morally flawed in any way, but which is perfectly holy/pure.** These propositions amplify the earlier part of the verse, enlarging upon the sense in which the church will be glorious. This is presented, first negatively, μὴ ἔχουσαν σπίλον ἢ ῥυτίδα "not having spot or wrinkle", then positively, ἁγία καὶ ἄμωμος "holy and unblemished".

Most of the commentators agree that μὴ ἔχουσαν σπίλον ἢ ῥυτίδα "not having spot or wrinkle" is a metaphorical reference to the appearance of a young bride who has no blemishes or wrinkles to spoil her beauty. According to Moore (p. 49), it is a figurative doublet. So, σπίλον "spot, blemish" and ῥυτίδα "wrinkle" represent moral or spiritual faults. It is difficult to see that there could be any particular distinction intended by the two words in either their non-figurative or figurative reference. The addition of ἤ τι τῶν τοιούτων "or anything of the kind" serves to emphasise the all-embracing nature of the doublet.

The amplification is completed by the positive clause, "that the church might be holy and blameless" or "the church might be perfectly holy/pure". This is in a relation of equivalence with the preceding clause "the church might not be morally flawed in any way" and serves to emphasise the glorious state of the church.

5:28a In the same manner [5:25b] also, a husband ought to love his wife as *he loves* his own body. There is discussion about the adverb οὕτως "so, likewise" and what it relates to. There are two possibilities:

1. It relates to what precedes, i.e. καθὼς καὶ ὁ Χριστὸς ἠγάπησεν τὴν ἐκκλησίαν "as also Christ loved the church" (5:25b).
2. It relates to what follows, i.e. ὡς τὰ ἑαυτῶν σώματα "as their own bodies".

The first option is the more usual reference of οὕτως and has most support. This provides the standard for both 5:25a and 5:28a.

There is discussion about the ὡς "as" in the phrase ὡς τὰ ἑαυτῶν σώματα "as their own bodies". The suggestions are:

1. It introduces a comparison and indicates manner. A husband ought to love his wife *as/in-the-same-way-that* he loves his own body. See, for example, Lincoln (p. 378), Mitton (p. 204).
2. It has the sense: "*as being* his own body". Christ and the husband are each "head" and, as the church is the body in relation to Christ, so is the wife in relation to the husband. As Christ loves the church as being his body, so should the husband love his wife as being *his* body. See, for example, Ellicott (pp. 109-110), Hendriksen (p. 254), Hodge (pp. 331-332), Lenski (p. 637).

There does not appear to be any discernible difference between a husband loving his wife as he loves his own body, and loving his wife as being his own body. In effect, both can be understood to refer to love for himself and, therefore, to mean that the love he has for his wife should be of the same kind as the love he has for himself.

5:28b The husband who loves his wife loves himself. This statement may be understood as providing an inference from the preceding clause, i.e. if a husband loves his wife as being his own body then he is loving himself. Alternatively, it may be an explanation of that clause and make clear that the focus of it is not on the husband's love for his own body, but on the degree of love which a husband should have for his wife. See, for example, Ellicott (p. 110), Hoehner (pp. 763-764).

It seems best to understand this statement as being an explanatory grounds for 5:28a. It is natural for a husband to love himself, and his love for his wife should be a natural extension of this.

5:29-30 The initial γάρ introduces a grounds in 5:29-30 for what immediately precedes in 5:28b. The reasoning seems to be as follows: A man who loves his wife loves himself, since, if he did not love her, he would be hating himself, and no one hates himself, but nourishes his body and cares for it, just as Christ loves the church. See, for example, Meyer (p. 517).

5:29a This is shown by the fact that This phrase expresses the function of the introductory γάρ as indicating a grounds for 5:28b.

no one ever hated his own body, Once again Paul uses a negative statement followed by a positive one to emphasise the point he wishes to make. The expression οὐδείς ποτε "no one ever" expresses a general rule which is not invalidated by exceptional examples which may occur.

The Greek noun σάρξ "flesh" has the sense here of "the body" viewed as physical substance rather than metaphorical uses it has elsewhere in Scripture.

but rather, he nourishes his body and cares for it, These two verbs ἐκτρέφει and θάλπει literally mean "he feeds" and "he warms". The first is also found in 6:4, the second in 1 Thessalonians 2:7 and nowhere else in the New Testament. In both Thessalonians and

Ephesians 6, there seems to be a sense of caring and tenderness involved so that "he nourishes and cares for it" might express the sense here.

5:29b just as Christ also cares for the church The Greek term καθώς "just as" introduces a comparison between the way in which a man cares for the well-being of his body and that in which Christ cares for the spiritual well-being of the church.

5:30 because we are parts of the body of Christ. The initial ὅτι introduces the reason for the preceding clause (5:29b), i.e. it is because of the closeness of the relationship between Christ and the church that Christ nurtures and cares for the individual believers who make up the church. In this metaphor, the relationship of individual believers to Christ is likened to that between the different parts of the human body.

The Greek noun μέλη literally means "members, parts, limbs". In the Greek text, it is forefronted for emphasis. It applies figuratively to the individual believers who make up the church.

There is some disagreement among commentators about the textual reading here regarding the phrase ἐκ τῆς σαρκὸς αὐτοῦ καὶ ἐκ τῶν ὀστέων αὐτοῦ "out of his flesh and out of his bones". The views are:

1. It should be included, following the reading of certain manuscripts. KJV includes the phrase.
2. It should be omitted. This is the strong recommendation of the UBS committee.

Most versions omit it, as does the display.

5:31 This [5:28-30] is in accordance with *the Scripture which says*, The expression ἀντὶ τούτου "for this cause" at the beginning of this verse has been understood in the following ways:

1. It has no clear meaning in this Ephesians context and "is used only because it is part of the text cited" (Bratcher and Nida, p. 146; see also Hendriksen, p. 256).
2. The connective phrase ἀντὶ τούτου is understood as functioning as part of Paul's argument in 5:25-31. See, for example, Candlish (p.116), Meyer (p. 520).

It is possible that Paul did not introduce the verse as being from Scripture because he wanted ἀντὶ τούτου "for this cause" to function directly as indicating support for his argument in this particular passage in Ephesians.

There is good support among commentators for understanding the quotation of Genesis 2:24 as referring directly to the union of Christ and his church, in view of the immediately preceding "we are members of his body" in 5:30. The first part of the quotation, "a man will leave his father and mother and be joined to his wife", may be understood as only a recitation of the verse for the purpose of putting the latter part of it in perspective. It is the latter part of the quotation which is relevant to Paul's purpose, "the two shall be one flesh", since it puts the focus on the union of Christ and the church. This agrees with 5:32 and Paul's statement there concerning Christ and the church. See Hodge (pp. 349-350), Lincoln (pp. 380-382), O'Brien (pp. 429-430).

However, it is possible that Paul wishes to confirm all that he has said in 5:28-30 concerning both aspects of the "one body", i.e. the union of Christ and the church and the union of husband and wife in marriage and to give it authority by recalling Genesis 2:24.

In 4:8 and 5:14, a passage from Scripture is introduced by the phrase διὸ λέγει "therefore, it says". This is similar to the context here in 5:31. In both 4:8 and 5:14 the introductory phrase has been analysed as indicating a grounds or confirmation of what has been said in the preceding verse. (In fact, many commentators take 4:8 as grounds.) In such contexts both the point being made and the quotation are thought of as proceeding from the same basis and may be represented either as "as it is written in the following Scripture" (4:8) or as "on the same basis the following is said in Scripture" (5:14).

A similar relationship to that in 4:8 and 5:14 is posited here in 5:31. What has been said in 5:28-30 is said to be in agreement with or on the same basis as the passage from Genesis as quoted in 5:31. It functions as a second grounds for what precedes. The relationship is shown in the display as "This [5:28-30] is in accordance with *the Scripture which says*".

This reference to Scripture is included in the display in order to make clear that the verse is a quotation from Scripture backing up what Paul is saying about the significance of "one body". CEV, NLT, REB, TEV also make clear the fact that 5:31 is a quote from scripture.

"A man shall leave his father and mother, and he shall be united to his wife, The use of the future tense in this verse, καταλείψει "he shall leave" and προσκολληθήσεται "he shall be joined to", indicates what ought to happen.

The verb προσκολληθήσεται "adhere closely to, be faithfully devoted to, be joined to" is generally agreed to refer to sexual union, cf. 1 Corinthians 6:16, where Paul also quotes from Genesis 2:24.

An expression such as "will be united to his wife" might be used, so that all aspects of the marriage bond are covered.

and the husband and the wife shall become *as* one body". In the clause καὶ ἔσονται οἱ δύο εἰς σάρκα μίαν "and the two shall be one flesh", οἱ δύο refers to the husband and the wife.

Lenski (p. 642) points out that in the expression σάρκα μίαν "one flesh" Paul reaches a climax towards which he has been working since 5:25. In that verse he speaks of husbands loving their wives. In 5:28, he speaks of wives as being compared with the husbands' own bodies, and compares the love of a husband for his wife with loving "himself". In 5:29, he speaks of the husband's "own flesh". Now in 5:31, he reaches the climax, which is literally, in Scripture, "the two shall be one flesh", the union in marriage of husband and wife.

This marital union is the physical counterpart of the spiritual union between Christ and the church. This has been expressed in the display as "the husband and the wife shall become *as* one body".

5:32a The secret-message which this *Scripture* [5:31] *expresses* is very important, As in its other occurrences in Ephesians (1:9; 3:3, 4, 9; 6:19), μυστήριον "mystery" is used to refer to something once hidden but now revealed by God, a secret disclosed which was "not discoverable by unaided human reason" (Graham, p. 513). The truth disclosed is described by μέγα "great" in the sense of "important" or "significant" or "profound".

Commentators suggest that τὸ μυστήριον τοῦτο "this mystery" may refer to:

1. The relationship of husband and wife in marriage.
2. The relationship between Christ and the church.
3. The comparison of human marriage with the union of Christ and the church.

At first glance, the first option seems the simplest as it refers to the immediately preceding quotation concerning the relation between husband and wife.

However, Paul is not thinking only of marriage, since he goes on immediately to refer to the relationship between Christ and the church. The comparison between the two relationships seems to be at the forefront of his thinking. And so it is more likely that the second option is the correct one. There is good support for this view. Lincoln says,

> Both the OT passage and the marriage relationship of which it speaks are connected with the mystery, but their connection is that they point to the secret that has now been revealed, that of the relationship between Christ and the Church (p. 381).

See also O'Brien (pp. 432–435) and Lenski (p. 643).

5:32b but I am speaking *specifically* about *the relationship between* Christ and the church. Paul uses variations of the formula ἐγὼ δὲ λέγω... "but I speak..." in various places in his letters where an explanation of something previously said is in view, e.g. 1 Corinthians 1:12; Galatians 3:17; 4:1; 5:16.

The δέ has a disjunctive force here. It indicates a change of ideas, introduces an explanation, and separates the explanation from the thing explained. It marks the fact that what follows is not a continuation of the discussion of the physical union of husband and wife. Rather, it is Paul's own application of the words of Scripture. He uses ἐγὼ δὲ λέγω... "but I speak..." to bring to their notice that, although the Genesis passage is relevant in exhorting a husband to care for his wife, the union he is specifically speaking of now is that between Christ and the church.

The mystery as presented in Genesis is profound, in the sense that it reveals the true nature of the relationship between Christ and the church. This is another aspect of the same mystery as that referred to in chapter three concerning the uniting of Jewish and Gentile believers into one body by their union with Christ.

As for describing the semantic relationship the second half of the verse has with the first half, it may be analysed as a clarifying identification of the mystery which Paul is now talking about.

5:33a Nevertheless, as for you, each husband should love his wife in the same way as *he loves* himself, Paul ends this unit with two further exhortations, summarising the duties and responsibilities of husbands and wives towards each other.

The conjunction πλήν with which this verse begins may be used:

1. In an adversative sense, i.e. "however" or "but".
2. In concluding a discussion and emphasising what is important.

In this verse, Paul ends the paragraph by these two summary exhortations, addressed to each husband and wife. The focus of the whole paragraph has been to make clear the true nature of the marriage relationship and its duties and responsibilities. This has been done in connection with an exposition of the analogous relation between Christ and the church. Although there has not been any digression from the topic, in 5:32 the statement which brings that verse to a close, ἐγὼ δὲ λέγω εἰς Χριστὸν καὶ εἰς τὴν ἐκκλησίαν "but I speak about Christ and the church", focusses only on the relationship between Christ and the church.

Now Paul wants to remind the Ephesians about the main point of the paragraph: the importance of the marriage relationship. He does so with this restatement of the earlier exhortations.

The phrase καὶ ὑμεῖς signals a switch of focus back to "you" after a gap of several verses.

The phrase οἱ καθ' ἕνα ἕκαστος "one by one each" focusses on each husband represented by the ὑμεῖς. There are to be no exceptions.

The Greek word ὡς "as" has the same comparative sense as in 5:28, "the husband should love his wife in the same way as he loves himself". See the notes on 5:28.

5:33b and the wife should respect her husband. In the clause ἡ δὲ γυνὴ ἵνα φοβῆται τὸν ἄνδρα "and the wife that she may fear/respect her husband" the ἵνα followed by the subjunctive φοβῆται is understood by most of the commentaries to have imperatival force, "the wife should respect her husband". See Ellicott (p. 113), Hodge (p. 353), Lenski (p. 645), Lincoln (p. 384), O'Brien (p. 436). This analysis is followed in the display.

As for the use of "fear" here, even in English it is too strong. It is preferable to use a verb like "to respect, honour".

BOUNDARIES AND COHERENCE

It is possible to regard these verses as two closely related paragraphs, 5:22-24 and 5:25-32, with 5:33 as a separate propositional cluster modifying both of them. However, in view of the cohesion and coherence factors listed below, they are analysed as a single complex paragraph.

The initial boundary has been discussed in the section on Boundaries and Coherence for 5:15-6:9.

The unit is brought to a conclusion in 5:33 with what amounts to a summary exhortation to husbands and wives and a completion of the chiasmus of 5:22a, 25a, 33a, 33b as follows:

A   Wives, submit yourselves to your husbands (5:22a).
  B   Husbands, love your wives (5:25a).
  B' Each husband should love his wife (5:33a).
A' Each wife should respect her husband (5:33b).

Also, the start of a new paragraph at 6:1 is marked by the vocative Τὰ τέκνα "children", as Paul begins to address a new group within the household: children and parents.

There is lexical cohesion in the repetition of the participants:

γυναῖκες "wives" (nine times)
ἄνδρες "husbands" (six times)
ὁ Χριστός "Christ" (five times)
ἐκκλησία "the church" (five times)

The metaphor of τὸ σῶμα "the body" (5:23, 28, 30) and its various parts representing the relationship between Christ and his church is a strong unifying factor. The vocabulary related to this is:

κεφαλή "the head" (5:23)
σάρξ "flesh" (5:29, 31)
μέλη "members" (5:30)

There is also vocabulary from the semantic field of "love":

ἀγαπάω and related words (5:25, 28, 33)
παρέδωκεν "gave (himself) up" (5:25)
σωτήρ "saviour" (5:23)
ἐκτρέφει καὶ θάλπει "nourishes and cherishes" (5:29)
ὑποτάσσω "submit" (5:24, implied verb of 5:22)
φοβῆται "respect" (5:33)

PROMINENCE AND THEME

Since the 5:22-33 paragraph is hortatory, both EXHORTATION₁ and EXHORTATION₂ are naturally prominent. The theme statement, therefore, is based upon both EXHORTATIONS. Both EXHORTATIONS function as CONGRUENCE components in CONGRUENCE-standard configurations. In each case, both CONGRUENCE and standard feature in the theme statement, since the standard is necessary to complete the full force of the exhortation in much the same way as the grounds usually does in a hortatory unit.

SECTION CONSTITUENT 6:1–4 (Hortatory Paragraph: Nucleus₄ of 5:15–6:9)

THEME: Children, obey your parents since, as believers in the Lord Jesus Christ, it is right that you do so. Fathers, bring up your children well, by training them according to the teaching given by the Lord Jesus Christ.

RELATIONAL STRUCTURE	CONTENTS
NUCLEUS₁ — NUCLEUS — EXHORTATION	6:1a Children, obey your parents,
⸤grounds₁	6:1b *since you are* united to (*or, believe* in) the Lord *Jesus Christ*.
⸤grounds₂	6:1c *Obey them,* since it is right *that you do so.*
AMPLIFICATION — EXHORTATION	6:2a Greatly respect (*or,* highly esteem) your father and mother.
orienter	6:2b *God* promised
condition	6:3a that *if you do this* [6:2a],
CONSEQUENCE₁	6:3b you will prosper,
⸤grounds — NUCLEUS ⸤CONSEQUENCE₂	6:3c and you will live a long time on the earth.
⸤amplification	6:3d *This* [6:2a] is the first law which *God* commanded in which *he* also promises something.
⸢negative exhortation	6:4a Fathers, do not *behave unreasonably towards* your children *with the result that* you cause them to become angry,
NUCLEUS₂ — POSITIVE EXHORTATION ⸤RESULT	6:4b but bring them up well,
⸤means	6:4c by means of your disciplining and instructing them in the way that the Lord *Jesus Christ* teaches that you should do so.

INTENT AND STRUCTURE

Paul's intent in 6:1–4 is to encourage good relations between parents and children based on the teachings of Scripture.

The hortatory nature of this unit is evident in that, of the seven finite verbs, four are in the imperative mood:

ὑπακούετε "obey" (6:1)
τίμα "honour" (6:2)
μὴ παροργίζετε "do not anger" (6:4)
ἐκτρέφετε "nurture" (6:4)

The paragraph is composed of two co-ordinate NUCLEI:

1. NUCLEUS₁ which consists of:

   an EXHORTATION (6:1a), supported by two grounds (6:1b, 1c),
   a hortatory AMPLIFICATION (6:2a) supported by a grounds (6:2b–3d).

The exhortations in NUCLEUS₁ are addressed to children urging them to obey and respect their parents.

2. NUCLEUS₂ which consists of:

   a negative exhortation (6:4a) and a POSITIVE EXHORTATION (6:4b) supported by a means proposition (6:4c).

There is no grounds stated for this exhortation.

This exhortation (NUCLEUS₂) is addressed to fathers (or parents) urging them to bring up their children well.

NOTES

6:1a–b Children, obey your parents, *since you are* united to (*or, believe* in) the Lord *Jesus Christ*. There is a textual issue regarding the phrase ἐν κυρίῳ "in (the) Lord":

1. Omit the expression. Several reliable manuscripts, for example, Codex Vaticanus, D*, do not have the phrase. REB follows these manuscripts.
2. Consider the expression as part of the original text as, for example, Papyrus 46, Codices Sinaiticus, Alexandrinus. Versions that follow

these manuscripts include NASB, NET, NIV, NJB, RSV, TEV and most others.

The UBS text includes it in brackets with a C "difficulty in deciding" rating. *The Greek New Testament according to the Majority Text* includes it.

Most commentators agree that the expression connects with ὑπακούετε, i.e. children are to obey "in the Lord". This is followed in the display.

It is generally agreed that ἐν κυρίῳ refers to "the Lord Jesus Christ". Children should obey their parents because they (the children) are united spiritually with Christ. They belong to him and, as believers, they should obey their parents. The phrase may be regarded as either one of manner or of grounds. The one would imply the other. In the display, it is analysed as grounds.

6:1c Obey them, since it is right *that you do so*. The γάρ "for" introduces the grounds for the obedience Paul commands.

The adjective δίκαιος "right" is used, not merely in the sense of "fitting", but in the sense of "righteous", that which is required by the law of Moses. This is confirmed by Paul's quotation from the ten commandments in the following verse.

6:2–3 There are two main opinions among commentators about the relationship between this cluster of propositions and 6:1. They suggest:

1. The relationship is that of a second grounds to 6:1a, following on 6:1c the clearly marked grounds, i.e. Children are to obey their parents, since it is right that they do so (6:1c) and since God commanded them to do so (6:2–3).
2. The relationship is that of restatement. The verses 6:2–3 restate 6:1, either as an amplification of it or an equivalent to it.

In the display, 6:2–3 is shown as an amplification of 6:1, rather than grounds. This analysis is supported by the fact that 6:2 is not introduced by a subordinating conjunction and the verb form in 6:2 is an imperative, as is ὑπακούετε "obey" in 6:1.

The restatement serves to reinforce the command of 6:1a. Eadie states,

> [It does not] give the ground of the preceding injunction, for δίκαιον contains a specific reason; but it is another form of the same injunction, based not upon natural right, but upon inspired authority (p. 438).

6:2a Greatly respect (*or,* highly esteem) your father and mother. This is a quotation from the fifth commandment (Exod. 20:12; Deut. 5:16).

It is difficult to express the full sense of τίμα "honour, revere". Possibly "highly esteem" or "greatly respect" might be acceptable.

6:2b–3d This provides the grounds for the exhortation of 6:2a.

6:2b *God* promised The abstract noun in the phrase ἐν ἐπαγγελίᾳ "with a promise" needs to be expressed in the display as an event and the agent in the event needs to be stated, e.g. "*God* promised". In the propositionalised text, this acts as orienter for 6:3.

6:3a that *if you do this* [6:2a], This provides the necessary condition for 6:3b–c. If children obey the command to honour their parents, then the blessings that God promised (6:3b–c) will be experienced.

6:3b–c you will prosper and you will live a long time on the earth. The quotation is from the LXX version of Exodus 20:12, but with the omission of the final phrase, "which the Lord thy God giveth thee". It is generally agreed that it has been omitted in order to generalise the promise, so that it is not confined to one land or people, but is intended for obedient children everywhere. Thus, ἐπὶ τῆς γῆς, which in the Old Testament originally refers to the land of Canaan, is here used in the general sense of "on the earth".

6:3d This [6:2a] is the first law which *God* commanded in which *he also* promises something. The construction ἐντολὴ πρώτη ἐν ἐπαγγελίᾳ "the first commandment with a promise" provides further information about the command stated in 6:2a. It stresses the importance of the commandment.

The Greek text order is 6:2a, 6:3d, 6:3b–c, i.e. this statement precedes the promise itself. In the reordering in the display, it is placed after the promise.

The main problem is how to understand πρώτη "first" in this context. It may have one of the following senses:

1. It is the first commandment, as far as order is concerned, connected with a promise.

2. It is the most important commandment which is accompanied by a promise.

There are difficulties with both options.

Paul is referring to the fifth commandment in the Decalogue. It is not true to say that this is the first commandment with a promise (the second also has a promise). It is also unlikely that anyone would describe it as the most important commandment.

Commentators produce many arguments to resolve these problems. However, none are completely satisfactory.

Most commentaries and versions follow the first alternative, despite its difficulties, and so this is represented in the display.

6:4 Paul now turns to address fathers/parents as regards their duty to their children. He does this first negatively (6:4a), and then positively (6:4b).

6:4a Fathers, It is not clear whether this command is addressed to fathers only or to both parents.

The argument for including both parents in the meaning here is that it would be consistent with 6:1–3 where both parents are included.

However, the use of πατέρες to include both parents is rare. And, in Paul's time, it was the father who was considered to rule the household and, therefore, have the responsibility to discipline his children.

So it is most likely that Paul wants to focus on "fathers". This is how it has been translated in most versions.

do not *behave unreasonably towards* **your children** *with the result that* **you cause them to become angry,** Paul is warning Christian fathers (parents) not to exercise authority over their children in a wrong manner, not in a way that will make it hard for their children to obey them. Rather, they should use that authority wisely and not make unreasonable, provocative demands of their children. Such demands would inevitably cause exasperation, friction, an angry reaction.

A literal translation of παροργίζετε "make angry" may not be adequate in this context. Legitimate fatherly discipline might cause a child to become angry. So it might be necessary to include some implications of this verb in translation, e.g. that what is being required by the father is unreasonable. This might possibly be expressed as "do not over-correct your children and so cause them to become angry" or "do not behave unreasonably towards your children with the result that you cause them to become angry".

6:4b but bring them up well, Now Paul introduces a positive exhortation with ἀλλά "but", in contrast to the negative one in 6:4a.

The verb ἐκτρέφω is used in 5:29 in its sense of "nourish". Here, it has the sense "rear, bring up".

6:4c by means of your disciplining and instructing them in the way that the Lord *Jesus Christ teaches that you should do so.* The Greek phrase here is ἐν παιδείᾳ καὶ νουθεσίᾳ κυρίου "in the discipline and instruction of the Lord".

In this context, it is best to understand the preposition ἐν "in" as introducing the means by which the children are brought up well. It is represented in the display here by a means proposition.

The two abstract nouns here are παιδεία "discipline, upbringing, training" and νουθεσία "instruction, admonition". Commentators regard them in three ways:

1. They are more or less synonymous. See, for example, Abbott (p. 178), Moore (p. 49).
2. They have different meanings: the first is general and the second more specific. See, for example, Hodge (pp. 359–360), Lincoln (p. 407).
3. They have different meanings: the first refers to training by means of rules and regulations, rewards and punishments; the second refers to training by means of the spoken word, involving encouragement and warning or reproof. See, for example, Ellicott (p. 115), Hendriksen (p. 262), Hoehner (pp. 797–798).

The distinction between the two terms is difficult to define. Many versions translate them by words such as "discipline" and "instruction" and these terms seem appropriate, especially if the word for "instruction" includes the idea of warning when needed.

Most commentators agree that κυρίου "of (the) Lord" refers to "the Lord Jesus Christ". This would agree with 4:20–21 which refers to believers learning Christ and being taught in him.

However, they discuss the meaning of the genitive παιδείᾳ καὶ νουθεσίᾳ κυρίου "in the discipline and admonition of (the) Lord":

1. Some understand it as a subjective genitive, i.e. the discipline and instruction are such as

the Lord prescribes or approves of. See, for example, Ellicott (p. 116), Hendriksen (pp. 262-263), Hodge (pp. 360-361), Hoehner (pp. 798-799), Stott (p. 249).

2. Others understand it as an objective genitive or a genitive of quality, i.e. parents should instruct their children about the Lord, or as Lincoln (p. 408) says, the instruction should have "the Lord as its reference point". See also Bruce (p. 122), O'Brien (p.447).

Most commentators support the first option and view the expression as a subjective genitive. This can, therefore, be expressed as "in the way that the Lord Jesus Christ teaches you to discipline/instruct your children", "according to how the Lord Jesus Christ teaches that you do this" or "in a way that is approved by the Lord".

BOUNDARIES AND COHERENCE

The initial boundary has been discussed in the section on Boundaries and Coherence for 5:22-33.

The final boundary is marked by a change of participants: Paul stops addressing children and parents (6:1-4) and, in 6:5-9, begins to address servants and their masters. Consequently, there is a change of semantic domain, from that relating to "immediate family" to that relating to "those serving their masters in the household or elsewhere".

The cohesion and resulting coherence of 4:1-4 as a paragraph consists of repeated references to the participants:

τέκνα "children"
γονεῖς "parents"
πατήρ "father"
μήτηρ "mother"

The cohesion is strengthened by the use of vocabulary belonging to the semantic domain of "right behaviour":

ὑπακούετε "obey" (6:1)
δίκαιον "right" (6:1)
τίμα "honour" (6:2)
ἐκτρέφετε "nurture" (6:4)
παιδεία "discipline" (6:4)
νουθεσία "instruction, admonition" (6:4)

Also, the occurrence of ἐν κυρίῳ "in (the) Lord" (6:1) and κυρίου "of (the) Lord" (6:4) enhances the unity of the paragraph.

PROMINENCE AND THEME

In 6:1-4, there are two naturally prominent NUCLEI, 6:1a and 6:4b. The propositional clusters in which they occur are linked by the conjunction καί "and" in 6:4a.

Since this is a hortatory paragraph, the theme statement is based on the NUCLEUS (6:1a) of the first set of exhortations and the POSITIVE EXHORTATION in 6:4b, plus the grounds (6:1b-c) for the first exhortation. A summary representation of the means (6:4c) is also included since this is needed to complete the exhortation in 6:4b.

SECTION CONSTITUENT 6:5–9 (Hortatory Paragraph: Nucleus₅ of 5:15–6:9)

THEME: Slaves, obey and serve your earthly masters wholeheartedly, since the Lord will reward each person for whatever good thing that person does. Masters, treat your slaves well, since you know that their Lord and yours deals with all people impartially.

RELATIONAL STRUCTURE	CONTENTS
EXHORTATION₁ —CONGRUENCE	6:5a Slaves, obey your earthly masters very respectfully [HYP] and sincerely,
└standard	6:5b just as you obey Christ.
EXHORTATION₁ AMPLIFIED — NUCLEUS₁ — POSITIVE ┬ negative	6:6a Obey your masters not only when they are watching you, nor only to impress them favourably,
│ ├ NUCLEUS₁	6:6b obey them as slaves of Christ *should*.
│ └ NUCLEUS₂	6:6c Do what God wants *you to do* wholeheartedly.
NUCLEUS₂ — NUCLEUS	6:7a Serve *your masters* zealously.
└manner ┬ POSITIVE	6:7b *Serve them zealously* as you would serve the Lord *Jesus*,
└ negative	6:7c and not *merely* as you would serve men.
motivational grounds ┬ orienter	6:8a *Do this* [6:5–7] *since* you know
├ CONSEQUENCE	6:8b that the Lord *Jesus Christ* will reward each person for whatever good thing that person has done,
└ condition	6:8c whether a person is a slave or a free person.
EXHORTATION₂ — GENERIC — NUCLEUS	6:9a And, you masters, treat your slaves *well*,
└ comparison	6:9b just as they should serve you *well*.
└ specific	6:9c *Specifically*, stop threatening them.
grounds ┬ orienter	6:9d *Do this* [6:9a–c], *since* you know
├ NUCLEUS₁	6:9e that the one who is both their Lord and your Lord is in heaven,
└ NUCLEUS₂	6:9f and he *deals with* all people impartially.

INTENT AND STRUCTURE

In this paragraph (6:5–9), Paul wants to encourage slaves and their masters to submit to one another (5:21) and to behave towards each other in a manner which is appropriate for those whom the Lord has called to be his people (4:1), who are controlled by the Holy Spirit (5:18).

NOTES

There are many similarities between this passage and the parallel passage in Colossians 3:22–4:1.

6:5a Slaves, obey your earthly masters The phrase τοῖς κατὰ σάρκα κυρίοις "masters according to the flesh" contrasts with ὑμῶν ὁ κύριός ἐστιν ἐν οὐρανοῖς "your Lord/Master who is in heaven" (6:9). It is a synecdoche, i.e. the part σάρξ "flesh" represents the human being as a whole person. Since an adjective ("human") rather than a noun is appropriate here, the whole phrase means "human/earthly masters".

very respectfully The expression μετὰ φόβου καὶ τρόμου "with fear and trembling" describes the nature of the obedience required. It is an idiom indicating a deeply respectful attitude. It is probably an example of a hendiadys serving as a hyperbole. That is, it does not mean that the slave is literally to tremble with servile fear before his master, but that he should show great respect for his master's authority. In the display, the two abstract nouns, φόβος "fear" and τρόμος "trembling", are expressed by an adverbial phrase qualifying the verb ὑπακούετε "obey": "obey...very respectfully". NJB translates the adverbial phrase as "with deep respect".

and sincerely, The expression ἐν ἁπλότητι τῆς καρδίας ὑμῶν "in singleness of your heart" further qualifies the verb ὑπακούετε "obey". The noun ἁπλότης means "simplicity, sincerity, uprightness, frankness". It is a Greek idiom used to describe behaviour which is sincere and without pretence.

6:5b just as you obey Christ. The phrase ὡς τῷ Χριστῷ "as to Christ" means that the obedience which the slaves should show their masters is the same kind/degree of obedience that they should show Christ.

Some ways to translate it are:

"as though you were serving Christ" (TEV)
"just as you would obey Christ" (NIV)
"Serve them...as you would serve Christ" (NLT)

The relationship between 6:5b and 6:5a is one of standard-CONGRUENCE. The obedience of the slaves to Christ is the standard against which their obedience to their human masters is to be measured.

6:6–7 These two propositional clusters amplify 6:5, further explaining the nature of the obedience which slaves should show to their masters. This is shown in a chiastic structure:

A Obey your masters not only to impress them favourably (6:6a).
  B Obey them as slaves of Christ should (6:6b).
    C Do what God wants you to do wholeheartedly (6:6c).
    C' Serve your masters zealously (6:7a).
  B' Serve them zealously as you would serve the Lord (6:7b).
A' Do not serve them merely as you would serve men (6:7c).

6:6 This propositional cluster contains a negative exhortation (6:6a) and a positive exhortation (6:6b–c). The positive exhortation is the more prominent.

6:6a Obey your masters not only when they are watching you, The Greek noun ὀφθαλμοδουλία "eye-service" refers to service which is performed only to attract attention and praise. Commentators differ about the sort of work it is referring to. They suggest:

1. It refers to good work being done only when the slave was actually being watched.
2. It refers to doing only such work as could obviously be seen.

In the context of this passage either alternative is acceptable, since it is their motivation that is in view and that is the same in both cases, i.e. they should be working well to please the Lord and not people.

In the clause μὴ κατ' ὀφθαλμοδουλίαν "do not (obey) by way of eye-service", there is an ellipsis of the imperative verb ὑπακούετε "obey". It is made explicit in the display.

nor only to impress them favourably, The Greek word ἀνθρωπάρεσκος is an adjective functioning as a complex noun. It means "one who tries to please men at the expense of principle". Here then, it refers to slaves who are not motivated by the desire to please God, nor by a desire to do a good job. Their motivation is to create a favourable impression. In the display, ἀνθρωπάρεσκοι is expressed as "only to impress them favourably".

The ὡς in the clause ὡς ἀνθρωπάρεσκοι "as men-pleasers" can have two meanings:

1. It indicates a comparison relation, i.e. "as men-pleasers do".
2. It may mean "as *being* men-pleasers".

The latter seems more appropriate in the context. NCV expresses it "You must do this not only while they are watching you, to please them". It might also be expressed:

"Obey your masters not only when they are watching you, nor only to impress them favourably".
"Do not obey your masters only when they are watching you, do not *merely* try to impress them favourably".

6:6b–c The positive side of the exhortation is now introduced by the conjunction ἀλλά "but". It consists of two co-ordinate NUCLEI.

6:6b obey them as slaves of Christ *should*. In the phrase ὡς δοῦλοι Χριστοῦ "as slaves of Christ", there is again an ellipsis of the verb ὑπακούετε "obey".

6:6c Do what God wants *you to do* wholeheartedly. The genitive construction here, τὸ θέλημα τοῦ θεοῦ "the will of God", may be expressed as "what God wants *you to do*".

The phrase ἐκ ψυχῆς "from the soul", which also occurs in Colossians 3:23, is an idiom meaning "wholeheartedly", "genuinely".

Commentators discuss how the phrase connects to the rest of the text. They suggest:

1. It is attached to ποιοῦντες τὸ θέλημα τοῦ θεοῦ "doing the will of God" (6:6c). See, for

example, Best (p. 578), Eadie (p. 450), Hodge (p. 365), Hoehner (p. 809).
2. It is attached to μετ' εὐνοίας δουλεύοντες "with goodwill serving as slaves" (6:7). See, for example, Abbott (p. 179), Alford (p. 142), Robinson (p. 211).

The first option has the best support. It fits well with the exhortation in 6:6 which is concerned with the attitude of the slave to his work. The majority view is followed in the display.

6:7a–c These three propositions provide the elements to complete the chiasmus begun in 6:6. See the notes on 6:6-7.

6:7a Serve *your masters* zealously. The present participle δουλεύοντες has the force of an imperative: "serve *your masters*".

The prepositional phrase μετ' εὐνοίας "with goodwill" qualifies δουλεύοντες and may be expressed as "willingly", "unreservedly", "unstintingly", "zealously", any expression which describes service which is ungrudgingly and cheerfully given.

6:7b–c *Serve them zealously* as you would serve the Lord *Jesus*, and not *merely* as you would serve men. Commentators suggest two ways in which ὡς introduces the two phrases ὡς τῷ κυρίῳ "as to the Lord" (6:7b) and καὶ οὐκ ἀνθρώποις "and not to men" (6:7c):

1. By means of a positive/negative comparison, these phrases clarify the way believing slaves are to serve their masters. This is similar to the parallel passage in Colossians 3:23.
2. ὡς introduces a grounds, i.e. "since you are serving the Lord Jesus Christ and you are not *merely* serving men".

Both make good sense, but ὡς is more commonly used to introduce comparisons, so the first option is followed in the display.

The phrase ὡς τῷ κυρίῳ "as to the Lord" is understood to refer to the Lord Jesus Christ here and in 6:8, in view of the fact in 6:5-6 servants are urged to serve their masters "as to Christ" and "as slaves of Christ".

6:8 This propositional cluster provides a motivational grounds for 6:5-7. Slaves should serve their earthly masters faithfully and diligently, whether or not their earthly masters reward them for their work. They should remember that they will receive good things from their heavenly Master as a reward for doing so.

6:8a *Do this* [6:5-7] *since* you know The participle εἰδότες "knowing" functions as an orienter for 6:8b–c. The content of the orienter provides a grounds for 6:5-7.

To show the relationships clearly, "*Do this* [6:5-7]" is made explicit in the display and the grounds relation is expressed as "*since*".

6:8b–c that the Lord *Jesus Christ* will reward each person for whatever good thing that person has done, whether a person is a slave or a free person. In the clause τοῦτο κομίσεται παρὰ κυρίου "this he will receive from (the) Lord", the verb κομίζω means "receive back, recover one's own". This is the normal meaning of the verb.

That which is to be "received back" is τοῦτο, which refers to τι ἀγαθόν "any good (thing)". The Lord will appropriately reward everyone for any good thing he has done. In the expression παρὰ κυρίου "from (the) Lord", the Lord probably refers to the Lord Jesus Christ. See the parallel passage in Colossians 3:24.

According to most commentators, this refers to the future. Hoehner (p. 812) says, "That future time most likely refers to the judgment seat of Christ when all believers will receive recompense for the deeds they have done (2 Cor. 5:10)".

6:9 Paul now addresses the masters and tells them how they should behave towards their slaves.

6:9a–b And, you masters, treat your slaves *well*, just as they should serve you *well*. The initial καί marks this exhortation as co-ordinate with that of 6:5a in which Paul addresses the slaves.

In the clause τὰ αὐτὰ ποιεῖτε πρὸς αὐτούς "the same (things) do to them", the pronoun αὐτούς refers to "the slaves".

Paul now exhorts the masters "to do the same things" to their slaves as the slaves do to them. Clearly, slaves and masters have different roles, so, for example, Paul is not telling the masters to obey their slaves. Both slave and master, however, have the same duty to serve the Lord. Therefore, just as the Lord requires a slave to serve his master honestly and wholeheartedly, so the master is required to treat his slaves well and with a concern for their welfare. He is to remember that Christ is just as much his Master as Master to his slaves.

The sense might be best expressed by two propositions, as shown in the display, with τὰ αὐτά "the same (things)" expressing a comparison of equality, hence the comparison proposition 6:9b.

6:9c *Specifically,* **stop threatening them.** This proposition is in a specific relationship with 6:9a.

The participle ἀνιέντες "give up, cease from" acts as an imperative. Paul is telling masters to cease/stop τὴν ἀπειλήν "the threatening" of their servants. The implication is that masters were in the habit of using threats to make their slaves obey them. Paul commands them to stop doing so.

6:9d *Do this* **[6:9a–c],** *since* **you know** The participle εἰδότες functions as an orienter, as it does in 6:8. It introduces a grounds for what precedes, i.e. *"since you know…"*.

6:9e–f that the one who is both their Lord and your Lord is in heaven and he *deals with* all people impartially. The word ὅτι "that" introduces the content of εἰδότες "knowing". These two propositions are co-ordinate, the Greek clauses being linked by καί.

There are a number of textual variations here, but καὶ αὐτῶν καὶ ὑμῶν ὁ κύριος "both of them and of you the Lord" is the best attested. It emphasises that both earthly masters and their slaves have the same heavenly Master.

In the clause προσωπολημψία οὐκ ἔστιν παρ' αὐτῷ "partiality is not with him" (6:9f), the pronoun αὐτῷ "him" refers to "the Lord". He treats all people the same and with complete justice. He is not influenced by a person's wealth or status, by whether the person is master or slave or even by an outward show of good behaviour. His judgements are based upon a person's inner attitudes and motivations, e.g. whether a person truly desires to serve and obey the Lord. This is made clear throughout this paragraph (6:5–9) by such phrases as "as to Christ" (6:5), "doing the will of God" (6:6) and "as to the Lord" (6:7).

Although most of the commentators consider that "Lord" here refers to Christ rather than God, there is no decisive evidence in favour of either one, since impartiality is attributed to both in Scripture. It is preferable, therefore, to leave the term Lord ambiguous, if possible. If a decision needs to be made, then the majority view may be followed.

In the context of 6:8, with its reference to rewards, it is possible that there may be an implicit reference to the final judgment in this clause. This might be expressed as "he *judges* all people impartially". Alternatively, the intention might be to make the masters conscious of their present accountability to the Lord, in which case it might be expressed as "he *deals with* all people impartially".

BOUNDARIES AND COHERENCE

The initial boundary has been discussed in the section on Boundaries and Coherence for 6:1–4.

The final boundary is marked by the start of a new section at 6:10. This is signalled by τοῦ λοιποῦ "for the rest, finally", as Paul turns from the list of specific exhortations linked to ἀξίως περιπατῆσαι "walk worthily" (4:1), to write a final hortatory unit related to the means by which the believer will be able to accomplish Paul's earlier exhortations.

There is also a change of semantic domain, from that of "right attitudes" between slaves and masters to that of "warfare", and a change of participants from "slaves" and "masters" to a more general second person plural.

There is lexical cohesion in this paragraph in the repetition of δοῦλος "slave" (6:5, 6), alongside κύριος "lord/master" (6:5, 9).

Also, there are other words belonging to the semantic domain of the master/servant relationship, having to do with obedience, service and the attitudes which are desirable in both master and slave.

PROMINENCE AND THEME

This hortatory paragraph comprises two complex EXHORTATIONS and two grounds. Since both exhortation and grounds are essential parts of a hortatory unit, the theme statement includes significant parts of each.

SUBPART CONSTITUENT 6:10–20
(Hortatory Section: Nucleus₂ of 4:1–6:20 [Climax])

THEME: At all times, rely wholeheartedly on the Lord Jesus Christ to strengthen you. Make use of every spiritual resource which God provides for you, in order to successfully resist the devil and all his powerful evil spirits. At the same time, persevere in prayer to God for all his people.

MACROSTRUCTURE	CONTENTS
NUCLEUS	6:10–13 At all times, rely wholeheartedly on the Lord Jesus Christ to strengthen you. Make use of every spiritual resource which God provides for you, in order to successfully resist the devil and all his powerful evil spirits.
AMPLIFICATION	6:14–20 Firmly resist the devil and all his evil spirits. Do this by relying on the truth, on your righteous conduct, on the good news which gives you peace, on your faith in the Lord Jesus Christ, on the fact that God has saved you and on the word which God has given you by means of his Spirit. At the same time, always be alert and persevere in prayer to God for all his people.

INTENT AND STRUCTURE

This 6:10–20 section ends the hortatory division of the epistle. Both paragraphs in this section are hortatory and their exhortations are similar.

In paragraph 6:10–13, Paul first urges the Ephesians to draw upon the mighty power of the Lord for their strength (6:10).

Then in 6:11–13, he explains why they need to be strong and how this mighty power is to be appropriated. They need to be strong spiritually if they are to be able to stand firm against the devil and all evil powers (6:12). In order to do this, they must make use of every spiritual resource which God makes available to them.

These resources are first introduced in general terms as "the whole armour of God" (6:11, 13). Then in paragraph 6:14–20, Paul repeats his exhortation to stand firm and describes in more detail the means to do so, that is, the various pieces of armour (6:14–17).

Finally (6:18–20), he emphasises persevering prayer as an essential accompaniment to everything else.

In a sense, these verses are both a summary of Paul's earlier exhortations and also the climax of the letter as a whole. See the discussion on 6:10–20 being a peak/climax in "Peak in Ephesians" under Epistle Constituent 1:3–6:20. Paul's intention is to sum up and reinforce the exhortations he has already made and, in this way, to stir the Ephesians to action.

In 4:1–6:9, he urged them to live in this world in a way which demonstrates that they are truly God's people. Now he refers to this as part of the larger struggle between the forces of good and evil. He wants them to resolutely resist Satan and all evil powers, using every spiritual resource which God has made available to them.

BOUNDARIES AND COHERENCE

The initial boundary has been discussed in the section on Boundaries and Coherence for 6:5–9.

The initial boundary of the next unit is marked by:

1. The use of δέ at the beginning of 6:21, introducing a change of subject matter.
2. Along with this, there is a tail-head link between 6:20 and 6:21. The topic of prayer begins in 6:18 with prayer for all believers. In 6:19–20, Paul asks for prayer for himself in relation to proclaiming the gospel. In 6:21 he leaves the topic of prayer, but retains the focus on his personal matters.

The topic of spiritual warfare gives coherence to this unit. Related to this is the use of the verbs:

ἐνδύω "put on" (6:11)
ἀναλαμβάνω "take up" (6:13, 16)
δέξομαι "take" (6:17)

Further evidence for the coherence of this unit is the use of the Greek root δυναμ- throughout, as in the following verb forms:

ἐνδυναμοῦσθε "be empowered" (6:10)
δύνασθαι "to be able" (6:11)
δυνηθῆτε "you may be able" (6:13)
δυνήσεσθε "you will be able" (6:16)

Other lexical items which are significant in the cohesion of this unit and express its coherence are the occurrences of ἵστημι and ἀνθίστημι:

στῆναι "to stand" (6:11, 13)
στῆτε "stand" (6:14)
ἀντιστῆναι "to stand-against/resist" (6:13)

Also significant are references to the devil and other forces of evil with whom the believer is to contend:

τοῦ διαβόλου "of the devil" (6:11)
τὰ πνευματικὰ τῆς πονηρίας "the spiritual forces of wickedness" (6:12)
τῇ ἡμέρᾳ τῇ πονηρᾷ "the evil day" (6:13)
τοῦ πονηροῦ "of the evil (one)" (6:16)

Verses 6:18–20 are also relevant to the topic of spiritual warfare. They focus on the necessity for prayer in the spiritual battle. They also provide a bridge with 6:21–22 which deals with more personal matters.

A number of versions begin a new paragraph at 6:18 (CEV, NASB, NRSV); others begin a new paragraph at 6:19 (NCV, NIV, NLT). Either is acceptable, since there is a switch of topic to "prayer" in 6:18 and there is a further switch to focus on Paul himself, in 6:19. However, it seems preferable to regard 6:18–20 as part of paragraph 6:14–20, since there are no non-subordinated finite verbs in 6:18–20, only participles, infinitives and subordinate clauses.

PROMINENCE AND THEME

This unit consists of a NUCLEUS (6:10–13) and AMPLIFICATION (6:14–20). The NUCLEUS is naturally prominent. However, since it is amplified at great length and because of its hortatory nature, the AMPLIFICATION is also prominent. The theme statement, therefore, is based on both the NUCLEUS and AMFLICATION.

SECTION CONSTITUENT 6:10–13 (Hortatory Paragraph: Nucleus of 6:10–20)

THEME: At all times, rely wholeheartedly on the Lord Jesus Christ to strengthen you. Make use of every spiritual resource which God provides for you, in order to successfully resist the devil and all his powerful evil spirits.

RELATIONAL STRUCTURE	CONTENTS
EXHORTATION₁	6:10 Finally, at all times, *rely wholeheartedly* on the Lord *Jesus Christ* to strengthen you *spiritually* by means of his own mighty power [HEN].
EXHORTATION₂ — MEANS — comparison	6:11a *Just as a soldier* puts on all *his* armour,
EXHORTATION₂ — MEANS — NUCLEUS	6:11b *so* you should make use of every *spiritual* resource which God *provides for you* [MET],
EXHORTATION₂ — purpose	6:11c in order that you may be able to *successfully* resist *when* the devil schemes *against you*.
grounds — negative	6:12a *You must do this* [6:11b] since we *believers* are not contending against human beings [SYN],
grounds — POSITIVE	6:12b but rather, we are contending against evil spirits who rule and have authority over all that is evil [MET] in this world. We are contending against evil spirits in heavenly places (*or,* unseen evil spirits which are everywhere).
EXHORTATION₂ restated — MEANS — comparison	6:13a Therefore, *just as a soldier* puts on all *his* armour,
EXHORTATION₂ restated — MEANS — NUCLEUS	6:13b *so* you should make use of every *spiritual* resource which God *provides for you* [MET].
PURPOSE — NUCLEUS₁	6:13c *Do this* [6:13b] in order that you may be able to *successfully* resist *the devil and all his powerful* evil *spirits* whenever they may attack you,
PURPOSE — NUCLEUS₂	6:13d and, in order that, *each time* you resist *them* to the utmost, you will remain resolute/undefeated *spiritually*.

INTENT AND STRUCTURE

This is a hortatory paragraph. This is signalled by:

1. The three imperatives:

   ἐνδυναμοῦσθε "be empowered" (6:10)
   ἐνδύσασθε "put on" (6:11)
   ἀναλάβετε "take up" (6:13)

2. Along with this is the use of ὅτι "because, since" (6:12) and διὰ τοῦτο "therefore" (6:13).

EXHORTATION₂ (6:11) is restated in 6:13. These two exhortations bracket 6:12 which provides the grounds for both of them and less directly for EXHORTATION₁. The restatement gives emphasis especially to EXHORTATION₂.

In this paragraph (6:11-13), Paul wants to make the Ephesians aware that it is not physical attacks they need to be ready for, but spiritual attacks from the devil and all other evil powers.

By this warning, he wants them to prepare for such attacks, so that, when they occur, the Ephesians will be able to resolutely resist. Paul assures them that all the Lord's power is available to them, as are all God's spiritual resources.

NOTES

6:10 Finally, The term τοῦ λοιποῦ "for the rest, finally" indicates the final point to be made in the presentation of the material in the BODY of the letter. It introduces the conclusion of the BODY, which gives directions as to how the Ephesian believers should prepare themselves for the struggle against Satan and every evil power.

Some manuscripts have the accusative τὸ λοιπόν "finally", which might have been expected here, instead of the genitive τοῦ λοιποῦ. However, it seems that they are used interchangeably.

In manuscripts with τὸ λοιπόν, ἀδελφοί μου "my brothers" occurs between τὸ λοιπόν and ἐνδυναμοῦσθε "be strong", but most versions do not include this phrase.

at all times, *rely wholeheartedly* on the Lord *Jesus Christ* to strengthen you *spiritually* The imperative ἐνδυναμοῦσθε may be:

1. Middle, i.e. "strengthen yourselves". See, for example, Bratcher and Nida (pp. 157-158), Lenski (p. 656).
2. Passive, i.e. "be strengthened". See, for example, Hoehner (p. 820), Lincoln (p. 441), O'Brien (p. 460).

Most commentators consider it to be passive, since this would indicate that the strength is to be drawn from an external source, the Lord. Further support for this view comes from Paul's prayer in 3:16, "that you may be strengthened with power through his Spirit".

Here, the present tense, literally "be being strengthened/empowered", indicates that the process is a continuous one. This is represented propositionally as "at all times".

Most commentators agree that ἐν κυρίῳ "in (the) Lord", in this context, refers to the Lord Jesus Christ.

In the phrase ἐνδυναμοῦσθε ἐν κυρίῳ "be strengthened/empowered in (the) Lord", the passive command might best be expressed actively as "*rely wholeheartedly/completely* on the Lord *Jesus Christ* to strengthen you".

by means of his own mighty power. The genitive construction ἐν τῷ κράτει τῆς ἰσχύος αὐτοῦ "in the might of his strength" recalls τοῦ κράτους τῆς ἰσχύος αὐτοῦ "of the might of his strength" in 1:19.

It is possible to consider the two nouns κράτος "might" and ἰσχύς "strength" in two ways:

1. A meaning distinction between the two nouns should be retained.
2. The two nouns are regarded as hendiadys, i.e. in "his mighty power".

Since only one concept is being referred to, i.e. "his strength/power", this second option seems appropriate and is followed in the display. The ἐν construction is expressed as "by means of his own mighty power". The ἐν "in, by" indicates the means or the source of the strengthening.

6:11a-b *Just as a soldier* puts on all *his* armour, *so* you should make use of every *spiritual* resource which God *provides for you*, Paul now amplifies what he said in 6:10. He explains how a believer can become strong spiritually and, therefore, able to resist all evil powers. The metaphor of a soldier and his armour is introduced. Just as a soldier should make use of all the armour that is available to him when he is going into battle, so a believer should make use of all the spiritual resources that God makes available to him when he needs to fight against Satan and all his evil powers.

Most commentators agree that the expression τὴν πανοπλίαν τοῦ θεοῦ "the whole armour of God" refers to the spiritual resources which God provides for the believer. The completeness of the provision is expressed by τὴν πανοπλίαν "the whole armour".

In the display, the image is expressed in 6:11a while the non-figurative meaning of the image is made explicit in 6:11b as: "you should make use of every *spiritual* resource which God *provides for you*".

6:11c in order that you may be able to *successfully* resist *when* the devil schemes *against you*. This proposition is in a purpose relationship with 6:11b, as indicated in the Greek by πρὸς τὸ δύνασθαι "in order to be able".

The military phrase στῆναι πρός "to stand against" means to stand firm in the face of attack. In this context, the attack is spiritual and it is τὰς μεθοδείας τοῦ διαβόλου "the schemes of the devil" which are to be resisted. This is expressed in the display as "*successfully* resist". It is unlikely that "stand against" in the Greek text needs to be analysed as a live metaphor in this context, the senses of the verb ἵστημι had long before been extended to include abstract senses such as in this context (cf. Rom. 11:20; 1 Cor. 7:37).

6:12a *You must do this* [6:11b] *since we believers* are not contending against human beings, The initial ὅτι "because, since" introduces a grounds relationship. The question is which of the two clauses in 6:11 does it support as grounds:

1. It is the grounds for Paul's reference to withstanding the schemes of the devil (στῆναι πρὸς τὰς μεθοδείας τοῦ διαβόλου).
2. It is the grounds for the command ἐνδύσασθε τὴν πανοπλίαν τοῦ θεοῦ "put on the whole armour of God".

The second option is followed in the display, since it incorporates the former.

The Greek noun πάλη "wrestling/struggle" (rendered as a verb in the display) comes from a sporting context, but can also refer to a hand-to-hand military battle. Here, it denotes the intense and personal nature of the struggle, as the believer contends with spiritual enemies.

The expression αἷμα καὶ σάρκα "blood and flesh" is a synecdoche for "human beings".

This proposition states negatively what is expressed positively by 6:12b.

6:12b but rather, we are contending against evil spirits who rule and have authority over all that is evil in this world. Unit 6:12b is the nucleus of the propositional cluster 6:12a–b.

The conjunction ἀλλά "but" introduces a statement concerning those against whom believers are fighting. This contrasts with human enemies in 6:12a. Believers are not fighting against people, but against evil spiritual powers. Since we are told in 6:12a that it is not human enemies that believers are to prepare to resist, the powers listed in 6:12b must be supernatural and, by implication, evil.

The repetition of πρός "against" before each "powerful being" is for emphasis. It draws attention to the variety and strength of the evil spiritual powers against which the believer must fight.

The powers listed in this verse are:

αἱ ἀρχαί "rulers"
αἱ ἐξουσίαι "authorities"
οἱ κοσμοκράτορες τοῦ σκότους τούτου "the world rulers of this darkness"
τὰ πνευματικὰ τῆς πονηρίας ἐν τοῖς ἐπουρανίοις "spiritual forces of wickedness in the heavenly places"

Similar lists are to be found in 1:21 and Colossians 1:16. As noted above, in this context, these terms refer to evil, supernatural powers, contrasting with the human powers referred to in 6:12a.

Some commentators suggest that the list of powers in 6:12b indicates a hierarchy of evil powers, but most commentators agree that the list is simply meant to indicate how varied and comprehensive the devil's power is. Callow, when commenting on the list of spirit beings in Colossians 1:16, says,

> Since it is generally agreed that precise distinctions were probably not intended, and that, if they were, they are no longer known, it is very difficult to translate the list as it stands (1983:75; 2002:45).

This seems to be the case here also.

In the genitive construction τοὺς κοσμοκράτορας τοῦ σκότους τούτου "the world rulers of this darkness", the reference to darkness recalls 5:8 and 5:11, where "darkness" is used as a picture of the past life from which believers have been delivered.

The sense of the construction here is "those who rule-over/control all that is evil in this world".

Although it may be difficult when translating into many languages to find a range of terms to describe and distinguish between different evil powers, it is good to use as wide a spectrum as possible.

We are contending against evil spirits in heavenly places (*or,* unseen evil spirits which are everywhere). In the genitive construction τὰ πνευματικὰ τῆς πονηρίας "the spiritual forces of wickedness", the noun πονηρίας "wickedness" signifies the wickedness and cruelty while πνευματικά indicates the fact that they are unseen spirits. Most commentators agree that the substantive phrase τὰ πνευματικὰ τῆς πονηρίας "the spiritual forces of wickedness" denotes evil spirits collectively. See, for example, Hendriksen (p. 272), Hodge (p. 379), Lincoln (p. 444), O'Brien (p. 467).

Most commentators agree that the phrase ἐν τοῖς ἐπουρανίοις "in the heavenly places" is attached to the preceding phrase τὰ πνευματικὰ τῆς πονηρίας, i.e. the spiritual forces of evil which are in the heavenly places. The phrase ἐν τοῖς ἐπουρανίοις "in the heavenly places" is also used in 1:3, 20; 2:6; 3:10 and, in each of these verses, it refers to a location.

However, it is not clear in this context which location Paul meant and there is no consensus among the commentators. They suggest:

1. It refers to heaven in a wide sense, as opposed to earth. See, for example, Hodge (pp. 380–381).
2. It refers to the lower heavens, the region above the earth, but below the heaven where God dwells. In 2:2, this is called the domain of the air. See, for example, Ellicott (pp. 121–122), Hendriksen (p. 273), Lenski (pp. 661–662).

It is not possible to be sure what Paul meant here. However, it serves to emphasise the nature of the forces ranged against them.

In context, Paul's point seems to be that these spirits are powerful. They are evil, they are unseen and, it may be inferred, they are everywhere.

6:13 One of the functions of aorist verb forms is to emphasise urgency. Four of the five aorist verbs in this verse, including ἀναλάβετε "take up", potentially have that function here. See Hendriksen, p. 273, fn. 171.

6:13a–b Therefore, The initial διὰ τοῦτο "because of this, therefore" refers back to the contents of 6:12. In that verse, Paul warned the Ephesian believers about the strength of the evil spirits opposing them. On the basis of this, the exhortation of 6:11 is reiterated in a slightly different form. This repetition gives further emphasis and urgency to it.

just as a soldier **puts on all** *his* **armour,** *so* **you should make use of every** *spiritual* **resource which God** *provides for you.* The image is expressed in 6:13a. The non-figurative meaning is made explicit in 6:13b.

6:13c *Do this* **[6:13b] in order that you may be able to** *successfully* **resist** *the devil and all his powerful* **evil** *spirits* **whenever they may attack you,** This purpose clause, introduced by ἵνα "in order that", reiterates the purpose clause 6:11c i.e. "in order that you may be able to resist the schemes of the devil".

The event represented by δυνηθῆτε ἀντιστῆναι "you may be able to withstand/resist" has an implied object: the devil and all the powers of evil referred to in 6:11 and 6:12. A number of commentators, for example, Hendriksen (pp. 273-274), Hodge (p. 381), Lenski (p. 663), suggest that ἀντιστῆναι has the sense of "to successfully resist" in this context. This is supported by what immediately follows: καὶ ἅπαντα κατεργασάμενοι στῆναι "and, having done everything, to stand firm". This implies that, despite the spiritual attacks of the devil and all other evil powers, believers will not have given way, but will have successfully resisted.

Commentators suggest a number of ways to understand ἐν τῇ ἡμέρᾳ τῇ πονηρᾷ "in the evil day". The main suggestions are:

1. It refers to a particular time of special tribulation immediately preceding the end of the world. See, for example, Meyer (pp. 541-542).
2. It refers to any time of particular crisis or trial which may come to an individual believer. See, for example, Hendriksen (p. 273), Hodge (p. 381), Lenski (p. 663), Stott (p. 275).
3. It refers to the present age as a whole, i.e. the time between the two comings of Jesus. It, therefore, may be synonymous with "the evil days" referred to in 5:16. See, for example, Bruce (p. 129).

Other commentators favour a combination of views.

It is difficult to decide which of these options is appropriate in this context and there are many detailed arguments in the commentaries related to this. It would seem that Paul's main concern is to prepare believers to be resolute in their resistance of evil in the present, ongoing conflict. However, on balance, a combination of views 2 and 3 makes good sense. See, for example Hoehner (p. 834), O'Brien (p. 471). They argue that while "the evil day" refers to the time between the two comings of Jesus, it also refers to regular attacks by the devil and his evil spirits, and times when the devil's attacks are particularly powerful.

The implication is that believers need to be prepared at all times, since no one knows when the "evil day" will occur. In the display, this is expressed as "whenever they may attack you", with "they" referring to "the devil and all his evil spirits".

6:13d and, in order that, *each time* **you resist** *them* **to the utmost, you will remain resolute/undefeated** *spiritually.* This proposition is connected to 6:13c by καί "and". Together they provide a purpose for 6:13a–b.

The verb κατεργάζομαι usually means "to do/accomplish", but in some contexts it can mean "to overpower" or "to overcome". It is used twenty-two times in the New Testament, always meaning "to do/accomplish".

In this context, commentators suggest:

1. It has its most common meaning here and so the aorist participial phrase ἅπαντα κατεργασάμενοι means "having done all". It then refers to a believer having completed all his preparations for the struggle against all evil spiritual powers. He is ready to resist them. See, for example, Best (p. 597), Lincoln (p. 446), O'Brien (p. 472).

2. It has its less frequent meaning here: "to overcome" and so the participial phrase ἅπαντα κατεργασάμενοι στῆναι means "having conquered all (things), to stand". It then refers to a believer's having accomplished all that is required of him in his struggle against evil spiritual powers, i.e. to have been fully prepared for the struggle and to have resisted the evil powers successfully. See, for example, Hodge (p. 382), TEV.

There are strong arguments in favour of both options, but there is no consensus among commentators as to its meaning. The second option is preferred in this analysis. The believer must make use of every spiritual resource which God provides in order to ensure that, each time he is attacked by the devil or other evil spirits, he will be able to resist the attack successfully and be ready for the next attack. The sense of this being an ongoing battle and not final victory is expressed as "*each time* you resist *them* to the utmost".

The conjunction οὖν in 6:14 is understood as being resumptive rather than inferential. The following paragraph (6:14-20) provides an amplification of 6:10-13. The occurrence of στῆναι "to stand" in final position in 6:13, followed by the imperative στῆτε "stand", occurring initially in 6:14, supports the view that οὖν should be understood in its resumptive sense.

BOUNDARIES AND COHERENCE

The initial boundary has been discussed in the section on Boundaries and Coherence for 6:5-9.

The final boundary is marked by the following features:

1. The initial οὖν "therefore" in 6:14 marks the beginning of a new unit, where it has resumptive force.
2. The aorist imperative στῆτε "stand" at the beginning of 6:14 functions as part of a tail-head link with 6:13, where the final verb is the infinitive στῆναι "to stand".
3. There is a change from the generic statement about spiritual warfare (6:11-13) to specific aspects of that struggle.

The parallel structure (A, B; A', B') of this unit provides the main unifying factor as can be seen below (the numbering is according to the clauses of the Greek text rather than that of the display):

A Put on the whole armour of God (6:11a)
   B in order to stand against the enemy (6:11b)
      C since we are fighting a spiritual battle (6:12).
A' Take up the whole armour of God (6:13a)
   B' in order to stand against the enemy (6:13b-c).

There is no conjunction linking 6:11 and 6:10. However, the juxtaposition of the two imperatival verbal clauses in these two verses, ἐνδυναμοῦσθε ἐν κυρίῳ... "be empowered in (the) Lord..." (6:10) and ἐνδύσασθε τὴν πανοπλίαν τοῦ θεοῦ... "put on the whole armour of God..." (6:11) links them. The second imperatival clause may be understood as explaining how the first is to be achieved: to be strong in the Lord, believers must put on the whole armour of God.

There is lexical cohesion and coherence in these verses in the use of the various terms describing:

the powerful evil spirits they are to resist (6:11, 12)
the mighty power of the Lord (6:10)
the repetition of πρός "against" (6:11, 12 [five times])
ἵστημι "to stand", i.e. to withstand, resist firmly (6:11, 13), along with ἀντιστῆναι "to resist" (6:13)
πανοπλία "the whole armour" (6:11, 13)

These serve to introduce and sustain the military metaphor, which is developed further in 6:14-17.

PROMINENCE AND THEME

In an exhortation-grounds paragraph, both units are generally considered to be thematic and should be included in the theme statement. In this paragraph, both EXHORTATION₁ and EXHORTATION₂ are represented in the theme statement. The two purpose units (6:11c, 6:13c-d) have marked prominence as indicated by their close resemblance. They, along with the grounds unit (6:12), function as motivational grounds for the exhortations. These motivational grounds units are summarised in the theme statement.

SECTION CONSTITUENT 6:14–20
(Hortatory Paragraph: Amplification of 6:10–13)

THEME: Firmly resist the devil and all his evil spirits. Do this by relying on the truth, on your righteous conduct, on the good news which gives you peace, on your faith in the Lord Jesus Christ, on the fact that God has saved you and on the word which God has given you by means of his Spirit. At the same time, always be alert and persevere in prayer to God for all his people.

RELATIONAL STRUCTURE	CONTENTS
GENERIC EXHORTATION — NUCLEUS	6:14a You must firmly resist *the devil and all his evil spirits*,
└ comparison	6:14b *just as a soldier* must stand firm *against the enemy* [MET].
GENERIC	6:14c *Prepare for this* [6:14a] *by doing the following:*
SPECIFIC₁ — NUCLEUS	6:14d Conform to the truth *which is revealed in the gospel, in order to be spiritually strong*,
└ comparison	6:14e *just as a soldier prepares to stand firm against the enemy by* putting on *his* belt [MET].
SPECIFIC₂ — NUCLEUS	6:14f Act/live righteously *in order to protect yourselves against the devil and all his evil spirits*,
└ comparison	6:14g *just as a soldier prepares to stand firm against the enemy by* putting on a breastplate *in order to protect his chest* [MET].
SPECIFIC₃ — NUCLEUS	6:15a *Study to know* the good news about *how people can be at peace with God*,
ENABLING EXHORTATIONS₁ └ comparison	6:15b *just as a soldier* prepares *himself to stand firm against the enemy by* putting *his* shoes on *his* feet [MET].
SPECIFIC₄ — NUCLEUS	6:16a In addition, believe firmly *in the Lord Jesus Christ. This will* enable you to protect yourselves from anything the devil *may do to harm you spiritually*,
└ comparison	6:16b *just as a soldier* carries *his* shield *in order that he* may protect *himself* against the fire-tipped arrows which the enemy *shoots at him* [MET].
SPECIFIC₅ — NUCLEUS	6:17a Also rely on *the fact that the Lord-Jesus-Christ/God* has saved you, *in order to protect yourselves against the devil and all his evil spirits*,
└ comparison	6:17b *just as a soldier* puts on *his* helmet *in order to protect his head* [MET].
SPECIFIC₆ — NUCLEUS	6:17c And rely on the words God has spoken *by means of* the *Holy* Spirit *in order that you may be able to resist the devil and all his evil spirits*,
└ comparison	6:17d *just as a soldier* takes hold of *his* sword *in order to resist the enemy* [MET].
NUCLEUS₁	6:18a *As you are doing this* [6:14–17], keep on praying *to God* at all times and in every situation,
ENABLING EXHORTATIONS₂ NUCLEUS₂	6:18b and always *let the Holy* Spirit *guide you when you pray.*
NUCLEUS₃	6:18c For this purpose [6:18a–b] always be ready to pray,

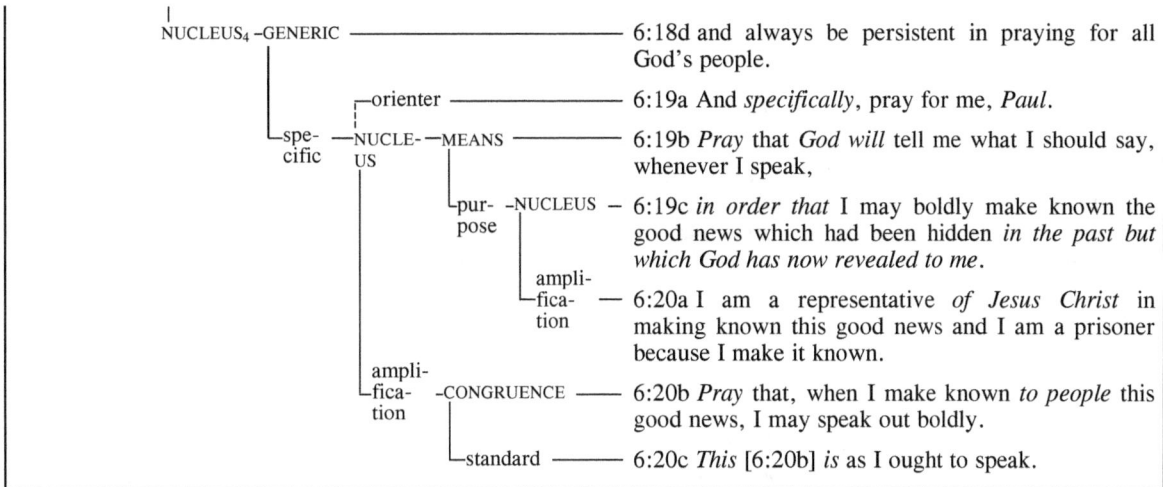

INTENT AND STRUCTURE

This 6:14-20 paragraph as presented in the display consists of a GENERIC EXHORTATION (6:14a-b) followed by two sets of ENABLING EXHORTATIONS: ENABLING EXHORTATIONS₁ (6:14c-17) and ENABLING EXHORTATIONS₂ (6:18-20).

In 6:14-16, there are four aorist participles:

περιζωσάμενοι "having girded"
ἐνδυσάμενοι "having put on"
ὑποδησάμενοι "having put shoes on"
ἀναλαβόντες "having taken up"

They all refer to actions to be taken before that of the aorist imperative στῆτε "stand" (6:14a). They function as imperatives and indicate the means by which the aorist imperative στῆτε "stand" is to be accomplished.

These actions enable a believer to be ready for spiritual warfare. They provide him with the means of resisting the attacks of Satan and all evil powers. The points of comparison between the military metaphors and the reality of the spiritual battle should not be understood too precisely. Paul applies them in a rather general manner, in order to make the point that God provides everything necessary for a believer to withstand the attacks of Satan.

In 6:18-20, Paul warns the believers that they need to be alert and prayerful at all times, in the face of Satan's attacks.

In this paragraph (6:14-20), Paul wants to encourage the Ephesian believers to be resolute in the face of all Satan's attempts to cause them to sin. Paul reminds them that the enemy they are fighting is not human but spiritual and, therefore, they need spiritual weapons to combat his attacks.

NOTES

6:14 The particle οὖν "therefore" may be inferential or resumptive. In this context, it is probably resumptive, indicating that Paul is going to continue with the topic of spiritual warfare, which he introduced in general terms in 6:10-13.

The fact that στῆναι "to stand" (6:13d) comes immediately before στῆτε "stand" (6:14a) is evidence that resumption is indicated here, so "therefore" is not included in the display.

In this paragraph, Paul describes in more detail the spiritual armour available to believers. This follows his exhortations, in 6:11 and 6:13, to put on that armour.

The EXHORTATIONS in this first set of ENABLING EXHORTATIONS are in an addition relation to each other as indicated by the use of καί "and" in 6:14, 15, 17 and in 6:16 by ἐπὶ πᾶσιν, or the alternative reading ἐν πᾶσιν, if the latter is also understood to mean "in addition to" (see note 6:16a-b).

Paul tells them that when they have prepared themselves by appropriating the spiritual resources represented by each piece of armour, they will be ready and able to resist the worst that Satan can do.

6:14a-b You must firmly resist *the devil and all his evil spirits, just as a soldier* must stand firm *against the enemy*. The verb ἵστημι "to stand" has already occurred in 6:11 and 6:13. Each occurrence is in a purpose clause. Here the aorist imperative στῆτε "stand" is used, emphasising the necessity of standing firm, ready to withstand the devil and all evil powers, in all situations and at all times. It is translated in different versions as "stand firm", "stand ready", "take your stand".

6:14c Prepare for this [6:14a] by doing the following: This proposition serves as a generic representation of the idea of preparation for standing firm implied in 6:14–17 and indicated by the use of the aorist tense in the participles that encode the events of putting on the armour.

6:14d-e Conform to the truth *which is revealed in the gospel, in order to be spiritually strong, just as a soldier prepares to stand firm against the enemy by* **putting on** *his* **belt.** In a Roman soldier's armour, the belt referred to by the verb περιζωσάμενοι "having girded (yourself)" was a leather apron which protected the thighs and was worn under the armour. It helped to keep the breastplate in place and supported the scabbard for the sword.

However, commentators do not agree about the meaning of the word ἀλήθεια "truth" in this context. There are three possibilities:

1. It refers to subjective truth, i.e. truth as an ethical quality, integrity, sincerity of character. See, for example, Bruce (p. 130), Hendriksen (p. 276), Lincoln (p. 448).
2. It refers to objective truth, the truth revealed by God in the gospel. See, for example, Lenski (p. 666), O'Brien (pp. 473–474).
3. It includes both ideas. See, for example, Ellicott (p. 123), Stott (pp. 277–278).

This last option seems appropriate in this context, since "one will not do without the other" (Gurnall, vol. 1, p. 291). The one who knows the truth as revealed in God's word must conform to its teaching and reveal it by a life of integrity.

6:14f-g Act/live righteously *in order to protect yourselves against the devil and all his evil spirits, just as a soldier prepares to stand firm against the enemy by* **putting on a breastplate** *in order to protect his chest.* The next piece of armour mentioned is the θώραξ "breastplate". This covered the soldier's chest and, possibly, his back, to protect it from weapons such as arrows, swords and spears. It is generally agreed that the allusion here is to Isaiah 59:17 and that the genitive construction τὸν θώρακα τῆς δικαιοσύνης "the breastplate of righteousness" is that of apposition, i.e. the breastplate is righteousness.

There is discussion among commentators as to the "righteousness" referred to in this context. There are two possibilities:

1. It is the righteousness imputed to the believer and which justifies him in the sight of God. See, for example, Hodge (p. 383), Lenski (pp. 666–667).
2. It is moral righteousness, the righteousness of character, which results from being justified in Christ. See, for example, Ellicott (p. 123), Hendriksen (pp. 276–277), Lincoln (p. 448), O'Brien (pp. 474–475).

The two options are closely linked. Imputed righteousness should result in a person's living a righteous life and it is impossible for someone to live a righteous life without first having the righteousness of Christ imputed to him. However, in this division of the letter (4:1–6:20), Paul's theme is urging the Ephesians to turn away from their old way of living and to live lives which are truly righteous. In this context, it seems appropriate to understand the righteousness referred to as being that of living a righteous life, maintaining a righteous character.

6:15a-b *Study to know* **the good news about how people can be at peace** *with God, just as a* **soldier** *prepares* **himself** *to stand firm against the enemy by* **putting** *his* **shoes on** *his* **feet.** The metaphor used here recalls Isaiah 52:7.

A Roman soldier wore heavy leather sandals with soles studded with nails. These enabled him to stand firm, even in difficult terrain. The point of comparison seems to be that, just as these sandals made the soldier ready for standing firm against the enemy, so should the believer be prepared for standing firm in spiritual conflict by means of "the gospel of peace".

The word "shoes" rather than "sandals" is used in the display text since in many cultures sandals are not thought of as footwear strong enough for battle.

The exact meaning of the double genitive construction ἐν ἑτοιμασίᾳ τοῦ εὐαγγελίου τῆς εἰρήνης "with the readiness/preparation of the gospel of peace" is unclear.

The first genitive construction ἑτοιμασία τοῦ εὐαγγελίου "preparation of the gospel" may be understood in two ways:

1. It refers to a state of readiness to resist evil which is produced by a *knowledge* of the gospel. See, for example, Ellicott (p. 124),

Hendriksen (p. 277), Hodge (p. 385), Lenski (p. 667), Lincoln (pp. 448–449).
2. It refers to being in a state of readiness to resist evil by *proclaiming* the gospel. See, for example, Bruce (p. 130), Stott (p. 280).

The first option seems more appropriate in the context, since the focus is on standing firm and resisting, rather than advancing, as can be seen in the main verb στῆτε "stand" in 6:14. The source of the preparedness is the gospel. Knowledge of the gospel message will prepare the hearts and minds of believers to be resolute when resisting evil.

In the second genitive construction τοῦ εὐαγγελίου τῆς εἰρήνης "the gospel of peace", the genitive "of peace" is generally agreed to mean the gospel which has peace as its message and brings peace. The peace referred to is probably the peace and reconciliation between human beings and God, which is at the centre of the gospel. The believer who knows and experiences this is well-prepared to withstand spiritual evil.

6:16a–b In addition, Some manuscripts have ἐπὶ πᾶσιν "besides all (these)", instead of ἐν πᾶσιν "in all (things)", but the latter appears in the UBS text with no mention of the former as a variant reading. However, the phrase ἐν πᾶσιν may also be understood to mean "besides all (these)", "in addition to". In fact, most commentaries favour this rendering, whether based on ἐπὶ πᾶσιν (Ellicott, p. 124; Hodge, p. 385; Stott, p. 281) or ἐν πᾶσιν (Lincoln, p. 449; O'Brien, p. 479, fn. 165). So, "in addition" is used in the display.

believe firmly *in the Lord Jesus Christ. This will* enable you to protect yourselves from anything the devil *may do to harm you spiritually, just as a soldier* carries *his* shield *in order that he* may protect *himself* against the fire-tipped arrows which the enemy *shoots at him*. The θυρεός "shield" used by a Roman soldier was large and used to protect most of the body from the eyes to the knees. It was usually made of light wood or formed on a rim of metal and covered with several layers of hide. It gave good protection against arrows which were often dipped in pitch and then set alight before they were fired.

The relationship between the nouns in the genitive construction τὸν θυρεὸν τῆς πίστεως "the shield of faith" is probably one of apposition, i.e. the shield which is faith. The faith referred to may be understood as the content of what is believed, or belief or confidence in God or Christ.

There is consensus among commentators that πίστις, in this context, refers to the act of believing in God or Christ. See, for example, Best (p. 601), Bruce (p. 131), Hendriksen (p. 278, fn. 175), Hoehner (p. 846), Lincoln (p. 449), O'Brien (pp. 479–480).

The point of comparison between the shield and faith is that, just as the soldier's shield gives him protection in battle, so the believer's trust in God gives him protection against all the temptations that Satan may use to try and harm him spiritually and will enable him not to succumb to them.

The phrase τοῦ πονηροῦ "of the wicked (one)" refers to the devil. It has the same referent as τοῦ διαβόλου in 6:11.

6:17a–b Also rely on *the fact that the-Lord-Jesus-Christ/God* has saved you, *in order to protect yourselves against the devil and all his evil spirits, just as a soldier* puts on *his* helmet *in order to protect his head*. After the sequence of aorist participles in 6:14–16, Paul now uses the imperative verb δέξασθε "take, receive" in relation to the last two pieces of armour.

Few commentators discuss the reason for Paul's shift from participles to an imperative form in this verse. Those who do suggest the following:

1. It is parallel to the preceding participles and linked to them by καί "and". See, for example, O'Brien (p. 480, fn. 178).
2. It is parallel to the imperative στῆτε "stand" in 6:14. See, for example, Hoehner (pp. 848–849).

In the display, it is analysed as being semantically parallel to the preceding participles, since it also continues to deal with additional items of the full armour of God.

The helmet worn by the Roman soldier was usually made of leather and strengthened with metal plates. Sometimes it was made of brass or iron. Its purpose was to protect the head from blows by a sword, club or axe.

In the genitive phrase τὴν περικεφαλαίαν τοῦ σωτηρίου "the helmet of salvation", the second noun is in apposition to the first semantically, i.e. the helmet which is salvation. The point of comparison is that just as a helmet will protect a soldier's head from the blows of various weapons, so, the assurance that God has saved him will protect a believer from succumbing to any temptation with which Satan will try to harm him spiritually.

6:17c-d And rely on the words God has spoken by means of the Holy Spirit in order that you may be able to resist the devil and all his evil spirits, just as a soldier takes hold of his sword in order to resist the enemy. The relative phrase ὅ ἐστιν ῥῆμα θεοῦ "which is (the) word of God" identifies τὴν μάχαιραν τοῦ πνεύματος "the sword of the Spirit", but the meaning of these two genitive constructions needs to be discussed.

Unlike some of the other weapons, where the apposition in the genitive constructions actually identifies the figure, here that relationship is between the sword and the word of God, while the genitive construction "the sword of the Spirit" is one of origin or source. That is, it is the Holy Spirit who inspires the word and/or makes the word powerful and effective.

In the second genitive construction ῥῆμα θεοῦ "(the) word of God", most commentators agree that the expression refers to Scripture.

However, there is no consensus as to whether it refers to its written or spoken form. The word ῥῆμα used here tends to emphasise the word as spoken or proclaimed. However, in effect, it is both the spoken and written forms of God's word which are effective against Satan's attacks. A believer who knows and understands the Scriptures is able to use them to defend himself against the devil, as Christ did.

The point of comparison in the metaphor, then, is that just as a soldier uses his sword to fight a physical enemy, so the believer should use the word of God, which the Holy Spirit inspired, to contend with evil spiritual powers.

6:18-20 These three verses comprise two propositional clusters, 6:18 and 6:19-20. The first of these two clusters consists of the four nuclei of the ENABLING EXHORTATIONS₂ set and NUCLEUS₄ of that set is in a GENERIC-specific relationship with the second propositional cluster, which consists of a personal appeal by Paul for prayer.

6:18 There is considerable discussion among commentators as to how this verse is connected to the preceding context:

1. It may be connected through διά "by means of, with, through" and have the relationship of means, manner or accompanying circumstance.

2. It may be connected through the participle προσευχόμενοι "praying" (possibly together with ἀγρυπνοῦντες "keeping alert, watching"). The prepositional phrase διὰ πάσης προσευχῆς καὶ δεήσεως "with all prayer and petition" (6:18a) relates to the participle προσευχόμενοι "praying", which follows it.

The latter has strong support. See, for example, Best (pp. 604-605), Ellicott (p. 126), Lincoln (p. 432). Ellicott (p. 126) states that διὰ πάσης προσευχῆς καὶ δεήσεως "with all prayer and petition" taken with προσευχόμενοι "praying" is not overly tautological but "simply and correctly denotes the earnest (because varied) character of the prayer".

A third question is which finite verb in 6:14-17 would 6:18 be connected to:

1. The two participles προσευχόμενοι "praying" and ἀγρυπνοῦντες "watching" are connected with the aorist imperative στῆτε "stand" in 6:14. See, for example, Best (p. 604), Ellicott (p. 126), Lincoln (p. 451), O'Brien (p. 483).
2. Grammatically, it would be more correct to connect these participles with the aorist imperative δέξασθε "take" in 6:17, since it is nearer. See, for example, Hoehner (p. 855).

However, this second option would indicate that Paul is urging the Ephesians to pray only in relation to the last-mentioned pieces of armour in 6:17, i.e. "salvation" and "the word of God". It seems preferable, therefore, to consider the connection of προσευχόμενοι "praying" and ἀγρυπνοῦντες "watching" to be with the main imperative στῆτε "stand" in 6:14. In support of this also is the prominence given to the concept of standing firm by the repetition of the forms of ἵστημι in 6:11, 13, 14.

The participles in 6:14-17 are aorist, denoting single acts, but in 6:18 Paul changes to present participles προσευχόμενοι "praying" and ἀγρυπνοῦντες "watching", denoting a continuous activity. Prayer should be a continuing accompaniment to the believer's resistance of Satan.

6:18a As you are doing this [6:14-17], keep on praying to God at all times and in every situation, In the phrase διὰ πάσης προσευχῆς καὶ δεήσεως "by means of all prayer and petition" the two nouns may be regarded in two ways:

1. As hendiadys, i.e. "every kind of petitionary prayer".
2. As a generic-specific doublet, i.e. "every kind of prayer, and specifically, every kind of petition".

There is greater support for the latter in the commentaries.

The repetition of the various forms of πᾶς "all, every" in 6:18 and the use of cognate words and synonyms to describe "prayer" reinforce the idea that prayer is an ongoing activity which should accompany the use of all the other resources God makes available to his people. They are to pray at all times and as is appropriate to every situation.

As Eadie says,

> The order of thought is—make preparation, take the armour, stand, fight, and all the while be praying (p. 474).

To show this relationship, "*As you are doing this* [6:14-17]" is supplied in the display at the beginning of 6:18a.

6:18b *and* always *let the Holy* Spirit *guide you when you pray*. The phrase ἐν πνεύματι "in the Spirit/spirit" is generally understood to refer to the Holy Spirit. The sense is that the Ephesians should be guided or empowered by the Holy Spirit to pray as they ought to pray.

6:18c For this purpose [6:18a-b] always be ready to pray, The phrase καὶ εἰς αὐτό "and to this end" refers back to the preceding clauses 6:18a-b for its purpose. In order to pray at all times under the guidance of the Holy Spirit, they are to be alert for every opportunity to pray. At the same time, 6:18c is a third exhortation and, in the display diagram, it is labelled as exhortation not as means.

6:18d and always be persistent in praying for all God's people. In the phrase πάσῃ προσκαρτερήσει καὶ δεήσει "all perseverance and petition", the two abstract nouns linked by καί represent the event of praying with perseverance, i.e. "you persevere in praying". As well as being alert to every opportunity to pray (6:18c), the Ephesian believers are to persevere in prayer. They are to pray for πάντων τῶν ἁγίων "all the saints". This refers to all believers, all God's chosen people.

6:19-20 This propositional cluster (6:19-20) may be regarded as constituting a sub-unit in which the focus is on Paul himself. It is in a specific relation to the GENERIC exhortation 6:18d.

6:19a And *specifically,* pray for me, *Paul*. The initial καί "and" relates this verse to the preceding one, continuing the sentence which began in 6:17. Paul has just been encouraging the Ephesians to pray for *all* believers. Now he makes a specific request that they pray for him personally.

6:19b *Pray* that *God will* tell me what I should say, whenever I speak, There are two ways to understand the ἵνα "that, in order that" which starts 6:19b:

1. It indicates the purpose of Paul's request that they pray for him. See, for example, Eadie (p. 477), Meyer (p. 550).
2. It introduces the content of the prayer that Paul asks them to pray for him. See, for example, Hendriksen (p. 282), Hodge (p. 393), Hoehner (p. 861), Lenski (p. 678).

Either makes good sense, but the second option has greater support. So it is followed in the display.

In the first part of Paul's request, μοι δοθῇ λόγος ἐν ἀνοίξει τοῦ στόματός μου "to me may be given speech in the opening of my mouth", it is necessary to supply the agent in the event "to me may be given". God is the one who gives the ability to speak and also supplies the message, so this is made explicit in the display.

There are a number of discussion points concerning what Paul asks them to pray for.

The Greek noun λόγος "speech" may denote:

1. A specific message. See, for example, Best (p. 607), Lincoln (p. 454).
2. Fluency and facility in speaking, i.e. what to say, or the ability to say it clearly and fluently. See, for example, Hodge (p. 393), O'Brien (p. 487).

Both are applicable in the context, but the first option has majority support and so is followed in the display.

The next issue for discussion is the meaning of the phrase ἐν ἀνοίξει τοῦ στόματός μου "in the opening of my mouth". Here there is consensus among commentators that the phrase indicates the beginning of an act of speaking. It means "when I open my mouth to speak". It usually indicates the beginning of a solemn and deliberate announcement or speech.

6:19c *in order that* I may boldly make known the good news which had been hidden *in the past but which God has now revealed to me.* The abstract noun παρρησία means "boldness, uninhibited speech, outspokenness, frankness of speech". In the phrase ἐν παρρησίᾳ "with boldness", it indicates the manner in which something is said.

Commentators do not agree about how ἐν παρρησίᾳ "with boldness" should be attached to the context. There are two possibilities:

1. It is connected to what precedes, i.e. "opening my mouth with boldness".
2. It is connected to what follows, i.e. "with boldness make known the mystery of the gospel".

In effect, it makes little difference to the meaning of the verse.

The event represented here by the infinitive γνωρίσαι "to make known" provides the purpose for 6:19a–b, "in order that I may boldly make known the mystery of the gospel".

In 1:9, the reference of μυστήριον "mystery" was to one particular purpose of the gospel, i.e. that all things are put under Christ's control. In 3:3, it is used of the union of Jewish and Gentile believers in one church. Here in 6:19c, μυστήριον is used in the genitive phrase τὸ μυστήριον τοῦ εὐαγγελίου "the mystery of the gospel". It probably refers to the whole gospel, the meaning of which had been hidden until God chose to reveal it. Paul is asking the Ephesians to pray that he might clearly and fearlessly make known to people the message which had once been hidden but which God has now revealed in Christ.

6:20a I am a representative *of Jesus Christ* in making known this good news and I am a prisoner because I make it known. Most commentators agree that the referent of ὑπὲρ οὗ "on behalf of which" is τὸ μυστήριον τοῦ εὐαγγελίου "the mystery of the gospel" in 6:19c. The mystery is the gospel. Semantically the reference also includes "making known...the gospel", since that is the reason that Paul was imprisoned.

The phrase ἐν ἁλύσει "in a chain" may be understood in two ways:

1. It can be understood literally, since Paul would be chained to the soldier guarding him.
2. It may be regarded as a metonymy for Paul's being in prison or in some other type of custody (cf. Acts 28:30).

There is little difference in the sense whichever is chosen.

Implicit in the concept of πρεσβεύω "I am an ambassador" is the one on whose behalf Paul is an ambassador, Jesus Christ. This may need to be made explicit in some languages.

This proposition amplifies 6:19c.

6:20b *Pray* that, when I make known *to people* this good news, I may speak out boldly. The ἵνα "that, in order that" which introduces this clause grammatically relates back to προσευχόμενοι "praying". It may indicate a relationship of content or purpose, both of which have support in the commentaries. However, since it is generally agreed that this clause is co-ordinate with that in 6:19b and since I have analyzed that as content, it seems appropriate to analyze this parallel clause in the same way. See, for example, Best (p. 609), Ellicott (p. 129), Hoehner (p. 861), O'Brien (p. 489, fn. 229). The similarity of meaning in 6:19b and 6:20b gives emphasis to it.

The referent of ἐν αὐτῷ "in it" is basically the same as for that of ὑπὲρ οὗ "on behalf of which", i.e. it refers to the infinitive clause γνωρίσαι τὸ μυστήριον τοῦ εὐαγγελίου "to make known the mystery of the gospel" in 6:19c. The whole clause then, ἵνα ἐν αὐτῷ παρρησιάσωμαι "that in it I may speak boldly", means that Paul wants the Ephesians to pray that when he is speaking the good news, he may do so freely and fearlessly, without any inhibition because of the difficulty or danger of his situation.

6:20c *This* [6:20b] *is* as I ought to speak. This clause, ὡς δεῖ με λαλῆσαι "as I ought to speak", qualifies the event of speaking boldly in 6:20b. As a chosen representative of Christ, this is how Paul ought to speak both regards content and manner. The relationship of 6:20b with 6:20c may be regarded as CONGRUENCE-standard.

BOUNDARIES AND COHERENCE

The initial boundary has been discussed in the section on Boundaries and Coherence for paragraph 6:10–13. The final boundary has been discussed in the section on Boundaries and Coherence for 6:10–20.

Coherence is provided by the topic, which amplifies paragraph 6:10-13 by presenting specific examples of how the Ephesian believers are to fulfil the exhortation to become spiritually resolute and to stand firm in the face of the devil's attacks. It does this by figurative language in 6:14-17.

Then, in 6:18-20, there is a change to non-figurative language, when the part played by prayer in the spiritual battle is dealt with.

There is conflict between the semantics and the grammatical structure of 6:14-20. A semantic division can be made at the end of 6:17 with the end of the military metaphor. However, grammatically, 6:18-20 could not stand alone as a unit since there is no independent verb, only participles. The idea of prayer is firmly connected to the other concepts expressed in 6:14-17 as a spiritual resource which should be used in conjunction with all the other resources mentioned. So these verses are regarded as a single, compound paragraph.

PROMINENCE AND THEME

Both the GENERIC EXHORTATION (6:14a) and ENABLING EXHORTATIONS$_1$ and ENABLING EXHORTATIONS$_2$ of 6:14c-18d are equally prominent. The theme statement, therefore, is based on all three.

EPISTLE CONSTITUENT 6:21–24 (Complex Section: Closing of the Epistle)

THEME: I am sending Tychicus to tell you what is happening to me and my fellow-workers, and to encourage you. I pray that God will cause you, fellow-believers, to have peace and to love one another. I also pray that he will continue to act graciously towards all who keep on loving our Lord Jesus Christ.

MACROSTRUCTURE	CONTENTS
NUCLEUS$_1$	6:21–22 I am sending Tychicus to tell you what is happening to me and my fellow-workers, and to encourage you.
NUCLEUS$_2$	6:23–24 I pray that God will cause you, fellow-believers, to have peace, to love one another and to keep on believing in Christ. I pray that God will continue to act graciously towards all who keep on loving our Lord Jesus Christ.

INTENT AND MACROSTRUCTURE

This section 6:21–24 brings the letter to a close. It consists of two units. In the first unit (6:21–22), Paul explains the task of Tychicus and commends him as his messenger. In the second unit (6:23–24), he prays that the Ephesians will have peace and love to accompany their faith and he gives a final benediction.

His intention in bringing the letter to a conclusion in this way is:

1. To encourage and reassure the Ephesians as to his own condition and circumstances. He refers to this here, but Tychicus will give them firsthand knowledge of how Paul is.
2. In the benediction (6:23-24), Paul communicates his love for the Ephesians. Verses 6:23 and 6:24 respectively open with the words εἰρήνη "peace" and ἡ χάρις "grace". These are commonly used in Paul's epistles in the openings and "grace" especially is used even in the benedictions of the epistles. So, it is difficult to know how specific a thematic connection Paul intended here with the other occurrences of these words in the BODY of the letter. Paul does mention "love" twice in 6:23-24. He prays that ἀγάπη μετὰ πίστεως "love with faith" may continue to be evident in the lives of the Ephesian believers. This recalls Paul's thanksgiving for their faith and love shown to one another (1:15) and his prayer that these two qualities might be fundamental in their lives (3:17).

In 6:24, Paul brings the letter to a close with the only explicit reference to the love which believers have for the Lord Jesus Christ. Lincoln (p. 466) suggests that in this way he draws attention to a believer's personal relationship and commitment to Christ.

BOUNDARIES AND COHERENCE

The initial boundary of this unit has been discussed in the section on Boundaries and Coherence for 6:10–20. The final boundary is the end of the epistle.

This unit consists of two closely-related paragraphs which bring the epistle to a close. The first paragraph, 6:21–22, is about a final, personal message concerning Paul's present situation, which Tychicus, sent by Paul, will make known to the believers there. The second paragraph, 6:23–24, consists of his final benediction to the believers at Ephesus and others who may have received the letter.

PROMINENCE AND THEME

Since the units in this section are co-ordinate with each other, the theme is a general statement incorporating the prominent elements of both paragraphs, 6:21–22 and 6:23–24.

SECTION CONSTITUENT 6:21–22 (Commissive Paragraph: Nucleus₁ of 6:21–24)

THEME: I am sending Tychicus to tell you what is happening to me and my fellow-workers, and to encourage you.

RELATIONAL STRUCTURE	CONTENTS
NUCLEUS — PURPOSE — NUCLEUS	6:21a In order that you, as well as *others*, may know about my circumstances,
└ amplification	6:21b how I am faring/doing,
MEANS (COMMISSIVE) — 'Tychicus'	6:21c *I am sending* Tychicus *to you, in order that* he will tell you everything *about me*.
└ confirmatory description	6:21d He *is* a brother *whom we (inc) love very much* and he serves the Lord faithfully.
amplification — MEANS	6:22a I am sending him to you for this very purpose [6:22b-c],
PURPOSE₁	6:22b in order that you might know about our (exc) circumstances,
PURPOSE₂	6:22c and in order that he might encourage you [SYN].

INTENT AND STRUCTURE

Structurally, the paragraph 6:21–22 consists of two propositional clusters which coincide with verses 6:21 and 6:22. The relationship between the two is that of NUCLEUS (6:21) and amplification (6:22).

A commissive proposition or unit is similar to an exhortation in that,

> [Both] are concerned with affecting future events, with changing states of affairs. But now it is the speaker who is envisaged as achieving this: he both wills the proposed activity or situation and is able to bring it about (K. Callow, p 112).

Here Paul is committing himself to sending Tychicus to the Ephesians to tell them how he is doing.

Paul wants to reassure and encourage the Ephesians about how he is. Paul's commendation in 6:21d will reassure the Ephesians that Tychicus is trustworthy.

NOTES

6:21–22 These two verses are similar to Colossians 4:7–8. It seems clear that Tychicus was entrusted with Paul's letters to the believers in both Colossae and Ephesus and for the same purpose.

6:21a–b In order that you, as well *as others*, may know about my circumstances, how I am faring/doing, The fronting of the ἵνα construction along with the conjunction δέ marks a transition to the new topic: the communication of Paul's present situation to the Ephesian believers. Many English versions do not translate δέ here as an explicit conjunction (NIV, NRSV, TEV).

The initial ἵνα "in order that" introduces Paul's purpose in sending Tychicus to the Ephesians. Grammatically it connects with πάντα γνωρίσει ὑμῖν Τύχικος "Tychicus will make known to you". However, Paul does not yet say explicitly that he is sending Tychicus to them. This information does not occur in the Greek text until 6:22. To make the meaning clear, this step in the action is made explicit earlier in the display (in 6:21c).

Commentators discuss how the καί "also" in the phrase καὶ ὑμεῖς "you also" should be understood. Most support the view that there were other groups concerned about Paul and his circumstances. Tychicus was delivering the same message to the Colossians (Col. 4:7–8) and possibly others also.

The expression τὰ κατ' ἐμέ is a Greek idiom which means "what concerns me", "my affairs", "what has been happening to me" (cf. Phil. 1:12). The phrase τί πράσσω "what/how I am doing", "how I fare", appears to say something very similar. Both refer to Paul's situation, and his circumstances. The absence of any connective between the two phrases indicates that they may be in either a generic-specific or contraction-amplification relationship.

The phrase τί πράσσω can be translated as:

1. "What I am doing". It refers to Paul's activities. See NAB, NIV, NJB, NRSV.

2. "How I am faring". It refers to Paul's state or condition. See KJV, NASB, TEV.

However, most commentators seem to agree that the second option is more likely; it refers to Paul's welfare, his condition, not his actions.

As mentioned above, the expressions τὰ κατ' ἐμέ "what concerns me" and τί πράσσω "what/how I am doing" appear to say something similar. Perhaps the difference between the two expressions is that the first refers to his circumstances, whereas the second refers more to his personal state, his reaction to those circumstances, their effect upon his feelings/attitude, etc. These two expressions are expressed in the display as "my circumstances" and "how I am faring/doing".

6:21c *I am sending* **Tychicus** *to you, in order that* **he will tell you everything** *about me.* The Greek simply states πάντα γνωρίσει ὑμῖν Τύχικος "Tychicus will make known to you everything", but, as stated above in the notes for 6:21a–b, it may be necessary to make explicit the fact that Paul is sending him to them. The implicit information in this proposition identifies the sending of Tychicus as the means whereby the Ephesians will hear about Paul's circumstances.

6:21d He *is* **a brother** *whom we (inc)* **love very much and he serves the Lord** *Jesus Christ* **faithfully.** This proposition describes Tychicus and presents him as someone whom the Ephesians can trust to give them a true picture of Paul's circumstances. It might be labelled a "confirmatory description", since it confirms his character as trustworthy.

brother *whom we (inc)* **love very much,** In this context ἀδελφός is used in the special sense of "brother in Christ" or "fellow-believer".

The first mention of Tychicus in the New Testament is in Acts 20:4 where he is named as one of Paul's companions when Paul went from Greece back to Asia. There may be no sure way to know when he first started out with Paul, but this point when he is first mentioned was probably not more than several months after Paul had to leave Ephesus. Also in Acts 20:4, Tychicus is said to be from the province of Asia Minor and must have been well-known to churches there. Note Hoehner's view:

> [Tychicus] and Trophimus were the two Asians who accompanied Paul immediately after the Ephesian riot (Acts 20:4). Tychicus may well have come from the vicinity of Ephesus or Colossae (p. 870).

The implicit agents of the event "love" could well be seen as inclusive, i.e. Paul, those associated with him at the time of writing this letter and some of those receiving the letter. The question could be asked, Why would the Ephesians need to receive a commendation regarding Tychicus from Paul if they already knew him? But he may well not have been known by all the believers there.

and he serves the Lord faithfully It is generally agreed that διάκονος "servant, minister", in this context, does not refer to an official office in the church, but to a servant or helper in a general sense.

Most commentators consider that the phrase ἐν κυρίῳ "in (the) Lord" is only connected to διάκονος, not to ἀδελφός as well.

There is, however, discussion about what the phrase means in this context. In some versions it is translated as "in the Lord's work". See NLT, REB, TEV.

This same phrase is used in an almost identical context in Colossians 4:7. Callow (2002:158; cf. 1983:225), suggests that, since Paul is simply describing Tychicus, the "ἐν κυρίῳ indicates the type of σύνδουλος he was, a Christian one". He, therefore, suggests that the simplest way to express this is to say "who serves the Lord together with *me*". In this context then, the sense of πιστὸς διάκονος ἐν κυρίῳ is "he serves the Lord faithfully".

6:22a I am sending him to you The relative pronoun ὅν "whom" refers back to Tychicus. The verb ἔπεμψα "I sent", is an "epistolary aorist". It is used in letters to refer to an action about to take place from the point of view of the writer, but which, from the standpoint of the recipients, was now past. Paul is going to send Tychicus with this letter, but, by the time he delivered it, the sending would be a past event. In English, the appropriate tense is the present continuous, but, strictly speaking, it means "I am about to send".

for this very purpose [6:22b–c], The phrase εἰς αὐτὸ τοῦτο "for this very (thing)" refers forward to the following ἵνα clauses, 6:22b and 6:22c, which explain what τοῦτο refers to. The αὐτό makes it emphatic, "for this very purpose" and the whole phrase gives the double purpose equal prominence with the MEANS, 6:22a.

6:22b in order that you might know about our (exc) circumstances, This is a restatement of 6:21a, except that Paul includes his fellow-workers with himself, ἡμῶν "us" (exclusive sense here) instead of ἐμέ "me".

6:22c and in order that he might encourage you. This gives the second purpose Paul had for sending Tychicus to Ephesus.

The phrase τὰς καρδίας ὑμῶν "your hearts" can be understood as a synecdoche, "hearts" being a representation of the whole person and so may be translated "you". However, as is the case with English "heart", a more specific reference, often language-idiosyncratic, would communicate the concept and connotations better than using "you".

This recalls 3:13 where the Ephesians are said to be in danger of becoming discouraged because of Paul's sufferings. The news Tychicus brings is meant to encourage them.

This cluster of propositions, 6:22a–c, provides an amplification of 6:21a–c.

BOUNDARIES AND COHERENCE

The initial boundary of this paragraph is marked in 6:21 by the conjunction δέ signalling a transition to a different subject. Paul moves from dealing with spiritual warfare to his own circumstances.

With an obvious benediction beginning in 6:23, the final boundary of this unit comes at the end of 6:22.

PROMINENCE AND THEME

The NUCLEUS of the paragraph is naturally prominent and its PURPOSE (6:21a) has marked prominence by reason of its amplification in 6:21b, 22b, 22c. The theme statement, therefore, is based on the NUCLEUS and the PURPOSE, along with their amplification.

SECTION CONSTITUENT 6:23-24
(Expressive Paragraph: Nucleus₂ of 6:21-24 [closing benediction])

THEME: I pray that God will cause you, fellow-believers, to have peace, to love one another and to keep on believing in Christ. I pray that God will continue to act graciously towards all who keep on loving our Lord Jesus Christ.

RELATIONAL STRUCTURE	CONTENTS
NUCLEUS₁	6:23 *I pray that* God *our* Father and the Lord Jesus Christ will cause *you*, fellow-believers, *to continue* to have peace, and to love *one another*, and to keep on believing *in Christ*.
NUCLEUS₂	6:24 *I pray that* God will *continue to* act graciously towards all those who keep on loving our Lord Jesus Christ.

INTENT AND STRUCTURE

Paul began this letter praying on behalf of the Ephesians for "grace" and "peace" (1:2). He now brings it to an end with two types of benedictions (6:23 and 6:24) in which he makes a similar reference to "grace" and "peace". It is difficult to know whether Paul intends more than he intends in 1:2 or in the opening and closing of his other letters where these terms are used.

Some commentators note that the peace referred to here recalls the peace of reconciliation between God and human beings which brings about reconciliation with each other (2:11-22; 4:3, etc.). These seem inseparable, the one flowing from the other. See, for example, Hendriksen (p. 284), Lincoln (pp. 465-466), O'Brien (p. 493). See more on the note for 6:23.

This paragraph comprises NUCLEUS₁ and NUCLEUS₂, which coincide with 6:23 and 6:24.

NOTES

6:23-24 These two verses are Paul's closing benediction and, as is common with such benedictions, there is no verb expressed in the Greek, but the verb "to be" is generally understood. In the display, "I pray that" is used to introduce this unit. It will depend upon the target language which form is appropriate as to how this will be expressed.

As has been stated, this recalls the beginning of the letter (1:2), except that there Paul addresses the Ephesians directly in the second person plural pronoun ὑμῖν "you", whereas here he refers to them in the third person as τοῖς ἀδελφοῖς "the brothers" (6:23). The reason most commonly given for this is that this form of address is more general and inclusive than the second person plural form and may indicate that the letter is not intended for one particular church, but for a number of churches.

See the note on 6:23.

6:23 *I pray that* **God** *our* **Father and the Lord Jesus Christ will cause** *you*, **fellow-believers,** *to continue* **to have peace,** Callow has a useful discussion of the meaning of εἰρήνη with reference to Colossians 1:2, χάρις ὑμῖν καὶ εἰρήνη ἀπὸ θεοῦ πατρὸς ἡμῶν "grace to you and peace from God our Father", which is similar to the passage we are dealing with here. I quote from that discussion here,

> It is generally agreed among the commentators that peace is the state enjoyed by the recipients of God's grace, and that it is similar in meaning to the Hebrew word *shalom* (often translated by εἰρήνη in the Septuagint). The Hebrew word, however, means more than internal peacefulness or outward freedom from war and strife. It corresponds more nearly to the English word *well-being*, a state of blessedness or prosperity of body and soul. How far the ideas associated with the Hebrew word carried over into the Greek εἰρήνη is hard to say, especially when used in a conventional salutation of a letter. Another problem, from the point of view of semantics, is that whereas 'grace' clearly comes from the Godhead, 'peace' is man's experience, so that the Greek preposition meaning 'from' has the meaning 'cause to come to pass' (2002:10-11; 1983:28).

There is general agreement that the prepositional phrase ἀπὸ θεοῦ πατρὸς καὶ κυρίου Ἰησοῦ Χριστοῦ "from God (the) Father and (the) Lord Jesus Christ" here in Ephesians 6:23 is attached both to εἰρήνη τοῖς ἀδελφοῖς "peace to the brothers" and ἀγάπη μετὰ πίστεως "love with faith".

Following the reasoning put forward in the Colossians SSA, we might translate Εἰρήνη τοῖς ἀδελφοῖς...ἀπὸ θεοῦ πατρὸς καὶ κυρίου Ἰησοῦ Χριστοῦ "Peace to the brothers...from God (the) Father and (the) Lord Jesus Christ" as "*I pray that* God *our* Father and the Lord Jesus Christ *will cause you,* fellow-believers, to experience/have peace".

However, in the context of Ephesians, we need to ask what Paul might have intended by this statement. Is he referring to well-being and inner peace in general, or is there a strong allusion to peace between believers and with God? In chapters two and four, and also in 6:15, the peace referred to is that of reconciliation between God and human beings or between believers.

Though there is potential allusion to this sense of peace here, it is not appropriate to propositionalise in the display with specific reference to peace with God or peace between the believers but to propositionalise similarly to the blessing at the beginning of the letter, χάρις ὑμῖν καὶ εἰρήνη ἀπὸ θεοῦ πατρὸς ἡμῶν καὶ κυρίου Ἰησοῦ Χριστοῦ "Grace to you and peace from God our Father and (the) Lord Jesus Christ" (1:2). Thus the display here is "will cause *you,* fellow-believers, *to continue* to have peace".

It is agreed that ἀδελφοί "brothers", in this context, is used in a figurative sense and refers to Christian brothers and sisters, fellow-believers.

Commentators who regard the epistle as written to more churches than the church at Ephesus alone, or at least grant that possibility, understand the term as referring to believers in various churches where the letter may be read. See, for example, Candlish (p. 131), Hoehner (p. 873), O'Brien (p. 493).

The term ἀδελφοί "brothers" probably describes the same people as those referred to in 6:24 as "all those that love our Lord Jesus Christ", i.e. all believers. The third person plural form τοῖς ἀδελφοῖς "to the brothers" appears to be used in the Greek Text with a view to making the benediction more inclusive. However, if its use is confusing in some languages, indicating rather, that the blessing is intended for a more *restricted* audience, and the second person "you" is more inclusive in its scope, then it may be preferable to use "you" or "you, fellow-believers".

Probably, as Paul is addressing his fellow-believers, wherever they meet together and read his letter, the use of the term ἀδελφοί "brothers" is intended to give them a sense of unity and belonging.

and to love *one another,* **and to keep on believing** *in Christ.* The preposition μετά is used to indicate a close connection between two nouns, the first of which is the one being emphasised (BDAG, p. 637.2f). Most commentators also agree that, in the phrase ἀγάπη μετὰ πίστεως "love with faith", μετά links "love" and "faith" in a close relationship. The two are together related to εἰρήνη "peace" by καί "and". Since believers are being addressed, they already have faith and so, presumably, Paul is praying that it may continue and be accompanied by love. The phrase recalls 1:15 where Paul praises the Ephesians for their faith and the love they show to all the saints.

The love referred to here is assumed to be love for other believers which should arise from their faith. In the case of both love and faith, God is the causer and believers are the agents.

Since the two events represented by the abstract nouns ἀγάπη "love" and πίστεως "faith" are concurrent, although the believing would have commenced before the loving of other believers, the relationship between them is expressed in the display by the same verb forms and the conjunction "and".

6:24 *I pray that* **God will** *continue to* **act graciously towards all those who keep on loving our Lord Jesus Christ.** The noun χάρις "grace" represents an event and, therefore, is expressed by a verbal phrase in the display. As in other SSAs "act graciously" is used, since there is no single English verb to represent the event. It is used in a special Christian sense.

The participants in the event are God and πάντων τῶν ἀγαπώντων τὸν κύριον ἡμῶν Ἰησοῦν Χριστόν "all those who love our Lord Jesus Christ".

There is discussion about how the phrase ἐν ἀφθαρσίᾳ "in incorruptibility, in immortality" connects with the rest of the verse. There are three main possibilities:

1. The phrase ἐν ἀφθαρσίᾳ "in incorruptibility, in immortality" connects with the participial clause πάντων τῶν ἀγαπώντων τὸν κύριον ἡμῶν "all the ones loving our Lord". It is understood to describe the quality of the love: those who love the Lord with undying/unfailing love. See, for example, Bruce (p. 136), Eadie (p. 484), Ellicott (p. 131), Hendriksen (p. 284), Hodge (p. 397), Hoehner (p. 877).

This analysis is followed by many versions (CEV, NCV, NET, NIV, NLT, NRSV, REB, TEV). Or, the phrase ἐν ἀφθαρσίᾳ means "incorruptible" in the sense of not being contaminated. Thus KJV has "Grace be with all them that love our Lord Jesus Christ in sincerity".

2. The phrase ἐν ἀφθαρσίᾳ "in incorruptibility, in immortality" is connected with χάρις "grace" and means "with immortality". Paul is therefore praying that grace and immortality might be granted to "all who love our Lord Jesus Christ". See, for example, Lenski (pp. 687–688), Lincoln (pp. 467–468), O'Brien (p. 494).

Although the second option makes good sense, it is problematic as the noun χάρις "grace" and ἐν ἀφθαρσίᾳ "in/with immortality" are distant from each other in the Greek text, ἐν ἀφθαρσίᾳ occurring finally in the sentence and χάρις occurring initially.

The first option has the most commentary support, so it is followed in the display.

BOUNDARIES AND COHERENCE

The initial boundary has been discussed in the section on Boundaries and Coherence for 6:21–22 and the final boundary coincides with the end of the epistle.

The coherence of this unit may be based on the fact that it consists of two benedictions.

PROMINENCE AND THEME

This paragraph consists of NUCLEUS$_1$ and NUCLEUS$_2$. Since they are co-ordinate and so equally prominent, the theme statement is based on both.

BIBLIOGRAPHY

COMMENTARIES, LEXICONS, AND OTHER GENERAL REFERENCES

Abbott, T. K. *A Critical and Exegetical Commentary on the Epistles to the Ephesians and to the Colossians*. The International Critical Commentary. Edinburgh: T. & T. Clark Ltd, 1979.

Alford, Henry. *The Greek Testament*, vol. 3. Pages 68-151. 1874. Revised by Everett F. Harrison. Chicago: Moody Press, 1968.

Banker, John. *A Semantic and Structural Analysis of Titus*. Dallas: SIL, 1987.

Banker, John. *A Semantic and Structural Analysis of Philippians*. Dallas: SIL, 1996.

Barry, Alfred. "Commentary on Ephesians and Colossians". *A New Testament Commentary for English Readers*. Edited by Charles J. Ellicott. London: Cassell Petter & Galpin, n.d.

Bauer, Walter. *A Greek-English Lexicon of the New Testament and Other Early Christian Literature*. Third ed. Revised and edited by Fredrick William Danker based on Walter Bauer's 6th ed. Chicago and London: University of Chicago Press, 2000.

Beekman, John, ed. "An Analysis of the Semantic Structure of the Epistle to the Colossians". Prepublication draft. Dallas: SIL, 1974.

Beekman, John, John Callow and Michael F. Kopesec. "The Semantic Structure of Written Communication". Prepublication Draft. Dallas: SIL, 1981.

Best, Ernest. *A Critical and Exegetical Commentary on Ephesians*. The International Critical Commentary. Edinburgh: T. & T. Clark Ltd, 1998.

Blass, R. and A. Debrunner. *A Greek Grammar of the New Testament and Other Early Christian Literature*. A translation and revision of the ninth-tenth German ed. incorporating supplementary notes of A. Debrunner by Robert W. Funk. Chicago and London: University of Chicago Press, 1961.

Bratcher, Robert G. and Eugene A. Nida. *A Translator's Handbook on Paul's Letter to the Ephesians*. New York: United Bible Societies, 1982.

Breeze, Mary J. "Hortatory Discourse in Ephesians: An Analysis of the Information Structure and the Implications for Understanding the Epistle". Draft of MA thesis. 1990.

Bruce, F. F. *The Epistle to the Ephesians: A Verse-by-Verse Exposition*. London: Pickering & Inglis, 1961.

Cadbury, H. J. "The Dilemma of Ephesians". *New Testament Studies* 5 (1958-59):91-102.

Callow, John. *A Semantic Structure Analysis of Second Thessalonians*. Dallas: SIL, 1982.

Callow, John. *A Semantic and Structural Analysis of Second Thessalonians*. Rev. ed. Dallas: SIL, 2000.

Callow, John. *A Semantic Structure Analysis of Colossians*. Dallas: SIL, 1983.

Callow, John. *A Semantic and Structural Analysis of Colossians*. 2d ed. Dallas: SIL, 2002.

Callow, Kathleen. *Man and Message*. Lanham, MD: University Press of America, 1998.

Calvin, John. *The Epistles of Paul the Apostle to the Galatians, Ephesians, Philippians and Colossians*. Calvin's Commentaries. Translated by T. H. L. Parker. Grand Rapids: Eerdmans, [1548] 1965.

Candlish, James S. *The Epistle of Paul to The Ephesians*. Edinburgh: T. & T. Clark, 1901.

Caragounis, Chrys C. *The Ephesian Mysterion: Meaning and Content*. Lund: CWK Gleerup, 1977.

Carson, D. A., Douglas J. Moo and Leon Morris. *An Introduction to the New Testament*. Grand Rapids: Zondervan, 1992.

Dunn, Phyllis, John Heins, Leslie Heyward, Michael Moxness and Larry Roettger. "Discourse analysis of Ephesians 2-6". Papers for Greek III. Dallas: SIL, 1982.

Eadie, John. *A Commentary on the Greek Text of the Epistle of Paul to the Ephesians*. Grand Rapids: Baker, [1883] 1979.

Ellicott, C. J. *A Critical and Grammatical Commentary on St. Paul's Epistle to the Ephesians*. London: John W. Parker and Son, 1855.

Foulkes, Francis. *The Letter of Paul to the Ephesians: An Introduction and Commentary*. Grand Rapids: Eerdmans, 1989.

Graham, Glenn H. *An Exegetical Summary of Ephesians*. Dallas: SIL, 1997.

Gurnall, William. *The Christian in Complete Armour*. Edinburgh: The Banner of Truth Trust, [1655, 1658, 1662 in 3 volumes] 1974.

Hart, George and Helen. *A Semantic and Structural Analysis of James*. Dallas: SIL, 2001.

Hendriksen, William. *New Testament Commentary: Ephesians*. London: The Banner of Truth Trust, [1967] 1972.

Hodge, Charles. *The Epistle to the Ephesians*. Grand Rapids: Eerdmans, [1856] 1964.

Hoehner, Harold W. *Ephesians: An Exegetical Commentary*. Grand Rapids: Baker, 2002.

Houlden, J. L. *Paul's Letters from Prison*. Harmondsworth: Penguin, 1970.

Jung, Minyoung, David F. Matti, Roland Milanese, Greg Pearson, Stephen J. Schooling and David L Seyer. "Discourse Analysis of Ephesians". Papers for Greek III. Dallas: SIL, 1984.

Keener, Craig S. *The IVP Bible Background Commentary (New Testament)*. Downers Grove: IVP, 1993.

Kopesec, Michael F. "A Literary-semantic Analysis of Ephesians (with primary focus on Ephesians 3 & 4)". Draft. Dallas: SIL, 1977.

Braune, Karl. "The Epistle of Paul to the Ephesians" in *Lange's Commentary on the Holy Scriptures*, vol. 11. Grand Rapids: Zondervan, [1870] 1960.

Lenski, R. C. H. *The Interpretation of St. Paul's Epistles to the Galatians, Ephesians, and to the Philippians*. Columbus: Wartburg Press, [1937] 1946.

Lincoln, Andrew T. *Ephesians*. Word Biblical Commentary, vol. 42. Dallas: Word, 1990.

Lloyd-Jones, D. Martyn. *God's Way of Reconciliation: Studies in Ephesians Chapter 2*. Grand Rapids: Baker Book House, 1972.

Lloyd-Jones, D. Martyn. *The Christian Warfare: An Exposition of Ephesians 6:10 to 13*. Edinburgh: The Banner of Truth Trust, 1976.

Lloyd-Jones, D. Martyn. *The Unsearchable Riches of Christ: An Exposition of Ephesians 3:1 to 21*. Edinburgh: The Banner of Truth Trust, 1979.

Lloyd-Jones, D. Martyn. *Christian Unity: An Exposition of Ephesians 4:1 to 16*. Edinburgh: The Banner of Truth Trust, 1980.

Louw, Johannes P., and Eugene A. Nida, eds. *Greek-English Lexicon of the New Testament Based on Semantic Domains*. 2 vols. New York: UBS, 1988.

Longacre, Robert E. *The Grammar of Discourse*. 2d ed. New York: Plenum, 1996.

Metzger, Bruce M. *A Textual Commentary on the Greek New Testament*. 2d ed. Stuttgart: German Bible Society, 1994.

Meyer, Heinrich August Wilhelm. "Critical and Exegetical Hand-Book to the Epistle to the Ephesians". In *Meyer's Commentary on the New Testament, Galatians and Ephesians*. Pages 277–561. Translated from the 4th German edition by Maurice J. Evans and the translation revised and edited by William P. Dickson, with a preface, translation of references, and supplementary notes to the American edition by Henry E. Jacobs. New York: Funk & Wagnalls, 1884.

Moore, Bruce. *Doublets in the New Testament*. Dallas: SIL, 1993.

Morris, Leon. *Expository Reflections on the Letter to the Ephesians*. Grand Rapids: Baker Books, 1994.

Moule, C. F. D. *An Idiom Book of New Testament Greek*. Cambridge: Cambridge University Press, 1960.

O'Brien, Peter T. *The Letter to the Ephesians*. The Pillar New Testament Commentary. Grand Rapids: Eerdmans, 1999.

Peckham, Jim. "Discourse analysis of Ephesians 5 & 6". Draft. Dallas: SIL, 1977.

Poole, Matthew. *A Commentary on the Holy Bible*, vol. 3. London: The Banner of Truth Trust, [1685] 1963.

Robinson, J. Armitage. *Commentary on Ephesians*. Grand Rapids: Kregel Publications, [1903] 1979.

Salmond, S. D. F. "The Epistle of Paul to the Ephesians". Pages 201–395. In *The Expositor's Greek Testament*, vol. 3. Ed. by W. Robertson Nicoll. Grand Rapids: Eerdmans, 1967.

Scott, E. F. *The Epistles of Paul to the Colossians, to Philemon and to the Ephesians*. The Moffatt New Testament Commentary. Ed. by James Moffatt. London: Hodder and Stoughton, 1930.

Stott, John R. W. *God's New Society: The Message of Ephesians*. The Bible Speaks Today. Downers Grove: InterVarsity Press, 1979.

Thompson, G. H. P. *The Letters of Paul to the Ephesians, to the Colossians and to Philemon*. The Cambridge Bible Commentary. Cambridge: University Press, 1967.

Wallace, Daniel B. *Greek Grammar Beyond the Basics: An Exegetical Syntax of the New Testament*. Grand Rapids: Zondervan, 1996.

Wood, A. Skevington. "Ephesians". Pages 1–92. In *The Expositor's Bible Commentary*, vol. 11. Ed. by Frank E. Gaebelein. Grand Rapids: Zondervan, 1978.

GREEK TEXTS AND TRANSLATIONS

Aland, Barbara, Kurt Aland, Johannes Karavidopoulos, Carlo M. Martini, and Bruce M. Metzger, eds. *The Greek New Testament*. 4th rev. ed. Stuttgart: United Bible Societies, 1993.

Brenton, Charles Lee. *The Septuagint Version of the Old Testament and Apocrypha with an English Translation*. 5th Zondervan printing. Grand Rapids: Zondervan, 1978.

Friberg, Barbara, and Timothy Friberg, eds. *Analytical Greek New Testament*. Grand Rapids: Baker, 1981.

Good News Bible: The Bible in Today's English Version. New York: American Bible Society, 1976.

Hodges, Zane C., and Arthur L. Farstad. *The Greek New Testament according to the Majority Text*. 2d ed. Nashville: Thomas Nelson, 1985.

Holy Bible: Contemporary English Version. New York: American Bible Society, 1995.

Holy Bible: New Living Translation. 2d ed. Wheaton: Tyndale House, 2004.

Holy Bible: New Revised Standard Version. Grand Rapids: Zondervan, 1990.

Net Bible: New English Translation. Version 9.206. Biblical Studies Press, L.L.C. Internet: www.NETBIBLE.COM, 1999.

The Bible: Revised Standard Version. New York: American Bible Society, 1971.

The Holy Bible: Authorized (or King James) Version. New York: American Bible Society, [1611] 1992.

The Holy Bible: New Century Version. Dallas: Word, 1993.

The Jerusalem Bible. Garden City: Doubleday, 1968.

The Living Bible, Paraphrased. Wheaton: Tyndale House, 1971.

The New American Bible. Camden, NJ: Thomas Nelson, 1971.

The New American Standard Bible. Text ed. Anaheim: Foundation Publications, Inc., 1997.

The New English Bible with the Apocrypha. Oxford study ed. New York: Oxford Univ. Press, 1976.

The New Jerusalem Bible. New York, London: Doubleday, 1990.

The New Testament in Modern English. Translated by J. B. Phillips. Revised Edition. New York: Macmillan, 1972.

The NIV Study Bible. London: Hodder & Stoughton, 1987.

The Revised English Bible with Apocrypha. Oxford: University Press, 1989.